The Behavioral Economics of Foreign Exchange Markets

European University Studies
Europäische Hochschulschriften
Publications Universitaires Européennes

Series V
Economics and Management

Reihe V Série V
Volks- und Betriebswirtschaft
Sciences économiques, gestion d'entreprise

Vol./Bd. 3178

PETER LANG
Frankfurt am Main · Berlin · Bern · Bruxelles · New York · Oxford · Wien

Robert Schmidt

The Behavioral Economics of Foreign Exchange Markets

A Psychological View on Human Expectation Formation in Foreign Exchange Markets

PETER LANG
Europäischer Verlag der Wissenschaften

Bibliographic Information published by Die Deutsche Bibliothek
Die Deutsche Bibliothek lists this publication in the Deutsche Nationalbibliografie; detailed bibliographic data is available in the internet at <http://dnb.ddb.de>.

Zugl.: Würzburg, Univ., Diss., 2005

D 20
ISSN 0531-7339
ISBN 3-631-54814-1
US-ISBN 0-8204-9838-6

www.peterlang.de

Preface

Die vorliegende Arbeit entstand während meiner Tätigkeit als wissenschaftlicher Mitarbeiter am Lehrstuhl für Geld und internationale Wirtschaftsbeziehungen an der Bayerischen Julius-Maximilians-Universität Würzburg. Im September 2004 wurde sie von der wirtschaftswissenschaftlichen Fakultät der Universität Würzburg als Dissertation angenommen.

Auf dem Weg zum erfolgreichen Abschluss meiner Dissertation wurde ich von vielen Menschen begleitet und unterstützt. Zu besonderem Dank bin ich meinem akademischen Lehrer, Herrn Prof. Dr. Peter Bofinger, verpflichtet. Er unterstützte mich stets bei meinem Dissertationsvorhaben und ermutigte mich, meine Forschungsergebnisse zu veröffentlichen. Seine kritische und zugleich realitätsbezogene ökonomische Denkweise hat mein Verständnis von Ökonomie sehr geprägt. Herrn Prof. Dr. Martin Kukuk danke ich für die Übernahme des Zweitgutachtens.

Meinen ehemaligen Kollegen am Lehrstuhl für Geld und internationale Wirtschaftsbeziehungen danke ich für die freundschaftliche Atmosphäre und die große Diskussions- und Hilfsbereitschaft, die weit über das gewöhnliche Ausmaß hinausging. Besonders zu erwähnen sind hier die Herren Dr. Oliver Hülsewig, Eric Mayer und Dr. Timo Wollmershäuser. Die gemeinsame Zeit mit ihnen hat mir sehr viel Spaß und Freude bereitet! Bedanken möchte ich mich auch bei meinen Studienfreunden Michael Bauer und Markus Besenbeck. Ihre Anwesenheit bei der gemeinsamen „wissenschaftlichen Ehrenrunde" erleichterte den beschwerlichen Weg der Erkenntnis und hat uns viele unvergessliche Stunden bereitet. Besonderer Dank gilt auch zwei scheinbar unbeteiligten Personen. Berit Rupp danke ich für ihre außerordentliche Leidensfähigkeit. Sie hat sich beim Korrekturlesen der Arbeit sicherlich mehrmals über Sinn und Unsinn wissenschaftlicher Arbeiten Gedanken gemacht. Auch meinem langjährigen Freund Bernd Schröder möchte ich an dieser Stelle von Herzen Danke sagen. Neben der Bereitstellung von makroökonomischen Daten und Prognosen, die für die vorliegende Arbeit elementar sind, hat er durch seinen freundschaftlichen Rat in allen Lebenslagen meinen Weg entscheidend begleitet.

Zuletzt, aber deswegen nicht weniger herzlich, möchte ich meiner Familie danken. Meine Eltern, Brüder und Christina haben mich während der gesamten Zeit immer vorbehaltlos unterstützt und ermutigt. Ohne sie wäre diese Arbeit nicht möglich gewesen. Danke! Die Arbeit ist ihnen gewidmet.

Düsseldorf, im September 2005 Robert Schmidt

Synopsis

Contents

Figures

Tables

Chapter I
Introduction

I.1 Aim

At the beginning of 1999, the Euro was formally launched as the new single currency in the European Monetary Union (EMU). Since then the EUR/USD exchange rate has gone through three different stages (see FIGURE I-1): at first, the Euro depreciated strongly for nearly two years against the US dollar; subsequently, the Euro moved sidewards against the US dollar in a narrow range between 0.85 and 0.95 US dollar per Euro; since February 2002 the Euro entered an appreciation phase against the US dollar.

Figure I-1: EUR/USD exchange rate from January 1999 to July 2004

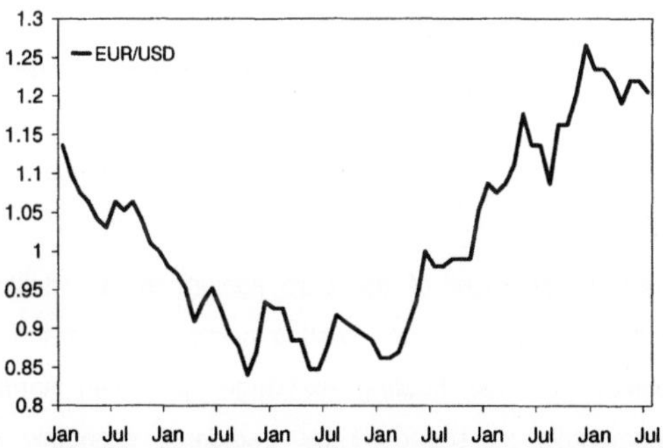

Almost all analysts found the actual development of the EUR/USD exchange rate rather astonishing. Hardly anyone would have foreseen such a course of the EUR/USD exchange rate. Consequently, the development of the EUR/USD exchange rate appears to be a mystery for many professional and scientific observers (see e.g. De Grauwe and Grimaldi [2001], European Economic Advisory Group at the CESifo [2002]). In particular, the initial depreciation of the Euro against the US dollar came quite surprisingly as it was expected that the Euro would appreciate against the US dollar because of the important synergies that analysts believed would quickly develop between the use of the Euro in foreign exchange transactions and in Euro area financial asset markets (see Salvatore [2002], Mundell [1998], Portes and Rey [1998] and Schneider [2003]). Also the recent appreciation of the Euro against the US dollar came rather unexpected for most of the professional analysts.

Many economists have tried to give reasonable explanations for the unexpected and astonishing development of the EUR/USD exchange rate. In line with the traditional economic approach, most of these explanations invoke macroeconomic fundamentals, whereas the GDP growth differences between the United States and Euroland have gained an outstanding prominence in the depreciation phase of the Euro. In the Euro's appreciation phase the large and probably not sustainable US current account deficit serves as an explanation for the appreciation of the Euro against the US dollar. However, both explanations only hold true for the specific time period in which they are used. For example, even in the appreciation phase of the Euro against the US dollar the US economy showed higher growth rates than the Euro economy. Thus, the Euro should have further depreciated. In contrast, the large US current account deficit existed also during the depreciation of the EUR/USD exchange rate. Consequently, it is completely right when Swann [2000] states:

> "The foreign exchange market is a capricious beast at the best of times. But the movements of the world's largest currencies have been particularly mystifying over the past year. Seldom has the divergence between economic fundamentals and the performance of currencies been so stark. Traditional currency analysis, based on economic growth, interest rates and current account balances would, for example, have dictated a rising euro and a falling yen. In fact, the reverse has happened. (Swann [2000], p. 4)

Overall, the mysterious development of the Euro against the US dollar is nothing new in economics. It rather belongs to a broader existing mystery in exchange rate economics. In general, the development of free floating exchange rates can hardly be explained by macroeconomic fundamentals as supposed by traditional economic theories. Therefore, prominent economists yet conclude that there exists an 'exchange rate disconnect puzzle' (see Obstfeld and Rogoff [2000]).

As a purely macroeconomic analysis of exchange rate movements appears to be futile, we choose an alternative way to identify important non-fundamental factors determining exchange rate movements. A reasonable starting point for this issue is to take a new explorative look at the observable exchange rate movements of free floating exchange rates. Conspicuous characteristics of free floating exchange rates are long and persistent trends. These trends are often disconnected from the macroeconomic development of the related economies so that they rather gather a momentum for its own.

Often the existing trends are attributed to an excessive speculative trading behavior of foreign exchange market participants. Already Keynes highlighted the importance of speculation in asset markets. According to Keynes, professional investors orientate their trading decisions rather on "waves of optimistic or pessimistic sentiments" (Keynes [1936], p. 154) than on "what an investment is really worth to a man who buys it for keeps" (Keynes [1936], p. 154-155). In this context, Keynes argued that in markets dominated by speculation psychological factors become particularly important. In our study we deal with the psychological factors, which may be important for understanding exchange rate movements. Thus, our study belongs to the new research field of behavioral economics, which considers the relevance of psychological factors in economic contexts. The main objective of behavioral economists is to develop a more realistic view of the actual human behavior in the context of economics. Therefore, behavioral economists often refer to the work of behavioral decision theorists, who introduced new concepts under the general heading of bounded rationality. Central to the concept of bounded rationality is the assumption that humans' actual behavior deviates from the ideal of economic rationality due to at least two reasons: first, decisions are usually based on an incomplete information basis (limited information) and, second, the information processing of human beings is limited by their computational capacities (limited cognitive resources). Due to these limitations people are forced to apply simplification mechanisms in information processing. Important simplification mechanisms, which play a decisive role in the process judgment and decision making, are simple heuristics. Simple heuristics can principally be characterized as simple rules of thumb, which allow quick and efficient decisions even under a high degree of uncertainty. In this study, our aim is to analyze the relevance of simple heuristics in the context of foreign exchange markets. In our view, the decision situation in foreign exchange markets can serve as a prime example for decision situations in which simple heuristics are especially relevant as the complexity of the decision situation is very high.

I.2 Organization of the study

The study is organized as follows. In Chapter II, we deal with the exchange rate disconnect puzzle. In particular, we discuss and check the main implications of the traditional economic approach for explaining exchange rate movements. The asset market theory of exchange rate determination implies that exchange rates are mainly driven by the development of macroeconomic fundamentals. Furthermore the asset market theory assumes that foreign exchange market participants form rational expectations concerning future exchange rate developments and that exchange rates are determined in efficient markets. Overall the empirical evidence suggests that the traditional approach for explaining exchange rate changes is at odds with the data.

Chapter III addresses the existence of long and persistent trends in exchange rate time series. We apply three different methods to determine empirically the trend length in foreign exchange markets. In particular, we apply a technical analysis tool, variance ratio tests and a Markov-Switching regression. Overall, our empirical analysis reveals that exchange rates show a clear tendency to move in long and persistent trends. Furthermore, we discuss the relevance of speculation in foreign exchange markets. With regard to the impact of speculation, economic theory states that speculation can have either a stabilizing effect or a destabilizing effect on exchange rates. Chapter III addresses both possible impacts of speculation on exchange rates on a theoretical basis and gives an overview on the empirical evidence. At the end of Chapter III, we examine the Keynesian view on the functioning of asset markets.

Chapter IV explores main insights from the new research field of behavioral economics. In particular, we give a brief description of the main implications of the logical theory of rational choice under uncertainty and summarize the empirical evidence for that theory. The empirical evidence suggests that actual human behavior is often inconsistent with the predictions of the theory of rational choice. A much discussed alternative to the traditional economic paradigm of rationality is the concept of bounded rationality first introduced by Herbert Simon [1955]. The concept of bounded rationality can be seen as the theoretical basis for most of the research in the field of behavioral economics. In the centre of the concept of bounded rationality is a psychological analysis of the actual human judgment and decision behavior. In Chapter IV, we discuss the concept of bounded rationality in detail and illustrate important insights of behavioral decision theories. In particular, we deal in Chapter IV with the relevance of simple heuristics in the context of foreign exchange markets.

Chapter V provides experimental and empirical evidence for the suggested relevance of simple heuristics in the context of foreign exchange markets. The experimental part of Chapter V is divided into two parts. In the first experiment, we deal with the human expectation formation. We compare point forecasts of the EUR/USD exchange rate surveyed from professional analysts and experimentally generated point forecasts of students for a simulated exchange rate time series. The results show that the forecasting performance of both groups differs substantially.

Afterwards we analyze the nature of expectation formation of both groups in detail to reveal similarities and differences, which allow us to draw reasonable explanations for the differences in the forecasting performances. In the second experiment, we analyze the expectation formation in an experimental foreign exchange market. This approach allows us to consider the relevance of expectation feedback as individuals' expectations directly influence the actual realization of the time series. Thus, Keynes' predictions on the importance of conventions in asset markets can be analyzed. Overall, both experiments reveal that the human beings tend to apply simple trend heuristics, when forming their expectations about future exchange rates. In the empirical part of Chapter V we deal with the usefulness of such simple trend heuristics in real world. Only if simple trend heuristics lead to profits in the specific environment of foreign exchange markets, their application can be recommended. Thus, we analyze the profitability of simple technical analysis tools in foreign exchange markets.

Finally, Chapter VI provides concluding remarks.

Chapter II
The exchange rate disconnect puzzle

In this chapter we deal with the evaluation of the 'modern' asset approach models to exchange rate determination. This special kind of exchange rate models arose in the mid 1970s and can be seen as the theoretical answer to the empirical regularities of the post Bretton Woods era. Since the collapse of the Bretton Woods System in the early 1970s freely floating exchange rates are mainly characterized by their high degree of short-term variability. However, the enormous variability of exchange rates could not be explained within the existing flow exchange rate models as they presume a rather sluggish exchange rate behavior. This is due to the fact that in this class of models exchange rate changes only occur if the demand and supply schedules for international goods and services shift. Thus, exchange rates in flow approach models are largely seen as a medium of exchange for executing international trade transactions. Correspondingly Mussa [1979] evaluates the usefulness of the flow models for explaining floating exchange rate behavior as follows:

> "In summary, an examination of the major empirical regularities in the behaviour of exchange rates and in the relationships between exchange rates and other variables does not indicate that the flow market model is of much use in understanding these regularities. It is reasonable to conclude, therefore, that the flow market model is not a very useful tool for understanding and explaining the behaviour of exchange rates." (Mussa [1979], pp. 37)

Consequently, the economic profession changed the way of modeling exchange rates in the direction of a stock/asset approach to exchange rate determination, which gave at least a theoretical basis for the observable volatile exchange rate movements. In the centre of the asset approach models are the expectations of market participants. The expectations concerning the future exchange rates, which depend on the future course of events influencing exchange rates, are the most important determinants of current spot exchange rates. With the monetary exchange rate models and the portfolio balance models, economists have developed theoretical models that connect exchange rates with macroeconomic fundamentals. Thus, current exchange rate movements are linked to the expected course of macroeconomic fundamentals. Although these models are theoretically persuasive, the asset approach models also miss an empirical validation at least for the short- and medium run, i.e. one to three years (see e.g. Sarno and Taylor [2002]). The lack of empirical validity of asset approach models let Obstfeld and Rogoff [2000] conclude that there exists an 'exchange rate disconnect puzzle', which is counted among the six major puzzles in international macroeconomics. According to Obstfeld and Rogoff [2000], the name exchange rate disconnect puzzle "alludes broadly to the exceedingly weak relationship (except, perhaps, in the longer run) between the exchange rate and virtually any macroeconomic aggregates" (Obstfeld and Rogoff [2000], p. 373).

> "For example, exchange rates are remarkably volatile relative to any model we have of underlying fundamentals such as interest rates, outputs, and money supplies, and no model seems to be very good at explaining exchange rates even ex post." (Obstfeld and Rogoff [2000], pp. 380)

In this Chapter we take a deeper look into the theoretical considerations of the asset approach models. The theoretical basis for all asset approach models of exchange rate determination is the asset market theory proposed by e.g. Frenkel and Mussa [1980]. The asset market theory is based on the assumption that traders in foreign exchange markets form rational expectations. Furthermore, the asset market theory of exchange rate determination hypothesizes that exchange rates are determined in an efficient market. Both assumptions imply several distinctive characteristics, which could be evaluated by means of empirical data. The remainder of this chapter is as follows: in the first section we illustrate the asset market theory and discuss both its central assumptions (rational expectations and efficient markets hypothesis). In the second section, we evaluate the validity of the most important empirical implications of the asset market theory for the behavior of exchange rates.

II.1 The 'modern' view on exchange rate modeling: the asset approach

II.1.1 Asset market theory of exchange rate determination

In contrast to the flow approach models of exchange rate determination, asset approach models treat exchange rates as a durable asset and thus as a store of value. Consequently, the asset approach requires the application of tools normally used for the determination of other durable asset prices like e.g. bond and share prices when analyzing the determinants of exchange rates (see Mussa [1979]). According to the asset market approach, the essential determinant of the current spot exchange rate can be seen in market expectations concerning future spot exchange rates and future economic conditions relevant for determining the appropriate value of the exchange rate. The most important implications of the asset view for exchange rate determination can be illustrated within the framework of the asset market theory to exchange rates (see e.g. Frenkel and Mussa [1980]).[1] Within the asset market theory to exchange rates the log of the spot exchange rate in period t, denoted by s_t, is determined by

$$s_t = Z_t + \beta\left(E_t s_{t+1} - s_t\right) \tag{II-1}$$

where Z_t represents a set of macroeconomic fundamentals that affect exchange rates in period t and $E_t s_{t+1} - s_t$ denotes the expected percentage change of the exchange rate between t and $t+1$ conditional on the available information set in t. The coefficient β ($0<\beta<1$) is a model parameter reflecting the sensitivity of the current exchange rate to its expected rate of change. Equation (II-1) represents a sufficiently general relation, which may be regarded as a 'reduced form' that can be derived by a variety of exchange rate models. The various models may differ in their emphasis on the fundamental determinants (Z_t), but they all share a similar reduced form (see Frenkel and Mussa [1980]). The central message of equation (II-1) is that the equilibrium spot exchange rate at time t is not only affected by the basic factors of supply and demand summarized by Z_t, but also by the expected exchange rate change. The expected exchange rate change provokes foreign exchange market participants to move assets either into or out of foreign exchange, depending on whether the price of foreign exchange is expected to rise or fall. To close the model, it is necessary to specify how market participants form their expectations. Within the framework of the asset pricing theory, it is usually assumed that expectations of future exchange rates are formed in a 'rational' manner, i.e. expectations are consistent with the validity of equation (II-1) in all future periods. This implies primarily that market participants use all available information, including the knowledge of the true model that determines the evolution of the exchange rate (see Muth [1961] and section II.1.2). Solving equation (II-1) for the current spot exchange rate s_t leads to

$$s_t = \frac{1}{1+\beta} Z_t + \frac{\beta}{1+\beta} E_t s_{t+1}, \tag{II-2}$$

---

[1] The asset pricing theory of exchange rates can be traced back at least to Mussa [1976]. Further contributions to the asset pricing theories can be found for example in Frenkel and Mussa [1980] and Mussa [1984]. For theoretical developments and applications of the asset market theory see Dornbusch [1976a], [1976b], and Frenkel [1976].

whereas it holds that $0 < \beta/_{1+\beta} < 1$, so that repeated forward iteration leads to:[2]

$$s_t = \frac{1}{1+\beta}\sum_{n=0}^{\infty}\left(\frac{\beta}{1+\beta}\right)^n E_t Z_{t+n} . \qquad \text{(II-3)}$$

Thus, the current spot exchange rate s_t depends on the expected discounted sum of all future values of the relevant macroeconomic fundamentals over an infinite horizon. In the absence of – current and future – changes in macroeconomic fundamentals, the spot exchange rate fully reflects the entire path of future macroeconomic fundamentals. Consequently, changes in the spot exchange rate only occur if exogenous shocks to the macroeconomic fundamentals arise, i.e. new information becomes publicly known. It is assumed that new information is immediately processed into exchange rate changes, so that unexploited profit opportunities do not arise (see Frenkel [1981]). This implication alludes to the efficient market hypothesis, which will be explored in more detail in section II.1.3.

Overall, the asset market theory to exchange rate determination places emphasis on at least two important interrelated building blocks: on the one hand, the asset market theory is mainly characterized by its inherent forward looking determination of the actual spot exchange rate. This implies that future expected exchange rates and the future expected stance of macroeconomic fundamentals are the major influencing factors for current exchange rates. Within the framework of asset market theory, it is usually assumed that market participants form the relevant expectations in a 'rational' manner. On the other hand, regarding exchange rates as an asset price implies that exchange rates are supposed to be determined in efficient markets. Both aspects will be presented in brief in the following two sections as the implications from both are afterwards used to evaluate the empirical validity of the asset market theory to exchange rate determination.

II.1.2 The role of expectations: rational expectations hypothesis

The economic profession distinguishes various concepts of expectation formation (e.g. regressive expectations, static expectations and adaptive expectations).[3] For asset pricing

---

2 If the transversality condition does not hold, exchange rates may be governed in part by an explosive bubble that will eventually dominate its behavior (see Mark [2001]). However, we ignore this possibility in the following illustration.

3 For an extensive discussion of the various concepts of expectations formation in economics we refer to Holden et al. [1985] and Chapter V of this study.

models, the rational expectations hypothesis is of crucial importance. The rational expectations hypothesis, first proposed by Muth [1960] and [1961], can be concretized as follows:

> "expectations of firms (or, more generally, the subjective probability distribution of outcomes) tend to be distributed, for the same information set, about the prediction of the theory (or the 'objective' probability distributions of outcomes)." (Muth [1961], p. 316)

Thus, rational expectations hypothesis states that agents' subjective expectations with respect to a variable (e.g. exchange rates) are equal to the mathematical expectations conditional on an information set containing all publicly available information. The conditional mathematical expectation value is thereby based on the true probability distribution of the variable. Within asset pricing models, the conditional mathematical expectation value is usually derived from the 'true' economic model and it is assumed that market participants behave as if they form their subjective expectations as the conditional mathematical expectations, so that subjective and objective expectations coincide. The corollary of the rational expectations hypothesis is therefore that the subjective density function of the exchange rate (f^*), based on the available information set Ω, coincides exactly with the objective conditional density function of the exchange rate (f):

$$f^*\left(s_t \middle| \Omega_{t-1}\right) = f\left(s_t \middle| \Omega_{t-1}\right). \tag{II-4}$$

According to the rational expectations hypothesis, market participants' expectations possess the following two important properties (see Baillie and McMahon [1990]): (a) expectation errors (ε) based on the available information set (Ω) are purely random,

$$\varepsilon_t = s_t - E\left(s_t \middle| \Omega_{t-1}\right), \quad \text{with } \varepsilon_t \sim \left(0, \sigma^2\right), \tag{II-5}$$

and, (b), expectation errors are serially independent,

$$E\left(\varepsilon_t \varepsilon_{t \pm i}\right) = 0 \qquad \text{for } i \geq 1. \tag{II-6}$$

The proof of these two propositions is quite straightforward. As the expectation error under rational expectations hypothesis is denoted as in equation (II-5), it follows that

$$E\left(\varepsilon_t \middle| \Omega_{t-1}\right) = E\left[s_t - E\left(s_t \middle| \Omega_{t-1}\right)\right]. \tag{II-7}$$

Using now the law of iterated expectations, it becomes obvious that

$$\begin{aligned} E(\varepsilon_t|\Omega_{t-1}) &= E(s_t|\Omega_{t-1}) - E\left[E(s_t|\Omega_{t-1})|\Omega_{t-1}\right] \\ &= E(s_t|\Omega_{t-1}) - E(s_t|\Omega_{t-1}) \\ &= 0 \end{aligned} \qquad \text{(II-8)}$$

This result holds for all subsets of Ω_{t-1}, say X_t (i.e. $X_t \subset \Omega_t$), so that we have

$$E(\varepsilon_t|X_t) = 0. \qquad \text{(II-9)}$$

Hence, the expectation error under rational expectations hypothesis based on the available information set has a zero mean.

The second property of expectations under rational expectations hypothesis can be derived from the fact that, for $i \geq 1$,

$$E(\varepsilon_t\varepsilon_{t-i}|\Omega_{t-i}) = \varepsilon_{t-i}E(\varepsilon_t|\Omega_{t-i}) \qquad \text{(II-10)}$$

and since $\Omega_{t-i}\ (i \geq 1)$ is a subset of Ω_{t-1}, then by (II-9) it follows that

$$E(\varepsilon_t\varepsilon_{t-i}) = 0, \qquad \text{for } i \geq 1. \qquad \text{(II-11)}$$

Hence, current expectations errors are uncorrelated with all past expectations errors. This result also holds for future expectations errors as

$$E(\varepsilon_t\varepsilon_{t+1}|\Omega_{t+i-1}) = \varepsilon_t E(\varepsilon_{t+i}|\Omega_{t+i-1}), \qquad \text{for } i \geq 1, \qquad \text{(II-12)}$$

and since under the rational expectations hypothesis $E(\varepsilon_{t+i}|\Omega_{t+i-1}) = 0$, then we also have

$$E(\varepsilon_t\varepsilon_{t+i}) = 0, \qquad \text{for } i \geq 1, \qquad \text{(II-13)}$$

Thus, current expectations errors are also uncorrelated with all future expectations errors, so that one can subsume together with (II-11) that the rational expectations hypothesis establishes that expectations errors ε_t are serially independent (see Baillie and McMahon [1990]).

Since the emergence of the rational expectations hypothesis in the early 1970s as a theoretical tool for modeling agents' expectations, it has been disputed. The main criticism is based on the assumption that agents are in a position to form expectations in accordance with the objective conditional density function as it is supposed by equation (II-4). On the one hand, equation (II-4) requires that economic agents are 'superior statisticians' (see Arrow [1978]). However, due to limited human computational abilities, this requirement seems to be rather unrealistic (see Shiller [1987] and Wärneryd [2001]). On the other hand, although economists routinely assume that economic agents form rational expectations, they normally do not ask how economic agents could logically know the objective conditional density function of the exchange rate (*f*). Obviously, rational expectations hypothesis is only applicable in cases where actually 'objective true' conditional expectations exist. This implies that market participants in the foreign exchange market can only – if at all – form rational expectations according to the future exchange rate movements in the case that there exists a stable link between macroeconomic fundamentals and exchange rates that is publicly known. However, we will see in section II.2.1 that this prerequisite is not fulfilled in reality.

II.1.3 Efficient market hypothesis for foreign exchange markets

The second important implication of the asset market theory to foreign exchange rate determination, which can be seen as a logical extension of the rational expectations hypothesis, is the suggestion that exchange rates are determined in efficient markets. The original concept of efficient markets, which has been the central proposition of finance for nearly thirty years, can be traced back to Fama [1965a], [1965b] and [1970]. Fama [1970] defines an efficient market as:

> "A market in which prices always 'fully reflect' all available information is called efficient." (Fama [1970], p. 383)

Thereby, an efficient market is primarily characterized as a market where a

> "large number of rational, profit-maximizers actively competing with each trying to predict future market values of individual securities, and where important current information is almost freely available to all participants". (Fama [1965a], p. 56)

Jensen [1978] gives a similar definition of market efficiency:[4]

> "A market is efficient with respect to information set Ω_t if it is impossible to make economic profits by trading on the basis of information set Ω_t." (Jensen [1978], p. 96)

---

[4] Jensen [1978] uses θ_t as symbol for the information set. We have changed this to the symbol Ω_t which will be used throughout the study.

Closely related to this definition, Malkiel [1992] provides the following definition:[5]

> "A capital market is said to be efficient if it fully and correctly reflects all relevant information in determining security prices. Formally, the market is said to be efficient with respect to some information set, Ω_t, if security prices would be unaffected by revealing that information to all participants. Moreover, efficiency with respect to an information set, Ω_t, implies that it is impossible to make economic profits by trading on the basis of Ω_t." (Malkiel [1992], p. 739)

All three definitions of market efficiency focus on the importance of the information set (Ω) adopted in tests of the efficient market hypothesis and the potential ability to exploit this information in a trading strategy. Both aspects will be discussed in the following.

If a financial market reveals the above mentioned characteristics of an efficient market, it should not be possible for any market participant to earn substantial abnormal profits. Formally, the efficient market hypothesis requires that the expected market excess return (ER_t) should be equal to zero

$$E\left(ER_t \left|\Omega_{t-1}\right.\right) = 0 . \qquad \text{(II-14)}$$

The excess market return is thereby defined as

$$ER_t = r_t - E\left(r_t \left|\Omega_{t-1}\right.\right) \qquad \text{(II-15)}$$

where r_t represents the actual rate of return at time t and $E\left(r_t \left|\Omega_{t-1}\right.\right)$ is the expected rate of return based on the available information at time t-1 (Ω_{t-1}). Furthermore, the efficient market hypothesis requires that the expected excess returns should be uncorrelated with any expected excess return in the past or future:

$$E\left(ER_t ER_{t\pm i}\right) = 0, \quad \text{for } i \geq 1 . \qquad \text{(II-16)}$$

If these two properties are fulfilled, the sequence $\{ER_t\}$ is a fair game with respect to Ω_t. In other words, the foreign exchange market is said to be efficient if on average expectations errors about returns are zero and these errors follow no systematic pattern that might be exploited to produce abnormal profits.

---

[5] Malkiel [1992] uses ϕ as symbol for the information set and we have changed this to Ω_t.

The above argumentation rests crucially on the assumption that all market participants are fully rational, i.e. they form rational expectations which correspond to the objective density function of the exchange rate (see Baillie and McMahon [1990]). However, according to the proponents of the efficient market hypothesis, the efficient market hypothesis holds even in cases where not all market participants are rational. For example, in a case where non-rational market participants trade randomly in the market and their trading strategies are uncorrelated, it is likely that their trades cancel each other out. Also in situations where trading strategies of non-rational market participants are correlated, the efficient market hypothesis may still hold due to arbitrage activities of rational-acting market participants (see Friedman [1953] and Fama [1965b]). The process of arbitrage ensures that asset prices remain close to their fundamental value even when some investors are not fully rational and their demands are correlated.[6]

For an empirical evaluation of the efficient market hypothesis, the above-given definition is too abstract. One needs to concretize what is meant by the relevant information set (Ω) and how the equilibrium model of pricing behavior is specified. With respect to the relevant information set (Ω), the literature generally distinguishes between three different variants of Ω and thus three different forms of market efficiency (see Roberts [1959]).

According to the *weak form of market efficiency*, the current exchange rate is considered to incorporate all information contained in past exchange rates. Thus, no market participant is able to generate significant excess returns by just using previous prices or returns for forecasting future developments as it is suggested by technical analysis. According to the *semi-strong form of market efficiency*, the current exchange rate incorporates all publicly known information, including its own past prices. An important property of the semi-strong form of market efficiency is that it encompasses the weak form, as information on past exchange rates is contained in the set of public information. Thus, a market that is semi-strong efficient is also weak-form efficient. If the foreign exchange market is semi-strong efficient, there are no under- or overvalued currencies, as new information is fully incorporated into exchange rates rather speedily. Therefore, the analysis of current fundamentals is futile since on that basis no substantial excess returns can be generated. The *strong form of market efficiency* states that the current exchange rate reflects all information that can possibly be known, including private information. This kind of market efficiency implies that there also exists no insider information

---

6 The three theoretical foundations of the efficient market hypothesis are discussed in more detail in Shleifer [2000]. In Chapter III it will be shown, however, that these arguments for the case of the efficient market hypothesis may not hold in all cases.

in the market that can be used for generating substantial excess returns (see e.g. Levich [2001]). As the semi-strong form of efficiency encompasses the weak form of efficiency, the strong form of efficiency encompasses both the semi-strong and the weak form of market efficiency.

The equilibrium model of pricing behavior is usually derived from the economic theory of exchange rate determination. In this context, a prominent model for testing the efficient market hypothesis is, for example, the uncovered interest rate parity (see Sarno and Taylor [2002]). However, the usage of economic models for testing efficient market hypothesis is inherently problematical, as such tests of efficient market hypothesis always imply a joint test of the assumed equilibrium model and the efficient use of information by the market participants (see Levich [1989]). Thus, for studies that reject this joint hypothesis, it is generally impossible to decide whether the rejection is due to an incorrect specification of the equilibrium rate or due to the fact that market participants are inefficient information processors. On the contrary, for studies that do not reject the efficient market hypothesis, it could be argued that the wrong equilibrium price or return process was assumed as the benchmark.

II.1.4 Important empirical implications of the asset market theory to exchange rate determination

Rational expectations hypothesis and the efficient market hypothesis entail some important implications for the behavior of foreign exchange rates. The most important implications are as follows:

1. ***There exists a stable link between macroeconomic fundamentals and exchange rate movements***

   The asset market theory of exchange rate determination suggests that there exists a stable link between macroeconomic fundamentals and exchange rates movements. The derivation of the relevant macroeconomic fundamentals was a major research goal in the early 1970s and resulted in the asset approach models, which will be represented in the section II.2.1.

2. ***Market participants form expectations in accordance with the rational expectations hypothesis***

   A second important implication of the asset market theory of exchange rate determination is the notion that foreign exchange market participants form rational expectations. That is, expectation errors are purely random and serially independent. In section II.2.2, we evaluate the rational expectations hypothesis by the means of survey expectations for the EUR/USD exchange rate.

3. *Exchange rate movements are only due to newly emerging information*

An additional important implication of the asset market theory of exchange rate determination is that the emergence of new information about macroeconomic fundamentals drives exchange rate movements. This can be illustrated by means of the basic equation for the exchange rate determination within the asset market theory. According to this approach, the actual spot exchange rate depends on both current fundamentals and the entire expected future path of fundamentals

$$s_t = \frac{1}{1+\beta}\sum_{n=0}^{\infty}\left(\frac{\beta}{1+\beta}\right)^n E_t Z_{t+n} \,. \tag{II-17}$$

To illustrate how news about macroeconomic fundamentals – defined as the deviation of (ex post) actual values of fundamentals from (ex ante) expected values of fundamentals – influence exchange rate movements consider that the at time *t-1* expected spot exchange rate in t is given by

$$E_{t-1}s_t = \frac{1}{1+\beta}\sum_{n=0}^{\infty}\left(\frac{\beta}{1+\beta}\right)^n E_{t-1} Z_{t+n} \,. \tag{II-18}$$

Now subtracting equation (II-18) from equation (II-17) gives

$$s_t - E_{t-1}s_t = \frac{1}{1+\beta}\sum_{n=0}^{\infty}\left(\frac{\beta}{1+\beta}\right)^n \left(E_t Z_{t+n} - E_{t-1} Z_{t+n}\right) . \tag{II-19}$$

Equation (II-19) clearly shows that unexpected exchange rate changes are caused by the emergence of new information about macroeconomic fundamentals (*Z*). Thus, new information that changes market participants' expectations concerning macroeconomic fundamentals is, according to the asset market theory, the driving force of exchange rate movements. In section II.2.3 we discuss the empirical impact of 'news' on exchange rate movements.

4. Exchange rates should move as random walks over time

This prediction of the efficient market hypothesis can be traced back at least to Samuelson [1965] and arises from the fact that, in an efficient market, the current exchange rate reflects all available information at that time and, hence, the expectation of future exchange rate based on that information set is simply the current exchange rate. This suggests that exchange rates in efficient markets should follow a martingale process. A stochastic variable X_t is said to follow a martingale process if it satisfies the following condition

$$E\left(X_{t+1}\middle|\Omega_t\right)=X_t. \tag{II-20}$$

or, equivalently,

$$E\left(X_{t+1}-X_t\middle|\Omega_t\right)=0. \tag{II-21}$$

Thus, the best forecast of all future values of $X_{t+j}\,(j\geq 1)$ is the current value X_t as no information in Ω_t helps to improve the forecast once the market participant knows X_t. A prominent example of a martingale process is a random walk. A time series, X_t, is said to follow a random walk if the change from one period to the next is purely random,

$$X_t=X_{t-1}+u_t, \tag{II-22}$$

or put differently

$$X_t-X_{t-1}=\Delta X_t=u_t, \tag{II-23}$$

where u_t follows a white noise process with zero mean and constant variance

$$E(u_t)=0 \qquad \text{and} \qquad \mathrm{Var}(u_t)=\sigma^2>0.^7 \tag{II-24}$$

7 However, the random walk is more restrictive than a martingale since a martingale does not restrict the higher conditional moments to be statistically independent (see Cuthbertson [1996]). In this context, Campbell et al. [1997] distinguish three different variants of random walk.

The random walk hypothesis has two important implications for exchange rate time series. First, the random walk hypothesis postulates a non-stationary time series, i.e. X_t exhibits a unit root, and, second, the increments of the random walk have to be uncorrelated at all leads and lags, so that

$$E(u_t u_\tau) = 0 \qquad \text{for all } t \neq \tau . \tag{II-25}$$

To illustrate that the current realization of a random walk, X_t, equals the sum of all previous realizations of u respectively forecasting errors, one can rewrite equation (II-22) as follows, if $X_0 = 0$,

$$X_t = \sum_{i=1}^{t} u_i . \tag{II-26}$$

This expression clarifies also that the variance of X_t is a linear increasing function in time, $Var(X_t) = t\sigma^2$, so that the variance of X_t becomes infinitely large as $t \to \infty$. However, as Levich [1989] annotates, it is not mandatory for exchange rates in an efficient market to follow random walk. In cases where the equilibrium value of exchange rates wander substantially and in a serially correlated fashion, randomly forecast errors with mean zero are not essential. However, substantially wandering equilibrium exchange rates should only be expected in the medium- and long-run. The random walk hypothesis for exchange rates will be investigated in section II.2.4.

5. Exchange rates remain at levels consistent with economic fundamentals

This prediction of the efficient market hypothesis is based on the considerations of Friedman [1953] and Fama [1965b]. As long as some market participants are fully rational, their trading behavior will ensure that current exchange rates remain closely related to the fundamental justified level. Otherwise rational market participants would neglect profit opportunities due to under- or overvalued currencies. Section II.2.5 deals with that topic.

II.2 The empirical validity of the asset market theory to exchange rate determination

This section deals with the empirical validity of the asset market theory of exchange rate determination. We discuss each of the listed implications of the asset market approach in detail and provide empirical evidence for each implication.

II.2.1 On the relationship between macroeconomic fundamentals and exchange rate movements

II.2.1.1 Asset approach models: theoretical considerations

Traditionally, a major research goal for economists studying flexible exchange rates is to find an acceptable model that explains exchange rate movements in terms of other macroeconomic fundamentals (see Baillie and McMahon [1990]). In this context, several macroeconomic exchange rate models have been developed in the past. A major requirement for the validity of the asset approach models is that capital is perfectly mobile, so that there are no international capital controls and covered interest rate parity holds. In general, the asset approach models can be divided with respect to the assumed degree of capital substitutability. Exchange rate models assuming perfect capital substitutability are subsumed under the term 'monetary approach'. The only assets considered in these models are domestic and foreign money. In the 'portfolio-balance approaches' the range of assets is expanded to include domestic and foreign bonds, which are assumed to display imperfect capital substitutability.

In the following, we briefly survey the most important versions of the asset approach models to derive the relevant macroeconomic fundamentals affecting exchange rates (extensive surveys of the asset approach models can be found, e.g., in MacDonald and Taylor [1992], Taylor [1995] and Sarno and Taylor [2002]).

II.2.1.1.1 Monetary approach to exchange rate determination

The monetary models of exchange rate determination are based on purchasing power parity and the quantity theory of money. The models start with the assumption that the exchange rate is the relative price of domestic and foreign money. Therefore, the exchange rate is modeled in terms of the relative supply of and demand for these two moneys. Within the monetary approach, one distinguishes between two prominent models which differ primarily with respect to the assumed degree of price flexibility. Whereas the monetarist alternative assumes perfectly flexible prices so that purchasing power parity holds continuously, the Dornbusch Overshooting model relaxes this strong assumption by allowing for price stickiness.

II.2.1.1.1.1 Flexible price monetary models: the monetarist model

The flexible-price monetary model rests on the assumptions that a) purchasing power parity is continuously valid and b) a stable demand function for money exists. Purchasing power parity can be defined as

$$s_t = p_t - p_t^* \tag{II-27}$$

where s is logarithm of the spot exchange rate and p and p^* are the logs of domestic and foreign price levels, respectively.[8] The domestic and foreign demand function for money are given by, respectively,

$$m_t = p_t + \phi y_t - \lambda i_t \tag{II-28}$$

and

$$m_t^* = p_t^* + \phi^* y_t^* - \lambda^* i_t^*, \tag{II-29}$$

where m is the log of the money supply, y is the log of the real income and i the nominal interest rate. The coefficients ϕ and λ denote the income elasticities of the demand for real money and the interest rate semi-elasticities. The demand functions for money are the central equations of the model as they determine the domestic respective foreign price levels. Equations (II-28) and (II-29) with equation (II-27) give the following equation for the determination of the spot exchange rate, assuming that the income elasticities and the interest rate semi-elasticities are equal for both countries

$$s_t = m_t - m_t^* - \phi\left(y_t - y_t^*\right) + \lambda\left(i_t - i_t^*\right). \tag{II-30}$$

According to the flexible price monetary model, an increase in the domestic money supply will lead to a depreciation of the domestic currency, and an increase of real domestic income is accompanied by an appreciation of the domestic currency. An increasing interest differential, furthermore, forces the domestic currency to depreciate. This is in contrast to the standard

---

8 Asterisks denote foreign quantities throughout the study.

Keynesian model described by Mundell [1968] and Fleming [1962]. In the Mundell-Fleming model an increase of the interest differential entails an appreciation of the domestic currency due to capital inflows.

II.2.1.1.1.2 Sticky-price monetary models: the overshooting model

Principally, the sticky-price monetary model is based on the same assumptions as the flexible price monetary model. However, the strong assumption of completely flexible goods prices is relaxed. Whereas the monetarist model assumes that speed of adjustment in goods markets is infinitively high, the sticky-price monetary model assumes that the speed of adjustment in goods markets is sluggish, so that purchasing power parity holds only in the long-run.

The essential characteristics of the sticky price monetary model can be illustrated as follows (see Rosenberg [1996]). According to Dornbusch [1976b], it is assumed that purchasing power parity holds only in the long-run,

$$\bar{s}_t = \bar{p}_t - \bar{p}_t^* \tag{II-31}$$

where the bars of the variables denote the long-run equilibrium. If we now substitute equation (II-31) for equation (II-27) in the derivation of the monetary model, it becomes obvious that the demand and supply for the respective moneys only determines the exchange rate in the long-run,

$$\bar{s}_t = \bar{m}_t - \bar{m}_t^* - \phi\left(\bar{y}_t - \bar{y}_t^*\right) + \lambda\left(\bar{i}_t - \bar{i}_t^*\right). \tag{II-32}$$

In the short-run, the sticky price monetary model assumes that the current spot exchange rate can deviate from its long-run equilibrium. However, the market expects that the current spot exchange rate will gradually converge on its long-run equilibrium level,

$$E_t s_{t+1} - s_t = \theta\left(\bar{s} - s_t\right). \tag{II-33}$$

The variable θ in equation (II-33) describes the speed of adjustment back to the long-run equilibrium level. To solve the sticky price monetary model for the current spot exchange rate we assume that the uncovered interest rate parity is valid, so that

$$E_t s_{s+1} - s_t = i_t - i_t^*. \tag{II-34}$$

It can then be shown that

$$i_t - i_t^* = \theta(\bar{s}_t - s_t), \tag{II-35}$$

so that the current spot exchange rate can be derived by rearranging

$$s_t = \bar{s}_t - \frac{1}{\theta}(i_t - i_t^*). \tag{II-36}$$

Combining equations (II-32) and equation (II-36) and solving for s gives the sticky price monetary model of exchange rate determination for the case where we assume current values for the explanatory variables are long-run equilibrium levels,

$$s_t = m_t - m_t^* - \phi(y_t - y_t^*) + \left(\lambda - \frac{1}{\theta}\right)(i_t - i_t^*). \tag{II-37}$$

To simplify equation (II-37) let $\eta = \lambda - 1/\theta$, so that

$$s_t = m_t - m_t^* - \phi(y_t - y_t^*) + \eta(i_t - i_t^*). \tag{II-38}$$

The sticky price monetary model is quite similar to the flexible price monetary model. Only the coefficient of the interest rate differential differs in the two models. Whereas the coefficient λ is positive in the flexible price monetary model, so that an increase of the interest rate differential will led to a depreciation, the coefficient η of the sticky price monetary model is expected to be negative as $1/\theta$ exceeds λ if $0 < \theta < 1$.

II.2.1.1.2 Portfolio-balance models

Contrary to the monetary models of the asset approach, the portfolio balance models assume that domestic and foreign assets are imperfect substitutes. Thus, the uncovered interest rate parity is extended by a risk premium. The basic structure of portfolio models can be illustrated by means of the composition of the net financial wealth of the domestic private sector (W). The net financial wealth can be divided into three components (see MacDonald and Taylor [1992], Taylor [1995]): domestic money (M), domestic bonds held by domestic residents (B) and foreign bonds denominated in foreign currency and held by domestic residents (B^*). Since, under a free float, a current account surplus on the balance of payments must be exactly matched by a capital account deficit, the current account must give the rate of accumulation of

B^* over time. The definition of wealth and the demand functions for its components are given as follows:

$$W \equiv M + B + S \cdot B^* \tag{II-39}$$

$$M = M\left(i, i^* + \Delta s^e\right)W, \frac{\partial M}{\partial i} < 0, \frac{\partial M}{\partial i^*} < 0, \frac{\partial M}{\partial W} > 0 \tag{II-40}$$

$$B = B\left(i, i^* + \Delta s^e\right)W, \frac{\partial B}{\partial i} > 0, \frac{\partial B}{\partial i^*} < 0, \frac{\partial B}{\partial W} > 0 \tag{II-41}$$

$$SB^* = B^*\left(i, i^* + \Delta s^e\right)W, \frac{\partial B^*}{\partial i} < 0, \frac{\partial B^*}{\partial i^*} > 0, \frac{\partial B^*}{\partial W} > 0 \tag{II-42}$$

where the domestic and the foreign interest rates are denoted by i and i^*, respectively, S is the spot exchange rate and Δs^e represents the expected rate of depreciation. Within the portfolio-balance model, the exchange rate is determined by solving equation (II-39) to (II-42) for given levels of M , B and B* and assuming that market participants form rational expectations. In the portfolio-balance models, exchange rate movements are caused by disturbances to the stocks of M, B and B* (see Flood and Taylor [1994]).

II.2.1.2 Empirical validity of the asset approach models

II.2.1.2.1 A selective survey of the existing literature

The existing exchange rate models have been thoroughly tested since at least twenty years. The results of this enormous empirical literature can be summarized by the following main conclusion (see e.g. Chinn and Meese [1995], Taylor [1995], Neely and Sarno [2002] and Sarno and Taylor [2002]):

1. In the short-run (1-3 years), macroeconomic exchange rate models perform worse than forecasts that do not rely at all on these fundamentals. Even if it is assumed that market participants can perfectly anticipate the future path of macroeconomic fundamentals, their forecasts are worse than naïve random walk forecasts. This result was originally put forth by Meese and Rogoff [1983a] and [1983b] who found that a random walk forecast typically outperforms a forecast based on a macroeconomic exchange rate model, although their forecasts were based on actual realized values of future explanatory variables. To date, the proposition that macroeconomic fundamentals do not account for movements in the

exchange rates is still valid (see e.g. Chinn and Meese [1995], Rogoff [1999], Flood and Rose [1999] and most recently Cheung et al. [2003]). Rogoff [2001] summarizes the present academic consensus accurately when he states:

> "To make a long story short not only have a subsequent twenty years of data and research failed to overturn the Meese-Rogoff result, they have cemented it..." (Rogoff [2001])

2. In the long-run (3-5 years), however, the recent empirical literature on the validity of macroeconomic exchange rate models suggests that fundamental based models have some explanatory power. Mark [1995] shows in his seminal paper that for long horizons there exists an economically significant predictable component in long-horizon changes in the log exchange rate. These systematic exchange rate movements are determined by economic fundamentals. Furthermore, the study of Mark [1995] reveals that the explanatory power of fundamental based forecasts measured by the coefficient of determination (R^2) increases with the forecast horizon and the out-of-sample point predictions generally outperform the driftless random walk at the longer horizons. Likewise Chinn and Meese [1995] and, more recently, Mark and Sul [2001] confirm the findings of Mark [1995]. Chinn and Meese [1995] examines the predictive power of structural exchange rate models using parametric and non-parametric techniques and found that, for longer horizons, error correction terms can explain exchange rate movements significantly better than a naïve random walk forecast. Mark and Sul [2001] study the long-run relationship between nominal exchange rates and monetary fundamentals for a panel of 19 countries and find that exchange rates are cointegrated with long-run determinants predicted by economic theory and that panel base forecast have a significant forecasting power. However, others remain still skeptical and began to criticize Mark's [1995] methodology and the resultant conclusions (see Kilian [1999], Berkowitz and Giorgianni [2001], Neely and Sarno [2002] and Faust et al. [2003]).
3. A further contradiction to the propositions of the asset market approaches is that the volatility of freely floating exchange rates exceeds the variability of the related macroeconomic fundamentals. Baxter and Stockman [1989] report that real exchange rates under a flexible exchange rate system tend to be more volatile than under a pegged exchange rate system. However, they find no evidence for systematic differences in the behavior of macroeconomic aggregates such as e.g. industrial production or consumption across both time periods. Flood and Rose [1995] point out that the observable volatility of exchange rates increased in the post Bretton Woods area, although the variability of macroeconomic fundamentals such as money or output do not change very much across

exchange rate regimes. These findings are crucial as they suggest that fundamental based exchange rate models are unlikely to be very successful. Flood and Rose [1999] therefore conclude that

> "macroeconomics appears to be irrelevant in explaining high and medium frequency exchange rate dynamics for low-inflation countries." (Flood and Rose [1999], p. F667)

4. For a fourth contradicting fact we refer to Goldberg and Frydman [2001]. Goldberg and Frydman [2001] maintain that the existing macroeconomic exchange rate models are able to explain the monthly or quarterly movements of exchange rates for some sub-periods reasonably well while for some other sub-periods their explanatory power completely disappears. This finding led them to suggest that empirical exchange rate models with fixed coefficients are unlikely to perform well either in sample or out of sample. Further evidence for unstable coefficients in empirical exchange rate models is given by De Grauwe and Vansteenkiste [2001]. They analyzed the relationship between exchange rates and fundamentals in a non-linear framework and found many significant switches in the coefficients. A further indication for instability in the coefficients of macroeconomic exchange rate models is given by Cheung et al. [2002] who report that, depending on model/specification/currency combinations, in one period favorable results can be obtained while in another period this combination will not necessarily work well.

Overall, it seems to be appropriate to conclude that the existing traditional macroeconomic exchange rate models fail to explain observable exchange rate movements consistently over various time periods. Or in the words of Kilian and Taylor [2003] who summarize the preceding evidence for fundamental based exchange rate models very accurately:

> "After nearly two decades of research since Meese and Rogoff's pioneering work on exchange rate predictability (...), the goal of exploiting economic models of exchange rate determination to beat naïve random walk forecasts remains as elusive as ever." (Kilian and Taylor [2003], pp. 85)

II.2.1.2.2 The link between macroeconomic fundamentals and the EUR/USD exchange rate

The negative empirical results for fundamental based exchange rate models are also confirmed by the EUR/USD exchange rate. The models of exchange rate determination discussed in section II.2.1.1 suggest that exchange rates are primarily determined by macroeconomic fundamentals such as domestic and foreign money supplies, real incomes, interest rates, price levels and the balance of international payments. For our basic evaluation of the relationship between the EUR/USD exchange rate and macroeconomic fundamentals, we refer to some descriptive statistics as suggested by Meese [1990]. The considered statistics include sample means, standard deviations, and a correlation matrix of the EUR/USD exchange rate and macroeconomic fundamentals. In particular, we use the following monthly differentials between Euro area and US macroeconomic fundamentals: short- and long-term interest rate differentials, differentials in consumer price indices, money supply differentials (M1 and M3) and differentials in the industrial production. This selection of fundamentals largely covers those variables, which are, according to economic theory, relevant for exchange rate determination. We analyze both levels and first differences (one period change) of the considered variables. The sample period starts in January 1999 and ends in June 2003.

Overall, the sample statistics reveal that the EUR/USD exchange rate is, in general, more variable (has larger standard deviation) than macroeconomic fundamentals except for the interest rate differentials (see Table II-1 and Table II-2). This finding corresponds with the results reported by Baxter and Stockman [1989] and Flood and Rose [1995] who report evidence for a higher volatility of exchange rates compared to macroeconomic fundamentals. Furthermore, the correlation matrix in Table II-2 indicates that there exists no systematic relationship between changes in the EUR/USD exchange rate and changes in macroeconomic fundamentals; none of the correlations appears to be statistically significant. In addition, the signs of many correlations between the EUR/USD level and their respective fundamentals are either insignificant or difficult to explain (see Table II-1). Both short- and long-term interest rate differentials show insignificant correlations to the level of the EUR/USD exchange rate. The sign of the correlation between the EUR/USD exchange rate and consumer price differentials is inconsistent with purchasing power parity. According to the purchasing power parity, a higher relative price level should be associated with a weaker currency. However, for the EUR/USD exchange rate higher relative price levels are associated with a stronger domestic currency. According to the economic theory, higher domestic money supply should involve a weakening of the domestic currency. Again the correlation between the EUR/USD exchange rate and the money supply is hard to reconcile with the economic intuition. Differences in M1 between the Euro area and the United States appear to be insignificantly correlated with the EUR/USD exchange rate. In addition, the correlation between the EUR/USD exchange rate and the M3 differential is in contrast with the economic theory, as higher domestic money supply measured by M3 leads to a appreciation of the domestic currency. Higher industrial production in the Euro area is associated with a depreciation of the Euro against the US dollar. This finding is somewhat astonishing as economists often hold higher growth activity responsible for appreciating currencies.

Overall, the results of our simple correlation analysis indicate that it is rather challenging if not impossible to explain exchange rates with macroeconomic fundamentals. However, it should also be mentioned that other sample correlations in Table II-1 and Table II-2 are also difficult to rationalize. This may be due to the fact that it is always dangerous to infer causal relations from simple correlations (see Meese [1990]). Therefore, we re-examine the relationship between macroeconomic fundamentals and the EUR/USD exchange rate. The second analysis is based on yearly figures provided by the OECD. Table II-3 shows yearly averaged figures for the EUR/USD, the GDP-growth differential, inflation differential, differences in government deficits, short- and long-tem interest rate differential – both nominal and real – and differences in the current account balances. Again the empirical evidence reveals that the link between exchange rates and macroeconomic fundamentals is exceedingly weak and unstable.

Table II-1: Sample moments of the level of US-$/€ exchange rate and macroeconomic fundamentals

No.	Variable	Mean	Standard Deviation
1	Log spot US-$/€	-0.0301	0.0897
2	Euro – U.S. Interest differential (1 month)	-0.3020	1.6990
3	Euro – U.S. Interest differential (10 years)	-0.2459	0.5556
4	Log European to U.S. prices (CPI)	-0.0400	0.0068
5	Log European to U.S. M1	0.5995	0.0512
6	Log European to U.S. M3	-0.3652	0.0295
7	Log European to U.S. industrial production	-0.0710	0.0226

		Correlation Matrix Variable no.						
		1	2	3	4	5	6	7
Variable no.	1	1						
	2	-0.1644	1					
	3	-0.2349	0.8884**	1				
	4	0.5437**	-0.4635**	-0.7011**	1			
	5	-0.2639	0.7246**	0.8624**	-0.7305**	1		
	6	0.5030**	-0.8691**	-0.9067**	0.7153**	-0.8230**	1	
	7	-0.2757*	0.9142**	0.9103**	-0.6584**	0.7663**	-0.8869**	1

Notes: *, ** denotes that correlation is significant at the 0.05, 0.01 level (two tailed)

Data sources: ECB Monthly Bulletin – Euro area statistics, Board of Governors of the Federal Reserve System and International Financial Statistics of the International Monetary Fund.

Reading the entries of the correlation matrix: the entry -0.2349 in the third row and first column is the sample correlation coefficient between the log of the €/US-$ exchange rate (variable 1) and the long-term Euro – U.S. Interest differential (10 years) (variable 3).

Table II-2: Sample moments of the first differences of US-$/€ exchange rate and macroeconomic fundamentals

No.	Variables	Mean	Standard Deviation
1	Log spot €/US-$	0.0001	0.0262
2	Euro – U.S. Interest differential (1 month)	0.0458	0.2044
3	Euro – U.S. Interest differential (10 years)	0.0243	0.1435
4	Log European to U.S. prices (CPI)	-0.0003	0.0030
5	Log European to U.S. M1	0.0035	0.0134
6	Log European to U.S. M3	-0.0013	0.0061
7	Log European to U.S. industrial production	0.0008	0.0069

	Correlation Matrix Variable no.						
Variable no.	1	2	3	4	5	6	7
1	1						
2	-0.1338	1					
3	0.2075	-0.1694	1				
4	-0.1302	0.1944	-0.2382	1			
5	-0.1658	-0.0970	-0.1007	0.1503	1		
6	0.2481	-0.1193	-0.1513	-0.0245	0.2653	1	
7	-0.0377	0.1375	0.0158	-0.0587	-0.0985	0.1899	1

Notes: *, ** denotes that correlation is significant at the 0.05, 0.01 level (two tailed)
Data sources: ECB Monthly Bulletin – Euro area statistics, Board of Governors of the Federal Reserve System and International Financial Statistics of the International Monetary Fund.
Reading the entries of the correlation matrix: the entry 0.2075 in the third row and first column is the sample correlation coefficient between the log of the €/US-$ exchange rate (variable 1) and the long-term Euro – U.S. Interest differential (10 years) (variable 3).

In 1999 and 2000 the growth differential between Europe and the United States was a very popular explanation for the development of the EUR/USD exchange rate (see Arestis et al. [2002]). However, since 2001 this argumentation is no longer compatible with the evidence of the observable exchange rate changes. In addition, in 1998 when the growth differential in favor of the United States was most pronounced, the depreciation of the Euro was rather weak. Thus, growth-differentials can not explain the EUR/USD exchange rate over the whole sample period. With regard to the inflation differential, we arrive at a similar conclusion. Although the inflation differential between the Euro area and the Unites States indicates a strong Euro for the time period of 1998 to 2001, the Euro actually depreciated against the US dollar. In 2002 the inflation differential suggests a weakening of the Euro against the US-dollar, however the actual rate appreciated. Thus, for the period of 1998 to 2002 the sign was wrong according to the purchasing power parity. Only in 2003 do the actual exchange rate movements correspond to the predications of purchasing power parity. In recent times, the actual appreciation of the

EUR/USD exchange rate is justified by the large current account deficit of the US economy. However, as Table II-3 shows, the larger current account deficit in the USA is nothing new. In fact, for the whole period the US current account deficit exceeds the European one so that it can not serve as a universal explanation for the observable movements of the Euro. The only macroeconomic variable that shows a consistent response of EUR/USD exchange rates over the whole period is the interest rate differential between the Euro area and the United States. Over the whole period of 1998 to 2003 the currency area with the higher interest rates experienced an appreciation of the domestic currency. However, this response of the exchange rate to interest differentials does not correspond to the intuition of economic theory. According to the uncovered interest rate parity, higher interest rates lead to a depreciation of the domestic currency.

Table II-3: US-$/€ exchange rate and macroeconomic fundamentals

	US-$/€	Δ US-$/€ (in %)	GDP-Growth (in %)	CPI	Nominal Interest Rate		Real Interest Rate		Current account balance (in % of GDP)
					Short-term	Long-term	Short-term	Long-term	
1998	1.11	-1.77	-1.5	-0.3	-1.6	-0.6	-1.3	-0.3	3.3
1999	1.06	-4.50	-1.3	-1	-2.4	-1	-1.4	0	3.5
2000	0.92	-13.21	-0.1	-1.2	-2.1	-0.6	-0.9	0.6	3.7
2001	0.89	-3.26	1.4	-0.4	0.6	0	1	0.4	4.1
2002	0.94	5.62	-1.5	0.7	1.5	0.3	0.8	-0.4	5.7
2003	1.12	19.15	-2.4	-0.3	1.1	0.2	1.4	0.5	5.4

Data source: Organisation for Economic Co-operation and Development [2003]

II.2.2 On the rationality of exchange rate expectations

A basic element of the asset market theory of exchange rate determination is the assumption of rational expectations. According to the rational expectations hypothesis, expectations of rationally acting subjects reveal several typical characteristics which can be used for an empirical evaluation of the rational expectations hypothesis. One of the central propositions of the rational expectations hypothesis is that expectation errors of rational agents (ξ_{t+h}) based on the available information set (Ω_t) should be purely random

$$\xi_{t+h} = s_{t+h} - E\left(s_{t+h} \middle| \Omega_t\right), \quad \text{with } \xi_{t+h} \sim \left(0, \sigma^2\right). \tag{II-43}$$

Thus, under the assumption of rational expectations, expectation errors are expected to be zero, i.e. they fluctuate randomly so that ex post no systematic deviations of the actual spot rate from the expected rate should be observed.

A second characteristic of rational expectations is that forecast errors of rational subjects are serially uncorrelated with past or future expectation errors,

$$E\left(\xi_t \xi_{t\pm h}\right) = 0 \quad \text{for } h \geq 1. \tag{II-44}$$

In addition, rational expectation hypothesis implies that rational subjects generate their forecasts by using all available information efficiently. This implication of rational expectations is often called the orthogonality hypothesis. According to the orthogonality hypothesis rational expectations incorporate all available information, so that their predictive power can not be improved by the inclusion of any variable that is known at the time of expectation formation. Consequently, expectations errors must be uncorrelated with any variable in the available information set Ω.

$$s_{t+h} - E_t s_{t+h} = \alpha + \beta X_t + \varepsilon_{t+h} \tag{II-45}$$

where X_t is a set of information known at time t and the orthogonality hypothesis holds if $\alpha = 0$ and $\beta = 0$.

II.2.2.1 Rational exchange rate expectations: a selective survey

The rationality of expectations is normally tested on the basis of survey data. The use of survey data is a reasonable choice as it allows for a direct analysis of expectations, instead of assuming a particular expectation formation model. However, the usage of survey data in this context is not undisputed. There is no assurance that the participants in the survey have enough incentives to disclosure their true expectations. Furthermore, there appears to be no precise link between average expectations and the actual exchange rate. However, given the fact that no better alternative exists for analyzing expectation formation in foreign exchange markets empirically, the literature based on survey data of exchange rate expectations has been expanding in recent years. Typically, the rationality of exchange rate expectations is evaluated by testing the unbiasedness and orthogonality hypothesis. The hypothesis of serially independent expectation errors is normally neglected. Extensive surveys on the literature related to the rationality of exchange rate expectations are given by Takagi [1991] and MacDonald [2000].

A common way to test the unbiasedness hypothesis is to regress the actual change in the spot exchange rate on the expected change according to the professional forecasts. Thus, the null hypothesis of unbiasedness implies that it is possible to decompose s_{t+h}-s_t as

$$s_{t+h} - s_t = \alpha + \beta(E_t s_{t+h} - s_t) + \varepsilon_{t+h} \tag{II-46}$$

where s is the logarithm of the nominal spot exchange rate, $\alpha = 0$, $\beta = 1$ and ε_{t+h} has a mean of zero and is uncorrelated with $E_t S_{t+h}$-S_t (see Cavaglia et al. [1994]).

Overall, the existing empirical results suggest that the unbiasedness hypothesis must be rejected in the context of exchange rate expectations. Dominguez [1992] rejects the unbiasedness hypothesis for various currencies against the US dollar using seemingly unrelated regressions. For short-term expectations (one-week and two-week) the slope coefficients of β are predominantly positive but close to zero. For longer horizons (one and three months) the slope coefficients of β are generally negative and close to - 0.5. This implies that forecasters over-predict the size of spot depreciation, and also get the direction of the exchange rate movements wrong. Cavaglia et al. [1993] reveal that the null hypothesis of β=1 is rejected for ten currencies relative to the US-Dollar. Furthermore, the sign of the β coefficient is in general significantly negative, so that the survey respondents predict the wrong direction of exchange rate depreciation. Sobiechowski [1996] finds comparable results. He reports that, except for the 12 month forecast horizon, the null hypothesis of β=1 is rejected and the joint null hypothesis of α=0 and β=1 is rejected for all forecast horizons and currencies under consideration. The forecast bias of survey data is ascribed to a systematic underestimation of the actual exchange rate change. Additionally, for some forecast horizons negative values of β are found so that respondents may even miss the direction of exchange rate change. Harvey [1999] performs empirical tests of the rational expectation hypothesis using survey expectations for the British Pound, the Deutsche Mark, the Japanese Yen and the Swiss Franc in the time period of January 1986 to June 1999. With regard to the unbiasedness hypothesis, his results strongly recommend a rejection of the rational expectation hypothesis. More recently, some researchers investigate the unbiasedness hypothesis using cointegration tests (see Liu and Maddala [1992a] and [1992b], Kim [1997] and Osterberg [2000]). Their results suggest that short-run expectations up to one month are unbiased predictors for future exchange rates. However, in the long-run unbiasedness hypothesis is rejected as well (see Miah et al. [2004]).

The second characteristic of rational expectations which has been often tested in the past is the orthogonality hypothesis. According to the orthogonality hypothesis, rational subjects make efficient use of all available information when forming their expectations so that their predictive power can not be improved by the inclusion of any variable that is known at the time of expectation formation. Consequently, forecast errors must be uncorrelated with any variable in the available information set. The orthogonality hypothesis is usually tested by regressing the ex post forecast errors against some known information available when market participants form their forecasts,

$$s_{t+h} - E_t s_{t+h} = \alpha + \beta X_t + \varepsilon_{t+h} \tag{II-47}$$

where X_t is a set of information known at time *t* and the orthogonality hypothesis holds if $\alpha = 0$ and $\beta = 0$. Typically, the information set X_t consists of forward discounts, nominal interest rate differentials or lagged spot exchange rates.

The preceding results of testing the orthogonality hypothesis provide also evidence against the rational expectations hypothesis. Frankel and Froot [1987] provide strong evidence against the orthogonality hypothesis as they find a strongly statistically significant estimate of β in equation (II-47). This result was confirmed by Froot and Frankel [1989] in their 1989 paper as they state that the rationality expectation hypothesis is rejected due to β being significantly greater than zero. Similar results are reported by Cavaglia et al. [1993] who also reject the orthogonality hypothesis for survey expectations covering ten currencies relative to the US-Dollar as the forward premium contains additional information for the exchange rate forecasts of the major currencies relative to the US-dollar. Beng and Siong [1993] took past forecast errors and past forward discounts as relevant information sets and found that currency forecasters could have improved their forecasts by better exploiting existing information. More recently, Sobiechowski [1996] analyses the orthogonality hypothesis by using lagged exchange rate changes, past forecast errors, and forward premiums. He concludes that market participants do not always use all available information efficiently especially in longer-term horizons. Similar results are also reported by Harvey [1999].

Overall, the preceding evidence suggests a rejection of the rational expectation hypothesis. Using survey data on exchange rate expectations leads to a consistent rebuttal of the unbiasedness hypothesis especially for longer-term forecast horizons. This holds also true for the orthogonality hypothesis which has proved to be problematic especially when considering longer forecast horizons.

II.2.2.2 Rationality of exchange rate expectations for the EUR/USD exchange rate

In this section, we analyze the rational expectations hypothesis for the EUR/USD exchange rate using survey data. To our knowledge, this is the first study analyzing professional exchange rate expectations for the EUR/USD exchange rate. Therefore, it appears to be of particular interest whether the introduction of a new currency has a discernable effect on the expectation formation of exchange rate analysts.[9]

II.2.2.2.1 Data

The analysis of professional exchange rate expectations is based on survey data provided by three different suppliers of financial data: Reuters, Consensus Economics and ZEW Finanzmarkttest from the Centre for European Economic Research (ZEW).[10] The period under consideration starts in January 1999 and ends in March 2003. The available forecast horizons vary depending on the supplier and are summarized in Table II-4. Figure II-1 shows the survey data that was received at a given date for different time horizons. The spot EUR/USD exchange rate is taken from the IFS CD-ROM of the International Monetary Fund (IMF). Here we use the end-of-month values of the preceding month since the market forecasts are given at the end or the beginning of a month: for instance, the December one-month forecast for January is typically made at the end of November/beginning of December. Thus, we compare this value with the actual end of the December spot rate.

Table II-4: Available survey data

	Period	**Forecast horizon**
Consensus Economics	1999/1-2002/12	3 months
Reuters	1999/1-2003/2	1, 3, 6 months
ZEW-Finanzmarkttest	1999/1-2002/12	6 months

[9] For a more detailed analysis of professional exchange rate expectations in the context of EUR/USD exchange rates, we refer to Bofinger and Schmidt [2003].

[10] Information about the suppliers of the survey data can be found on www.consensuseconomics.com, www.reuters.com and www.zew.de. Consensus Economics and Reuters also provide survey data of exchange rate expectations for longer time horizons. However, due to the special topic of this study – especially in Chapter V – we analyze here only expectations up to a forecast horizon of six months. For an evaluation including forecast horizons of 12 and 24 months, we refer to Bofinger and Schmidt [2003].

Figure II-1: Available professional exchange rate forecasts

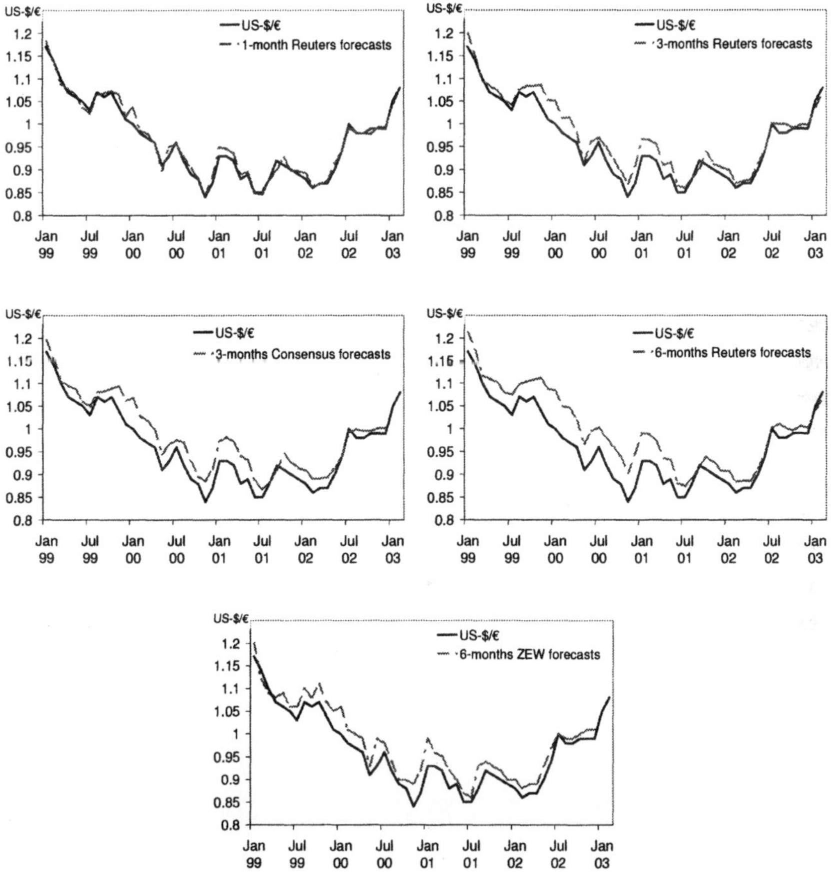

Note: The professional exchange rate forecasts are shifted back to the time of forecast formation.

II.2.2.2.2 Empirical results

For the empirical evaluation of the rational expectation hypothesis in the context of EUR/USD exchange rate expectations we refer to the three discussed characteristics of rational expectations. Concerning the unbiasedness hypothesis, already a simple graphical analysis of the professional expectation errors illustrates that those expectations are difficult to reconcile with rational expectation hypothesis (see Figure II-2). Instead of fluctuating randomly, the expectation errors exhibit systematic deviations. In particular, this becomes apparent for the three and six month professional expectations. Overall, the professional expectations errors reveal that until the spring of 2002 almost all expectations were too optimistic for the Euro exchange rate vis-à-vis the US dollar; after that date they were too pessimistic.

Figure II-2: Expectations errors of survey data

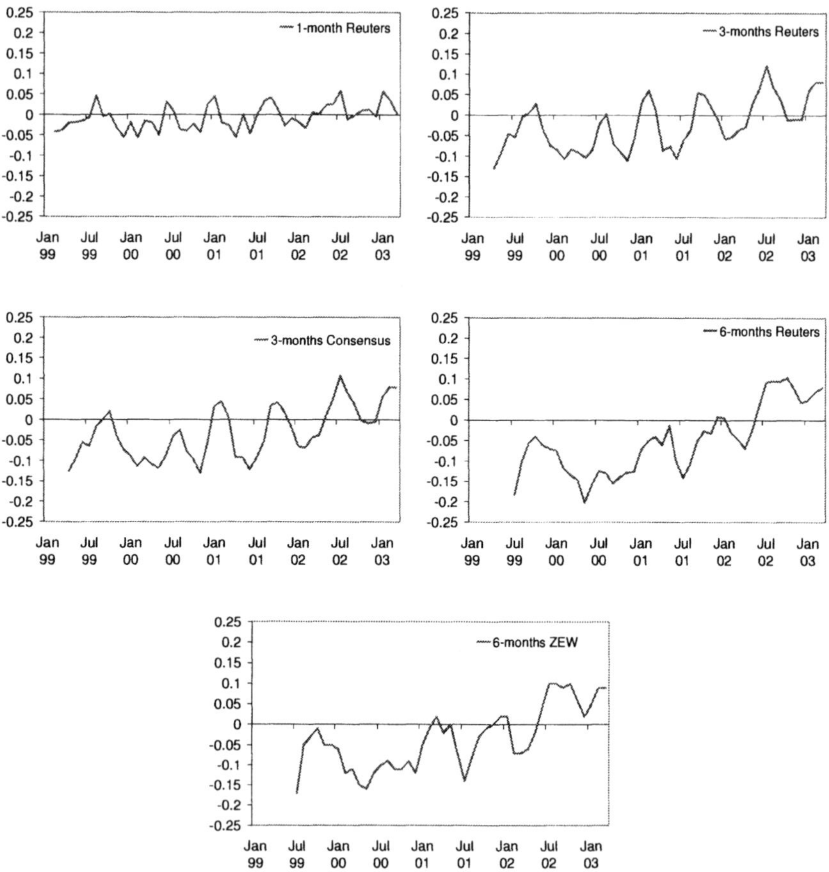

For evaluating the unbiasedness hypothesis empirically, we estimate equation (II-46) for each professional exchange rate expectation over the three different forecast horizons via ordinary least squares (OLS). Since Hansen and Hodrick [1980] demonstrate that, when the forecast horizon is larger than the observational frequency, the forecast error ε_{t+k} will be serially correlated. We decide to account for the autocorrelation in the residuals on the one hand by using the Newey and West [1987] estimation procedure (see Cavaglia et al. [1994]) and on the other hand by an explicit modeling of the autocorrelation structure of residuals. Both estimation procedures imply some advantages but also some drawbacks.[11] The results are summarized in Table II-5.

For all market expectations the results indicate that the unbiasedness hypothesis is rejected. Figure II-3 illustrates that the slope coefficients (β) for all professional exchange rate expectations over all three forecasting horizons are negative instead of being approximately one. Consequently, the regression results indicate that although the α coefficients are almost close to zero, the β coefficients clearly depart from one. The Wald-Tests suggest that for all professional expectations the null hypothesis of $\alpha = 0$ can not be rejected. However, the null hypothesis of $\beta = 1$ and the joint hypothesis of $\alpha = 0$ and $\beta = 1$ can not be maintained. Interestingly, the different estimation procedures result in divergent statements about the relationship between the actual exchange rate change and the expected. Whereas the results of the Newey and West [1987] estimation procedure suggest that professional exchange rate expectations clearly fail to anticipate the direction of change (β is significantly smaller than zero), the results of the AR regression indicate that no correlation between expected exchange rate changes and actual exchange rate changes exist. Overall, the results reported for the EUR/USD exchange rate expectations are consistent with the results reported in the literature.

[11] For a description of the applied estimation procedures see APPENDIX A.

Figure II-3: Scatter diagrams for the unbiasedness hypothesis of professional exchange rate expectations

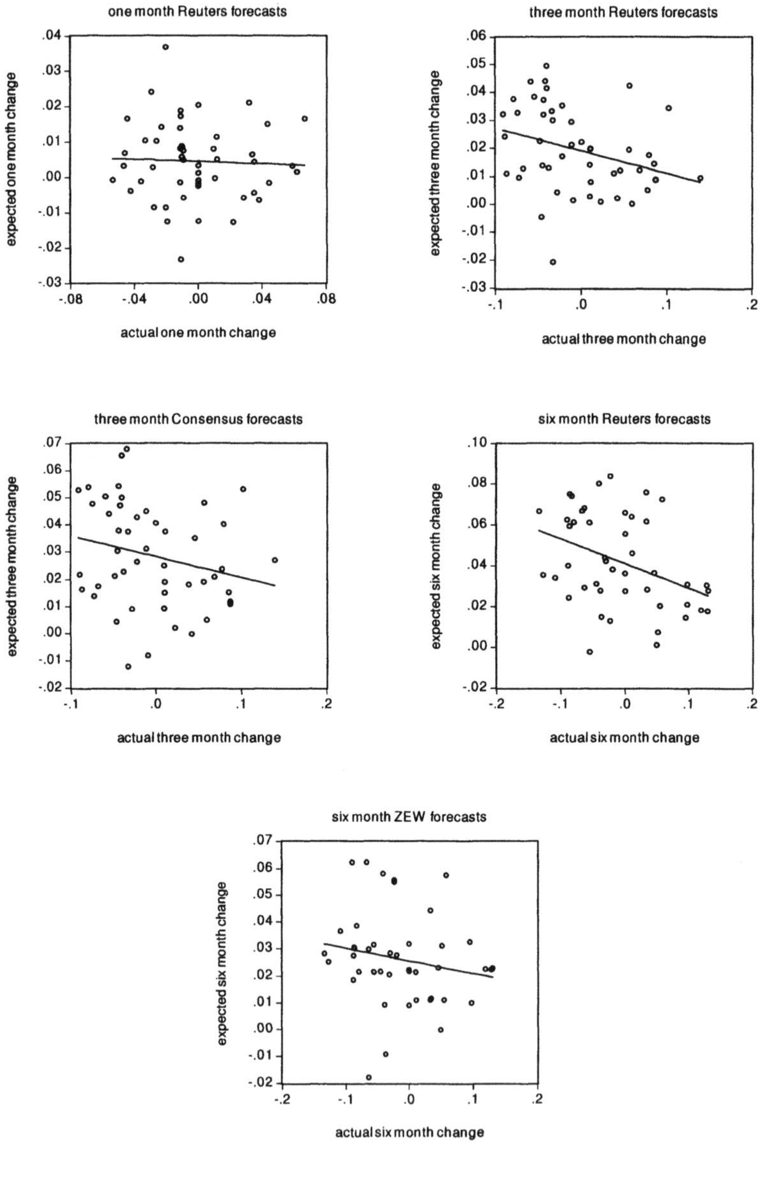

Table II-5: Unbiasedness of market expectations

	Estimation procedure	Q-Statistic	α	$H_0: \alpha = 0$	β	$H_0: \beta = 1$	$H_0: \alpha = 0, \beta = 1$
1-month Reuters	NW	--	-0.0011 (0.0046)	0.0585 [0.8099]	-0.1117 (0.2928)	14.4100 [0.0004]	7.3039 [0.0017]
	ARMA	Q(12) = 0.127 Q(24) = 0.090	-0.0005 (0.0048)	0.0111 [0.9168]	0.0603 (0.4090)	5.2775 [0.0269]	3.2583 [0.0489]
3-months Reuters	NW	--	0.0197 (0.0185)	1.1276 [0.2938]	-1.2012 (0.5865)	14.0873 [0.0005]	12.8717 [0.0000]
	ARMA	Q(12) = 0.340 Q(24) = 0.234	0.0039 (0.0175)	0.0488 [0.8263]	0.0787 (0.2710)	11.5580 [0.0016]	6.1459 [0.0049]
3-months Consensus	NW	--	0.0166 (0.0181)	0.8406 [0.3640]	-0.7093 (0.4068)	17.6537 [0.0001]	15.6519 [0.0000]
	ARMA	Q(12) = 0.467 Q(24) = 0.264	-0.0038 (0.0208)	0.0333 [0.8562]	0.3749 (0.2432)	6.6045 [0.0142]	3.8948 [0.0289]
6-months Reuters	NW	--	0.0418 (0.0352)	1.4074 [0.2420]	-1.1948 (0.6104)	12.9287 [0.0008]	17.8645 [0.0000]
	ARMA	Q(12) = 0.223 Q(24) = 0.535	0.2264 (0.9089)	0.0621 [0.8048]	0.3582 (0.4628)	1.9237 [0.1750]	1.0271 [0.3696]
6-months ZEW	NW	--	-0.0128 (0.0272)	0.2227 [0.6394]	-0.8225 (0.5865)	9.6576 [0.0033]	9.1256 [0.0005]
	ARMA	Q(12) = 0.390 Q(24) = 0.379	-0.1639 (0.2803)	0.3419 [0.5627]	0.2610 (0.2468)	8.9665 [0.0052]	4.5542 [0.0179]

Notes: Standard errors are in parenthesis, p-values in brackets.
NW denotes the Newey & West estimation procedure; ARMA denotes the ARMA estimation procedure.

The orthogonality hypothesis is empirically evaluated by a variant of equation (II-45). In particular, we use in our regression approach four lags of the (log) spot exchange rate as information set X_t, so that the regression equation is given as

$$s_{t+h} - E_t s_{t+h} = \alpha + \beta_1 s_t + \beta_2 s_{t-1} + \cdots + \beta_4 s_{t-3} + \varepsilon_{t+h} . \qquad \text{(II-48)}$$

Table II-6 shows the corresponding results which are obtained by using general least squares (OLS). Again, we run each regression twice by using Newey and West [1987] estimation procedure as well as the explicit modeling of the autocorrelation structure of the residuals. For an evaluation of the null hypothesis $\alpha = \beta_1 = \beta_2 = ... = \beta_4 = 0$, we carry out Wald tests. The corresponding F-statistics are also summarized in Table II-6. The results for the orthogonality hypothesis are somewhat mixed. For the one month professional exchange rate expectations the results indicate that the orthogonality hypothesis can be maintained.[12] However, the estimation results for the three and six months expectations suggest that the orthogonality

[12] Note that this does not necessarily mean that the monthly exchange rate expectations could not have been improved, just not necessarily with the data tested.

hypothesis must be rejected. This conclusion is also largely confirmed by the corresponding F-statistics of the Wald-tests analyzing the null hypothesis of $\alpha = \beta_1 = \beta_2 = \ldots = \beta_4 = 0$. Overall, our results are in line with previous evidence. Sobiechowski [1996] also reports that the orthogonality hypothesis has to be rejected especially for the longer forecast horizons.

Table II-6: Orthogonality test for professional exchange rate forecasts

	Estimation procedure	Q-Statistic	α	β_1	β_2	β_3	β_4	H_0: $\alpha = \beta_1 \ldots \beta_4 = 0$
1-month Reuters	NW	--	-0.0088 (0.0070)	0.2149 (0.1320)	-0.3343 (0.1832)	-0.0098 (0.2301)	0.0528 (0.1509)	1.4351 [0.2322]
	ARMA	Q(12) = 0.645 Q(24) = 0.191	-0.0088 (0.0061)	0.2149 (0.1720)	-0.3343 (0.2640)	-0.0098 (0.2699)	0.0528 (0.1712)	1.0041 [0.4275]
3-months Reuters	NW	--	-0.0412 (0.0173)	-0.0499 (0.3085)	-0.3238 (0.3038)	-0.3639 (0.3718)	0.4324 (0.2861)	1.9666 [0.1053]
	ARMA	Q(12) = 0.617 Q(24) = 0.242	-0.0892 (0.0926)	-0.9529 (0.2038)	-0.1666 (0.2028)	-0.3860 (0.2016)	0.2656 (0.1992)	6.0016 [0.0004]
3-months Consensus	NW	--	-0.0476 (0.0180)	0.1734 (0.3182)	-0.5075 (0.3019)	-0.3130 (0.3923)	0.3866 (0.3149)	2.2048 [0.0733]
	ARMA	Q(12) = 0.638 Q(24) = 0.370	-0.0917 (0.1032)	-0.7637 (0.2002)	-0.3429 (0.1993)	-0.3438 (0.1981)	0.2521 (0.1956)	5.1309 [0.0011]
6-months Reuters	NW	--	-0.0834 (0.0234)	-0.3506 (0.4186)	0.0927 (0.4262)	-0.0718 (0.3530)	-0.2534 (0.3483)	2.9412 [0.0251]
	ARMA	Q(12) = 0.534 Q(24) = 0.622	0.0129 (0.1987)	-0.5469 (0.1913)	0.1407 (0.1925)	0.1297 (0.2012)	0.1111 (0.2041)	2.1530 [0.0827]
6-months ZEW	NW	--	-0.0663 (0.0219)	-0.7121 (0.3710)	0.3733 (0.3613)	0.1247 (0.3597)	-0.3224 (0.3496)	2.9830 [0.0236]
	ARMA	Q(12)= 0.165 Q(24) = 0.125	0.0449 (0.1761)	-0.6859 (0.1966)	0.3722 (0.1987)	0.3574 (0.2088)	0.0333 (0.2122)	4.1948 [0.0045]

Notes: Standard errors are in parenthesis, p-values in brackets.
NW denotes the Newey & West estimation procedure; ARMA denotes the ARMA estimation procedure.

The hypothesis of serially uncorrelated expectation errors (ξ) can directly be tested by estimating the following regression equation

$$\xi_t = \alpha + \beta_1 \xi_{t-1} + \beta_2 \xi_{t-2} + \cdots + \beta_n \xi_{t-n} + \varepsilon_t . \qquad \text{(II-49)}$$

The hypothesis of serially uncorrelated forecast errors implies that $\alpha = \beta_1 = \beta_2 = \ldots = \beta_n = 0$. Table II-7 summarizes the results for evaluating the hypothesis of serially uncorrelated expectation errors. The results are obtained by estimating equation (II-49) considering four lagged expectation errors via OLS.[13]

[13] In this context, we forbear from applying both different estimation procedures as the structure of the estimation equation is autoregressive so that the probability of autocorrelated residuals is rather low.

Overall, a similar pattern compared to the results for the orthogonality hypothesis is found. For the one month professional exchange rate expectations the expectation errors appear to be correlated of order one. However, the corresponding F-statistic testing the joint null hypothesis of $\alpha = \beta_1 = \beta_2 = \beta_3 = \beta_4 = 0$ indicates that the null hypothesis can not be rejected. The results for the three and six month expectation errors imply that those expectation errors are clearly correlated with lagged expectation errors. This conclusion is, consequently, also supported by the F-statistics of the Wald-tests.

Table II-7: Test for serial correlation in professional forecast errors

	α	β_1	β_2	β_3	β_4	$H_0: \alpha = \beta_1 ... \beta_4 = 0$
1-month Reuters	-0.0044 (0.0052)	0.3085 (0.1563)	0.0001 (0.1693)	-0.0231 (0.1695)	-0.1832 (0.1622)	1.3742 [0.2545]
3-months Reuters	-0.0045 (0.0068)	1.0722 (0.1493)	-0.1756 (0.2111)	-0.5726 (0.2147)	0.3755 (0.1530)	20.3089 [0.0000]
3-months Consensus	-0.0051 (0.0070)	1.1854 (0.1482)	-0.2817 (0.2265)	-0.5357 (0.2297)	0.3965 (0.1531)	29.8217 [0.0000]
6-months Reuters	-0.0016 (0.0076)	1.1892 (0.1695)	-0.4043 (0.2626)	0.1223 (0.2625)	0.0153 (0.1698)	51.3124 [0.0000]
6-months ZEW	-0.0032 (0.0080)	1.1288 (0.1711)	-0.3220 (0.2550)	-0.0023 (0.2518)	0.0519 (0.1659)	26.7208 [0.0000]

Notes: Standard errors are in parenthesis, p-values in brackets.

On the whole, the results for the professional EUR/USD exchange rate expectations show that rational expectation hypothesis must be rejected. Solely for the short-run expectations of one month the hypothesis of orthogonality and serially uncorrelated expectation errors can be maintained. However, these results may only be due to the selection of the included lags and using longer lags may result in a rejection of rational expectations hypothesis.

II.2.3 On the link between exchange rate dynamics and 'news'

This section deals with the implication of the asset market approach that exchange rate changes should be associated with surprises in macroeconomic fundamentals. As equation (II-19) shows, unexpected exchange rate changes are caused by new information about macroeconomic fundamentals. Thus, news is an important factor driving exchange rates.

II.2.3.1 A selective survey of the existing literature

A considerable amount of academic research has been employed to ascertain whether the predicted reaction of exchange rates to 'news' can be supported by empirical evidence. Most tests for 'news'-effects on exchange rates are based on estimating some version of equation (II-50)

$$s_t - s_{t-1} = \alpha + \beta NEWS_t + \varepsilon_t \tag{II-50}$$

where $NEWS_t$ is a vector containing news variables (see Jansen and De Haan [2003]). One strand of the literature on news and exchange rates uses univariate or multivariate time series methods to extract news in macroeconomic fundamentals; related studies are for example Frenkel [1981] and Edwards [1983]. Their results indicate that unexpected exchange rate changes could be linked to unexpected changes in the corresponding fundamentals. However, the usage of time series methods to generate news in fundamentals is afflicted with various problems. First, it is implicitly assumed that the market participants know the true statistical process of the fundamentals. Second, the models are typically estimated on the basis of monthly of even quarterly data which does not allow for an accurate record of the arrival of new information. These problems are overcome by a second strand of the literature, which uses official announcements of macroeconomic fundamentals and expectations about these fundamentals collected from surveys. The main advantage of this approach is that the impact of news on exchange rates can be evaluated on a daily or intra-daily basis (see Galati and Ho [2003]). Hardouvelis [1988] for example analyses the news effect for various currencies against the US-Dollar on a day-to-day basis by using survey forecasts for a wide variety of US macroeconomic indicators. He reports that markets respond primarily to monetary news but also to news about the trade deficit, domestic inflation, and variables that reflect the state of the business cycle. However, the overall fit of his regression approach is rather low with adjusted R^2 lying around 0.02 to 0.04. Tanner [1997] investigates the daily exchange rate response to unanticipated information about US economic fundamentals for the time period October 1987 to December 1991. His results suggest that news in trade deficit and consumer price index announcements affect the DM/USD exchange rate. Contrary, news in the US industrial production, producer price index, unemployment and money supply announcements are statistically insignificant and the estimation fit is also very low. In a related study Edison [1997] examines the response of exchange rates on economic news announcements and finds that daily dollar exchange rates systematically react to news about GDP growth, but not to news on inflation, unemployment, industrial production and retail sales. Galati and Ho [2003] investigate the news effect for the EUR/USD exchange rate using both US and European macroeconomic fundamentals. On a day-to-day basis their results suggest that macroeconomic news can explain part of the daily EUR/USD exchange rate movements during the first two years of the European Monetary Union (EMU). In addition, Galati and Ho [2003] reveal that the market reacts significantly to news in the US NAPM manufacturing index and the German ifo-index, also news about inflation is found to be statistically significant (US CPI, German CPI, and PPI EU 11). However, macroeconomic news about the real US and European Economy failed to be statistically significant.

Overall, the empirical results for daily news effects on exchange rates suggest that it is difficult to detect systematic and meaningful effects of macroeconomic news on exchange rates at a daily frequency. A logical reason for this result may be that other (potentially non-fundamental) factors affect exchange rates so that the considered news-effect at a daily frequency is drowned out. Furthermore, the results indicate that the news which influences exchange rates can change over time and/or the influence of certain news may vary over time as the sign of the coefficient estimates varies across the different periods of investigation. Table II-8 illustrates a selective sample of studies investigating the news-effect on exchange rates. It becomes apparent that the sign of news effects varies over different time periods and currencies. For example, the results of Hardouvelis [1988] suggest that a positive surprise in CPI leads to an appreciation of the US dollar against the Deutsche Mark and the Japanese Yen. However, the evidence reported by Tanner [1997] and in part by Edison [1997] indicates a reversed impact. Similar conclusions can also be drawn for the industrial production and retail sales.

Table II-8: Sign of regression coefficients for US macroeconomic announcements – a selective survey

US NEWS	Hardouvelis [1988]		Tanner [1997]	Edison [1997]				Galati and Ho [2001]	Ehrmann and Fratzscher [2004]
	DM/USD	Yen/USD	DM/USD	DM/USD	DM/USD	YEN/USD	YEN/USD	EUR/USD	EUR/USD
	Oct '79 – Aug '84	Oct '79 – Aug '84	Oct '87 – Dec '91	Feb '80 – Feb '95	Feb '84 – Feb '95	Feb '80 – Feb '95	Feb '84 – Feb '95	Jan '99 – Dec '00	Jan '93 – Feb '03
CPI	-	-	+	-	-	+	-	-	-
PPI	-	+	+	+	+	+	+	n.a.	-
IP	-	+	+	+	+	-	+	+	+
RS	-	-	n.a.	+	+	0	+	+	+
TD	+	+	-	n.a.	n.a.	n.a.	n.a.	n.a.	+
UN	+	-	-	-	-	-	-	-	-

Notes: The signs of Tanner [1997] are reversed as he defines news conversely. CPI = consumer price index, PPI = producer price index, IP = industrial production, RS = retail sales, TD = trade deficit, UN = unemployment rate, n.a. = not available

The disappointing results of empirical studies using daily exchange rate data motivated a switch to high-frequency exchange rate data, in the hope of more accurately capturing the effects of news on exchange rates. Tanner [1997] investigates the effect of 'news' in US macroeconomic indicators on intraday dollar/mark spot rates. The results illustrate that news in the trade deficit and the consumer price index significantly influence the intra-daily DM/USD exchange rate. However, in contrast to the trade deficit news, which was immediately processed by the market, CPI news take longer to be processed by the market. Almeida et al. [1998] analyze the impact of macroeconomic news for the US and German economy on the DM/USD exchange rate using high frequency data. Overall, the results reveal a strong, quick impact of macroeconomic news. However, this impact seems to be quantitatively small and the overall effect of news on lower frequency exchange rate changes decays quite rapidly toward insignificance (see Almeida et al. [1998]). Furthermore, Almeida et al. [1998] report that there seem to be differences between U.S. and German announcements in the exchange rate reaction time pattern. Andersen et al. [2003] use a new data set consisting of six years of real time exchange rate quotations (5 minutes intervals), macroeconomic expectations, and macroeconomic realizations to characterize the conditional means of the US-$ exchange rates. They find that intra-daily exchange rate changes can be linked to announcement surprises for US macroeconomic variables including inter alia non-farm payroll, NAPM index, retail sales, consumer confidence, CPI, PPI, industrial production, and GDP. However, the impact of German macroeconomic news on the DM/USD rate is not as pronounced as that of US news. Only news in M3 and industrial production produce significant reactions in the exchange rate. Furthermore, Andersen et al. [2003] find sign effects which refer to the fact that the market reacts to news in an asymmetric fashion as bad news has greater impact on exchange rate changes than good news.

In addition to studies analyzing news effects for exchange rates by the means of scheduled macroeconomic announcements, some interesting studies try to discover the relevance of unscheduled news such as e.g. policy statements of leading politicians or official interventions in the foreign exchange markets (see e.g. Tivegna [2001]). Fatum and Hutchison [2002] investigate the impact of intervention-related news on the EUR/USD exchange rate. Their results suggest that official statements denying ECB interventions or questioning the efficacy of intervention have been viewed as important news and worked to depreciate the value of the Euro against the US dollar. Furthermore, it is found that rumors and speculation of intervention in support of the Euro is associated with an increase of the USD/EUR exchange rate. However, the effect is not persistent. On the contrary, official statements in support of the Euro seem to be ignored by the market. Most recently, Jansen and De Haan [2003] study the effect of statements of ECB officials on the level and volatility of the EUR/USD exchange rate. Their results suggest that the effects of ECB statements on the level of the EUR/USD exchange rate are comparatively small and often not persistent. However, in the case of volatility, ECB statements have had considerable influence as policy statements of ECB officials increase the EUR/USD exchange rate volatility. Concerning the EUR/USD exchange rate development, efforts of the ECB to 'talk up' the Euro have been futile as the official statements only led to higher volatility. In contrast, according to the results of Jansen and De Haan [2003] official statements about the (potential) intention to intervene in the foreign exchange market may have had some effects on the level of exchange rate. Thus, talking about intervention before conducting it may describe a reasonable strategy of central banks (see Jansen and De Haan [2003]). Furthermore, Jansen and De Haan [2003] find evidence for an asymmetric response of exchange rates to news. Markets respond differently to positive or negative news from the same category.

Summarizing the preceding evidence leads to the conclusion that the occurrence of news can only explain exchange rate movements to some extent. Some surprises in macroeconomic announcements have in fact significant impact on exchange rate developments. This holds true in particular for US macroeconomic variables and in the very short-run. However, much news seems to have no significant impact on exchange rates. Furthermore, the magnitude of news effects is quite low and the fit of the regression equations, especially for studies using daily exchange rate changes, is generally too low to explain the observable exchange rate variability. Additionally, recent studies like Galati and Ho [2003] on a daily basis and Andersen et al. [2003] on a intra-daily basis report evidence for an asymmetric response of exchange rates to news. This clearly contradicts the proposition of the asset market theory to exchange rate determination.

II.2.3.2 The link between macroeconomic 'news' and the EUR/USD exchange rate

II.2.3.2.1 Data

For the analysis of the impact of macroeconomic news on the EUR/USD exchange rate we use daily EUR/USD exchange rates between January 1999 and June 2003. The applied exchange rate time series is reported by the Federal Reserve Bank of New York and consists of the noon buying rates in New York for cable transfers. It is taken from Thomson Financial Datastream (mnemonic: E.U$FR2). We choose the noon rates in New York to capture the overall impact of news about both European and US announcements which occur on a specific day but at different points in time during the day, appropriately (see Galati and Ho [2003]). The main reason for using daily rather than intra-daily exchange rates is that empirical studies using intradaily data often come to the result that the effects of news are very transient (see e.g. Andersen et al. [2003]). However, from an economic perspective, news about macroeconomic fundamentals should have a sustained impact on the development of exchange rates so that exchange rates are driven by news on a daily frequency (see Ehrmann and Fratzscher [2004]). Admittedly, using daily exchange rates has the drawback that due to the large amount of news that hits the market at a particular trading day the measured impact of any given macroeconomic announcements includes a lot of noise from other news during the day.

Our selection of US and Euro area macroeconomic announcements largely corresponds to the selection of other related studies (see Kettell [2000]). Furthermore, we choose those variables that are judged by market participants to be important 'market movers'. On this point we refer to the discussion of economic indicators given by Mattern [2000]. For the European economy we only choose German macroeconomic announcements. This can be justified for several reasons: first, the German economy accounts for the largest economic weight in the Euro area; second, traders seem to orientate predominately on German macroeconomic announcements (see Galati and Ho [2001]); and third, German macroeconomic announcements are chronologically before the European wide macroeconomic announcements so that the German variables anticipate much of the European wide announcement. The considered macroeconomic announcements are summarized in Table II-9.

Table II-9: Macroeconomic announcements

United States	Unit	Ranking
Real gross domestic product	Percentage change, q/q	1
Change in non-farm payrolls	000's	2
Unemployment rate	Percentage	3
Consumer price index ex food & energy	Percentage change, m/m	4
Producer price index	Percentage change, m/m	5
NAPM / ISM – Index	Index	6
Industrial production	Percentage change, m/m	7
Retail sales	Percentage change, m/m	8
Durable goods orders	Percentage change, m/m	9
Goods & services trade balance	Billions $	10
Germany	**Unit**	**Ranking**
Real gross domestic product	Percentage change, q/q	1
Unemployment, sa m/m	000's	2
Ifo index	Index	3
Consumer price index	Percentage change, m/m	4
Producer price index	Percentage change, m/m	5
Industrial production	Percentage change, m/m	6
Retails sales, real nsa[14]	Percentage change, y/y	7
Manufacturing orders	Percentage change, m/m	8

The market expectations and the releases for the considered macroeconomic announcements are taken from the Money Market Survey (MMS). Money Market Survey conducts a survey of about 30 participants on the Friday the week before the release of each variable under consideration (see Edison [1997]). As a proxy for the market expectations we decided to use the median of the survey. Following the common approach in the literature we define the news of the announcement k as the differences between the actual announcement ($A_{k,t}$) and the market's prior expectations ($E_{k,t}$). Table II-10 presents the sample statistics of the measured news associated with the chosen macroeconomic announcements.

[14] Data for German retail sales are incomplete. Missing data are: December 1999, November 2000, May 2002, June 2002 and January 2003.

Table II-10: Sample statistics of the news variables

United States	**Mean**	**St error**	**Min**	**Max**	**Positive news (%)**
Real gross domestic product	0.1269	0.0769	-1.2	1.6	60
Change in non-farm payrolls	35.9815	14.7208	-328	188	44
Unemployment rate	-0.0278	0.0202	-0.3	0.3	43
Consumer price index ex f&e	-0.0028	0.0126	-0.2	0.2	42
Producer price index	-0.0074	0.0653	-1.3	1.2	41
NAPM / ISM – Index	-0.0722	0.2853	-4.5	4.7	43
Industrial production	-0.0157	0.0384	-0.6	0.7	43
Retail sales	0.0788	0.1175	-1.8	5	51
Durable goods orders	0.1694	0.4755	-7.5	10.85	54
Goods & services trade balance	-0.3324	0.3218	-5.7	7.3	42
Germany	**Mean**	**St error**	**Min**	**Max**	**Positive news (%)**
Real gross domestic product	-0.0611	0.0354	-0.4	0.1	33
Unemployment	3.1815	2.7816	-54	53	62
Ifo index	-0.1259	0.1495	-3	2.3	43
Consumer price index	0.0185	0.0200	-0.2	0.4	54
Producer price index	0.0056	0.0378	-0.6	0.8	45
Industrial production	-0.2870	0.1996	-3.6	2.7	40
Retails sales	-0.6306	0.3366	-5.4	5.8	45
Manufacturing orders	0.0778	0.3062	-4.1	4.9	57

In the regression analysis the news components enter normalized by dividing the news by its sample standard deviation (σ_{A_k}):

$$X_{k,t} = \frac{A_{k,t} - E_{t-1}\left(A_{k,t}\right)}{\sigma_{A_k}}. \tag{II-51}$$

The advantage of using normalized news measures in the regression analysis is a direct comparability of the news impact on exchange rates for different macroeconomic announcements. Furthermore, this approach allows the aggregation of news across macroeconomic variables, while preserving the magnitude of the news (see Galati and Ho [2003]).

II.2.3.2.2 Empirical results

For analyzing the impact of macroeconomic 'news' on exchange rate movements we refer to the empirical framework often used in the related literature (see section II.2.3.1). In particular, we investigate the impact of 'news' on the EUR/USD exchange rate changes by regressing the news variables on the log exchange rate changes:

$$\Delta s_t = \alpha + \sum_{k=1}^{K} \beta_{k,t} X_{k,t} + \varepsilon_t \qquad \text{(II-52)}$$

The coefficients of X_k measure the impact of macroeconomic 'news' about each announcement, allowing for this impact to depend on the magnitude of surprise. All regressions are run by using the Newey and West [1987] estimation procedure, since exchange rate time series often show heteroscedatisity in the returns. The results of estimating equation (II-52) are summarized in Table II-11.

Table II-11: News impact for the US-$/€ exchange rate, estimation equation (II-52)

	Coefficient	t-stat	Sign level
US announcements			
Non-farm payrolls	-0.1178	-1.6809	0.0931
Unemployment rate	0.2205	2.8524	0.0044
Consumer price index	0.2649	2.0114	0.0445
GDP	-0.1527	-1.5532	0.1206
Retail sales	-0.0248	-0.3460	0.7294
Industrial production	-0.1487	-1.8047	0.0714
Durable orders	-0.1538	-1.3344	0.1823
NAPM (ISM)	-0.3017	-2.7591	0.0059
Trade balance	-0.1152	-1.2643	0.2064
Producer price index	0.0091	0.1059	0.9156
German announcements			
GDP	0.2325	1.7430	0.0816
Industrial production	0.0724	1.2752	0.2025
Producer price index	0.1048	1.9233	0.0547
Consumer price index	-0.1252	-1.5475	0.1220
Unemployment	-0.0533	-0.6101	0.5419
ifo-Index	0.2714	3.0519	0.0023
Retail sales	-0.0341	-0.4896	0.6245
Manufacturing orders	0.0166	0.2051	0.8375

$R^2 = 0.04$
Adjusted $R^2 = 0.03$
D.W. = 1.95

The results indicate that some macroeconomic news have a significant impact on daily EUR/USD exchange rate movements during the period of January 1999 to June 2003. However, consistent with the literature, the overall explanatory power of news for the observable daily exchange rate movements is rather low. Macroeconomic news only accounts for around 4% of daily EUR/USD exchange rate movements. The results further indicate that most of the news components show the correct sign in that an improvement of the real economic conditions in the United States leads to an appreciation of the US dollar. Analogously, the good news for the German economy causes an appreciation of the Euro against the US dollar. However, the impact of US news appears to be more salient than that of German news. Most of the US macroeconomic variables have a significant news effect on the EUR/USD exchange rate whereas only a minor proportion of German macroeconomic news seem to affect the exchange rate significantly. According to our results, news about the ISM-index and the ifo-index show the largest impact on the EUR/USD exchange rate. A surprise of one standard deviation in the ISM index leads, on average, to a 0.30% appreciation of US dollar and a surprise of one standard deviation in the ifo-Index induces on average a 0.27% appreciation of the Euro. To sum up, it is fair to conclude that news about macroeconomic fundamentals has an appreciable but small impact on exchange rate movements.

In a next step, we intend to analyze whether the occurrence of macroeconomic news per se influences the exchange rate movements. Therefore, we carry out a regression based solely on dummy variables, which take the value one if the news is positive (i.e. the actual realization exceeds the expected value), minus one if the news is negative and zero otherwise. However, in case of unemployment a higher actual than expected realization has the opposite economic connotation so that the observed surprises in the unemployment rate are aggregated with the reversed sign. For inflation related news a similar problem exists, however it is a priori not necessarily clear whether positive surprises in consumer or producer price indices should induce the exchange rate to appreciate or depreciate. On the one hand, a higher than expected inflation may result in an expected tightening of monetary policy and consequently an appreciation of the home currency. On the other hand, according to the purchasing power parity higher inflation leads, to a depreciation of the nominal exchange rate. As Table II-11 shows, US CPI and PPI news tend to induce the US dollar to depreciate so that the second argumentation may be adequate. Thus, CPI and PPI news are also aggregated with the reversed sign (see Galati and Ho [2003] and Ehrmann and Fratzscher [2004]).

The only difference to the first approach is the substitution of the 'news vector' (X_k) by a 'news occurrence dummy' (D_k). The corresponding regression equation is given as

$$\Delta s_t = \alpha + \sum_{k=1}^{K} \beta_{k,t} D_{k,t} + \varepsilon_t . \tag{II-53}$$

The results of estimating equation (II-53) are summarized in Table II-12. Overall, the results are rather similar to that of the previous news regression. Some macroeconomic news has per se a significant impact on daily EUR/USD exchange rate movements. In particular, the very publication of US macroeconomic news is relevant for explaining the observable exchange rate movements. However, the overall explanatory power of news for the empirical exchange rate movements is again rather low. The regression approach using news dummies can only account for round about 4% of the daily EUR/USD exchange rate movements.

Table II-12: News impact for the US-$/€ exchange rate estimation equation (II-53)

	Coefficient	**t-stat**	**Sign level**
US announcements			
Non-farm payrolls	-0.2433	-3.2298	0.0013
Unemployment rate	-0.1797	-2.2553	0.0243
Consumer price index	-0.2702	-2.0052	0.0452
GDP	-0.0534	-0.5149	0.6067
Retail sales	-0.0615	-0.6993	0.4845
Industrial production	-0.0627	-0.6675	0.5046
Durable orders	-0.0740	-0.7384	0.4604
NAPM (ISM)	-0.2684	-2.8321	0.0047
Trade balance	-0.0668	-0.7412	0.4587
Producer price index	-0.0406	-0.4292	0.6679
German announcements			
GDP	0.2733	1.6352	0.1023
Industrial production	0.0593	0.8089	0.4187
Producer price index	-0.0952	-1.2620	0.2072
Consumer price index	0.0897	1.0429	0.2972
Unemployment	0.0612	0.7478	0.4547
ifo-Index	0.2647	2.9506	0.0032
Retail sales	0.0269	0.3868	0.6989
Manufacturing orders	0.0285	0.3198	0.7492

R^2 = 0.04
Adjusted R^2 = 0.02
D.W. = 1.94

Overall, the results of our investigation of the news effect for the EUR/USD exchange rate is broadly in line with the results of earlier studies. News about macroeconomic fundamentals can not explain the variability of EUR/USD exchange rate very well as indicated by the low values for the coefficient of determination (R^2 and adjusted R^2). Furthermore, much of the macroeconomic news appears to be statistically insignificant and thus plays only a minor role in the evaluation of market participants. However, some macroeconomic news shows a significant impact on EUR/USD exchange rate changes. This is in particular true for U.S. macroeconomic news.[15]

II.2.4 On the random walk behavior of exchange rates: an application of variance ratio tests

The efficient market hypothesis implies that exchange rates should follow a random walk process – at least in the short-run. In principle, there are two implications of a random walk that could be used for testing foreign exchange market efficiency. On the one hand, one may look for a unit root in the exchange rate series and on the other hand the exchange rate series may be analyzed with respect to uncorrelated increments. Our approach focuses on the uncorrelated increments aspect of a random walk (see equation II-26) as unit root tests cannot detect some important departures from the random walk (see Lo and MacKinlay [1989]).[16] Additionally, the autocorrelation aspect may provide some interesting insights concerning the time series properties of foreign exchange rates.

In particular, we refer to variance ratio tests for evaluating the efficiency of foreign exchange markets.[17] The variance ratio test exploits the fact that the variance of the increments in a random walk must be linear in the sampling interval. That is, if a time series follows a random walk, the variance of its q-differences would be q times the variance of its first difference.

$$Var\left(X_t - X_{t-q}\right) = q\left(Var\left(X_t - X_{t-1}\right)\right). \tag{II-54}$$

[15] For an extended analysis of the impact of news on exchange rate movements see Appendix B.

[16] The unit root test focuses on establishing whether a times series is difference stationary or trend stationary and are known to have low power and cannot detect some departures from random walk (see Campbell et al. [1997]). Lo and MacKinlay [1989] show that the variance ratio test is more reliable for detecting unit root components than the Dickey-Fuller test developed by Dickey and Fuller [1979].

[17] For detailed discussion of the Variance Ratio Test we refer to Campbell et al. [1997].

Therefore, the relevant null hypothesis of the variance ratio test implies that the following variance ratio is equal to one:

$$VR = \frac{\sigma^2(q)}{\sigma^2} = 1, \tag{II-55}$$

where $\sigma^2(q)$ is $1/q$ times the variance of the q-th period returns and σ^2 is the variance of the one-period returns. Given a sample of nq holding-period returns, the unbiased estimates of $\sigma^2(q)$ and σ^2 can be computed as follows:

$$\sigma^2(q) = \frac{1}{M}\sum_{t=q}^{nq}(X_t - X_{t-q} - q\hat{\mu})^2, \tag{II-56}$$

where

$$M = q(nq - q + 1)\left(1 - \frac{q}{nq}\right), \tag{II-57}$$

$$\hat{\mu} = \frac{1}{nq}\sum_{t=1}^{nq}(X_t - X_{t-1}) = \frac{1}{nq}(X_{nq} - X_0), \tag{II-58}$$

and

$$\sigma^2 = \frac{1}{nq-1}\sum_{t=1}^{q}(X_t - X_{t-1} - \hat{\mu})^2. \tag{II-59}$$

The asymptotic variance of the variance ratio under homoscedasticity, $\phi(q)$, is given by:

$$\phi(q) = \frac{2(2q-1)(q-1)}{3q(nq)}. \tag{II-60}$$

The standard normal test statistic under homoscedasticity, $Z(q)$, is then:

$$Z(q) = \frac{VR(q) - 1}{[\phi(q)]^{1/2}} \sim N(0,1). \tag{II-61}$$

Since financial time series often posses time varying volatilities and deviate from normality, we also calculate Lo and MacKinlay's heteroscedastisitcy-consistent standard normal test statistic. The heteroscedasticity-consistent asymptotic variance of the variance ratio, $\phi^*(q)$, is given by:

$$\phi^*(q)=\sum_{j=1}^{q-1}\left[\frac{2(q-j)}{q}\right]^2\hat{\delta}(j), \tag{II-62}$$

where

$$\hat{\delta}(j)=\frac{\sum_{t=j+1}^{Nq}(X_t-X_{t-1}-\hat{\mu})^2(X_{t-j}-X_{t-j-1}-\hat{\mu})^2}{\left[\sum_{t=1}^{Nq}(X_t-X_{t-1}-\hat{\mu})^2\right]^2}, \tag{II-63}$$

The heteroscedasticity-consistent standard normal test statistic, $Z^*(q)$, is then calculated as follows:

$$Z^*(q)=\frac{VR(q)-1}{\left[\phi^*(q)\right]^{1/2}}\sim N(0,1). \tag{II-64}$$

As noted above, a main advantage of the variance ratio test compared to other efficiency tests is that it provides some insights concerning the autocorrelation structure of the considered time series. With regard to the autocorrelation structure of time series, Cochrane [1988] shows that the variance ratio, VR(q), can be approximated by the following expression:

$$VR(q)\approx 1+2\sum_{j=1}^{q-1}\frac{q-j}{q}\hat{\rho}_j, \tag{II-65}$$

where $\hat{\rho}_j$ denotes the jth-order autocorrelation coefficient estimator of the first differences of X_t (see Cochrane [1988]). Equation (II-65) provides a simple interpretation for the variance ratios computed with an aggregation value q: they are approximately linear combinations of the first q-1 autocorrelation coefficient estimators of the first differences with arithmetically declining weights (see Lo and MacKinlay [1999]). Thus, variance ratios larger than one indicate the presence of positive serial correlation in the series which is consistent with trend behavior in exchange rate series and, in contrast, variance ratios smaller than unity suggest the presence of negative serial correlation which is consistent with a mean reverting behavior in exchange rate series. In the next section we provide a short summary of the preceding evidence for the foreign exchange markets efficiency using variance ratio tests. Afterwards we carry out variance ratio tests for the DM/USD and YEN/USD exchange rate using daily and weekly data.

II.2.4.1 Random Walk behavior of exchange rates: a selective survey of the existing evidence

To our knowledge, the first empirical study that applied variance ratio tests to analyze the random walk behavior of exchange rates is presented by Liu and He [1991]. They investigate five weekly currencies against the US dollar in the time period of August 1974 to March 1989 and find evidence for rejecting the random walk hypothesis for most tested currencies. In their study the rejection of the random walk hypothesis is largely due to positive autocorrelation in the returns as almost all variance ratios are significantly larger than one. Their results appear to be robust to heteroscedasticity and to two sub-sample periods. Pan et al. [1996] use heteroscedasticity-robust variance ratio tests to evaluate the short-term behavior of exchange rates. In particular, they analyze weekly data for the British Pound, the Canadian dollar, the Deutsche Mark, the Japanese Yen and the Swiss franc vis-à-vis the US dollar in the time period of August 1974 to December 1987. Their results indicate a rejection of the random walk hypothesis for the British Pound, the Japanese Yen, and the Swiss franc. However, for the Deutsche Mark and the Canadian dollar the hypothesis of random walk can be maintained. Overall, the pattern of the variance ratio estimates indicates that all exchange rate returns are positively correlated except for the Deutsche Mark and the Canadian dollar. Similar results are reported by Ajayi and Karemera [1996] who analyze the currencies of eight Pacific Basin economies using daily and weekly data. Their results suggest that for both daily and weekly data the random walk hypothesis is rejected for the majority of the considered exchange rates. The rejection of the random walk hypothesis is related to the presence of serial correlation as well as heteroscedasticity. However, with regard to the nature of serial correlation, the given evidence contradicts the preceding evidence as exchange rate returns show a clear tendency for negative autocorrelation. Recently, Wright [2000] proposes an alternative variance ratio test based on the ranks and signs of a time series to test for the martingale hypothesis. He applies his test to five exchange rate series and finds that the martingale hypothesis is rejected by the data. As all rejections are in the right tail of the distribution, evidence for positive serial autocorrelation in returns is reported. Contrary to the above-mentioned studies, Lee et al. [2001] report evidence in favor of random walk behavior of exchange rates. They analyze nine daily Asian exchange rates vis-à-vis the US dollar in the period January 1988 to December

1995. The results of a joint variance ratio test indicate only little evidence of serial correlations in exchange rate returns except for the Korean Won.

Overall, the existing evidence for random walk behavior of exchange rates using variance ratio tests suggests that the random walk hypothesis is largely rejected. In particular, the rejection is primarily due to positive serial correlation in the exchange rate returns.

II.2.4.2 Empirical evidence against Random Walk behavior of DM/USD and YEN/USD exchange rates

II.2.4.2.1 Data

To test the random walk null hypothesis for the DM/USD and YEN/USD exchange rate series we carry out the variance ratio test proposed by Lo and MacKinlay [1988]. The exchange rate data were taken from the Datastream of Thomson Financial. As no continuous exchange rate series exists for DM/USD and YEN/USD exchange rates for the considered time period of January 1975 to June 2003 we refer to the corresponding cross rates via the British Pound. The mnemonics are DMARKER, USDOLLR and JAPAYEN. To test the robustness of our results of the variance ratio test to sampling frequencies, we apply daily as well as weekly data for both exchange rate time series. The variance ratio test is conducted by using log spot exchange rates.

II.2.4.2.2 Empirical results

In the following we present the results of performing the variance ratio test on the DM/USD exchange rate and the YEN/USD exchange rate using daily and weekly data. Table II-13 and Table II-14 summarize the results for the DM/USD exchange rate and Table II-15 and Table II-16 the results for the YEN/USD exchange rate. The variance ratio estimates VR(q) and the corresponding standard normal test statistic under homoscedasticity, Z(q), are calculated for each data set for the cases q = 2, 4, 8, 12, 16, 20, and 24.[18] In addition a heteroscedasticity-consistent variance ratio test is performed by calculating the heteroscedasticity-consistent test statistic $Z^*(q)$ for each of the cases q = 2, 4, 8, 12, 16, 20, and 24.

[18] The selection of the reported multiples of each sampling frequency q corresponds to those of other related studies (see e.g. Liu and He [1991] and Ajayi and Karemera [1996])

For the daily DM/USD exchange rate our results indicate that the hypothesis of random walk behavior is rejected. Except for Z(2), all homoscedasticity-consistent test statistics Z(q) indicate a rejection of the null hypothesis. In principle, the rejection of the random walk may either be due to heteroscedasticity in the data or to serial correlation. The heteroscedasticity-consistent variance ratio test is also implemented, to investigate this issue. The results indicate that most of the rejections under homoscedasticity are robust to heteroscedasticity. Thus, the variance ratio estimates differ from one due to autocorrelation rather than to heteroscedasticity. In other words, the random walk is rejected because of autocorrelations of daily increments in the DM/USD exchange rate series. As all variance ratio estimates are greater than one, the results suggest that the daily DM/USD exchange rate exhibit positive autocorrelation in returns.

Table II-13: Results of the Variance Ratio Test for the daily DM/US-$ exchange rate (January 1975 – June 2003)

Lags	Variance Ratio	Z(q)	Z*(q)
2	1.0171	1.4724 (0.1409)	1.1775 (0.2390)
4	1.0408	1.8807 (0.0600)	1.5228 (0.1278)
8	1.0717	2.0893 (0.0367)	1.7155 (0.0862)
12	1.1032	2.3729 (0.0176)	1.9642 (0.0495)
16	1.1295	2.5369 (0.0112)	2.1152 (0.0344)
20	1.1431	2.4830 (0.0130)	2.0828 (0.0373)
24	1.1649	2.5952 (0.0095)	2.1888 (0.0286)

Note: p-values are given in parenthesis.

In order to check whether our results for the daily DM/USD exchange rate are robust to sampling frequencies, we also perform the variance ratio test for weekly data. Overall, the results for the weekly data correspond to those for the daily data. All variance ratio estimates are greater than one, with most of these estimates appearing to be statistically significant. As for the daily exchange rate data, the rejection of the random walk hypothesis is largely due to serial correlation rather than heteroscedasticity. Altogether, we have to conclude that the random walk hypothesis is rejected for the DM/USD exchange rate in the considered time period. The rejection can largely be attributed to positive autocorrelation in returns.

Table II-14: Results of Variance Ratio Test for the weekly DM/US-$ exchange rate (January 1975 – June 2003)

Lags	Variance Ratio	Z(q)	Z*(q)
2	1.0302	1.1654 (0.2438)	1.0679 (0.2856)
4	1.0820	1.6906 (0.0909)	1.4770 (0.1397)
8	1.1527	1.9894 (0.0467)	1.7193 (0.0856)
12	1.1997	2.0533 (0.0400)	1.7923 (0.0731)
16	1.2437	2.1339 (0.0328)	1.8804 (0.0601)
20	1.2800	2.1718 (0.0299)	1.9312 (0.0535)
24	1.3037	2.1361 (0.0327)	1.9141 (0.0556)

Note: p-values are given in parenthesis.

The results for the YEN/USD exchange rate are akin to those of the DM/USD exchange rate. Applying the variance ratio test to daily YEN/USD exchange rates shows that all variance ratio estimates are greater than one. The corresponding homoscedasticity-consistent test statistics Z(q) are almost above the critical values, so that the estimates are statistically different from one. For daily YEN/USD exchange rates the phenomena of heteroscedasticity seems to play a more decisive role as up to $q = 8$, the rejection of the random walk hypothesis is due to heteroscedasticity rather than serial correlation. For longer multiples of the sampling frequency however serial correlation seems to be responsible for the rejection of the random walk hypothesis. As all variance ratio estimates are greater than one, we suspect positive autocorrelation in daily YEN/USD exchange rate returns.

Again, we check the robustness of our results for the daily YEN/USD exchange rate using weekly data as well. Overall, the results are in line with our previous findings. All variance ratio estimates are statistically significant on common levels: this holds true for the case of homoscedastisity as well as heteroscedastisicty. Thus, the reason for the rejection of the random walk behavior for weekly YEN/USD exchange rates can be found in serial correlation. As all variance ratio estimates are greater than one, we again conjecture that those exchange rate returns exhibit a clear tendency for positive autocorrelation.

Table II-15: Results of Variance Ratio Test for the daily ¥/US-$ exchange rate (January 1975 – June 2003)

Lags	Variance Ratio	Z(q)	Z*(q)
2	1.0166	1.4343 (0.1515)	0.9739 (0.3301)
4	1.0389	1.7931 (0.0730)	1.2742 (0.2026)
8	1.0617	1.7985 (0.0721)	1.3398 (0.1803)
12	1.1059	2.4362 (0.0148)	1.8621 (0.0626)
16	1.1559	3.0530 (0.0023)	2.3794 (0.0173)
20	1.1906	3.3069 (0.0009)	2.6175 (0.0089)
24	1.2248	3.5375 (0.0004)	2.8316 (0.0046)

Note: p-values are given in parenthesis.

Table II-16: Results of the Variance Ratio Test for the weekly ¥-US-$ exchange rate (January 1975- June 2003)

Lags	Variance Ratio	Z(q)	Z*(q)
2	1.0591	2.2796 (0.0226)	1.8439 (0.0652)
4	1.2014	4.1504 (0.0000)	3.4938 (0.0005)
8	1.3552	4.6286 (0.0000)	3.9893 (0.0001)
12	1.4121	4.2372 (0.0000)	3.6907 (0.0002)
16	1.4874	4.2684 (0.0000)	3.7577 (0.0002)
20	1.5466	4.2395 (0.0000)	3.7661 (0.0002)
24	1.5820	4.0941 (0.0000)	3.6621 (0.0003)

Note: p-values are given in parenthesis.

Totaling the above-presented results for the DM/USD and YEN/USD exchange rate time series, we can conclude that the hypothesis of random walk behavior must be dismissed. The rejection of Random Walk behavior is largely due to serial correlation in the returns rather than heteroscedasticity. As all estimated variance ratios are greater than one for all considered time series, those exchange rate returns exhibit a clear tendency for positive autocorrelation. This positive serial correlation in exchange rate returns may indicate that exchange rates show a trend behavior in the levels at least in the short-run. This result is in line with the seminal findings of Poterba and Summers [1988] and Cutler et al. [1991], who report evidence for positive autocorrelation in returns over short horizons.

II.2.5 On exchange rate misalignments

Exchange rate misalignment can be defined as the departure of nominal exchange rate from its long-run fundamental equilibrium level. Misalignments can be either due to over- or undervaluation of the currency relative to fundamentals. Measuring misalignments is always difficult and imprecise as it requires an estimation of what is termed the fundamental equilibrium exchange rate. However, the concept of equilibrium exchange rate is not an integrated concept, but a large number of equilibrium exchange rate concepts have been proposed.

The most widely applied approach to calculating equilibrium exchange rates is the theory of purchasing power parity (see Rogoff [1996]). The theory of purchasing power parity is based on the arbitrage logic of the 'law of one price'. The law of one price states that once prices are converted to a common currency the same good should have the same price across different countries if no transportation costs, tariffs, or non-tariff barriers exist. In economics usually two different versions of the theory of purchasing power parity are distinguished: first, absolute purchasing power parity and, second, relative purchasing power parity. According to the absolute version of purchasing power parity, the logarithm of the ominal exchange rate (s) is determined by the difference between the price levels of the two countries:

$$s_t = p_t - p_t^* \tag{II-66}$$

where p and p^* denote the log domestic and foreign price level. Given the difficulties with the construction of an appropriate common goods basket for implementing absolute purchasing power parity, a weaker version of purchasing power parity is often considered (see Rogoff [1996], Isard [1995]). According to this relative version of purchasing power parity, the nominal exchange rate (s) should bear a constant proportionate relationship to the ratio of the price levels of the two countries:

$$s_t = k + p_t - p_t^*, \qquad \text{(II-67)}$$

where k represents a constant parameter. The relative purchasing power parity is often expressed in first difference form

$$\Delta s_t = \Delta p_t - \Delta p_t^* = \pi_t - \pi_t^*, \qquad \text{(II-68)}$$

where π_t and π_t^* are the domestic and foreign inflation rates respectively at time t. Hence, the inflation differential between two countries is balanced by a corresponding relative change in the spot exchange rate. When purchasing power parity holds the real exchange rate should be equal to a constant. Thus, any movements in the real exchange rate represent deviations from the theory of purchasing power parity.[19]

Figure II-4: DM/USD and purchasing power parity

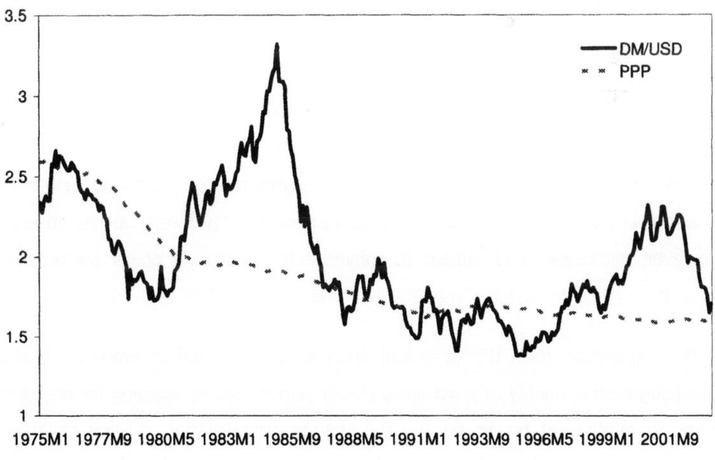

---

[19] The real exchange rate expresses the terms of trade for domestic and foreign goods and services and is defined as the nominal exchange rate adjusted by the relative price between domestic and foreign goods and services. When absolute purchasing power parity is valid, the real exchange rate corresponds to one. In case of relative purchasing power parity, the real exchange rate is equal to k.

Figure II-5: YEN/USD and purchasing power parity

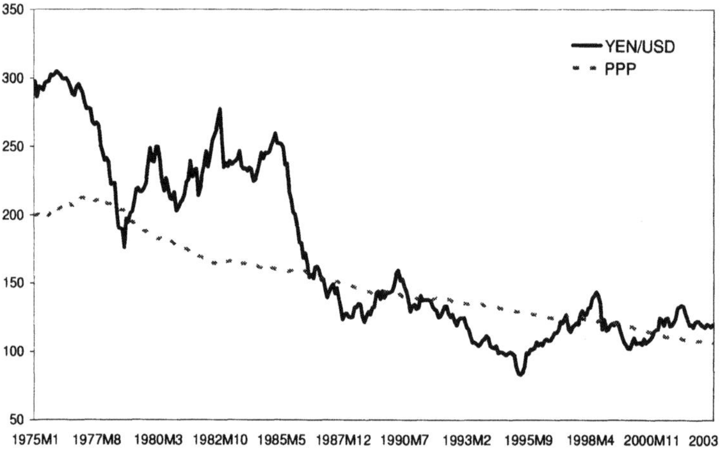

For a graphical analysis of the theory of purchasing power parity in the context of the DM/USD and YEN/USD exchange rate we compute the purchasing power parity level for both exchange rates. For the calculation we use consumer price indices. As starting point for the determination of the purchasing power exchange rates we decide to use the actual exchange rates for the DM/USD and the Yen/USD at the time of the Louvre Accord in February 1987 (see Destler and Henning [1989]). As both figures reveal (Figure II-4 and Figure II-5), the real DM/USD and real YEN/USD exchange rate is anything but constant. Furthermore, prolonged deviations of the nominal and real exchange rates from purchasing power parity levels can be observed in the past. However, exchange rates appear to converge to purchasing power parity levels in the long-run as the cyclical behavior of real exchange rates around PPP levels suggests.

Overall, the impression from the graphical analysis is confirmed in empirical studies. Early studies investigate the validity of purchasing power parity without allowing for any dynamics of adjustment to purchasing power parity. The results indicate that, outside of hyperinflation periods, a continuous validity of purchasing power parity is strongly rejected (see Froot and Rogoff [1995]). The disappointing results of the early studies encouraged an alternative approach. By investigating the time series properties of real exchange rates it was attempted to evaluate whether real exchange rates are non-stationary. If real exchange rates are non-stationary it is suggested that the real exchange rates follow a random walk, i.e. deviations from purchasing power parity are permanent. In case of stationarity, real exchange rates exhibit a tendency to mean reversion, i.e. purchasing power parity is at least in the long-run a valid equilibrium. The early literature on the validity of purchasing power parity normally failed to reject the hypothesis of random walk behavior of real exchange rates, so that purchasing power parity appeared to be invalid even in the long-run (see Rogoff [1996]). However, as Frankel [1986] and [1990] indicates, the early empirical results may be due to a lack of power of the empirical tests as they only include the most recent period of floating exchange rates. Using long-span data and panel data, various economists have shown that real exchange rates tend to reveal a mean reversion behavior so that evidence for a long run validity of PPP is found in the data (see e.g. for studies using long-span data Frankel [1986], Edison [1987], Diebold et al. [1991], Lothian and Taylor [1996] and e.g. for studies using panel data Wei and Parsley [1995], Frankel and Rose [1996], Oh [1996], Wu [1996], Papell [1997], Papell and Theodoridis [1998], Sarno and Taylor [1998] and Taylor and Sarno [1998]).[20,21]

However, it can take a relatively long time before the real exchange rates converge to the equilibrium purchasing power parity level as most studies report a size of the half-life of deviations from purchasing power parity, that is about three to five years (see Rogoff [1996], Engel and Morley [2001] and Murray and Papell [2002]). This large degree of persistence in the real exchange rates can be seen as the second generation of the PPP puzzle. The high degree of persistence in real exchange rates can not be satisfactorily explained just with standard economic explanations like nominal shocks.[22] More recently, Taylor [2001] has illustrated that the high degree of persistence in real exchange rates may be biased upwards due to the possibility of nonlinear adjustment of real exchange rates. Taylor et al. [2001] provide evidence of nonlinear mean-reversion in a number of major real exchange rates during the post Bretton Woods era. The nonlinearity in real exchange rates is according to Taylor et al. [2001] established by the different behavior of real exchange rates depending on current deviation of

---

[20] See for a critical evaluation of the use of long-span data for testing the validity of PPP Frankel and Rose [1996]. They argue that the long samples required to generate a reasonable level of statistical power with standard univariate unit root tests may be unavailable for many currencies so that may be a "survivorship bias" is produced in long-span tests. Furthermore, it is sometimes argued that long-span studies do not take into account the fact that real exchange rate behavior may differ across different historical periods and different nominal exchange rate regimes (see Baxter and Stockman [1989] and Hegwood and Papell [1998]). For the usage of panel studies for analyzing the empirical validity of PPP Taylor and Sarno [1998] critically note that the probability of rejecting the null hypothesis *all of the series are generated by unit-root processes* may be quite high when as few as just one of the series under consideration is a realization of a stationary process (see Taylor et al. [2001]).

[21] However, some researchers find negative results for PPP as e.g. Baum et al. [1999] and Engel [2000].

[22] Nominal shocks can only have strong effects over a time frame in which nominal wages and prices are sticky (see Sarno and Taylor [2002]).

the real exchange rate from the long run equilibrium. The closer real exchange rates are to long run equilibrium the more do real exchange rates behave like unit-root processes. On the contrary, the further they are from long run equilibrium the more mean reverting behavior can be observed. Thus, only for shocks occurring around the long run equilibrium, Taylor et al. [2001] find half-lives of deviation from purchasing power parity in the range of 3 to 5 years (see Taylor et al. [2001]).

Overall, the empirical results for the validity of the purchasing power parity suggest that a continuous validity of purchasing power parity is clearly rejected. Real exchange rates exhibit a tendency for prolonged deviations from its equilibrium level. However, in the (very) long-run purchasing power parity has some meaning as a fundamental equilibrium, as real exchange rates show mean reversion behavior in the long-run. Nonetheless, in the meantime it is likely that actual exchange rates are clearly misaligned and not in accordance with purchasing power parity. Furthermore, purchasing power parity can not explain the prolonged deviations of actual exchange rate, so that it can only serve as an approximate, long-term exchange rate equilibrium concept. Consequently, the usage of purchasing power parity as an equilibrium exchange rate concept is not undisputed in the existing literature. Many researchers indicate that the assumption of constant real exchange rates is too restrictive. In reality there are good reasons to assume that real exchange rates should exhibit prolonged fluctuations due to macroeconomic fundamentals. In particular, the following factors have been discussed in the literature: differences in the productivity development, unsynchronized business cycles, and differences in the monetary and fiscal policy stance (see Akram et al. [2003]). These factors are taken up by two more sophisticated concepts for the equilibrium exchange rate.[23] The first one is an a-theoretical, statistical approach that takes into account the possibility that fundamentals generate swings in real exchange rates. As this approach is not explicitly based on a structural model it is denoted as behavioral equilibrium exchange rate approach (BEER). The advantage of leaving a structural model aside is that the results do not depend on a model that may be mis-specified, as one can never be sure of assuming the correct model (see Stein [2002]). In contrast, the second approach is based on a structural approach. According to the fundamental equilibrium exchange rate approach (FEER), the fundamental equilibrium rate is the real exchange rate that is explicitly consistent with the internal and external balance. The FEER

[23] A detailed illustration of the various concept for the determination of the equilibrium exchange rate can be found in Wren-Lewis and Driver [1998].

approach can be characterized as normative since the fundamental equilibrium exchange rate is consistent with 'ideal' economic conditions. However, even more sophisticated approaches for determining the fundamental equilibrium exchange rate show that actual exchange rates are clearly misaligned over long-lasting periods. Table II-17 summarizes various studies using BEER, FEER or PPP approaches to determine the fundamental exchange rate of the EUR/USD rate. Overall, the results indicate that the Euro was under-valuated against the US dollar in the considered periods. However, the exact magnitude of the undervaluation is hard to quantify as the range of the available estimates is rather broad. This assessment is also shared by the European Central Bank in the January Monthly Bulletin 2002:

> "As early as the second half of 1999, the vast majority of these empirical applications recorded some negative deviation of the actual exchange rate of the euro from its measured 'equilibrium exchange rate' derived from fundamental based models. This assessment was consolidated during 2000, and in autumn 2000 virtually all the models surveyed indicated that exchange rates had moved out of line with fundamentals." (European Central Bank [2002], p. 52-53)

Overall, the proposition of the asset market theory that actual exchange rates remain at levels largely consistent with macroeconomic fundamentals must be rejected for the EUR/USD exchange rate. The empirical evidence on this issue rather suggests that floating exchange rates are characterized by large and persistent deviations of the actual exchange rate from its fundamental equilibrium level.

Table II-17: Selected estimates of the euro's "equilibrium" exchange rate

Study	Methodology	Refernce currency	Reference period	"Equilibrium" rate US-$/€ or under(-)/over(+) valuation(%) for the reference period
Wren-Lewis and Driver [1998]	FEER	US-$	2000	1.19-1.45
Gern et al. [2000]	BEER, UIP	US-$	2000Q1	Around US-$/€ 1.03
Clostermann and Schnatz [2000]	BEER	US-$	1999Q4	US-$/€ 1.13
Lorenzen and Thygesen [2000]	BEER	US-$	1999	Long-run: US-$/€ 1.28
			End 1999	Medium-run US-$/€ 1.19
			Mid-2000	Short-run: US-$/€ 1.09
Alberola et al. [1999]	PEER	US-$	End 1998	US-$/€ 1.26
Stein [2002]	NATREX	US-$	2001Q1	US-$/€ 1.17
Borowski and Couharde [2000]	FEER	US-$	First half of 1999	US-$/€ 1.23-1.31
International Monetary Fund [2000]	Saving-investment approach	US-$	Summer 2000	US-$/€ -30% or more
Schulmeister [2000]	PPP for tradebales	US-$	Mid-2000	US-$/€ 0.87
OECD PPP estimates	GDP PPP	US-$	2000	US-$/€ 1.09

Source: Koen et al. [2001], European Central Bank [2002] and Schneider [2003]

II.3 Summary

Our discussion of the empirical validity of the asset market theory of exchange rate determination has revealed that there exists a huge amount of evidence contradicting the traditional economic model. For all important implications of the asset market theory to exchange rate determination, counterevidence is easily found:

1. The link between macroeconomic fundamentals suggested by economic exchange rate models and exchange rates appears to be exceedingly weak. No existing exchange rate model can explain actual exchange rate movements at horizons up to 3 years. Or in the words of Sarno and Taylor [2002], p. 4:

   > " an emerging stylised fact is that, while macroeconomic fundamentals appear to be an important determinant of exchange rate movements over relatively long horizons [...], there seem to be substantial and often persistent movements in exchange rates which are largely unexplained by macroeconomic fundamentals."

   No existing exchange rate model can predict future exchange rate movements better than naïve random walk forecasts. The volatility of exchange rates exceeds that of macroeconomic fundamentals by an order of magnitude. Furthermore, the volatility of exchange rates increased in the Post Bretton Wood era, although the volatility of the fundamentals did not.

2. Exchange rate expectations can not be reconciled with the important concept of rational expectations. Professional exchange rate expectations appear to be a biased predictor of future exchange rates. Furthermore, those expectations are made without exploiting all available information efficiently. Finally, expectation errors are correlated with past errors, which contradicts the rational expectation hypothesis.

3. Exchange rate movements can not systematically be linked to news in the relevant fundamentals. Additionally, if an impact of news is found it appears to be asymmetric.

4. Foreign exchange market efficiency implies that exchange rates should move as random walk processes. However, according to the results of our variance ratio test and the preceding evidence, the random walk hypothesis is rejected by the data. Furthermore, the results of our variance ratio test suggest that exchange rates exhibit a tendency for trend behavior, which can potentially be exploited by technical trading techniques.

5. With regard to the proposition of the asset market theory to exchange rate determination that actual exchange rates remain closely linked to levels consistent with macroeconomic fundamentals, we have to conclude that floating exchange rates are rather characterized by prolonged deviations from fundamental rates.

Overall, our survey on the empirical validity of traditional economic exchange rate models reveals conclusively the empirical failure of those models. Thus, after roughly 30 years of free floating exchange rates, the economic profession is unable to offer convincing explanations for the observable exchange rate movements in a consistent manner. This dismal result is the starting point for our attempt to provide a new view on foreign exchange rates. In the next Chapter, we take a new view on the observable exchange rate movements in order to discover identifiable patterns. We will see that exchange rates movements are largely characterized by trends, which are often related to speculation in foreign exchange markets. Consequently, we discuss afterwards the impact of speculation on foreign exchange rates on theoretical and empirical basis and represent the view of Keynes on the functioning of asset markets.

Chapter III
Patterns of exchange rate dynamics and the role of speculation

The striking results concerning the empirical validity of the existing asset market theory to exchange rate determination demonstrate that a purely fundamental, macroeconomic approach clearly fails. Only for long time horizons do fundamental macroeconomic factors seem to drive exchange rate movements in the predicted way. In the short- and medium run, however, other factors seem to have a decisive impact on exchange rate movements.

The aim of this study is to reveal important non-fundamental factors for the short- and medium run exchange rate movements. In our opinion, a reasonable starting point for this issue is to take a new, explorative look at the observable exchange rate movements of free-floating exchange rates. Apparently, an eye-catching characteristic of those exchange rates is their tendency to move in long and persistent trends. The observable exchange rate trends appear to be largely disconnected from fundamental developments in the related economies. This chapter deals with the empirical exchange rate dynamics. In particular, we analyze the supposed trend behavior of exchange rates in more detail. Our results indicate a persistent trend behavior for the DM/USD and YEN/USD exchange rates. As such trends in exchange rate time series are often related to an excessive speculative trading behavior of foreign exchange dealers, we discuss subsequently the role of speculation in the context of foreign exchange markets. In doing so, we dwell on two different kinds of speculation discussed in the literature. On the one hand, economists often state that speculation is beneficial for the economy as it assures that asset prices always coincide with the fundamental value. On the other hand, in many cases foreign exchange dealers apply trading practices which result in destabilizing tendencies due to speculation. At the end of this chapter we discuss Keynes' view on the functioning of asset markets as it provides in our view a very proper description of the essential elements which affect human behavior in asset markets.

III.1 Long swings of free floating exchange rates

Section III.1 deals with the empirical investigation of the supposed trend behavior in free floating foreign exchange rates. In particular, we apply a trend criterion derived from the technical analysis literature, variance ratio tests and Markov-switching regression models to evaluate the trend behavior in exchange rates.

III.1.1 Exchange rate trends according to technical analysis

In order to analyze the trend behavior of foreign exchange rates, we first of all have to define the term 'trend' more precisely. Therefore, we revert to the technical approach of investment as it is "a reflection of the idea that prices move in trends which are determined by the changing attitudes of investors toward a variety of economic, monetary, political, and psychological forces" (Luca [2000], p. 2). One simple, basic technique for identifying trends in exchange rate series is the peak-and-trough-progression. This technique is based on the observation that a rising market moves in a series of waves, each peak and trough being higher than its predecessor. When the series of rising peaks and troughs is interrupted, a trend reversal is indicated (see Luca [2000]). Correspondingly, an upward trend is defined as a sequence of successively higher peaks and troughs, where the exchange rate at time t is described as a peak if it is higher than both the exchange rate at time t-1 and t+1, and where a trough is defined as just the opposite direction. According to Saacke [1999], this can be written as:

$$\begin{aligned} PEAK_t &= \{S_i : S_{i-1} < S_i, S_{i+1} < S_i; i \le t-1\} \\ &= \{p_t^1, p_t^2, \dots, p_t^n\} \end{aligned} , \quad \text{(III-1)}$$

$$\begin{aligned} TROUGH_t &= \{S_i : S_{i-1} > S_i, S_{i+1} > S_i; i \le t-1\} \\ &= \{tr_t^1, tr_t^2, \dots, tr_t^m\} \end{aligned} , \quad \text{(III-2)}$$

where S_t is the exchange rate at time t and $PEAK_t$ ($TROUGH_t$) is the set of peaks (troughs) in the considered exchange rate time series, which occur before t. Given these conventions, a sufficient condition for the existence of an upward trend at time t is:

$$\left(p_t^n > p_t^{n-1}\right) \wedge \left(tr_t^m > tr_t^{m-1}\right). \quad \text{(III-3)}$$

Correspondingly, a sufficient condition for the existence of a downward trend at time t is:

$$\left(p_t^n < p_t^{n-1}\right) \wedge \left(tr_t^m < tr_t^{m-1}\right). \qquad \text{(III-4)}$$

Depending on the frequency of the applied data, this definition is appropriate for analyzing short-term as well as long-term trends. The focus of our study is the analysis of long swings in exchange rates. Hence, we decided to use exchange rate time series with a quarterly frequency. Figure III-1 and Figure III-2 illustrate the exchange rate time series of the DM/USD and, respectively, YEN/USD for the period of 1974 – 2003. The marked trends in the figures reflect the trends derived from the above criteria. The average trend length for the DM/USD time series is about 11 quarters, for the YEN/USD the average trend length is approximately 10 quarters. Compared to fundamental exchange rate models, these exchange rates seem to overreact in the short-run and to adjust only gradually towards its fundamental justified value in the (possibly very) long run. This hypothesis is supported by several empirical studies (see e.g. Mark [1995], Chinn and Meese [1995], Mark and Choi [1997] and Lothian and Taylor [1996]).

Figure III-1: Trends in the DM/USD exchange rate, 1975:1 to 2003:2

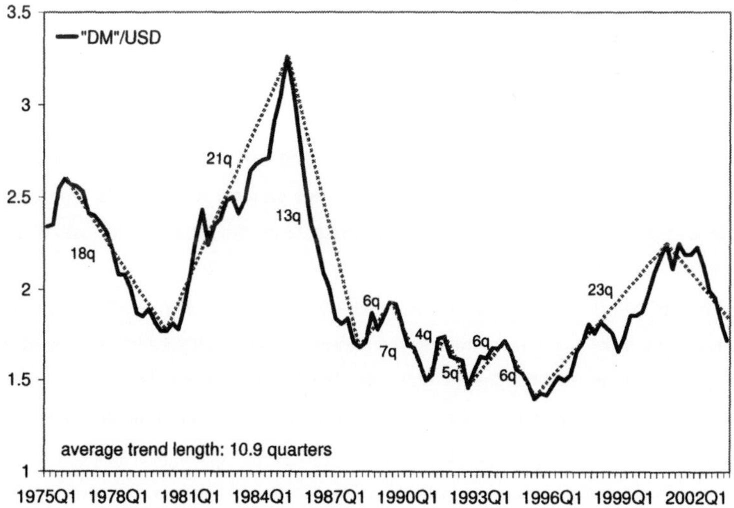

Figure III-2: Trends in the YEN/USD exchange rate, 1975:1 to 2003:2

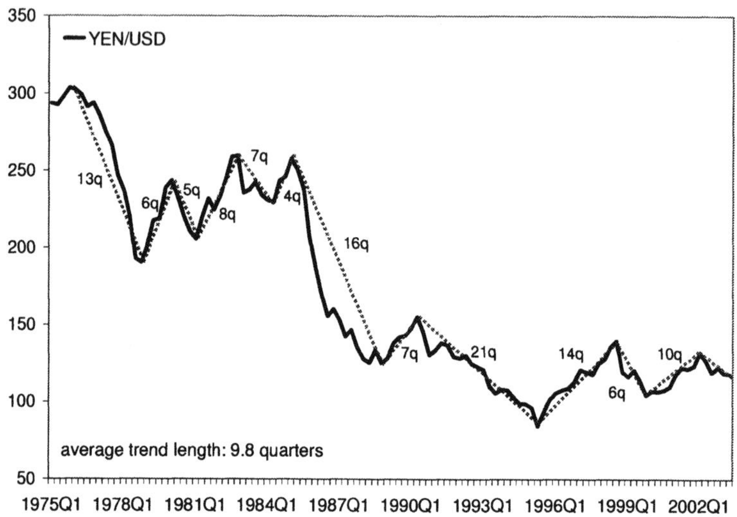

III.1.2 Exchange rate trends according to variance ratio tests

In this section we go back to the variance ratio tests conducted in II.2.4, but now we use the variance ratio test to determine the length of trends in exchange rates. Following Frennberg and Hansson [1993] and Chang and Ting [2000], we perform the variance ratio test for the DM/USD and YEN/USD exchange rates considering large values of q, i.e. we consider the autocorrelation structure of high multiplies of the sampling frequencies. However, it should be noted that this long-horizon results have to be interpreted with caution as Richardson and Stock [1989] point out that "a commonly recognized feature of these statistics is that even though the sample may be large, the number of non-overlapping observations can still be small ... this suggests that there is not much independent information in a long time series of multiyears returns, which in turn suggests that conventional large sample approximations to sampling distributions might perform poorly in practice" (Richardson and Stock [1989], p. 324).

For the DM/USD exchange rate the results are illustrated in Figure III-3 and Figure III-4. Figure III-5 and Figure III-6 show the variance ratio estimates for the YEN/USD exchange rate. The corresponding variance ratio estimates and test statistics are reported in Table III-1, Table III-2, Table III-3 and Table III-4. For both weekly exchange rate time series the variance ratio test indicates that up to q = 150 positive autocorrelation is found for the DM/USD and YEN/USD exchange rates. Subsequently, the variance ratio estimates decline, indicating evidence for negative autocorrelation in returns for large q's. Overall, the results for the weekly data indicate that both exchange rate time series feature a trend behavior tendency for approximately 150 weeks, which is equivalent to about three years.

On the whole, the results for the daily DM/USD and YEN/USD exchange rates confirm the results for the weekly data. The variance ratio estimates for both daily time series also indicate negative autocorrelation in the returns for large q's, while for smaller values of q positive autocorrelation is found. Up to q = 800 the variance ratio estimates increase gradually, afterwards a decline is observed. This corresponds approximately with a trend behavior in daily DM/USD and YEN/USD exchange rates for also about three years.

Figure III-3: Variance ratio estimates for large q's, DM/USD (daily data)

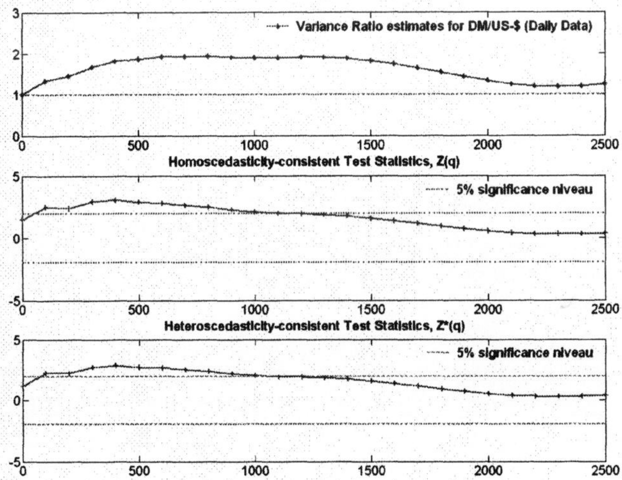

Figure III-4: Variance ratio estimates for large q's, DM/USD (weekly data)

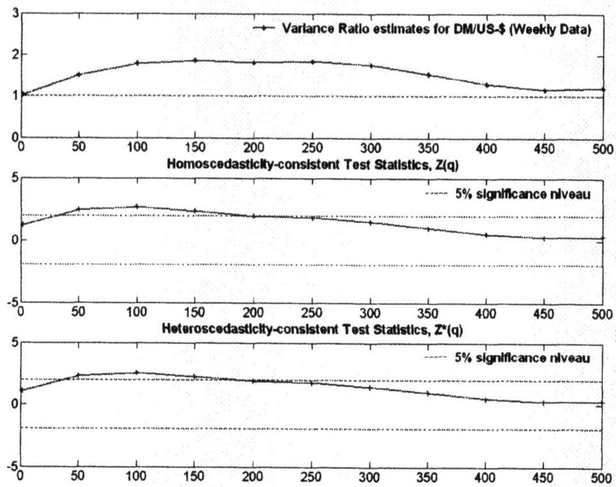

Table III-1: Variance ratio estimates for large q's, DM/USD daily exchange rates

q's	100	200	300	400	500	600	700	800	900	1000	1100	1200
VR	1.3334	1.4560	1.6825	1.8194	1.8635	1.9217	1.9296	1.9383	1.9158	1.8907	1.8961	1.9072
Z(q)	2.5080 (0.0121)	2.4164 (0.0157)	2.9493 (0.0032)	3.0647 (0.0022)	2.8876 (0.0039)	2.8130 (0.0049)	2.6262 (0.0086)	2.4793 (0.0132)	2.2810 (0.0225)	2.1046 (0.0353)	2.0187 (0.0435)	1.9565 (0.0504)
Z*(q)	2.2413 (0.0250)	2.2225 (0.0262)	2.7471 (0.0060)	2.8798 (0.0040)	2.7327 (0.0063)	2.6778 (0.0074)	2.5128 (0.0120)	2.3826 (0.0172)	2.2003 (0.0278)	2.0369 (0.0417)	1.9595 (0.0501)	1.9044 (0.0569)
q's	**1300**	**1400**	**1500**	**1600**	**1700**	**1800**	**1900**	**2000**	**2100**	**2200**	**2300**	**2400**
VR	1.9104	1.8873	1.8225	1.7428	1.6487	1.5467	1.4424	1.3338	1.2443	1.2023	1.1924	1.2123
Z(q)	1.8863 (0.0593)	1.7716 (0.0765)	1.5865 (0.1126)	1.3871 (0.1654)	1.1752 (0.2399)	0.9625 (0.3358)	0.7582 (0.4484)	0.5575 (0.5772)	0.3983 (0.6904)	0.3221 (0.7474)	0.2996 (0.7645)	0.3237 (0.7461)
Z*(q)	1.8409 (0.0656)	1.7332 (0.0831)	1.5559 (0.1197)	1.3634 (0.1728)	1.1577 (0.2470)	0.9501 (0.3421)	0.7499 (0.4533)	0.5525 (0.5806)	0.3955 (0.6925)	0.3204 (0.7487)	0.2986 (0.7653)	0.3232 (0.7465)

Note: p-values are given in parenthesis

Table III-2: Variance ratio estimates for large q's, DM/USD weekly exchange rates

q's	50	100	150	200	250	300	350	400	450	500	550	600
VR	1.5164	1.7991	1.8641	1.8289	1.8524	1.7652	1.5473	1.2918	1.1585	1.2101	1.1478	1.0380
Z(q)	2.4753 (0.0133)	2.6880 0.0072)	2.3671 (0.0179)	1.9641 (0.0495)	1.8052 (0.0710)	1.4766 (0.1398)	0.9787 (0.3278)	0.4881 (0.6255)	0.2498 (0.8027)	0.3142 (0.7534)	0.2108 (0.8331)	0.0519 0.9596)
Z*(q)	2.2751 (0.0229)	2.5217 (0.0117)	2.2493 (0.0245)	1.8849 (0.0594)	1.7465 (0.0807)	1.4387 (0.1502)	0.9594 (0.3374)	0.4811 (0.6305)	0.2475 (0.8045)	0.3127 (0.7545)	0.2107 (0.8331)	0.0522 (0.9584)

Note: p-values are given in parenthesis.

Figure III-5: Variance ratio estimates for large q's, Yen/USD (daily data)

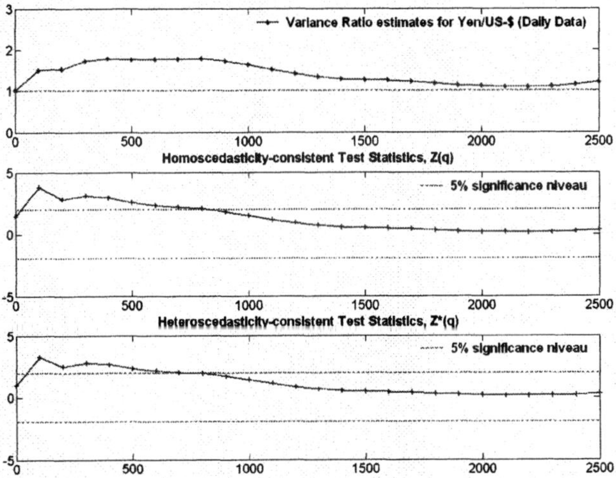

Figure III-6: Variance ratio estimates for large q's, Yen/USD (weekly data)

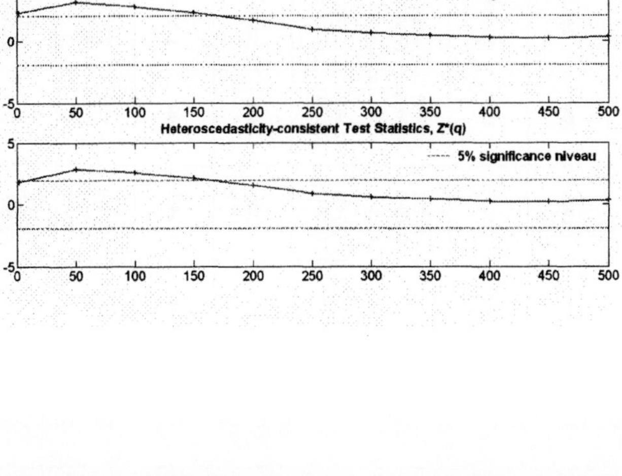

Table III-3: Variance ratio estimates for large q's, YEN/USD daily exchange rates

q's	100	200	300	400	500	600	700	800	900	1000	1100	1200
VR	1.5035	1.5302	1.7138	1.7829	1.7558	1.7604	1.7595	1.7835	1.7201	1.6338	1.5138	1.4053
Z(q)	3.7878 (0.0002)	2.8099 (0.0050)	3.0849 (0.0020)	2.9282 (0.0034)	2.5276 (0.0115)	2.3208 (0.0203)	2.1456 (0.0319)	2.0703 (0.0384)	1.7937 (0.0729)	1.4977 (0.1342)	1.1575 (0.2471)	0.8741 (0.3821)
Z*(q)	3.2452 (0.0012)	2.4803 (0.0131)	2.7745 (0.0055)	2.6687 (0.0076)	2.3265 (0.0200)	2.1538 (0.0313)	2.0059 (0.0449)	1.9482 (0.0514)	1.6978 (0.0896)	1.4247 (0.1542)	1.1060 (0.2687)	0.8386 (0.4017)
q's	**1300**	**1400**	**1500**	**1600**	**1700**	**1800**	**1900**	**2000**	**2100**	**2200**	**2300**	**2400**
VR	1.3455	1.2821	1.2684	1.2443	1.2223	1.1760	1.1343	1.1162	1.0925	1.0878	1.1035	1.1442
Z(q)	0.7159 (0.4741)	0.5633 (0.5732)	0.5176 (0.6047)	0.4563 (0.6482)	0.4028 (0.6871)	0.3099 (0.7566)	0.2302 (0.8180)	0.1941 (0.8461)	0.1507 (0.8802)	0.1398 (0.8888)	0.1612 (0.8719)	0.2198 (0.8260)
Z*(q)	0.6894 (0.4906)	0.5444 (0.5862)	0.5019 (0.6157)	0.4440 (0.6571)	0.3932 (0.6942)	0.3035 (0.7615)	0.2262 (0.8211)	0.1914 (0.8482)	0.1491 (0.8815)	0.1387 (0.8897)	0.1604 (0.8725)	0.2194 (0.8263)

Note: p-values are given in parenthesis

Table III-4: Variance ratio estimates for large q's, YEN/USD weekly exchange rates

q's	50	100	150	200	250	300	350	400	450	500	550	600
VR	1.6561	1.8111	1.8213	1.6874	1.4145	1.3075	1.2432	1.1463	1.1204	1.2249	1.3059	1.3152
Z(q)	3.1446 (0.0017)	2.7282 (0.0064)	2.2498 (0.0245)	1.6289 (0.1033)	0.8778 (0.3801)	0.5942 (0.5524)	0.4350 (0.6636)	0.2447 (0.8067)	0.1898 (0.8495)	0.3362 (0.7367)	0.4361 (0.6628)	0.4301 (0.6671)
Z*(q)	2.8876 (0.0039)	2.5736 (0.0101)	2.1547 (0.0312)	1.5775 (0.1147)	0.8563 (0.3919)	0.5830 (0.5599)	0.4293 (0.6677)	0.2430 (0.8080)	0.1897 (0.8496)	0.3380 (0.7354)	0.4409 (0.6593)	0.4375 (0.6618)

Note: p-values are given in parenthesis.

III.1.3 Exchange rate trends according to Markov Switching regressions

A further useful tool for modeling trend behavior in exchange rates empirically is Markov Switching models. Markov Switching models were first performed by Hamilton [1988, 1989] and can be assigned to the class of non-linear time series models. The purpose of Markov Switching Models is to detect discrete switches in the data governing process and, thus, to capture more complex dynamic patterns. Applications of Markov Switching models to exchange rate dynamics can be found for example in Engel and Hamilton [1990], Kaminsky [1993], Engel [1994] and Klaassen [2001].

III.1.3.1 Data and estimation procedure

Our analysis of the DM/USD and YEN/USD exchange rate is based on quarterly data taken from the International Financial Statistics of the International Monetary Fund (IMF).[24] The time period under consideration starts in the first quarter of 1975 and ends with the second quarter of 2003. The considered time series are shown in Figure III-7 to Figure III-10. The quarterly returns (y) of the exchange rates (s) are defined as the first log differences multiplied times 100:

$$y_t = (s_t - s_{t-1}) * 100. \qquad \text{(III-5)}$$

Since Markov Switching models postulate a stationary time series, we have carried out an augmented Dickey-Fuller (ADF) test (see Dickey and Fuller [1979, 1981]) to test for the presence of a unit root in the data. The ADF test is based on the following regression equation:

$$\Delta y_t = \phi + \sum_{i=1}^{k} \psi_i \Delta y_{t-i} + \pi y_{t-1} + \varepsilon_t, \qquad \text{(III-6)}$$

where $\Delta y_t = y_t - y_{t-1}$ and k represents the number of lags, which should be chosen sufficiently large enough to render the error term empirically white noise. The ADF test consists of testing the null hypothesis H_0: $\pi=0$ against the alternative H_1: $\pi<0$. The null hypothesis of a unit root is rejected when the value of the test statistic $t(\hat{\pi})$ is lower than the critical value.

[24] The corresponding identification codes on the IFS CD-ROM are for the Euro/USD rate 163..RF.ZF, for the DM/USD rate 134..RF.ZF and for the YEN/USD 158..RF.ZF.

Figure III-7: Quarterly DM/USD exchange rate

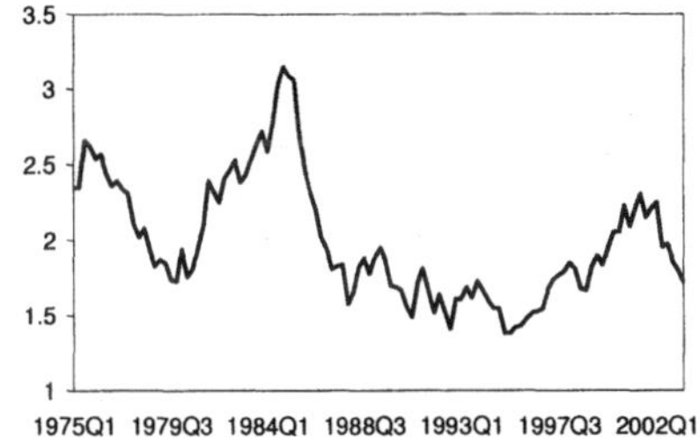

Figure III-8: Quarterly YEN/USD exchange rate

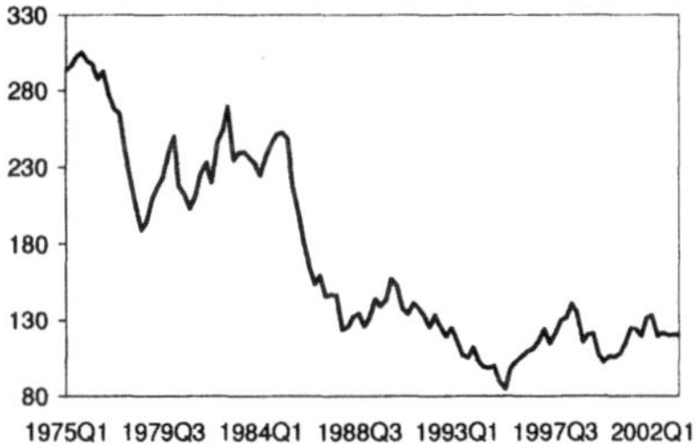

Figure III-9: Quarterly DM/USD exchange rate returns

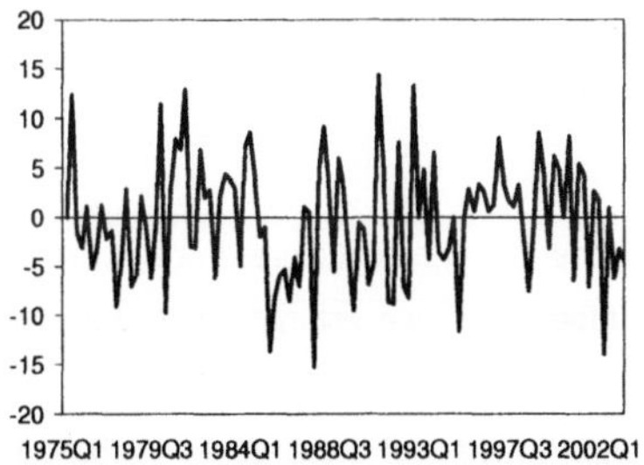

Figure III-10: Quarterly YEN/USD exchange rate returns

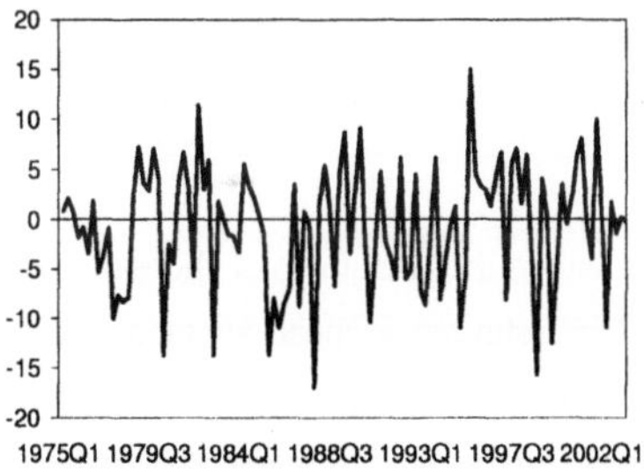

Table III-5 and Table III-6 show the results of the ADF test for the (log) levels and the (log) first differences of the DM/USD and YEN/USD exchange rate. Besides the test statistics $t(\hat{\pi})$ of the ADF test, the tables show also the number of lags included in the ADF regression. The lag length (k) has been determined by choosing the smallest lag length such that the residuals of the ADF regression do not indicate any significant autocorrelation as measured by the Ljung-Box test statistic. The ADF regression includes a constant for the levels of the exchange rate and no intercept for the first differences. The results indicate that while the levels of both the DM/USD exchange rate and the YEN/USD exchange rate are non-stationary, the corresponding first differences are stationary. This suggests that the DM/USD and YEN/USD exchange rate can be treated as integrated of order one, i.e. I(1). Therefore, we will use the first differences of the log DM/USD and log YEN/SUD exchange rate in the following regression analysis.

Table III-5: Results for the ADF test, DM/USD exchange rate

	$t(\hat{\pi})$	k
Levels (logs)	-1.8518 (-2.8872)	1
First differences	-7.6423 (-1.9429)	0

MacKinnon [1991] critical values for the 5% significance level are in parenthesis.

Table III-6: Results for the ADF test, YEN/USD exchange rate

	$t(\hat{\pi})$	k
Levels (logs)	-1.8292 (-2.8872)	3
First differences	-4.5239 (-1.9429)	2

MacKinnon [1991] critical values for the 5% significance level are in parenthesis.

To evaluate the usefulness of choosing a non-linear time series model instead of a linear model, we first estimate a linear AR model of order p. Afterwards, we estimate a 2 state Markov Switching model with the same AR(p) in each state so that we can compare the fits of both models. In general, a linear univariate autoregressive model of order p for exchange rate returns can be described as follows:

$$y_t = \alpha_0 + \alpha_1 y_{t-1} + \alpha_2 y_{t-2} + \ldots + \alpha_p y_{t-p} + \varepsilon_t \tag{III-7}$$

where y_t is defined as in equation (III-5) and ε_t is a white noise disturbance term. The choice of the appropriate lag length in the autoregressive regression is somewhat arbitrary. We decided to include all lags up to the order for which the partial autocorrelations are at last significant. Thus, for the DM/USD exchange rate we choose a lag length of one (see Figure III-11) and for the YEN/USD exchange rate a lag length of three (see Figure III-12). The results of estimating equation (III-7) for the returns of the DM/USD and YEN/USD exchange rates are illustrated in Table III-7 and Table III-9, respectively.

Figure III-11: Partial correlation of changes in the log DM/USD

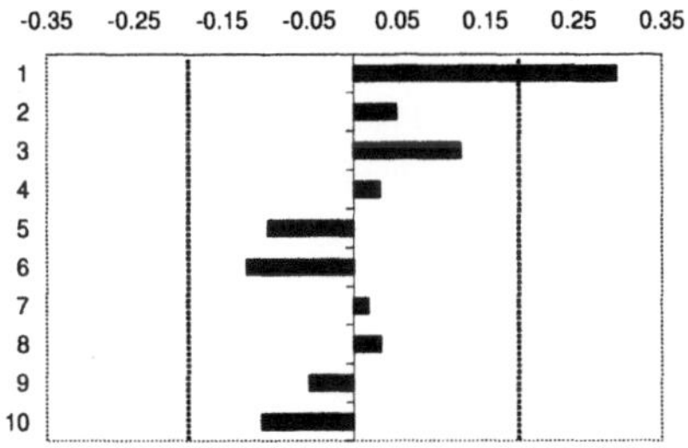

Figure III-12: Partial correlation of changes in the log Yen/USD

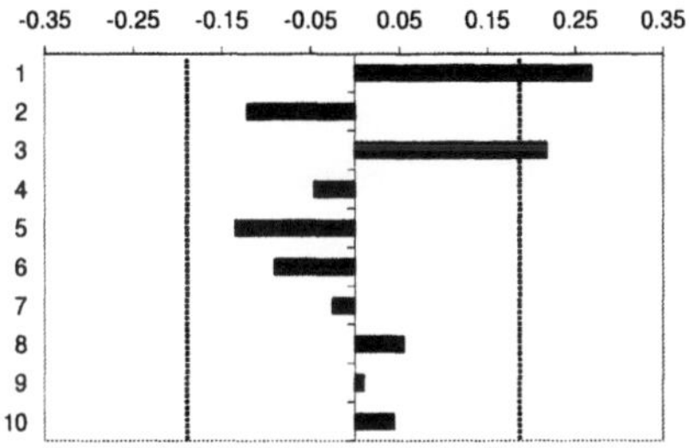

(dotted lines are the approximate two standard error bounds computed as $\pm \frac{2}{\sqrt{T}}$)

The 2 state Markov Switching regression is based on a univariate autoregressive structure in each state. Thus, the corresponding regression equation is given by:[25]

$$y_t = \begin{cases} \alpha_{0,1} + \alpha_{1,1} y_{t-1} + \alpha_{2,1} y_{t-2} + \ldots + \alpha_{p,1} y_{t-p} + \varepsilon_t & \text{if } h_t = 1, \\ \alpha_{0,2} + \alpha_{1,2} y_{t-1} + \alpha_{2,2} y_{t-2} + \ldots + \alpha_{p,2} y_{t-p} + \varepsilon_t & \text{if } h_t = 2, \end{cases} \tag{III-8}$$

where y_t denotes the returns of the exchange rate and ε_t is a white noise error term. The state variable h_t describes the unobservable state of the world. It is assumed that h_t follows an ergodic, irreducible first-order Markov process, which can be characterized by the following matrix P consisting of the transition probabilities p_{ij} from state i to state j ($p_{ij} = \Pr(h_t = j | h_{t-1} = i)$):

$$P = \begin{bmatrix} p_{11} & p_{21} \\ p_{12} & p_{22} \end{bmatrix}, \text{ where } \sum_{i=j}^{2} p_{ij} = 1 \; \forall \; i, j \in \{1,2\}. \tag{III-9}$$

The unconditional probabilities for both states, $P(h_t = i)$ for i = 1,2, can be derived from the theory of ergodic Markov chains (see Hamilton [1994]):

[25] A detailed discussion of Markov Switching Models can be found in Hamilton [1994], Krolzig [1997] and Franses and van Dijk [2000].

$$P(h_t = 1) = \frac{1 - p_{22}}{2 - p_{11} - p_{22}},$$
$$P(h_t = 2) = \frac{1 - p_{11}}{2 - p_{11} - p_{22}}. \tag{III-10}$$

As Engel and Hamilton [1990] have pointed out, modeling exchange rates empirically by the means of Markov Switching regression allows for a variety of potential exchange rate behaviors. For example, Markov Switching models are consistent with asymmetric behavior in different states, e.g. short but sharp downward moves and long but gradual upward trends. Markov Switching models can also capture random walk behavior of exchange rates. Within Markov Switching regressions this hypothesis would imply that the transition probabilities p_{11} and p_{22} are equivalent. Thus it is reasonable to conclude that Markov Switching models do not inevitably require exchange rates to move in long swings (see Engel and Hamilton [1990] and De Grauwe and Vansteenkiste [2001]).

Since the state variable s_t is not observable, the estimation of the 2 state Markov switching model is highly non-standard. Maximum likelihood techniques are used for the parameter estimation. The aim of the estimation procedure is to obtain the parameters in the autoregressive models in each state and the probabilities of the transition matrix P as well as the probabilities with which each state occurs at each point of time (see Franses and van Dijk [2000]). The maximum likelihood estimates are derived by relying on the Expectation Maximization (EM) algorithm as described by Franses and van Dijk [2000].[26]

III.1.3.2 Empirical results for DM/USD and YEN/USD exchange rates

The results of the Markov Switching AR(1) model for the DM/USD exchange rate returns are summarized in Table III-7. Obviously, the fit of the 2 state Markov Switching model is clearly in excess of the fit of the linear alternative. The adjusted R^2 for the linear AR(1) regression is about 0.08 compared to 0.60 for the 2 state Markov Switching model. Similarly, the higher log likelihood of the Markov Switching model indicates that this model performs better than the linear autoregressive regression. However, this hypothesis can not be tested empirically by standard likelihood ratio tests since one of the regularity conditions necessary for this test does not hold (see Hamilton [1994] and [1996]). We therefore carried out Wald tests for evaluating

[26] The estimates of the Markov Switching models are generated by using the Gauss codes provided by Philip Franses and Dick van Dijk (see http://www.few.eur.nl/few/people/djvandijk/nltsmef/nltsmef.htm).

the existence of two different states (see Engel and Hamilton [1990], Dewachter [1997]). The considered Wald tests allow for testing at least two hypotheses. First, it can be used to test for systematically alternating states in contrast to arbitrarily alternating states, i.e. H_0: $p_{11}=1-p_{22}$. The corresponding test statistic is given by (see Engel and Hamilton [1990]):

$$\frac{\left[\hat{p}_{11}-\left(1-\hat{p}_{22}\right)\right]^2}{\widehat{\text{var}}\left(\hat{p}_{11}\right)+\widehat{\text{var}}\left(\hat{p}_{22}\right)+2\widehat{\text{cov}}\left(\hat{p}_{11},\hat{p}_{22}\right)}\approx\chi^2(1). \tag{III-11}$$

The second application of the Wald test accounts for testing against the null hypothesis of identical parameters in the different states. The corresponding test statistic is given by (see Engel and Hamilton [1990]):

$$\frac{\left[\hat{\alpha}_{p,1}-\hat{\alpha}_{p,2}\right]^2}{\widehat{\text{var}}\left(\hat{\alpha}_{p,1}\right)+\widehat{\text{var}}\left(\hat{\alpha}_{p,2}\right)-2\widehat{\text{cov}}\left(\hat{\alpha}_{p,1},\hat{\alpha}_{p,2}\right)}\approx\chi^2(1). \tag{III-12}$$

Both Wald tests are used to evaluate the appropriateness of using a non-linear 2 state Markov Switching model instead of a linear AR(p) model. The critical value for the 5% significance level is 3.841 (d.f. =1). The related results for DM/USD exchange rate are summarized in Table III-8. They show that the 2 state Markov Switching model appears to be a reasonable description for the DM/USD exchange rate. The results of testing for the null hypothesis H_0: $\alpha_{p,1} = \alpha_{p,2}$ show that the constants in each state deviate significantly from each other. However, the autoregressive components of each state do not differ significantly. A further indication for the existence of two different states in the DM/USD exchange rate time series are the estimates for the transition probabilities in the Markov Switching model. Both are relatively high, indicating the existence of two fairly persistent states. This is also confirmed by testing the null hypothesis H_0: $p_{11} = 1-p_{22}$ by means of a Wald test. The result indicates that the hypothesis of arbitrarily alternating states is rejected in favor of systematically alternating states. Thus, it is reasonable to conclude that the 2 state Markov Switching model describes the DM/USD exchange rate returns rather well. As expected, the Markov Switching model identifies an appreciation state and a depreciation state for the DM/USD. Thereby, the average depreciation rate of the DM/USD rate in state one is about 3% per quarter and the average appreciation in state two is about 3.7% per quarter. The expected duration of each state (E(D)) can be evaluated according to Kim and Nelson [1999] as follows:

$$E(D)=\frac{1}{1-p_{ii}}. \tag{III-13}$$

For the DM/USD exchange rate the expected duration of each state is, according to the estimation results, round about 5 quarters. Figure III-13 illustrates the respective probabilities for state 1 at each point in time and the DM/USD exchange rate.

Table III-7: Results for the DM/USD exchange rate returns

	Linear AR(1) model	State	Non-Linear AR(1) model
α_0	-0.2108 (-0.4749)	1	3.1462 (3.5536)
		2	-3.2551 (3.7372)
α_1	0.3025 (3.3088)	1	-0.0163 (-0.1777)
		2	0.1283 (0.8703)
p_{11}			0.7950 (6.7436)
p_{22}			0.8045 (8.8243)
P(h_t = 1)			0.4881
P(h_t = 2)			0.5119
Log Likelihood	-331.05		-328.144
R^2	0.0905		0.6210
Adjusted R^2	0.0823		0.5996
Test for autocorrelation in residuals			
Q-Stat(4)	2.5882 [0.629]		5.3279 [0.255]
Q-Stat(8)	4.4801 [0.811]		8.5036 [0.386]
Q-Stat(12)	7.9435 [0.790]		14.083 [0.295]
Estimated Mean of return	-0.3022	1	3.0957
		2	-3.7342
Expected duration of each state	--	1	4.8780
	--	2	5.1151

Notes: t-statistics are given in parenthesis, p-values in brackets.

Table III-8: Wald tests for the DM/USD exchange rate returns

	H_0: $\alpha_{p,1} = \alpha_{p,2}$		H_0: $p_{11} = 1-p_{22}$
	Constant	**AR(1)**	
Test statistics	26.9069	0.3621	37.1829

Figure III-13: DM/USD exchange rate and state probabilities

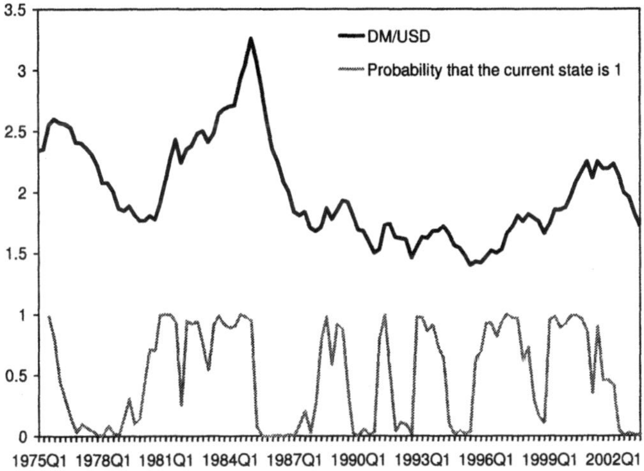

The estimation results for the YEN/USD exchange rate using Markov Switching regression are summarized in Table III-9. Overall, the results correspond to those for the DM/USD exchange rate. The fit for the 2 state Markov Switching AR(3) model clearly exceeds that of the linear AR(3) model, as the adjusted R^2 for the linear model is about 0.10 and that of the Markov Switching model about 0.55. The log likelihood is higher for the non-linear model and the Wald tests suggest that significant differences in the 2 states can be observed. According to the estimation results, an appreciation state of the Yen vis-à-vis the US dollar is identified with an average appreciation rate of 3.6 % per quarter. For the depreciation state an average rate of 2.9 % per quarter is expected. The expected duration of a depreciation phase is, according to our results, approximately 5 quarters. An appreciation phase is expected to be longer with about 9 quarters. Figure III-14 shows the respective probabilities of state 1 at each point in time and the YEN/USD exchange rate.

Table III-9: Results for the YEN/USD exchange rate returns

	Linear AR(3) model	State	Non-Linear AR(3) model
α_0	-0.5502 (-1.0966)	1	4.0157 (3.5385)
		2	-3.2839 (-4.1833)
α_1	0.3272 (3.4532)	1	-0.1443 (-0.7839)
		2	0.1850 (1.6174)
α_2	-0.1886 (-1.9163)	1	-0.2125 (-1.4635)
		2	-0.3628 (-3.3791)
α_3	0.2205 (2.3198)	1	-0.0395 (-0.3178)
		2	0.2719 (2.4628)
p_{11}			0.8117 (10.9367)
p_{22}			0.8897 (17.7615)
$P(h_t = 1)$			0.3694
$P(h_t = 2)$			0.6306
Log Likelihood	-333.85		-330.32
R^2	0.1294		0.5879
Adjusted R^2	0.1048		0.5475
Test for autocorrelation in residuals			
Q(4)	0.1375 [0.998]		0.7290 [0.948]
Q(8)	3.8694 [0.869]		2.8692 [0.942]
Q(12)	4.8221 [0.964]		4.0782 [0.982]
Estimated Mean of return	-0.8585	1	2.876
		2	-3.6250
Expected duration of each state		1	5.3107
		2	9.0662

Notes: t-statistics are given in parenthesis, p-values in brackets

Table III-10: Wald tests for the YEN/USD exchange rate returns

	$H_0: \alpha_{p,1} = \alpha_{p,2}$				H_0: $p_{11} = 1-p_{22}$
	Constant	AR(1)	AR(2)	AR(3)	
Test statistics	29.8881	2.4847	0.7266	3.8931	80.7354

Figure III-14: Yen/USD exchange rate and state probabilities

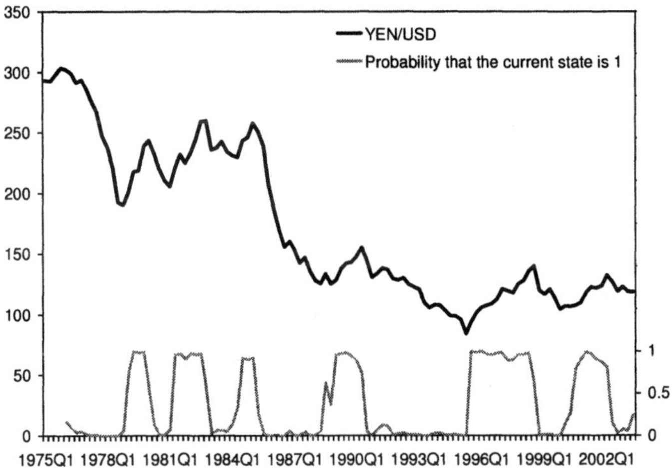

Overall, the analysis of the DM/USD and YEN/USD exchange rates by the means of Markov Switching regressions has revealed that both exchange rate time series are characterized by two distinguishable states rather than random walk behavior. Furthermore, the results indicate that DM/USD and YEN/USD exchange rates can be best described by appreciation and depreciation phases. However, the estimated duration of each state is well below that suggested by technical analysis of variance ratio tests.

III.2 Speculation in foreign exchange markets

The foregoing analysis of the empirical exchange rate dynamics suggests that free floating exchange rates tend to move in long persistent trends. Table III-11 summarizes the estimated trend length of DM/USD and YEN/USD exchange rates. The results reveal that free-floating exchange rates are characterized by long-trends. However, the observed long trends are judged to be disconnected from macroeconomic fundamentals (see Table III-12). This assessment of practitioners coincides also with the results of section II.2.5.

Table III-11: Summary of trend length in quarters

	DM/USD	YEN/USD
Technical analysis (appreciation)	9.8	11.3
Technical analysis (depreciation)	12	8.2
Variance ratio test (daily data)	12	12
Variance ratio test (weekly data)	12	12
Markov-Switching (appreciation)	5.1	5.3
Markov-Switching (depreciation)	4.9	9.1

The disconnect puzzle of foreign exchange rates is often explained by an excessive, speculative trading behavior of foreign exchange market participants. Due to speculation, it is argued, exchange rates deviate substantially from their intrinsic fundamental value. For example, Cheung and Wong [2000] and Cheung and Chinn [2001] carried out a systematic survey of Asian and U.S. foreign exchange traders and asked for the reasons why actual exchange rates do not reflect fundamental values (see Table III-13). According to their results, foreign exchange traders believe that the most important reason for deviations of exchange rates from their fundamental value is 'excessive speculation'. For the Asian survey of foreign exchange traders, Cheung and Wong [2000] report that round about 83 per cent agree with the hypothesis that 'excessive speculation' prevents exchange rates from reflecting fundamental value. A very similar role of 'excessive speculation' is reported by Cheung and Chinn [2001] for the U.S. foreign exchange market. According to this poll, 'excessive speculation' is also the most important reason for deviations of exchange rates from fundamental value.

Table III-12: Fundamentals and exchange rate movements

Do you believe exchange rate movements accurately reflect changes in the fundamental value?				
		Short-run	Medium-run	Long-run
Cheung et al. [2000]	Yes	3	57.8	87
	No	97	42.2	12
	No opinion	0	0	1
Cheung and Wong [2000]♣	Yes	5.2	51.6	80.3
	No	91	38.1	10
	No opinion	3.8	10.3	9.7
Cheung and Chinn [2001]	Yes	1.43	58.69	88.4
	No	94.24	31.88	7.97
	No opinion	4.31	9.42	3.62

♣ Figures are averages for the trading centers of Hong Kong, Tokyo and Singapore

Table III-13: The role of speculation in Asian and U.S. foreign exchange markets

Reasons exchange rate movements do not reflect changes in the fundamental value: Excessive speculation?			
Trading centre	Yes	No	No opinion
U.S. market	74.19%	18.54%	7.25%
Hong Kong	85.8%	8.5%	5.7%
Tokyo	75.0%	16.7%	8.3%
Singapore	88.5%	5.1%	6.4%

Sources: Cheung and Wong [2000], Cheung and Chinn [2001]

In this section we deal with the role of speculation in foreign exchange markets. In particular, we try to answer the question whether speculative trading behaviors can be held responsible for exchange rate developments that are disconnected from macroeconomic fundamentals. We first define the general meaning of the term 'speculation'. Afterwards, we analyze the major characteristics of foreign exchange markets and evaluate to what extent these characteristics are likely to promote speculation.

III.2.1 Relevance of speculation in foreign exchange markets

A prominent definition of speculation is given by Kaldor [1939] in his influential work on speculation and economic stability. He defines speculation as the

> "[...] purchase (or sale) of goods with a view to re-sale (or re-purchase) at a later date, where the motive behind such action is the expectation of a change in the relevant prices relatively to the ruling price..." (Kaldor [1939], p. 1)

Analogously, the Oxford Universal Dictionary defines speculation as

> "the action or practise of buying and selling goods, stocks and shares, etc., in order to profit by the rise or fall in the market value." (quoted in Tirole [1992], p. 514)

Both definitions reveal that speculation has to be distinguished from investment activities as they are carried out to gain from the use of the asset by interest payments, dividends etc.. Furthermore, speculation is separated from arbitrage, which is exclusively conducted to profit from price differences in different sub-markets (see Krüger [1996]). Both definitions of speculation illustrate that speculative trading always contains two central attributes:

- First, speculative trading activities always rest upon expectations concerning the future development of the corresponding market value.
- Second, as the future development of the market value can not be predicted for sure, speculative transactions are always accompanied by a high degree of uncertainty, so that speculation is always risky.

Given the above definitions of speculation, all foreign exchange market transactions whose returns largely depend on the change in exchange rates can be seen as speculation. Thus, all open positions of foreign exchange market participants, whose value will change with a change in exchange rates, can be considered as speculation, since the return on those positions is clearly dominated by changes in the exchange rate, whereas interest rates play only a minor role (see Krüger [1996]). A natural way for determining the extent of speculation in foreign exchange markets would be to measure the number of open positions held by foreign exchange market participants. However, such data are not available on a broad basis. Therefore, we opt for an indicative approach to evaluate the role and extent of speculation in foreign exchange markets. According to Kaldor [1939], a good or asset can only be an object of speculation if at least two main conditions are fulfilled: the existence of a perfect market and low carrying costs.

In this context, Aschinger [1995] lists the following main factors that promote speculation:

a) the existence of a broad and almost perfectly functioning market in which a homogenous good is traded,

b) the existence of high liquidity in the market , i.e. the good is often traded,

c) the existence of low transaction costs, i.e. the spread between bid and ask quotes should be low,

d) the existence of high volatility in the market, and

e) the traded good should be storable.

In the following, we contrast the institutional characteristics of foreign exchange markets with the listed factors that are likely to promote speculation to evaluate the role of speculation in foreign exchange markets.

Currency is unambiguously a *perfect standardized (homogeneous)* and *storable good.* It is traded in a *broad* and almost *perfectly functioning market.* Although the foreign exchange market exhibits a rather complex market structure, which is characterized by its decentralism, it ensures a smooth functioning of the market. Figure III-15 illustrates schematically the structure of the foreign exchange market. In principle, the foreign exchange market can be divided into two segments according to the involved transaction partners. The first segment covers trading between foreign exchange market dealers and brokers. Accordingly, it is often called the inter-dealer market.[27] Dealers in foreign exchange markets are normally large commercial banks acting as market makers (MM).[28] Brokers are financial corporations, who match dealers in the inter-dealer market without taking own positions and thus facilitate transactions between different market makers.[29] In the second segment of the foreign exchange market, market

---

[27] The foreign exchange inter-dealer market is also often called foreign exchange inter-bank market. This notion reflects the dominant role of commercial banks in the foreign exchange inter-dealer market. However, their importance has been reduced over the past years as investment banking firms and other financial institutions have become emulators. Thus, it is more accurate to allude to an inter-dealer market (see Cross [1998]).

[28] This implies that dealers in foreign exchange markets provide double-auction quotes, i.e. both bid and ask prices.

[29] According to Bjønnes and Rime [2000], the three most important reason for trading via brokers are: a) the initiating party stays anonymous, b) dealers can enter one-way prices (bid or ask) without being worried about revealing their position, and c) the quoting party chooses when to place a quote, opposed to direct trading.

makers trade with customers according to the needs of the customers. Customers in foreign exchange markets are small banks, which are not members of the inter-dealer market, managed funds, hedge funds, insurance companies, non-financial corporations, individuals and central banks (see Luca [2000]).

Figure III-15. Schematic structure of the foreign exchange market

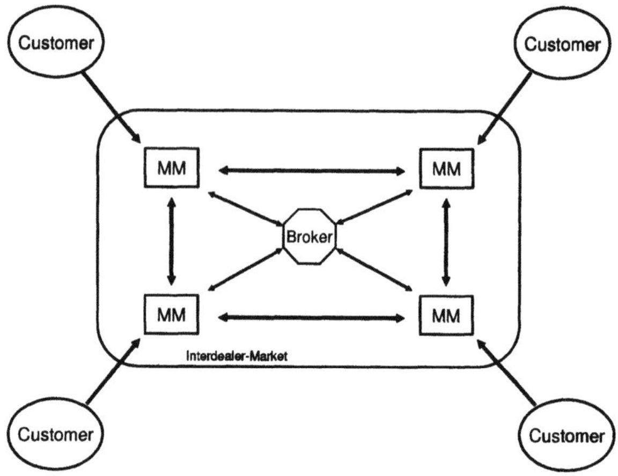

Trading in foreign exchange markets is dominated by market makers. Market makers are involved in every transaction in foreign exchange markets, with inter-dealer-market trading accounting for the largest proportion (see Table III-14). According to the latest figures of the Bank for International Settlements [2002], trading in the inter-dealer market accounts for about 60 per cent of the total daily turnover in foreign exchange markets. The trading activity of market makers with financial customers comprises roughly 30%, trades with non-financial customers cover merely 10 per cent of total foreign exchange turnover. In this context, Lyons [2001b] states however that the share of inter-dealer trades is likely to be underestimated by the survey, as the category 'other financial institutions' includes some non-reporting dealers.

Table III-14: Reported foreign exchange market turnover by counterparty (daily averages in April, in billions of US-$)

		1992	1995	1998	2001
Total turnover		776 (100%)	1137 (100%)	1430 (100%)	1173 (100%)
Inter-dealer trade		540 (70%)	729 (64%)	908 (63%)	689 (59%)
Customer trade	**Financial**	97 (12 %)	230 (20%)	279 (20%)	329 (28%)
	Non-financial	137 (18%)	178 (16%)	242 (17%)	156 (13%)

Source: Bank for International Settlements [2002]

A further factor that promotes speculation in a market is a *high degree of liquidity*. The foreign exchange market is the most liquid market of the world with an impressive overall trading volume. The foreign exchange market has experienced a spectacular growth in volume ever since the breakdown of the Bretton Woods system. While the daily turnover in 1977 was about 5 billions of US dollar, it increased to 590 billions of US dollar in 1989 and reached an absolute peak in 1998 with about 1,490 billions of US dollar. At present, the daily foreign exchange market turnover is estimated to amount to 1,200 billions of US dollar (see Figure III-16).[30]

Figure III-16: Foreign exchange market turnover (daily averages in April, in billions of US-$)

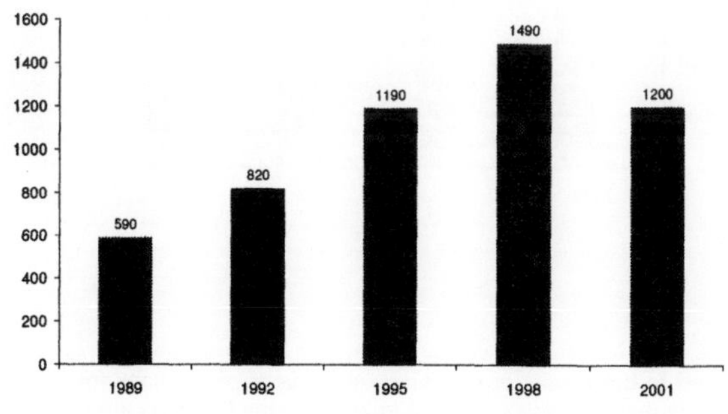

[30] The latest Triennial Central Bank Survey of the Bank for International Settlements (BIS) covers a broad range figures describing the most important characteristics and developments of foreign exchange markets; see Bank for International Settlements [2002].

The dimension of these figures becomes even more obvious if one compares the daily trading volume of a single currency pair with the daily trading volume per stock on the New York Stock Exchange (NYSE); whereas the daily per stock trading volume in 1998 amounts 'only' to 10 millions of US dollar, the daily trading volume of the DM/US dollar is about 300 billions of US dollar (see Evans and Lyons [2002b]). For the EUR/USD the most recent figure in 2001 is about 350 billions of US dollar (see Bank for International Settlements [2002]).[31] Furthermore, a comparison of the annual world merchandise trade with the annual foreign exchange turnover demonstrates the tremendous dimension of foreign exchange trading. The total world merchandise trade with about 12,453 billions of US dollar in 2001 accounts only for scarcely 4 % of the total yearly foreign exchange turnover with 300,000 billions US dollar.[32] Thus, the annual volume of foreign exchange trading is about 24 times larger than annual world merchandise trade (see Figure III-17).

Figure III-17: Foreign exchange market turnover and world merchandise trade (annual figures, in billions of US-$)

[31] However, compared to the results of the foregoing surveys of the Bank for International Settlements the foreign exchange market activity declined in 2001 for the first time after more than two decades of significant growth (see Figure III-16). According to Galati [2001], this drop in overall foreign exchange market turnover does not reflect a substantial change in the pattern of exchange rate volatility, but is the consequence of various factors as e.g. the introduction of the Euro as the common European currency, the growing share of electronic brokering in the spot market, a clear tendency of consolidation in the banking industry and international concentration in the corporate sector (see for more details Galati [2001]).

[32] Merchandise trade is the sum of exports and imports of goods. The yearly total foreign exchange turnover is calculated by assuming 250 trading days per year. Trade figures are taken from the IFS-CD-Rom of the International Monetary Fund (IMF) (see International Monetary Fund [2004]).

The high trading volume in foreign exchange markets can mainly be ascribed to the trading practice of market makers. Market makers are continuously willing to quote bid-ask spreads to the corresponding counterparties. By doing so, market makers assure the immediacy and hence the efficient functioning of the foreign exchange market, so that any foreign exchange market participant can deal according to his needs at any time. In order to supply this liquidity service to the other market participants it is necessary that market makers buy and sell currencies on their own account. Consequently, their foreign exchange inventory varies with the arriving requests of counterparties. To manage the associated inventory risk, a market maker passes almost all of his positions on to other market makers, who in turn sell it to another market maker and so on. This process of inter-dealer risk management is often denoted as 'hot potato trading' and implies that 'trading begets trading'. Burnham [1991] describes the process of hot potato trading quite vivid:

> "... the marketmaker's equilibrium position has been disturbed by its receipt of a currency position occasioned by its willingness to quote two-way prices. It now seeks to restore its own equilibrium by going to another marketmaker or the broker market for a two-way price. A game of "hot potato" has begun. Eventually, another party willing to accept the position at the market price is found, or a new market price is established and at least one marketmaker accepts a loss on the position. It is this search process for a counterparty who is willing to accept a new currency position that accounts for a good deal of the volume in the foreign exchange market." (Burnham [1991], p. 135).

Lyons [1996] reports empirical evidence supportive for the hot potato trading hypothesis in foreign exchange markets. A central result of this trading practice is that the trading volume in the inter-dealer market is tremendously high, but in return it assures that foreign exchange markets are highly liquid so that a continuous pricing is guaranteed.[33] Thus, the trading practice of market makers also promotes speculative behavior as it ensures a smooth functioning of foreign exchange markets by providing liquidity to the market.[34] This assessment is in line with Kirman [1995], who reports a quotation of an economist:

> "These [foreign] exchange transactions began as a means to smooth and facilitate the flows of traditional trade and investment. But this FX 'tail' has grown to be some

[33] The volume of interdealer trading decreased in the last view years, reflecting the increasing use of electronic brokers (see Bank for International Settlements [2002], p. 7).

[34] Interestingly, it should also be noted that the observable high trading volume in foreign exchange markets clearly conflicts with the traditional asset approach models to exchange rate determination. Frankel and Froot [1990] clarify the conflicting aspect: "When a new piece of information becomes available, if all investors process the information in the same way and are otherwise identical, no trading needs to take place. The price of the asset should simply jump to its new value." (Frankel and Froot [1990], p. 92).

> hundred times larger than the original 'dog' ... FX is a speculators' paradise." (see Kirman [1995], p. 286)

A by-product of the high liquidity in foreign exchange markets are *low transaction costs*. Trading in foreign exchange markets is judged to be very inexpensive. Krause [1991] states that

> "the foreign exchange market is said to have perhaps the lowest transactions costs and thus is as close to being a 'perfect' market (a market where the bid and ask prices are identical) as any in existence." (Krause [1991], p. 67).

This rating coincides also with the assessment of an equity strategist employed by the Dresdner Bank. He claims the following order of trading costs in various asset markets (ascending order): foreign exchange trading, fixed income trading and equity trading (see Schröder [2004]).

Furthermore, the high liquidity also results in high volatility in foreign exchange markets. Figure III-18 shows the courses of monthly DM/USD and YEN/USD exchange rates compared to the monthly price development of consumption goods. Obviously, exchange rates show more distinctive price movements than consumption goods. Overall, this very short comparison reveals that exchange rates are rather volatile compared to normal consumption goods. Thus, exchange rates are a likely objective of speculation.

Figure III-18: Price movements of consumption goods and exchange rates

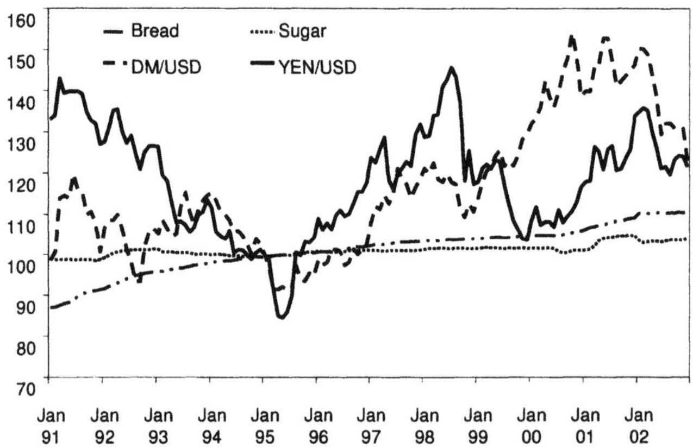

Source: IMF Financial Statistics; Federal Statistical Office Germany

The extent to which prices in a market are dominated by speculation depends to a large extent on the specific characteristics of the market. Summarizing the institutional characteristics of the foreign exchange market leads to the conclusion that the foreign exchange market shows all factors that are likely to promote speculation. Thus, we can conclude that the foreign exchange market must be regarded as prime example for a market whose specific characteristics promote speculative transactions.

III.2.2 The impact of speculation on foreign exchange rates

The impact of speculation on exchange rate movements depends primarily on the nature of speculators' expectations. Traditionally, the economic profession assumes that expectations about future exchange rates are formed rationally, i.e. speculators orientate their speculative engagements on the fundamental value of currencies. This vision of speculation goes at least back to the influential contributions of Friedman [1953] and Fama [1965a, 1965b] who suggest that rationally acting market participants ensure that prices correspond always to their fundamental values. Consequently, speculation is judged to be beneficial to the whole economy as it stabilizes exchange rates around their intrinsic fundamental values. In this view, the possibility that irrational speculators can have a substantial influence on exchange rate movements is ruled out, as they would suffer permanent losses (see Friedman [1953]).

In recent times, more and more economists scrutinized the traditional view on the impact of speculation. On the one hand, there exists a strong theoretical doubt that rational speculators always stabilize exchange rates to the full extent. This criticism is mainly attributed to the institutional constraints of speculators in foreign exchange markets, which induce limits to arbitrage (see Shleifer [2000]). On the other hand, it can be shown that Friedman's [1953] hypothesis that non-rational speculators must suffer losses, does not hold in all instances. On the contrary, some theoretical models show that non-rational speculation can be very profitable.

In the following we deal with the subject of speculation in more detail. First, Friedman's [1953] view of speculation is illustrated and discussed. Afterwards the impact of noise traders (i.e. non-rational speculators) on asset prices will be examined, whereby two different models are considered. The implications of these models show that under the existence of noise traders rational speculators do not fully stabilize prices, or rather may themselves even cause destabilizing price movements. Finally, we analyze the results of survey studies with regard to the actual trading behavior of foreign exchange market participants, to assess whether their trading behavior can be described as fundamentally oriented, i.e. stabilizing speculation, or as non-fundamentally oriented, i.e. destabilizing speculation.

III.2.2.1 The case of stabilizing speculation

Friedman´s [1953] view of speculation is dominated by the idea that exchange rates reflect the relative macroeconomic performance of two countries. Thus, it is based on macroeconomic exchange rate models. In this context, speculation can be interpreted as the exploitation of occurring exchange rate deviations from their fundamental values. Consequently, speculation is clearly fundamental-oriented and ensures an efficient functioning of foreign exchange markets as it stabilizes exchange rates around their fundamental values. By doing so, fundamental-oriented rational speculators earn substantial profits, as they always buy (sell) exchange rates when the current rate is below (above) the fundamental equilibrium rate. According to Friedman [1953], this stabilizing speculation is the only practicable kind of speculation because non-fundamental and possibly destabilizing speculation must be – in his opinion – always unprofitable and speculators following non-fundamental strategies lose their money and so must leave the market:

> "It is said that speculators will take a decline in the exchange rate as a signal for a further decline and will thus tend to make the movements in the exchange rate sharper than they would be in the absence of speculation. The special fear in this connection is of capital flight in response to political uncertainty or simply to movements in the exchange rate. ...People who argue that speculation is generally destabilizing seldom realize that this is largely equivalent to saying that speculators lose money, since speculation can be destabilizing in general only if speculators on the average sell when the currency is low in price and buy when it is high. It does not, of course, follow that speculation is not destabilizing; professional speculators might on the average make money while a changing body of amateurs regularly lost larger sums." (Friedman [1953], p. 175)

The main lines of Friedman´s [1953] argumentation can be analyzed in terms of a simple demand and supply analysis, which is based on a partial equilibrium model (see e.g. Johnson [1976], Aschinger [1995]). The model relies on the following basic assumptions:

a) A homogenous good is traded in market under perfect competition.

b) The model considers two periods, whereby at the beginning of period one no speculators exist. In period one, speculators take open positions to achieve profits because of expected price changes.

c) The share of speculators in the market is low, so that speculators orientate on the expected decisions of the non-speculators.

d) For the moment it is assumed that speculators can anticipate the future development of supply and demand correctly.

The case of partially stabilizing speculation is shown in Figure III-19. At the beginning of period one, no speculators are in the market and the equilibrium is given at E_1. It is now assumed that speculators, who possess superior information concerning the future demand[35] and expect a rising price, enter the market and buy $\bar{Q}$ quantities of the homogenous good. Thus, the good's demand curve shifts from D_1 to D_1^S and a new equilibrium is found at E_1^S. In period two, the non-speculative demand for the good shifts from D_1 to D_2. Subsequently, speculators sell the quantity $\bar{Q}$ bought in period 1 and the supply curve shifts from S_1 to S_2^S. Without speculative trading activities the equilibrium in period two would have been at E_2. However, with speculation the equilibrium is at E_2^S. Thus, the trading activities of speculators had a stabilizing impact on the price of the homogeneous good; without speculation the price would have risen from P_1 to P_2 compared to a rise from P_1^S to P_2^S with speculative trading activities.

The welfare implications of partially stabilizing speculation can also be evaluated by means of Figure III-19. In the first period, speculation generates a net welfare gain for the non-speculators of $E_1E_1^SB$, which is related to the increase of producers' surplus due to the increasing price ($P_1 \rightarrow P_1^S$). In period two, non-speculators again receive a net welfare gain ($CE_2^SE_2$). This is related to the increasing consumer surplus due to the falling price ($P_2 \rightarrow P_2^S$). Thus, on the whole the welfare effects of speculation for non-speculators are positive. Also speculators generate profits by speculation whereby the extent is determined by $\bar{Q}(P_2^S - P_1^S)$ and corresponds to DFE_2^SC. The total welfare gain of speculators and non-speculators is given by $E_1^SGE_2^SE_2$.

[35] This is completely in line with Friedman's view that speculators in foreign exchange markets are traders with better than average insight and foresight into the market process (see Krause [1991]).

Figure III-19: Partially stabilizing speculation

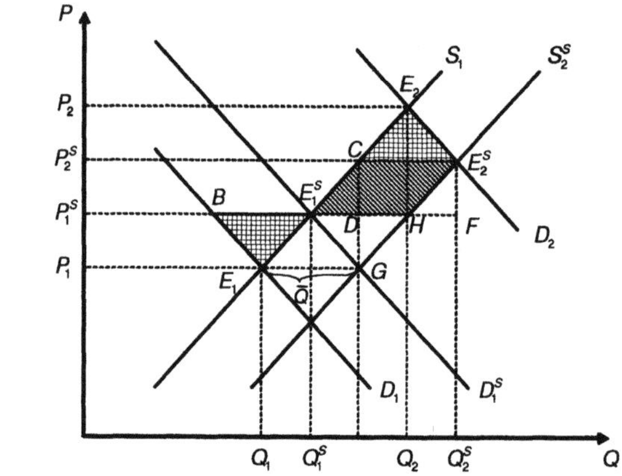

If the trading activities of speculators lead to a perfect stabilization of the price, the net welfare gain of non-speculators increases compared to Figure III-19. However, speculators do not generate profits by their trading activities (see Figure III-20).

Figure III-20: Perfect stabilizing speculation

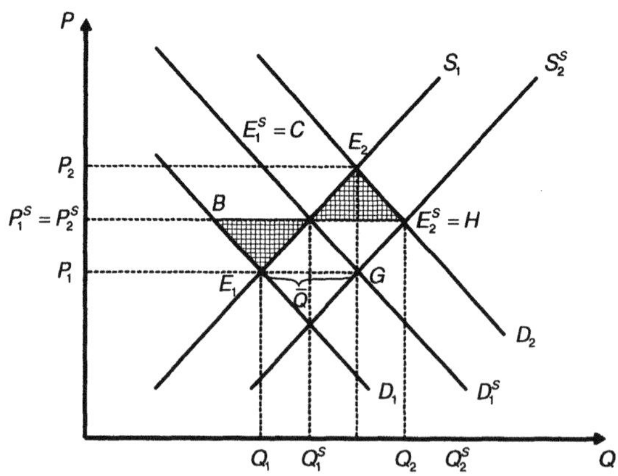

The case of destabilizing speculation is shown in Figure III-21. It is assumed that speculators do not anticipate the future demand of non-speculators correctly or behave irrationally by buying (selling) too much of the good in period one (period two).[36] Due to the increased extent of speculation, non-speculators get a large net welfare gain. However, speculators suffer financial losses of $\bar{Q}\left(P_2^S - P_1^S\right)$ which is represented by $E_1^S HKB$. On the whole the welfare losses of speculators exceed the welfare gains of non-speculators, so that $E_1^S G E_2^S E_2$ is the net welfare loss for all market participants. As the trading activities of speculators increase the price fluctuation from $P_1P_2 \rightarrow P_1^S P_2^S$, it is usually judged to be destabilizing.

Figure III-21: Destabilizing speculation

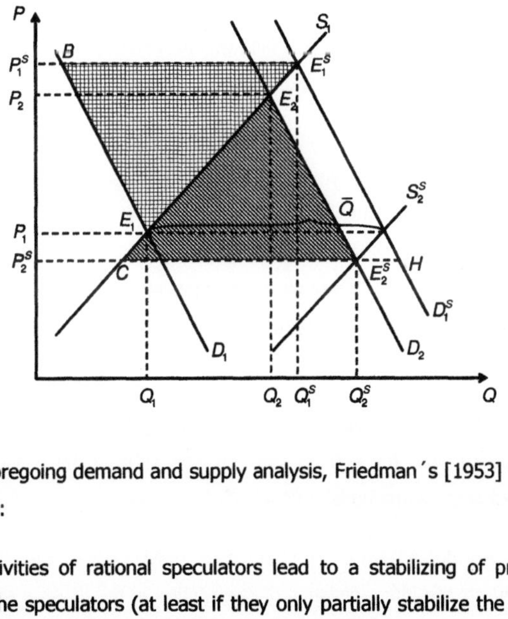

Summarizing the foregoing demand and supply analysis, Friedman's [1953] view of speculation becomes very clear:

1. Trading activities of rational speculators lead to a stabilizing of prices and generate profits for the speculators (at least if they only partially stabilize the price). In addition, speculative trading is beneficial to the whole economy as a total welfare gain occurs.

[36] Meade [1951] claimed that destabilizing speculation is due to 'perverse' (wrong sign) or 'grossly excessive' (overestimation of changes) market forecasts. In both cases, speculators' expectational errors 'destabilize' the market causing either temporary perverse adjustments, as in the first case, or temporary overshooting, as in the second case. Such speculation is deemed destabilizing because the exchange rate becomes more volatile than it would have been in the absence of such speculative trading (see Krause [1991]).

2. Only if non-rational speculators, who mispredict future demand, enter the market destabilizing price movements are expected. However, those speculators sustain losses and thus must leave the market. In addition, rational speculators will trade against the less rational investors and by doing so counter the deviations of prices from fundamentals and stabilize them (see De Long et al. [1990b]).

However, the validity of the simple causalities 'rational speculation is stabilizing speculation and generates profits' and 'irrational speculation is destabilizing speculation and generates losses' is not undisputed in the economic literature. Already Kaldor [1939] emphasizes that the above line of argumentation only holds if speculative transactions are a minor part of total demand or supply. In this context, Menkhoff [1995] summarizes three main lines of argumentation which can explain the existence of destabilizing and at the same time profitable speculation (see Menkhoff [1995] and Krause [1991]):

- First, although destabilizing speculation might be unprofitable on average, it could be profitable for a sub-group. For example, if destabilizing speculation occurs in two stages the sub-group called 'insiders' destabilize the price in the first stage. Then in the second stage before the market turns they sell out to a group of 'outsiders' who are attracted by the chance of high profits. Thus, although speculation is unprofitable for speculators on the whole, a sub-group of 'insiders' could profit.[37]

- Second, in cases of non-linear demand and supply curves, destabilizing speculation can be profitable as demand and supply schedules may generate two stable equilibria and speculators bounce the price from one to the other. Thus, speculation would be destabilizing and at the same time profitable.[38]

- Baumol [1957] provides a third and perhaps more realistic counter-example. He argues that Friedman's view on the characteristics of speculation is based on a static view about the fundamental equilibrium price. In contrast, Baumol [1957] assumes that the fundamental equilibrium price moves in a cyclical manner and speculators are confronted with a high degree of uncertainty about its current level. In such situations it may be reasonable for speculators to buy in upswings and to sell in downswings. Baumol [1957] argues that

[37] A necessary condition for this argumentation is that demand and supply of outsiders coincide with the needs of "insiders".

[38] However, this counter-example is quite unrealistic and can be treated as empirically irrelevant. Thus, Friedman's argumentation still holds in general, only in seemingly insignificant circumstances it may disappear (see Krause [1991]).

speculators can hope to identify price peaks and troughs more accurately in retrospect and so reduce their risks. Such behavior implies that speculation is both stabilizing and destabilizing.

> "It will have some stabilizing influence in that, if profitable, it involves higher priced sales than purchases thereby forcing the higher price down and vice versa. But it must also have a destabilizing influence in accelerating both upward and downward movements because speculative sales occur when prices are falling, and purchases are made when prices have begun to rise. For this reason the speculative activity may be profitable, yet be on balance destabilizing." (Baumol [1957], pp. 263)

In general, the theoretical considerations have shown that profitable speculation need not necessarily be fundamental-oriented and at the same time stabilizing, as predicted by Friedman [1953]. On the contrary, as Baumol [1957] has shown, it may be reasonable for speculators to carry out speculation based on a simple trend chasing behavior. As long as arbitrageurs have short horizons and must worry about liquidating their investment in a misvalued asset, their aggressiveness will be limited even in the absence of fundamental risk. In this case irrational trading behavior can lead to a large divergence between market prices and fundamental values.

III.2.2.2 The case of destabilizing speculation

The relevance of destabilizing speculation becomes apparent by two quotations of famous speculators in asset markets. First, John Maynard Keynes stated that "markets can remain irrational, longer than you can remain solvent" (quoted from Rubin and Weisberg [2003], p. 82) and second, Soros [1994] states:

> "The market mechanism fails to bring currencies back into alignment. On the contrary, speculation tends to exaggerate currency moves. [...] The system of freely floating currencies is cumulatively destabilizing." (Soros [1994], p. 328)

In recent years, the impact of non-fundamental, irrational speculation on asset prices has been a major topic in the modern financial literature (see Menkhoff [1998]). The related approaches usually introduce heterogeneous groups of market participants. Thereby, at least one group is characterized by non-fundamental, irrational trading behaviors, defined as trading on information which is not related to any relevant fundamentals. This point was originally put forth by Black [1986], who emphasizes that "people sometimes trade on noise as if it were information" (Black [1986], p. 529). Thus, traders sometimes base their trading decisions on noisy pseudo-signals, which are unrelated to fundamentals. Black [1986] states in this context:

> "Noise trading is trading on noise as if it were information. People who trade on noise are willing to trade even though from an objective point of view they would be better off not trading. Perhaps they think the noise they are trading on is information. Or perhaps they just like to trade." (Black [1986], p. 531)

Traders who trade on noise are, according to Black [1986], described as "noise traders". The existence of noise traders in a market creates divergences between current market prices and fundamental values (see De Long [1992]). The noise trading approach is possibly the single most influential attempt to offer an alternative to the efficient market hypothesis (see Menkhoff [1998]). It relies on two core propositions (see Shleifer and Summers [1990]):

a) At least some investors are not fully rational and their demand and supply is affected by their beliefs or sentiments that are not fully justified by fundamental news.

b) Arbitrage is assumed to be risky and therefore limited. As a consequence, rational traders are unable to fully counteract the trading of "noise traders".

In the following two sections, we examine two different noise trader models, which have attracted much interest by academics and practitioners in recent years. The results of both models show that the simple causalities of 'rational speculation is stabilizing speculation and generates profits' and 'irrational speculation is destabilizing speculation and generates losses', which is the logical consequence of Friedman´s [1953] view, are not necessarily valid. The first approach assesses the possibility that noise trading creates an additional risk for rational arbitrageurs when their speculation horizon is limited. Due to this risk, rational arbitrageurs reduce their stabilizing speculation. The second approach assesses the possibility that due to noise trading rational speculators themselves skip to a destabilizing trading behavior.

III.2.2.2.1 Noise trading and limits to arbitrage

The model of De Long et al. [1990a] contains two types of agents: rational arbitrageurs and noise traders. Noise traders choose their investment strategies according to pseudo-signals like e.g. technical analysis or market sentiment. Thus their expectations may be subject to systematic biases. For rational arbitrageurs the optimal investment strategy in the presence of noise traders is to exploit these misperceptions. So, rational arbitrageurs buy when noise traders depress prices and sell when noise traders push prices up. In consequence, rational arbitrageurs would stabilize prices around the fundamental value. However, this argumentation neglects the existing noise trader risk for rational arbitrageurs when their speculation horizon is limited to short periods. This point is taken up by the approach of De Long et al. [1990a].[39] It consists of an overlapping generations model with agents who live for two periods. Within the first period, agents pick an investment strategy and in the second they liquidate their investments and consume the proceeds. This assumption ensures that the speculation horizon is limited (see Shleifer [2000]).[40] Agents can choose between two different types of assets that pay each the identical, certain real dividends r. The only difference between both assets is the assumed degree of supply elasticity. For the safe asset (s) perfectly elastic supply is assumed, whereby its price is fixed at one per unit. On the contrary, the risky asset (u) is not in elastic supply but exists in a fixed and unchangeable quantity normalized at one unit. If the price of u were equal to the present value of its dividends (i.e., its intrinsic value), then assets u and s would be perfect substitutes and would sell at the same price in all periods. However, the model will show that there might be sustained deviations of the price of the risky asset u from its intrinsic value.

De Long et al. [1990a] introduce two types of agents; first, rational arbitrageurs (denoted by i) and, second, irrational noise traders (denoted by n). The proposed share of noise traders is given by μ and, correspondingly, the share of rational arbitrageurs by $1-\mu$. All agents of a given type are identical. Within the first period, both types of agents choose a combination of the safe and risky asset in order to maximize their perceived, subjectively expected utility. Here, De Long et al. [1990a] presume that the representative rational arbitrageur anticipates the distribution of returns from holding the risky asset correctly, whereas the representative noise trader misperceives it by an independent and identically distributed normal variable ρ_t:

$$\rho_t \sim N\left(\rho^*, \sigma_\rho^2\right). \tag{III-14}$$

Each agent, now, maximizes his utility with regard to the expected wealth ($\bar{W}$), whereby it is assumed that the utility function can be described by a constant absolute risk aversion function (CARA) of wealth:

$$U = -e^{-(2\gamma)\bar{W}}, \tag{III-15}$$

[39] For the illustration of the De Long et al. [1990a] model we refer to the original version of the model published in the Journal of Political Economy, 1990.

[40] The short horizons of rational arbitrageurs are important. If their horizons are long relative to the duration of the noise traders misperceptions, they can carry out fundamental stabilizing speculation being confident that they can sell when prices revert to their fundamental value. Only if the duration of noise traders' misperceptions is of the same order or longer than the speculation horizon of rational speculators, is noise trader risk a substantial hindrance for stabilizing speculation (see Shleifer [2000]).

where γ is the coefficient of absolute risk aversion. In case of normally distributed returns for holding a unit of the risky asset (u), the maximization of equation (III-15) corresponds to maximizing the following mean-variance utility (see Samuelson [1970]):

$$\bar{w} - \gamma\sigma_w^2, \tag{III-16}$$

where σ_w^2 is the one period ahead variance of wealth.

As the model consists only of two assets, the choice of young agents in period one can be represented by uniquely specifying the quantity of the risky asset (u) to be purchased. To obtain the demand for the risky asset (u) the respective expected utility must be maximized with respect to the quantity of the risky asset (see De Long et al. [1990a]). The results reveal that the demand of rational arbitrageurs for the risky asset (λ_t^i) equals

$$\lambda_t^i = \frac{r + {}_tp_{t+1} - (1+r)p_t}{2\gamma\left({}_t\sigma_{p_{t+1}}^2\right)}, \tag{III-17}$$

and the demand of noise traders for the risky asset (λ_t^n) corresponds to

$$\lambda_t^n = \frac{r + {}_tp_{t+1} - (1+r)p_t}{2\gamma\left({}_t\sigma_{p_{t+1}}^2\right)} + \frac{\rho_t}{2\gamma\left({}_t\sigma_{p_{t+1}}^2\right)}. \tag{III-18}$$

The demand for the risky asset of both types of agents – rational arbitrageur and noise trader – is proportional to its perceived excess return and inversely proportional to its perceived variance. The only difference between the demand of the rational arbitrageur and the noise trader is the last term in equation (III-18), which reflects the noise trader's misperception of the expected return of the risky asset. Within the model, rational arbitrageurs exert a stabilizing influence on the price of the risky asset as they offset the volatile positions of the noise traders. Furthermore the demand functions clarify the relevance of noise trader risk in the model. The variance of the risky asset's price, which appears in the denominators of both demand functions, is derived solely from the existence of noise traders. It entails that both – rational arbitrageurs and noise traders – reduce their demand for the risky asset because of the uncertainty of the future price of u. In the model, the uncertainty about the future price of u arises solely from the uncertain beliefs of the next period's young noise trader generation. Thus, noise trader risk limits the position taking of all agents and in particular keeps rational arbitrageurs from driving the price for u to its fundamental value (see Shleifer [2000] and Thaler [1992]).

To calculate the equilibrium price of the risky asset (u), we make use of the fact that the old sell their holdings to the young and thus demand must equal one in equilibrium:

$$(1-\mu)\lambda_t^i+\mu\lambda_t^n=1 \qquad \text{(III-19)}$$

De Long et al. [1990a] show that the price for the risky asset (u), in which the price depends only on exogenous factors of the model and on public information about present and future misperception by noise traders, is given by

$$p_t=1+\frac{\mu(\rho_t-\rho^*)}{1+r}+\frac{\mu\rho^*}{r}-\frac{(2\gamma)\mu^2\sigma_\rho^2}{r(1+r)^2} \qquad \text{(III-20)}$$

The last three terms of the pricing rule clarify several interesting aspects of the impact of noise traders on the price for the risky asset u within the framework of De Long et al. [1990a]. If there are no noise traders in the economy ($\mu=0$), the pricing rule in equation (III-20) suggests that the market price for the risky asset equals its fundamental value. The second term of equation (III-20) reflects the fluctuations of the risky asset due to the variation in noise traders' misperception. Although asset u is not subject to any fundamental risk (the dividend of the risky asset is fixed at r) and is known to a large class of agents, its price will shift if the misperception of noise traders shifts. For example, if a generation of noise traders is more optimistic than the average generation, they push up the price of the risky asset and vice versa. The third term in equation (III-20) illustrates the average misperception of all noise traders which may be responsible for a divergence of the price of the risky asset from its fundamental value. If noise traders are optimistic on average ($\rho^*>0$) the price of u is higher than it would otherwise be and vice versa. De Long et al. [1990a] characterize the last term in equation (III-20) as the heart of their model. It captures the effect of noise trader risk on the price of the risky asset. According to this term the mere presence of noise traders introduces risk about future prices for which both types of agents obtain a compensation. However, one must stress that this risk is only due to the existence of noise traders and not due to fundamental risk. That's why De Long et al. [1990a] state that

> "noise traders [...] 'create their own space': the uncertainty over what next period's noise traders will believe makes the otherwise riskless asset u risky and drives its price down and its return up." (De Long et al. [1990a], p. 712)

According to equation (III-20) noise traders have a substantial impact on the price of risky assets. However, Friedman [1953] emphasizes that noise traders, who affect prices, should earn lower returns than rational arbitrageurs and consequently leave the market (see Shleifer [2000]). In the model of De Long et al. [1990a], it can be shown that noise traders possibly earn higher returns than rational arbitrageurs. Therefore one has to consider the difference between the returns of rational arbitrageurs and noise traders (ΔR_{n-i}):

$$\Delta R_{n-i} = \left(\lambda_t^n - \lambda_t^i\right)\left[r + p_{t+1} - p_t\left(1+r\right)\right]. \tag{III-21}$$

Given equal initial wealth, the difference corresponds to the product of the difference between the demands for the risky asset and the excess return paid by a unit of the risky asset. The expected value of this difference is given by (see De Long et al. [1990a])

$$E\left[\Delta R_{n-i}\right] = \rho^* - \frac{\left(1+r\right)^2 \left(\rho^*\right)^2 + \left(1+r\right)^2 \sigma_\rho^2}{\left(2\gamma\right)\mu\sigma_\rho^2} \tag{III-22}$$

In order for noise traders to earn higher expected returns than rational arbitrageurs, equation (III-22) requires that mean misperception ρ^* is positive.

Overall, the model of De Long et al. [1990a] has shown that a short speculation horizon combined with risk aversion limits the willingness of rational arbitrageurs to take stabilizing positions and thus drive the price of the risky asset back to its fundamental value, even if there is no uncertainty about fundamentals. The main cause for this result is the existence of noise trader risk, which implies that the future price is unpredictable for rational arbitrageurs due to random demand of noise traders (see Brunnermeier [2001]). Nonetheless, the trading of rational arbitrageurs leads to a partial stabilization of price movements, as it brings prices to move – at least – in the direction of fundamentals.

III.2.2.2.2 Noise trading and destabilizing behaviors of rational speculators

The second model of De Long et al. [1990b] illustrates that rational arbitrageurs may even exert a destabilizing impact on asset prices due to the existence of noise traders.

The model of De Long et al. [1990b] considers four periods (0,1,2, and 3). There are two assets: cash and stock. Cash is in perfectly elastic supply and pays no net return. Stock is in zero net supply and is liquidated in period three, whereby it pays a risky dividend equal to $\Phi+\theta$. Thereby, Φ represents a random variable that takes on the values $-\phi$, 0, ϕ with equal probability and θ is a model parameter that is distributed normally with mean zero and variance σ_θ^2 and is promulgated in period three. The value of Φ becomes publicly known in period two and a signal ε about Φ is exclusively received by the rational arbitrageurs in period one. In the model, three different types of investors exist:

(1) positive feedback traders (noise traders), present in a measure of one and denoted by f;

(2) informed rational speculators, who maximize utility as a function of consumption in the third period. They are present in a measure of μ and denoted by r;

(3) passive investors are present in a measure of 1-μ and denoted by e. Their demand depends in all periods only on the price relative to its fundamental value.[41]

Following De Long et al. [1990b], we begin the illustration of the model in the third period and then go back up to period 0.[42] In the third period no trading occurs in the market. All investors pay each other according to the positions they hold in the stock and the publicly known dividend $\Phi+\theta$. The stock price is equal to $\Phi+\theta$ as now the dividend is known for sure and rational investors keep the stock price to its fundamental value $\Phi+\theta$.

In period two, both rational and passive investors receive the value of Φ.[43] The second period's demand of positive feedback traders is determined by

$$D_2^f = \beta(p_1 - p_0) = \beta p_1 \qquad \text{(III-23)}$$

where p_1 is the price in period 1, p_0 is the price in period 0 (which is set equal to 0) and $\beta>0$ is a positive feedback coefficient. Equation (III-23) shows that positive feedback traders only trade due to past price changes. The actual price in period two (p_2) does not influence their trading decisions. Rational informed investors choose their demand in period two by maximizing

---

41 The total of passive investors and informed rational speculators is held constant to derive comparative static results on the effect of changes in the number of informed rational speculators, holding constant the risk-bearing capacity of the market (see De Long et al. [1990b], p. 384).

42 The illustration of the model draws heavily on the original source of De Long et al. [1990b]. In addition, we orientate our illustration on that of Stadtmann [2002] and Frenkel et al. [2004].

43 In this context De Long et al. [1989] note that the realized value of Φmust be sufficiently small "so as not to upset the mean-variance approximation used in deriving informed speculators' demands. In this setup, period 2 news is about the fundamental of the stock. The conclusions also hold if Φ represents a "noise" shock – a temporary shock to noise traders' demand but not to the fundamental value of the stock. For an analysis of such a model, see the earlier working paper version of the paper." (De Long et al. [1989], p. 9).

a mean-variance utility function with a Arrow–Pratt measure of absolute risk aversion γ. In concrete terms, the demand of rational investors in period two is given by

$$D_2^r = \frac{(\Phi - p_2)}{2\gamma\sigma_\theta^2} = \alpha(\Phi - p_2), \tag{III-24}$$

where α is defined as $1/(2\gamma\sigma_\theta^2)$. Obviously, the willingness of rational investors to bet on a stock price reversion to its fundamental value is limited due to the risky dividend in period three. Since passive investors possess the same utility function as rational investors, their demand depends also negatively on the price in period two:[44]

$$D_2^e = \alpha(\Phi - p_2). \tag{III-25}$$

In period one, informed rational investors get a signal $\varepsilon \in \{-\phi, 0, \phi\}$ about the fundamental news Φ in period two.[45] The Rational investors' demand in period one is equivalent to their demand in period two and is therefore given by

$$D_1^r = \alpha(\Phi - p_1). \tag{III-26}$$

The demand of passive investors in period one also corresponds with that in period two, i.e.

$$D_1^e = -\alpha p_1. \tag{III-27}$$

Since there are no past price movements in period 1 the demand of feedback traders in this period equals zero:

$$D_1^f = 0. \tag{III-28}$$

Period 0 serves as reference period; the market participants receive no signals about Φ; the stock price is equal to its initial fundamental value ($p_0 = 0$) and there is no trading. As no trading occurs in period 0 or three, the market clearing conditions are automatically satisfied in those periods. For the period one and two the market clearing condition is given by,

---

44 To ensure stable solutions De Long et al. [1990b] assume that α > β (see De Long et al. [1990b], p. 386).

45 De Long et al. [1990b] consider in their paper two different scenarios for the information content of the signal ε: first, rational investors receive a noiseless signal ε, i.e. ε=Φ, and, second, rational investors receive a noisy signal ε. As both scenarios lead in general to the same conclusion, we confine our illustration of the model to the first scenario.

$$0 = D_1^f + \mu D_1^r + (1-\mu) D_1^e, \tag{III-29}$$

respectively,

$$0 = D_2^f + \mu D_2^r + (1-\mu) D_2^e. \tag{III-30}$$

To illustrate the development of the asset price within the model, De Long et al. [1990b] consider the case of a positive demand shock, i.e. $\Phi = +\phi$. Assuming that the signal ε in period one is perfectly correlated with the demand shock Φ in period two denotes that there is no uncertainty in period one about the stock price in period two. Thus, as long as some rational investors ($\mu > 0$) are in the market, their arbitrage activities ensure that the price in period one is equal to that in period two; however, if no rational investor is present ($\mu=0$), the stock price in period one comes to zero, as no market participant has information about the fundamental value of the stock in period three ($\Phi + \theta$):

$$\begin{aligned} p_1 &= p_2 \quad if\, \mu > 0, \\ p_1 &= 0 \quad if\, \mu = 0. \end{aligned} \tag{III-31}$$

Substituting (III-23), (III-24) and (III-25) in the market clearing condition for period two leads to the following equilibrium condition in period two:

$$\begin{aligned} 0 &= \beta p_1 + \mu\alpha(\phi - p_2) + (1-\mu)\alpha(\phi - p_2) \\ &= \beta p_1 + \alpha(\phi - p_2). \end{aligned} \tag{III-32}$$

Consequently, we obtain the following two expressions for the stock price by combining (III-32) with (III-31);

$$p_1 = p_2 = \frac{\alpha\phi}{\alpha - \beta} \quad if\, \mu > 0, \tag{III-33}$$

$$p_1 = 0, p_2 = \phi \quad if\, \mu = 0. \tag{III-34}$$

As De Long et al. [1990b] assume that $\alpha > \beta$, the price of stock is necessarily further from its fundamental value (ϕ) when rational investors are present than when they are absent. Thus, in the model of De Long et al. [1990b] the existence of rational investors leads to a destabilization of prices in the case of a noiseless signal. Figure III-22 summarizes the results of the model in the case of a noiseless signal ε.

Figure III-22: Price development with a noiseless signal

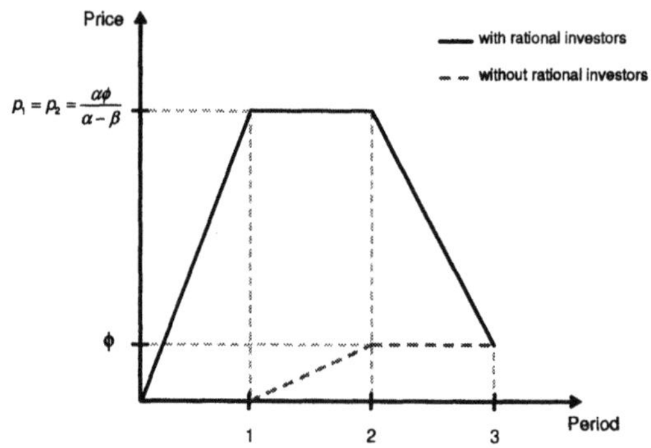

III.2.3 Empirical evidence on the actual trading practice of foreign exchange traders

So far, we have seen that excessive speculation is held responsible for misaligned exchange rates. However, from a theoretical point of view, speculation can exert stabilizing fundamental-oriented and destabilizing non-fundamental oriented effects on exchange rates. According to the assessment of foreign exchange traders, the actual impact of speculation on exchange rates is ambiguous. Cheung and Wong [2000] and Cheung and Chinn [2001] asked foreign exchange traders whether speculation leads to movements of exchange rates towards their fundamental values or away from fundamental values. The given answers show that market participants believe in both effects of speculation (see Table III-15).

Table III-15: Effects of speculation on exchange rates

	US	Hong Kong	Tokyo	Singapore
Away from fundamental value	29.3	53.3	43.1	46.2
Towards fundamental value	60.7	46.7	56.9	53.8

Source: Cheung and Wong [2000] and Cheung and Chinn [2001]

Nevertheless, to arrive at conclusions with regard to the impact of speculation on exchange rates, we consult more results of survey data. First, the survey responses allow us to assess to what extent rational fundamental and irrational non-fundamental factors like e.g. bandwagon-effects, technical analysis, affect exchange rate movements.[46]

Table III-16: Factors determining exchange rate movements (in %)

		Intraday	Medium-run (≤ 6 months)	Long-run (> 6 months)
UK Foreign Exchange Market (Cheung et al. [2000])	Rational fundamental factors	0.6	31.4	82.5
	Irrational non-fundamental factors	97.7	67.2	15.4
Asian Foreign exchange markets* (Cheung and Wong [2000])	Rational fundamental factors	0.7	32.2	79.6
	Irrational non-fundamental factors	99.3	67.8	20.4
US Foreign exchange market (Cheung and Chinn [2001])	Rational fundamental factors	0.8	32.1	87.4
	Irrational non-fundamental factors	98.6	66.8	9.4

* Values represent the average of the three Asian trading centers Hong Kong, Tokyo, and Singapore

Table III-16 shows that for the short and medium-run horizons market participants consider irrational non-fundamental factors as most important for the determination of exchange rates. This holds for all three regional foreign exchange markets. Only in the long-run are rational fundamental factors seen to be the most important determinants. However, even in the long-run a non-negligible part of market participants judge irrational non-fundamental factors to be important. Overall, Table III-16 can be interpreted as a first empirical indication for the existence of noise traders and thus destabilizing speculation in foreign exchange markets.

A second indication of the relevance of destabilizing speculation in foreign exchange markets is given in Table III-17. Table III-17 summarizes the relevance of different trading practices according to the assessment of market participants themselves. Fundamental and technical analysis best describe about 30% of the actual trading behavior. However, the importance of technical analysis has increased in recent times. The rest of the trading is characterized as either flow analysis/customer orders and jobbing. Thus, it is reasonable to conclude that large parts of the actual trading behavior can be delineated as destabilizing speculation. However, it

[46] For a detailed specification of the possible categories we refer to Cheung et al. [2000], p. 31, question 15.

is up to now not clear which characteristics customer orders possess. This will be evaluated at the end of this section.

Table III-17: Trading methods – Which method best describes your own trading practice

	Date of survey	Fund. Analysis	Technical analysis	Flow/ customer	Jobbing	Other
Menkhoff [1997]	1992	50.2	27.8	9.8	--	12.2
Cheung et al. [2000]	1993	31.2	13.8	33.0	53.2	--
	1998	33.6	32.7	37.3	36.4	--
Cheung and Chinn [2001]	1993	23.0	19.4	23.4	31.1	--
	1998	24.9	29.5	22.4	21.1	--
Gehrig and Menkhoff [2004]	2001	29.4	35.8	17.4	--	17.4

Notes: Cheung et al. [2000] and Cheung and Chinn [2001] survey FX dealers; Menkhoff [1997] and Gehrig and Menkhoff [2004] survey FX dealers and fund managers. The responses in Cheung et al. [2000] do not add to 100 % due to multiple answers.

In addition to the studies cited in Table III-17, further surveys also provide evidence for the relevance of technical analysis in foreign exchange markets. In 1988, Taylor and Allen [1992] conducted a questionnaire survey among foreign exchange dealers based in London. Their results indicate that there is "a skew towards reliance on technical, as opposed to fundamentalist, analysis at shorter horizons" (Taylor and Allen [1992], p. 304). However, with increasing time horizons the importance of fundamental analysis increases. Lui and Mole [1998] conducted a survey of foreign exchange dealers in Hong Kong and report also a skew towards reliance on technical analysis at shorter horizons. Again, the importance of fundamental analysis is judged to be more relevant for longer horizons. In this context, Lui and Mole [1998] suggest that fundamental models may perform poorly as they neglect the impact of trading decision based on technical analysis. Furthermore, the survey participants state that technical analysis is thought to be superior in predicting both trends and turning points compared to fundamental analysis. Oberlechner [2001] surveyed over 320 European foreign exchange traders and 59 financial analysts. His results reveal that Chartism is vitally important, especially for shorter forecasting horizons. However, the survey responses also show that across all forecasting horizons, traders use a mixture of fundamental and technical methods in their forecasting approach. Similar to the results summarized in Table III-17, Oberlechner [2001] reports an increasing role of Chartism among foreign exchange traders over time. Overall, the results of the various survey studies conducted in recent years show that destabilizing non-fundamental speculation may play a decisive role in foreign exchange markets. In particular, the widespread usage of technical analysis can be seen as an indication for destabilizing speculation. Furthermore, the development of the survey responses over time reveal that the impact of non-fundamental factors even seems to have risen in recent years.

Besides studies investigating the actual trading behavior of foreign exchange traders, two other survey studies explicitly deal with the topic of noise trading in foreign exchange markets. Both studies use surveys to evaluate important hypotheses of the noise trading approach in foreign exchange markets. The first study is provided by Menkhoff [1998] and examines three basic assumptions of the noise trading approach: a) there are limits of arbitrage in foreign exchange markets due to the short horizons of rational arbitrageurs, b) noise trading is mainly based on beliefs or sentiments which are disconnected from fundamentals, and, c) there are two different groups of traders (rational arbitrageurs and noise traders). By and large, the survey results support the three assumptions of the noise trading approach (see Menkhoff [1998]): there are indications for the existence of limited arbitrage activities of rational speculators, as there are constraints to the time horizons which effectively restrict rational arbitrageurs. In addition, Menkhoff [1998] provides evidence for the relevance of beliefs and sentiments. However, Menkhoff [1998] fails to distinguish two different groups of traders as suggested by the noise trading approach. Menkhoff [1998] attributes this result to a point made by Shleifer and Summers [1990], who hint at the possibility that rational arbitrageurs might try to exploit noise traders. In this case, it is hard to discriminate between rational arbitrageurs and noise traders as "arbitrageurs begin to look like noise traders themselves". (Shleifer and Summers [1990], p. 26). This point was also mentioned by Black [1986] who stresses that "there will always be a lot of ambiguity about who is an information trader and who is a noise trader" (Black [1986], p. 532).

The second study that deals explicitly with the relevance of the noise trading approach is given by Ahn et al. [2002]. They likewise analyze the relevance of the noise trading approach for the Korean foreign exchange market by using questionnaires. The results of the survey largely confirm the noise trading approach:

- noise trading – defined as Chartism and flow analysis – appears to be a widely used in the Korean foreign exchange market;
- there is only little evidence for the hypothesis that irrational noise traders are eliminated due to their inferior investment strategies as suggested by Friedman [1953]; and

- the hypothesis that noise trading is random so that irrational trading practice may cancel itself out is also rejected by the survey results. On the contrary, noise trading is used in the Korean foreign exchange market due to its self-fulfilling character.

Overall, both studies on the relevance of the noise trading approach in the context of foreign exchange markets have shown that it is rather likely that destabilizing non-fundamental trading practices play an important role in the determination of exchange rates.

The results summarized in Table III-17 show that many foreign exchange traders orientate their trading decision on the basis of order flows.[47] In this context, Lyons [2001b] shows that especially financial-customer order flows play a decisive role in foreign exchange markets. Thus, it is essential to consider also their trading behavior, in order to assess to what extent stabilizing or destabilizing trading occurs in foreign exchange markets. With regard to the trading behavior of financial customers, the ECB provides a useful review of the foreign exchange market structure (see European Central Bank [2003]). The European Central Bank [2003] review divides the group of financial customers into three groups: institutional funds and institutional asset managers, leveraged funds and active currency overlay management. According to the European Central Bank [2003] report, institutional funds and asset managers are often characterized as 'real money' funds that manage their foreign exchange positions by "separately identifying and managing currency exposures." Thus, the main objective of institutional funds and assets managers is to manage the risk associated with foreign exchange positions as changes in the underlying currency add volatility to the reported returns of funds. However, the European Central Bank [2003] report notes that, due to lower equity returns in recent years, equity fund mangers focus more on currency returns to yield positive returns. Overall, the group of institutional funds and asset managers are mainly engaged with risk management in foreign exchange markets, but to a lesser extent also in speculation. Admittedly, the European Central Bank [2003] report provides no indication of the nature of this speculation.

With regard to the group of leveraged funds, the European Central Bank [2003] report concludes that many of them trade in foreign exchange markets using proprietary models, which are based on quantitative models. Those models are often exclusively based on historic price movements such as trend-following momentum models, which generate trading signals when prices move through historic moving averages. Furthermore, the European Central Bank

[47] In Appendix C we discuss the role of order flow in exchange rate economics in more detail.

[2003] report assesses that "the investment horizon of model-driven funds is often very short, at most a week or two and sometimes intraday." (European Central Bank [2003], p. 20). According to the authors of the report this implies "that, while the currency risk being run by these funds at any point in time may be small [...], the FX market turnover they generate may be relatively large." (European Central Bank [2003], p. 20). Furthermore, foreign exchange market participants have suggested that model-based trading has become more popular in recent times. Hence, the report on the trading practice of leveraged funds can be interpreted as an indication for a destabilizing speculative trading behavior. A similar conclusion can be drawn for the group of active currency overlay management. In addition to hedging financial risk associated with international transactions, active currency overlay management covers also position taking with a view to generating additional returns (see European Central Bank [2003]). Thereby, currency overlay managers apply a variety of trading approaches. In this context, the European Central Bank [2003] report stresses again the importance of trend-following trading strategies. Thus, indications of destabilizing speculation are clearly discernible. Further evidence for destabilizing trading practices in foreign exchange markets is provided by Froot et al. [2001]. They analyze daily international portfolio flows into and out of 44 countries within the time period of 1994 through 1998. Using variance ratio tests Froot et al. [2001] show that international portfolio flows are persistent as all estimated ratios are statistically greater than one and display very large magnitudes. Furthermore, international portfolio flows appear to be strongly influenced by past returns, i.e. international inflows are influenced by trend following trading behaviors. Similar results are also reported by Froot and Ramadorai [2002], who analyze cross-border foreign exchange transaction data for 19 countries/currency areas in the time period of 1994 to 2001. Their results indicate that flows are correlated with contemporaneous and lagged exchange rates. Moreover, flows contain useful information about future excess currency returns, whereas this information can not be linked to future macroeconomic fundamentals.

Overall, the results of the various surveys of foreign exchange market participants and the description of the trading practices of financial customers provided by the European Central Bank [2003] suggest that non-fundamental, irrational factors play a decisive role in foreign exchange markets. Consequently, the impact of speculation in foreign exchange markets is likely to be destabilizing rather than stabilizing.

III.3 Keynes' view on the functioning of asset markets

Piron [1991] compares views about the noise trading approach from the article of Shleifer and Summers [1990] with those expressed by Keynes [1936] in his General Theory. The comparison impressively shows that Keynes' view about the functioning of asset markets can be closely linked to that of the modern noise trading approach. Piron [1991] demonstrates the similarity of Keynes and the proponents of the noise trading approach by comparing three quotations respectively. Thereby he concentrates on the topics of origins of noise trading, positive feedbacks and bubbles and possible cures. We decide to illustrate the connection between Keynes and the noise trading approach by a quotation of Keynes [1936] on the role of sentiments for the development of asset prices:

> "... the market will be subject to waves of optimistic and pessimistic sentiments, which are unreasoning and yet in a sense legitimate where no solid basis exists for a reasonable calculation." (Keynes [1936], p. 154)

Akin to Keynes [1936], Shleifer and Summers [1990] two of the originators of the noise trading approach also place emphasis on the relevance of sentiments in asset markets:

> "Some shifts in investor demand for securities are completely rational. [...] But not all demand changes appear to be so rational; some seem to be a response to changes in expectations or sentiment that are not fully justified by information. Such changes can be a response to pseudo-signals that investors believe convey information about future returns but that would not convey information in a fully rational model." (Shleifer and Summers [1990], p. 23)

As a relationship exists between Keynes and the noise trading approach, it appears fruitful to analyze Keynes´ [1936] view on the functioning of asset markets in more detail. In chapter 12 of the General Theory, Keynes [1936] discusses the role of expectations in speculative asset markets. In this context, it becomes apparent that, according to Keynes [1936], an exclusively fundamental oriented trading is futile in speculative markets.

> "The outstanding fact is the extreme precariousness of the basis of knowledge on which our estimates of prospective yield have to be made. Our knowledge of the factors which will govern the yield of an investment some years hence is usually very slight and often negligible. [...] In fact, those who seriously attempt to make any such estimate are often so much in the minority that their behaviour does not govern the market." (Keynes [1936], p. 149-150)

Consequently, market participants are according to Keynes [1936]

> "concerned, not with what an investment is really worth to a man who buys it 'for keeps', but with what the market will value it at, under the influence of mass psychology, three month or a year hence." (Keynes [1936], p. 154-155)

So that

> "the professional investor is forced to concern himself with the anticipation of impending changes, in the news or in the atmosphere, of the kind by which experience shows that the mass psychology of the market is most influenced." (Keynes [1936], p. 155)

The Keynesian view of the functioning of asset markets, also stresses the relevance and importance of expectations for asset price determination. However, in contrast to the traditional economic view, Keynes [1936] negates the existence of rational expectations. In our opinion, his view can be traced back to a different assessment of the impact of uncertainty on the expectation formation in speculative markets. While in the traditional economic view uncertainty is regarded as merely adding stochastic to the decision problem, Keynes states that uncertainty is more fundamental for the decision problem. In his understanding of uncertainty, uncertainty entails that a reliable judgment of probability is rather difficult for individuals, so that the basis for rational decisions is greatly weakened (see Koppl [1991]). In the following we discuss the different notions with regard to the term "uncertainty" and show how individuals behave under fundamental uncertainty.

III.3.1 The role of uncertainty in asset markets

According to Pesaran [1988], 'decision making under uncertainty' can be described in a very general way as a process in which an individual decision maker is not perfectly aware of the consequences of his own action. This loose description of uncertain decision situations can be aligned to different dimensions of uncertainty. From a theoretical point of view, at least two different sources of uncertainty can be distinguished (see Pesaran [1988] and Figure III-23):

- exogenous uncertainty, and
- endogenous/behavioral uncertainty.

'Exogenous uncertainty' covers uncertainty due to exogenous environmental factors (e.g. in the context of foreign exchange markets, the development of macroeconomic fundamentals). The essential characteristic of exogenous uncertainty is that it is randomly initiated by 'mother nature' and independent from an individual's action (see Muthoo [1999]). 'Endogenous uncertainty' can be attributed alternatively to the impact of actions chosen by some other market participants. In that case, the state is strategically determined by some other traders' actions, because the state is a strategy choice of some other traders (see Muthoo [1999]). As endogenous uncertainty arises from the behavior of other market participants, it is also characterized as 'behavioral uncertainty'. Under behavioral uncertainty the probability of the occurrence of a certain state is not an invariable result of an individual's action. The existence and prevalence of behavioral uncertainty is rather due to the capacity of individuals to adapt and react to another in a non-negligible manner (see Pesaran [1988]). The extent of behavioral uncertainty is closely related to the degree to which individuals may be able to influence the actions of others by their own actions, or to what extent they are themselves influenced by others' actions. Pesaran [1988] concludes that in reality all decentralized systems of economic-decision making are subject to behavioral uncertainty. As the foreign exchange market is characterized by a decentralized market structure in which speculation may dominate the trading behavior of many market participants, we assume that behavioral uncertainty plays a crucial role in foreign exchange markets.

Figure III-23: Uncertainty in foreign exchange markets

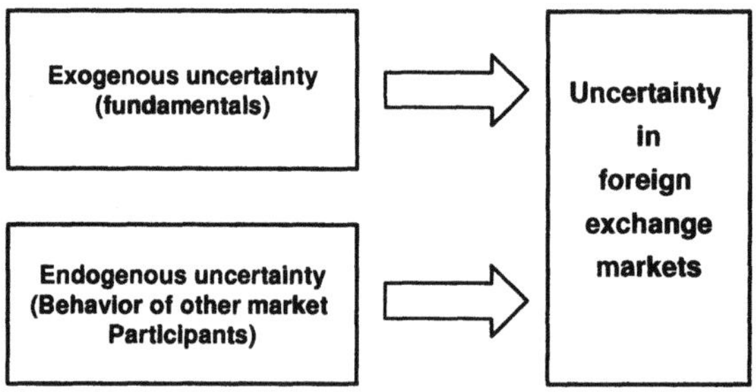

Both sources of uncertainty are closely related to the differentiation between 'risk' and 'true uncertainty' that was first proposed by Knight [1921]. In Knight's [1921] interpretation, 'risk' refers to situations where a decision maker can assign mathematical probabilities to the randomness which he is faced with. In contrast, in situations characterized as 'true uncertainty' the existing randomness can not be expressed in terms of mathematical probabilities. Reasons for the inability to assign a mathematical probability distribution may be seen in the unfamiliarity with the situation in which the decision maker is placed or in the complexity of the operation of assigning probabilities to events. The basis of Knight´s [1921] differentiation between 'risk' and 'true uncertainty' lies in the question of whether randomness can be measured by the means of mathematical probabilities or not. A similar view is also represented by Keynes [1973] in his response to his critics in 1937 where he states:

> "By 'uncertain' knowledge, let me explain, I do not mean merely to distinguish what is known for certain from what is only probable. The game of roulette is not subject, in this sense, to uncertainty; nor is the prospect of a Victory bond being drawn. Or, again, the expectation of life is only slightly uncertain. Even the weather is only moderately uncertain. The sense in which I am using the term is that in which the prospect of a European war is uncertain, or the price of copper and the rate of interest twenty years hence, or the obsolescence of a new invention, or the position of private wealth owners in the social system in 1970. About these matters there is no scientific basis on which to form any calculable probability whatever. We simply do not know." (Keynes [1973], p. 113-114)

Moreover, Keynes [1973] added

> "... the hypothesis of a calculable future leads to a wrong interpretation of the principles of behaviour." (Keynes [1973], p. 122)

Basically, the problem of measurability of randomness may arise regardless of whether the source for uncertainty is exogenous or endogenous. However, as Pesaran [1988] rightly argues, 'true uncertainty' in the sense of Knight [1921] or Keynes [1973] is obviously more likely in situations characterized by 'behavioral uncertainty'.

III.3.2 Decision behavior under "true behavioral uncertainty"

The last section has revealed that in speculative asset markets an essential source for uncertainty can be ascribed to the uncertain actions taken by some other market participants. This behavioral uncertainty is likely to be accompanied by the existence of 'true uncertainty' so that market participants can not assign mathematical probabilities to the randomness they are faced with. Keynes [1936] provides a very thorough description of the individual behavior in situations characterized by 'true behavioral uncertainty' and identifies two factors that influence the expectation formation under such conditions:

- expectations are driven by current facts, and
- expectations are driven by others' expectations.

The first point refers to the response of individuals to the need for decisions in an environment characterized by 'true uncertainty'. Obviously, in this context Keynes [1936] would have rejected the view of Muth [1961] that individuals form rational expectations in the sense that "expectations of firms (or, more generally, the subjective probability distribution of outcomes) tend to be distributed, for the same information set, about the prediction of the theory (or the 'objective' probability distributions of outcomes)" (Muth [1961], p. 316). In contrast, Keynes [1936] suggests that individuals adopt practices which, although they may not lead to an optimal decision, nevertheless are reasonable, as they can be seen as the best response to decision situations under 'true uncertainty' (see Rundes [1991]). For example, Keynes [1936] argues that individuals will tend to favor information about which they are relatively more 'confident' or orientate their decision on the 'facts of the existing situation':

> "It would be foolish, in forming our expectations, to attach great weight to matters which are very uncertain. It is reasonable, therefore, to be guided to a considerable degree by the facts about which we feel somewhat confident, even though they may be less decisively relevant to the issue than other facts about which our knowledge is vague and scanty. For this reason the facts of existing situation enter, in a sense disproportionately, into the formation of our long-term expectations; our usual practise being to take the existing situation and to project it into the future, modified only to the extent that we have more or less definite reasons for expecting a change." (Keynes [1936], p. 148).

Thus, expectations formed under 'true uncertainty' tend to be to a considerable extent backward-looking as they project past or current situational factors into the future instead of being exclusively forward-looking as suggested by the rational expectations hypothesis.

The second point covers the response of individuals to an environment that is mainly characterized by 'behavioral uncertainty'. This point has received much attention in the corresponding literature on Keynes [1936] as he gave a very prominent and illustrative description of the individual's decision behavior in an environment that is primarily characterized by behavioral uncertainty. Keynes [1936] compared the individual decision situation in asset markets with the decision situation of a participant in a beauty contest organized by a newspaper:

> "...professional investment may be linked to those newspaper competitions in which the competitors have to pick out the six prettiest faces from a hundred photographs, the prize being awarded to the competitor whose choice most nearly corresponds to the average preferences of the competitors as a whole: so that each competitor has to pick, not those faces which he himself finds prettiest, but those which he thinks likeliest to catch the fancy of other competitors, all of whom are looking at the problem from the same point of view. It is not a case of choosing those which, to the best of one's judgment, are really the prettiest, nor even those which average opinion genuinely thinks the prettiest. We have reached the third degree where we devote our intelligence to anticipating what average opinion expects the average opinion to be." (Keynes [1936], p. 156)

The objective of the beauty contest is to guess which picture will get the most votes. The appropriate behavior for participants is not to choose the picture favored by themselves, but to elect the picture favored by most of the other participants. Consequently, they have to estimate "what average opinion expects the average opinion to be" (Keynes [1936], p. 156). According to Carabelli [1988], Davis [1994] and Arestis [1996] this kind of uncertainty about the others' expectations is the fundamental source of general uncertainty (see Rosser [2001]). Keynes [1936] describes this purpose as the information of the third degree. The implication of Keynes' parable is that an understanding of financial markets not only requires an understanding of market participants' evaluation about assets' future returns, but also an understanding of market participants' evaluation about other market participants' evaluation and higher order evaluations (Allen et al. [2003]). Or, in the words of Keynes [1936] himself:

> "For most of these persons are, in fact, largely concerned, not with making superior long-term forecasts of the probable yield of an investment over its whole life, but with foreseeing changes in the conventional basis of valuation a short time ahead of the general public. They are concerned, not with what an investment is really worth to a man who buys it "for keeps", but with what the market will value it at, under the influence of mass psychology, three months or a year hence. [...] Thus the professional investor is forced to concern himself with the anticipation of impeding changes, in the news or in the atmosphere, of the kind by which experience shows that the mass psychology of the market is most influenced." (Keynes [1936], pp. 154)

From a theoretical point of view, the solution of the Beauty Contest Problem can be found in the concept of focal points. Focal points are cues that induce people to behave in a similar manner. The focal solution of a decision-making problem under behavioral uncertainty emerges because a group of people has come to believe that the members of this group will behave consistently with this equilibrium, but which solution is a priori unknown and depends on the co-ordination problem and the decision-making environment (see Young [1996]). Arrow [1987] notes that in this context the solution of such decision-making problems calls for a rationality that refers to social phenomena. As soon as one particular solution is known to be focal, it becomes reasonable or "rational" for each decision-maker to expect that all others will decide consistently with this solution and to act on this expectation. An important characteristic of focal points is that nobody has an incentive to change once a common expectation has been established. Consequently, the expectations, which rely on existing focal points, feature a high degree of persistence (see Duncan and Isaac [2000]). Closely related to the concept of focal point is the concept of convention. A convention is typically defined as "a pattern of behavior that is customary, expected and self-enforcing" (Young [1996]). The main characteristic of convention is that everyone conforms to it, everyone expects others to conform to it, and everyone has good reason to conform because conforming is in each person's best interest when everyone else plans to conform (Young [1996]). The main feature of a convention is that, out of a host of conceivable choices, only one is actually used. Hence, conventions resolve problems of indeterminacy in interactions that have multiple equilibria. In general, one may discern two ways in which conventions become established: first, by authority, and second, by the gradual accretion of precedent. At first glance, in the context of asset markets, the second process by which conventions may emerge seems to be of particular interest. The idea is that, in a repeated co-ordination game, one particular way of interaction emerges successively as a superior way of resolving the game. Thus, it reaches a greater degree of prominence, which in turn entails that more people notice it, which leads to more people using it, and so forth. Consequently, a positive feedback loop is created.

The relevance and importance of conventions in situations characterized by true behavioral uncertainty can be found in many statements of Keynes. In chapter 12 of his General Theory, Keynes asked how the market participants evaluate stocks in practice, given that they are unable to calculate exact solutions of the possible outcomes of their investment decision. His answer to this question is:

> "In practice we have tacitly agreed, as a rule, to fall back on what is, in truth, a convention. The essence of this convention [...] lies in assuming that the existing state of affairs will continue indefinitely, except in so far as we have specific reasons to expect a change." (Keynes [1936], p. 152)

Keynes concretized this point of view in his 1937 Quarterly Journal of Economics reply to his critics:

> "Knowing that our own individual judgment is worthless, we endeavour to fall back on the judgment of the rest of the world which is perhaps better informed. That is, we endeavour to conform with the behaviour of the majority or the average. The psychology of a society of individuals each of whom is endeavouring to copy the others leads to what we may strictly term a *conventional judgment.*" (Keynes [1973], p. 114)

The conventional judgment described by Keynes implies an imitative behavior of market participants. Using this imitative behavior, market participants try to manage the fact that they do not have a clear idea of what the future holds (see Muchlinski [1997] and Bibow et al. [2004]). For this, they try to conform to the behavior of the majority or average. Furthermore, Keynes states in this context that the valuation of assets based on conventions is rather 'arbitrary' as "... the market will be subject to waves of optimistic and pessimistic sentiments, which are unreasoning and yet in a sense legitimate where no solid basis exists for a reasonable calculation." (Keynes [1936], p. 154 and Koppl [1991]). Anecdotal evidence for this point of view can be found in a trader's comment. He states that the prevailing convention on asset markets is not necessarily related to fundamentals.

> "Ninety percent of what we do is based on perception. It doesn't matter if that perception is right or wrong or real. It only matters that other people in the market believe. I may know it's crazy, I may think it's wrong. But I lose my shirt by ignoring it. This business turns on decisions made in seconds. If you wait a minute to reflect on things, you're lost. I can't afford to be five steps ahead of everybody else in the market. That's suicide." (Bruns [1994], p. 103)

III.4 Summary

In this Chapter, we took a new look at the observable exchange rate movements. The application of various analysis tools has revealed that exchange rate time series can be described rather well by long-lasting trends. These trends in exchange rates are often ascribed to excessive speculation in foreign exchange markets. Thus, our interest in this chapter was to evaluate the impact of speculation on foreign exchange markets. In principle, speculation may exert either stabilizing or destabilizing impacts on exchange rate movements. Thus, speculation is either beneficial for the economy as it ensures that exchange rate reflect true economic values or speculation is harmful as it leads to mispriced exchange rates which may be associated with high economic costs. The empirical evidence on the actual trading practices of foreign exchange market participants suggests that destabilizing non-fundamental speculation is predominant most of the time. In the recent literature, the effects of non-fundamental, irrational trading practices are discussed in the context of noise traders. Although noise trader models are rather new in economics, the roots of those models can be traced back at least to John Maynard Keynes. The discussion of the Keynesian view of the functioning of asset markets has revealed that Keynes seriously queries the traditional economic view that under uncertainty individuals make rational decisions which are based on an optimized calculation. Instead of an optimized calculation, Keynes argues that individuals base their decisions on a 'conventional judgment'. The practice of 'conventional judgment' must not be rated as irrational as it is a reasonable response to the environmental structure and allows for an efficient use of scarce human cognitive resources (see Lawson [1985]).

These two points – the impossibility of exactly calculating expected values of an asset and the use of convention – implicitly highlight the relevance of psychology for explaining the actual human behavior in financial markets, as both topics are picked out as a central theme in psychology. On the one hand psychology deals with the actual decision behavior and tries to reveal systematic human behaviors. On the other hand, psychology analyses the impact of social interaction on the decision behavior. Keynes [1936] also stresses the relevance of psychology explicitly within his General Theory. In many statements, Keynes refers to the importance of psychological phenomena. However, Keynes [1936] fails to put his subjective suppositions on the actual human decision behavior on a firm theoretical/psychological footing. Nevertheless, it was Keynes who paved the way for a more realistic view on the functioning of asset markets based on psychological considerations.

In the following chapter, we discuss the relevance of psychological considerations in more detail. We will see that the Keynesian view on the functioning of asset markets is largely in line with the main psychological insights with regard to the human decision behavior.

Chapter IV

Behavioral economics as an alternative approach

The foregoing chapters have revealed that traditional exchange rate theory is in crisis. The economic profession is unable to provide a reliable exchange rate model, which would allow a systematic description of observable exchange rate movements on the basis of macroeconomic fundamentals. However, exchange rate time series show a striking characteristic. As the analysis in section III.1 has shown, exchange rate movements are dominated by trends, which are often remarkably long lasting. In this context, it is important to note that the observable trends are largely detached from any macroeconomic fundamentals. Furthermore, the trend behavior of exchange rates is at odds with the hypothesis of efficient foreign exchange markets, which is essential for traditional exchange rate economics. The results of section II.2.4 indicate that the efficient market hypothesis does not hold for either DM/USD or YEN/USD exchange rates.

A possible explanation for the deviation of actual exchange rates from the predicted economic level and the rejection of the efficient market hypothesis may be found in the behavior of market participants. Economic exchange rate theories state that market participants act as rational agents orientating their expectations on macroeconomic fundamentals. However, psychological evidence raises strong doubts on the economic concept of rationality. Thus, a closer look at the actual behavior of market participants and the underlying psychological processes may help us to understand the interaction of market participants in foreign exchange markets and the resulting exchange rate movements more accurately. Such an approach pursues the newly emerging research area of behavioral economics. Herbert Simon, possibly the most prominent representative of behavioral economics, characterizes behavioral economics as follows:

> "...behavioural economics is best characterized not as a single specific theory but as a commitment to empirical testing of the neoclassical assumptions of human behaviour and to modifying economic theory on the basis of what is found in the testing process."
> (Simon [1987a], p. 221)

This definition of behavioral economics highlights two important tasks for economic research. On the one hand, behavioral economics requires a discerning evaluation of the neoclassical assumptions, in particular the assumption of economic rationality. On the other hand, behavioral economics requires a propagation of a new approach based on more realistic assumptions concerning actual human behavior. According to Camerer and Loewenstein [2004], behavioral economics tries to improve the explanatory power of economic analysis by providing it with more realistic psychological foundations:

> "At the core of behavioral economics is the conviction that increasing realism of the psychological underpinnings of economic analysis will improve economics on its own terms – generating theoretical insights, making better predictions of field phenomena, and suggesting better policy." (Camerer and Loewenstein [2004], p. 3)

Within the research field of behavioral economics many different problems are discussed. For example, behavioral economics deals with macroeconomics and savings (see e.g. Shefrin and Thaler [2004] and Shafir et al. [2004]) and labor economics (see e.g. Fehr and Gächter [2004] and Gneezy and Rustichini [2004]). In the context of financial markets, the sub-area of behavioral finance is of particular relevance. Stracca [2004] provides a recent definition of behavioral finance:

> "Behavioral finance rejects a vision of economic agents' behavior based on the maximization of expected utility. At the root of this rejection is the overwhelming evidence available that agents, both in controlled experiments and in real life situations, behave in a way so as to violate the axioms of expected utility [...]. It should be emphasized that the focus of behavioral finance is on a *positive* description of human behavior especially under risk and uncertainty, rather than on a *normative* analysis of behavior which is more typical of the mainstream approach. One of the key objectives of behavioral finance is to understand the systematic market implications of agents' psychological traits." (Stracca [2004], p. 374)

In line with the definition of behavioral economics, behavioral finance focuses also on the validity of the traditional economic model of human behavior in the context of financial markets. Furthermore, behavioral finance deals with a positive description of actual human behavior by trying to describe the "actual, often intuitive behavior of decision makers, whether plausible or irrational" and predicting "the behavior before during and after a decision [...]" (Goldberg and von Nitzsch [2001], p. 11). In this context, a detailed analysis of the perception, selection and processing of information and the resulting decisions is of particular importance (see Goldberg and von Nitzsch [2001]). In addition to these objectives, which are concentrated on the level of individuals, behavioral finance also deals with the repercussions of humans' psychological characteristics on the market level.[48] Thus, behavioral finance is also concerned with the results of psychological processes in a market environment. Consequently, behavioral finance can provide important assistance for economic policy.

The structure of the following sections is based on the main objectives of behavioral economics and behavioral finance. First of all, we discuss in a nutshell the standard economic model of human behavior. We dwell on the logical theory of economics from a theoretical as well as from an empirical/experimental perspective. Subsequently, we review the concept of bounded rationality as an alternative approach to the traditional economic point of view. The concept of bounded rationality can be seen as the theoretical basis for all models of behavioral economics. Afterwards we take a closer look at the psychological view on human behavior. Hereby, we concentrate in particular on the relevance of simple decision rules in human judgment and decision making processes. In Chapter V we are concerned with an experimental and empirical verification of the psychological implications for decision making foreign exchange markets.

IV.1 The traditional economic model of human behavior – a critique

IV.1.1 The logical theory of rational choice under uncertainty

Rational choice theory is basically a normative approach for optimal choice behavior of individuals. According to the standard approach in economics, human behavior is driven by rational decisions. A choice is characterized as 'rational', if the agent chooses that alternative which is preferred to all others, or in the words of Simon [1978]:

> "The rational man of economics is a maximizer, who will settle for nothing less than the best. Even his expectations [...] are rational" (Simon [1978], p. 2).

In case of uncertain outcomes, rational choice behavior is described by the expected utility theory (EUT) first proposed by von Neumann and Morgenstern [1947]. It constitutes the basis for all normative decision theories in social sciences and is furthermore a central building block

[48] This point holds of course also for behavioral economics: "Behavioral Economics is the combination of psychology and economics that investigates what happens in markets in which some of the agents display human limitations and complications." (Mullainathan and Thaler [2000]).

of modern asset market theories like portfolio selection models and capital asset market models. According to the expected utility theory, rational subjects always choose the risky alternative (x) which leads to the highest expected utility. Formally this decision rule can be represented as follows:

$$Max\ EU\left(x|\Omega_t\right). \quad \text{(IV-1)}$$

Equation (IV-1) shows the central components of a rational choice according to the expected utility theory: (a) Max represents the optimization objective of rational agents; (b) EU( ) stands for the preference ordering of rational agents; and (c) Ω_t contains the available information set. In the following, we will briefly discuss the underlying assumptions and corresponding implications of each component of rational choice:

Ad (a): Optimization objective

In economics it is usually assumed that rational agents maximize their utility by making deliberate decisions. This implies, on the one hand that rational agents always choose the best alternative out of all possible alternatives. On the other hand, rational agents are aware of the fact that a choice between different alternatives has to be made. Thus, only deliberate decisions are considered in the rational choice theory; impulsive, habitual or conventional behavior that are based on non-deliberated decisions are judged to be irrational (see Gerrard [1993]).

Ad (b): Preference ordering

The preference ordering provides an ordinal ranking with respect to the preferences of a rational agent over different alternative risky prospects. Thereby, the pairwise comparison between any two alternative risky prospects, x and y, can be represented in a preference relation, which is usually denoted by $\succeq$. Technically, $\succeq$ denotes the binary relation on the set of alternatives X, so that a pairwise comparison between any two alternatives, x, y $\in$X, is feasible. The relation $x \succeq y$ indicates, for example, that 'x is at least as good as y'. The preference relation $\succeq$ enables us to derive two other important preference relation, which are needed to constitute the basic axioms of rational choice (see Mas-Colell et al. [1995], Schotter [1997]). The strict preference relation, $\succ$, is defined by $x \succ y$ if and only if $x \succeq but\ not\ y \succeq x$ and denotes that 'x is strictly preferred to y'. The indifference relation, $\sim$, is defined by

$x \sim y$ if and only if $x \succeq and\ y \succeq x$ and denotes that 'x is indifferent to y'. With these three preference relations we are now in a position to derive the basic axioms of rational choice:

- **Axiom 1 (Ordering)**: The axiom of ordering ensures that preferences of rational agents are complete and transitive.

  Completeness requires that for all risky prospects x, y $\in$ X, either $x \succeq y$, $y \succeq x$ or $x \sim y$ must hold. It ensures that rational agents are able to express a preference or indifference between any pair of alternatives, so that no gaps in the agent's preference ordering exist.

  Transitivity entails that for all risky prospects x, y and z $\in$ X must hold that if $x \succeq y$ and $y \succeq z$, then $x \succeq z$.

  According to the transitivity condition, rational agents are able to rank all alternatives consistently. This is clearly a necessary condition for the existence of rational choice.[49]

- **Axiom 2 (Continuity):** Continuity requires that for all risky prospects x, y and z $\in$ X where $x \succeq y$ and $y \succeq z$, there exists a unique probability p such that $(x, p; z, 1-p) \sim y$, where $(x, p; z, 1-p)$ represents a compound prospect that results in x with probability p and in z with probability 1-p.

[49] A very illustrative example for the consequences of intransitive preferences is given by Schotter [1997]: "Say a person exists whose preferences are intransitive. For instance, assume the person prefers good a to good b, good b to good c, but good c to good a, and this person is willing to pay at least $10 to switch from one good to a preferred good. Further assume that this person currently has good b, but that you have good a and c. [...] You offer the person a trade of good a for his good b. You say: "I will give you good a if you give me good b plus $10." Because the person prefers good a to good b even though it will cost him $10, he accepts the deal and receives good a. You then have $10 and good b and c. However, you find out that the person prefers good c to good a, so you offer the following deal: "I will give you good c, if you give me good a plus $10." Again, the person accepts the deal. You have then collected $20 and hold goods b and a, while the person with intransitive preferences has paid out $20 and holds good c. Finally, you learn that the person prefers good b to good c, and you therefore offer the following deal: "I will give you good b if you give me good c plus $10." Once again, the person accepts the deal. You now have $30 and goods a and c. As a result of these deals, we see that the person has paid out $30 and has returned to his starting position – again holding only good b. You can now start the trading process over again and become infinitively rich (or at least take all the other person's wealth by repeated trading)." (Schotter [1997], p.22).

- **Axiom 3 (Independence):** The axiom of independence requires that for all risky prospects x, y and z $\in$ X if $x \succeq y$ then $(x,p;z,1-p) \succeq (y,p;z,1-p)$ for all p $\in$ (0,1). In other words, the axiom of independence implies that if we mix two risky prospects with a same third risky prospect, then the preference ordering of the two resulting mixtures is independent of the third risky prospect.

If all three axioms hold, preferences can be represented by a numerical utility index, and the utility of a prospect x corresponds to the utility of its possible outcomes $u(x_i)$ weighted with the known probabilities p_i. Thus, the functional form for the expected utility is given by

$$EU(x) = \sum_{i=1}^{n} p_i \cdot u(x_i). \qquad \text{(IV-2)}$$

According to the traditional economic paradigm, rational agents choose the risky prospect with the highest expected utility, so that the decision rule is given by equation (IV-1).

Ad (c): Available information set

The third important element of rational choice theory is the assumption that rational agents know all relevant information so that they are able to determine the optimal choice. Sub-optimal decisions due to a lack of knowledge are excluded. Furthermore, rational choice theory assumes that rational agents have no problem in handling all relevant information in a proper style, so that they can actually determine the risky prospect with the highest expected utility.

The main advantage of the normative approach of rational choice theory is that it allows economists to provide concise predictions of rational behavior without studying the actual human decision behavior (see Simon [1990]). The only necessary information to derive the rational solution for a decision problem is the utility function of the decision maker. If the utility function is known, rational choice theory allows with mathematical simplicity and clearness predictions of the rational response to all decision problems. However, as the next section will show, actual human behavior often contradicts the predictions of rational choice.

IV.1.2 Empirical evidence for the theory of rational choice

In recent years, several decision phenomena have been explored by economists as well as psychologists that contradict the economic paradigm of rational choice. These phenomena are usually characterized as anomalies and represent the starting point for most of the criticism on rational choice theory. According to Rabin and Thaler an anomaly can be defined as follows:

> "An empirical result qualifies as an anomaly if it is difficult to 'rationalize', or if implausible assumptions are necessary to explain it within the paradigm" (e.g. Rabin and Thaler [2001], p. 219).

A central assumption of the rational choice approach is the idea of utility maximization. Accordingly, economists assume that all choices of individuals reflect their foregoing maximization of utility. However, psychological evidence raises strong doubts on the human possibility of utility maximization. Due to cognitive limitations – in particular limits on human computational and information processing capabilities – agents need to adopt short cuts which allow for an efficient dealing with scarce cognitive resources (see Stracca [2004]).[50]

In addition, there exists a large body of evidence indicating that actual choice behavior contradicts the main axioms of expected utility theory. In particular, violations of the axiom of independence are reported. Very prominent examples for violations of the axiom of independence are given by Allais [1953]. Allais [1953] asked in an experiment a number of people to choose between two mutually exclusive alternatives. The concrete alternatives were given by a and b

a) 1 million French Franc with certainty.

b) 5 million French Franc with probability 0.1, 1 million French Franc with probability 0.89 and 0 French Franc with probability 0.01.

In a second round the participants had to choose again between two risky prospects. Now the two alternatives were given by c and d:

c) 1 million French Franc with probability 0.11 and 0 French Franc with probability 0.89.

d) 5 million French Franc with probability 0.10 and 0 French Franc with probability 0.90.

---

[50] The relevance of mental short cuts, so-called decision heuristics, will be discussed in detail in section IV.3.2.

Most of the participants choose a over b, but d over c (see Allais [1953]). This choice pattern clearly contradicts the expected utility theory as it violates the axiom of independence. A rational agent with expected utility preferences should either choose a and c or b and d across this pair of problems. The results of Allais [1953] have been replicated in many following studies (see Camerer [1995]), whereby Kahneman and Tversky [1979] have shown that the enormous amounts of money in the original formulation are not essential (see Thaler [1991]).

Further experimental evidence suggests that the failure of expected utility theory may run deeper than violations of the axiom of independence. Utility theories usually make several implicit background assumptions which seem to be so natural for economists that their empirical validity is often taken for granted. According to Starmer [2004], expected utility theory implicitly assumes

- procedure invariance, i.e. preferences over prospects are independent of the method used to elicit them; and
- description invariance, i.e. preferences over different prospects are purely a function of the probability distributions of consequences implied by prospects and do not depend on how those given distribution are described.

For economists both assumptions appear to be appropriate and their relevance is usually not really questioned. However, experimental evidence suggests that both assumptions fail in the real world. With regard to procedure invariance, the psychologists Sarah Lichtenstein and Paul Slovic provide in a series of experiments impressive counterevidence. The procedure invariance refers to the assumption of expected utility theory that for each individual subject a stable preference ordering exists, that should be recoverable in any number of alternative elicitation procedures (see Thaler [1991]). Experiments in the context of procedure invariance usually consist of two different tasks. The first task is called the choice task as participants have to choose between two distinct prospects: the first prospect offers a high probability for winning a small amount of money (often called the 'p-bet'); the second prospect offers a small probability for winning a high amount of money (often called the '$-bet'). The expected value of both prospects is usually about the same. The second task for the participants in the experiment – the judgment task – is to assign monetary values to the two distinct prospects that indicate their minimum selling prices for the two prospects. Contrary to the predications of expected utility theory, a large number of participants in the experiments, who preferred the 'p-bet' in the choice task assigned a larger value to the '$-bet' in the judgment task (see Lichtenstein and Slovic [1971] and Thaler [1991]). This result is rather puzzling for economists because both tasks in the experiments include essentially the same question for the participants: "Which of these two prospects do you prefer?" However the preference with regard to the two prospects is reversed by the elicitation method. Thus, this phenomenon is denoted as the preference reversal effect. It has been confirmed in many other studies (see for example Slovic [1995] and Starmer [2004]).

Also the assumption of description invariance is disproved by experimental evidence. The most famous violations of the description invariance are 'framing effects'. The impact of framing on the decision behavior can be illustrated by the means of the famous experiment conducted by Tversky and Kahneman [1981]. The participants in the experiment were divided into two groups and told that a new disease is expected to kill 600 people and that they can choose between two alternatives to combat the disease. The experiment was conducted in two different settings where the alternatives given to the participants change (see Table IV-1). Although both experimental settings show the same outcomes with regard to the saved people, i.e. A and C and B and D are equivalent in terms of lives lost or at risk, the presentation of the decision problem changes significantly the choices of the participants in the experiments. In the 'positive frame' most people choose alternative A over B. Contrarily, in the 'negative frame' most subjects prefer alternative D over C.

Table IV-1: Framing effects according to the experiment of Tversky and Kahneman [1981]

Experiment 1 (N=152)	**Choice**	**Experiment 2 (N=155)**	**Choice**
A: 200 people saved	72%	C: 400 people die	22%
B: ▪ 600 saved with probability 1/3 ▪ 0 saved with probability 2/3	28%	D: ▪ 0 die with probability 1/3 ▪ 600 die with probability 2/3	78%

Source: Tversky and Kahneman [1981]

A further effect that is hard to reconcile with the expected utility theory is the reference point effect. Reference points can be interpreted as a base from which expected changes are assessed. For a classical rational agent only the final outcome of risky alternatives matters and thus the reference point is irrelevant. However, in the real world a reference-dependence choice behavior can be observed (see McFadden [1999]).

The list of anomalies could be easily extended as the quotation of Starmer [1999] clarifies (see for an extensive discussion Camerer [1995]):

> "One thing we have learned for sure [...] is that EUT is *descriptively false*. Mountains of experimental evidence reveal systematic (i.e., predictable, non random) violations of the axioms of EUT, and the more we look, the more we find." (Starmer [1999], p. F8)

However, as our primary objective is not an extensive overview on existing anomalies but rather an experimental and empirical analysis of behavioral phenomena within the context of foreign exchange markets, we finish at this point and move on to an alternative concept of modeling human behavior.

IV.2 The alternative concept of bounded rationality

The foregoing section has revealed that expected utility theory is at odds with the empirical evidence. Another approach to attacking the economic rationality paradigm was made by Herbert Simon [1955], [1956] and [1978], who based his criticism more on the logical appeal of arguments than on empirical evidence (see Goldstein and Hogarth [1997]). Simon's animadversion on the rationality paradigm is mainly based on two implications of economic rationality: first, human beings possess all relevant information when making their decisions and, second, human beings have always the computational capabilities to determine the optimal solution. Herbert Simon regarded both implications as an inaccurate description of actual human behavior. According to Simon [1987b], the inaccuracy of the assumptions of rationality stems from at least two different sources:

a) limited information, i.e. decisions are usually based on an incomplete information basis, and

b) limited cognitive resources, i.e. the information processing of human beings is limited by their computational capacities.

For these both reasons, people can not conform to the ideal of economic rationality as it is proposed, for example, by the expected utility theory. The concept of bounded rationality can be seen as a central theme in behavioral economics. It is the most known and acknowledged alternative to the traditional economic concept of rationality. Principally, models of bounded rationality are concerned with the way people actually arrive at their decisions and how this decision process actually influences the decisions that are reached (see Simon [1987b]). Thus, models of bounded rationality try to answer the question, how people actually behave under limited information and limited cognitive resources (see Gigerenzer [2004a]).

However, although many economists have applied the notion of bounded rationality to express their criticism on the economic rationality paradigm and to introduce their own alternatives, bounded rationality does not represent a unified theory as its antagonist expected utility theory. It rather denotes a label for behavioral approaches analyzing actual human decision making. Unfortunately, the diffuse application of the term bounded rationality in the literature causes a multi-faceted understanding of bounded rationality in the corresponding literature (see e.g. Gigerenzer [2004b]). To remove the existing equivocality, we first discuss the original vision of bounded rationality provided by Herbert Simon. Afterwards, we present different interpretations of Simon's vision of bounded rationality found in the literature and verify to what extent these three different interpretations of bounded rationality are in line with Simon's original vision.

IV.2.1 Herbert Simon on bounded rationality

Herbert Simon, an early and persistent critic of the economic rationality paradigm, can be seen as the originator of the concept of bounded rationality (see Klaes and Sent [2002]). The starting point for his criticism of the economic paradigm of rationality is found in his conviction that an implementation of economic rationality requires people to be 'superior statisticians', which is far beyond human cognitive capabilities (see Goldstein and Hogarth [1997]). Instead of the economic model of human decision behavior, Herbert Simon introduced the notion of bounded rationality that should be used to

> " ... designate rational choice that takes into account the cognitive limitations of the decision-maker – limitations of both knowledge and computational capacity. Bounded rationality is a central theme in the behavioural approach to economics, which is deeply concerned with the ways in which the actual decision-making process influences the decisions that are reached." (Simon [1987b], p. 266)

Simon [1987b] definition of bounded rationality clarifies the crucial elements of models of bounded rationality:

- first, models of bounded rationality allow for cognitive limitations of the decision-maker and should provide, consequently, a more realistic view on how people actually make decisions, and
- second, Simon [1987b] stresses the importance of analyzing the actual decision-making process to gain deeper insights about the actual decision behavior of individuals.

With regard to the first element, Simon argues that people are usually not able to obtain all relevant information by the time a decision has to be made. Thus, the information on which decisions are usually based is incomplete. Additionally, Simon states that even if all information were available people could not perceive it accurately. This fact is justified by humans' limited information processing skills (see Schwartz [2002] and Hayakawa [2000]). These existing cognitive limitations induce people to handle their limited cognitive resources efficiently when making their decisions. Thus, according to Simon's vision of bounded rationality, people are keen to apply mechanisms, which allow them to use their limited cognitive resources in an efficient way. In this context, Simon [1995] states that recognition and heuristic search mechanisms play a pivotal role (see Simon [1990] and Munier and Selten [1999]). Both mechanisms help decision makers to simplify the structure of their decision problem:

> "For the first consequence of the principle of bounded rationality is that the intended rationality of an actor requires him to construct a simplified model of the real situation in order to deal with it. He behaves rationally with respect to this model, and such behavior is not even approximately optimal with respect to the real world. To predict his behavior, we must understand the way in which this simplified model is constructed, and its construction will certainly be related to his psychological properties as a perceiving, thinking, and learning animal." (Simon [1957], p. 199)

With regard to the second basic element of bounded rationality, Simon emphasizes the relevance of considering the decision making process instead of solely focusing on the optimal decision outcome. This is obviously in stark contrast to the common economic view on decision making as economic theories like the expected utility theory merely serve as an apparatus for predicting the optimal outcome of a rational choice given a certain utility function. The associated decision process is blended out by assuming that rational agents behave as if they were maximizing their expected utility (see Simon [1978] and [1987b]). Thus, the results of rational behavior depend only on the objectives of the rational agent, which are represented in his utility function. The rational 'super-calculator' always reaches the decision that is objectively, or substantively, best in terms of the given utility function (see Simon [1986]). Therefore, Simon denotes the traditional economic vision of rationality as substantive rationality, which refers to a rational behavior that optimally achieves given goals within the limits imposed by given conditions and constraints of the real world (see Simon [1976]).

Unlike the traditional economic vision of rationality, Herbert Simon stresses the role of the decision making process within his vision of bounded rationality. This approach is justified by the influence of limited cognitive capabilities on the decision behavior (see Simon [1986]). If knowledge and computational power are limited, agents are unable to determine optimal choices objectively. They are, rather, forced to a selective information-perception and an efficient information processing in terms of cognitive resources. Consequently, the real world and the agent's perception of it are likely to diverge. Furthermore, the reasoning about the real world is likely to diverge from substantive rationality. Thus, the objective of bounded rationality is to explain how particular aspects of reality, rather than other aspects, come to the decision makers' attention and which reasoning processes are applied by decision makers to reach their decisions (see De Bruijin [1999]). Thus, rationality is defined as the efficient use of scare cognitive resources within the decision process. Herbert Simon denotes this kind of rationality as procedural rationality. An exploration of procedural rationality necessitates an extensive analysis of the actual human decision behavior as it is conducted within psychological research. Or in the words of Simon [1955]:

> "One is tempted to turn to the literature of psychology for the answer" (Simon [1955], p. 99-100).

In this context, Augier [2001] illuminates a precise description of Simon's understanding of psychology:

> "Psychology represents, according to Simon, a field in which we can find basis for the fact that people only can process a limited amount of information; that people have a tendency to let feelings, or 'intuition', overcome logic, and that they tend to take shortcuts when making decisions." (see Augier [2001], p. 318)

Thus, models of bounded rationality describe how judgments or decisions are reached (i.e. what approximate methods are used) rather than merely the outcome of the decision (see Gigerenzer and Selten [2001]).

As Todd and Gigerenzer [2003] argue, most people recognized what Herbert Simon was criticizing, namely the concepts of full substantive rationality including maximization of expected utility, the ideal of 'Homo Oeconomicus' and just plain optimization. However, the alternative concept of bounded rationality introduced by Herbert Simon appeared to be broad enough to be understood in many different ways. Unfortunately, the consequence of the diverse interpretations of bounded rationality is a very broad and diffuse understanding of bounded rationality in the existing literature. In the next section, we discuss three different interpretations of the concept of bounded rationality and examine their conformity to the original understanding of Herbert Simon.

IV.2.2 Different perspectives on bounded rationality in the literature

Simon's term bounded rationality itself has been associated with at least three disparate programs: a) optimization under constraints, b) cognitive illusions, and c) ecological rationality (see Todd and Gigerenzer [2003] and Gigerenzer [2004b]). These different interpretations of bounded rationality will now be examined with regard to their conformity to Herbert Simon's understanding of the concept of bounded rationality.

IV.2.2.1 Bounded rationality as optimization under constraints

A popular interpretation of bounded rationality includes an optimization behavior of individuals under certain constraints (see e.g. Sargent [1993]). Models belonging to this vision of bounded rationality draw upon the criticism that models of unbounded rationality assume all relevant information is available at no cost. In reality, however, people need to search actively for the relevant information about alternatives. This search is inevitably associated with costs in terms of consuming limited resources (see Gigerenzer and Selten [2001]). As normally economic models assume that no free lunch should be possible, these models of bounded rationality introduce a deliberation cost parameter, which reflects information costs or search times. Thus, the bounds in bounded rationality are just another name for constraints and bounded rationality is just a case of optimizing under constraints (see Todd and Gigerenzer [2003]). As a result, decision makers in models of this vision of bounded rationality have to calculate the benefits and costs of searching for further information and stop searching as soon as the costs outweigh the benefits (see Dudey and Todd [2001]). Examples for models of bounded rationality as optimization under constraints can be found in e.g. Stigler [1961] or Sargent [1993].[51]

Although introducing real constraints does indeed make the outcome of these models more realistic, the adherence to the ideal of optimization still leads to psychologically implausible assumptions concerning the actual human decision making, as optimization is simply shifted to the problem of determining when to finish the search (see Chase et al. [1998]). This shift invokes new kinds of omniscience because it implies that the decision maker is able to foresee

---

[51] Further references can be found in Conlisk [1996] and Rosser [2003]. Collectively, these models show how a deliberation technology can merge standard modeling ingredients (optimization, rational expectations, market equilibrium) with boundedly rational ingredients (satisficing, learning, rules of thumb). In such a context the "degree of rationality" of a decision, relative to the decision that would prevail under unbounded rationality, is endogenously determined, along with other model outcomes, by economic forces (see Conlisk [1996]).

what additional information and further search would bring, what it would cost, and what opportunities he would forgo during that search (see Todd and Gigerenzer [2003]). In the end, models of optimization under constraints can require even more knowledge and computational capacities than models of unbounded rationality (see Vriend [1996] and Dudey and Todd [2001]). Furthermore, these models of bounded rationality do not contribute to a better understanding of actual human decision making, as the ultimate decision process is still kept unobserved. Also, Herbert Simon articulated criticism on interpreting bounded rationality as optimization under constraints:

> "Limits and costs of information are introduced, not as psychological characteristics of the decision maker, but as part of his technological environment. Hence, the new theories do nothing to alleviate the computational complexities facing the decision maker – do not see him coping with them by heroic approximation, simplifying and satisficing, but simply magnify and multiply them. Now he needs to compute not merely the shapes of his supply and demand curves, but the costs and benefits of computing those shapes to greater accuracy as well. Hence, to some extent, the impression that these new theories deal with the hitherto ignored phenomena of uncertainty and information transmission is illusory." (Simon [1979], p. 504)

In addition, these models of optimization under constraints are criticized because they lead to an infinite regression problem. Taking into account deliberation costs, one necessarily comes to a more complex meta-optimization procedure that includes both the basic decision problem and how many resources to allocate to that original decision problem. As meta-optimization is also costly, and even more so, this approach leads to an infinite regression (see e.g. Vriend [1996], Rosser [2003] and Gigerenzer and Selten [2001]).

All things considered, bounded rationality as optimization under constraints does not appear to be a very promising research strand with regard to the objectives of Herbert Simon's view on bounded rationality. Therefore, we will disregard this approach in the following. In doing so, we align ourselves with the originator of bounded rationality, Herbert Simon, who once remarked that he has considered suing authors who misuse his concept of bounded rationality to construct ever more complicated and unrealistic models of human decision making (see Gigerenzer and Todd [1999a]).

IV.2.2.2 Bounded rationality as cognitive illusions

The probably most known vision of bounded rationality focuses on the cognitive limitations of human beings and the resulting systematic biases (see e.g. Camerer [1998] and Rabin [1998]). Thereby, most research on individual decision making has taken some normative decision theory like e.g. the expected utility theory as null hypothesis about rational behavior, and tested this hypothesis in psychological experiments. The objective is to test whether the supposed norm of rationality is systematically violated and to propose alternative theories to explain the observed violations. For example, Camerer [1995], who summarizes many decision biases in his article "Bounded rationality in individual decision making", calls this way of proceeding the "exploration of procedural (bounded) rationality of individuals" (Camerer [1995], p. 179). Thus, the focus of the research subsumed under the notion of bounded rationality as cognitive illusions is the investigation of decision errors or biases compared to some normative decision theory. But why study errors in decision making rather than the appropriateness of human reasoning? Psychologists study errors because if people use simplified procedures to judge and choose, those procedures may be seen most clearly through the errors they cause. For economists, the frequency of errors is important because errors might affect economic efficiency, and methods for removing errors could be useful policy tools (see Camerer [1995]).

The most important contribution of the research related to this vision of bounded rationality is that it has impressively demonstrated that substantive rationality is an inadequate description of actual human decision behavior. Furthermore, proponents of this vision of bounded rationality always attach importance to the investigation of the actual process of decision making. Bounded rationality as cognitive illusions has its origins in the research program of Daniel Kahneman and Amos Tversky. Both psychologists deal with humans' cognitive limitations, which express themselves in errors in judgment and decision making. The observed errors are usually denoted as cognitive biases. Prominent examples of cognitive biases are e.g. the base rate neglect, overconfidence bias and sunk-cost effect (see e.g. Tversky and Kahneman [1999]). Also Herbert Simon acknowledged the relevance and importance of bounded rationality as cognitive illusions when he stated that "[..] Kahneman and Tversky have decisively disproved economists' rationality model" (quoted in Gigerenzer [2004b], p. 396).

While bounded rationality as cognitive illusions can be mainly attributed to the research of psychologists, it has a strong connection to economics. This strong link becomes apparent when Conlisk [1996] ends a section of his paper on "Evidence of bounds on rationality" by saying

> "the bias evidence suggests that people are capable of a wide variety of substantial and systematic reasoning errors relevant to economic decisions." (Conlisk [1996], p. 672).

Most of the existing literature related to the field of behavioral economics can be classified in this interpretation of the concept of bounded rationality. On behalf of many economic proponents of behavioral economics, Richard Thaler provides the following characteristic definition of bounded rationality in economics:

> "The possibility of cognitive error is of obvious importance in light of what Herbert Simon has called bounded rationality. Think of the human brain as a personal computer, with a very slow processor and a memory system that is both small and unreliable. I don't know about you, but the PC I carry between my ears has more disk failures than I care to think about." (Thaler [1992], pp. 2)

Although bounded rationality as cognitive illusions is very popular in economics and psychology, some researchers criticize this interpretation of Herbert Simon's bounded rationality in recent times (see for example Todd and Gigerenzer [2003], Gigerenzer [2004b]). The main reason for their expressed criticism is found in the implicit adherence of bounded rationality as cognitive illusions to the economic norm of rationality. The study of cognitive illusions and biases suggest that human beings behave due to their cognitive limitations in a non-rational manner. However, the economic norm of rationality may not be adequate and the rationality of certain cognitive processes may be analyzed with respect to the respective environment (see Todd and Gigerenzer [2003]). In this context, Todd and Gigerenzer [2003] state that "a true theory of Bounded Rationality need not rely on optimization theories, neither as descriptions nor as norms of behavior" (Todd and Gigerenzer [2003], p. 146). The reasons for his point of view are given in the next section.

IV.2.2.3 Bounded rationality as ecological rationality

The proponents of the third vision of bounded rationality refer to Simon's famous scissors blade metaphor. According to Simon [1990],

> "human rational behavior [...] is shaped by a scissors whose two blades are the structure of task environments and the computational capabilities of the actor." (Simon [1990], p. 7).

Simon's scissors metaphor implies that one has to consider for a sound understanding of human behavior both aspects – limited cognitive resources and the structure of the decision environment. The proponents of bounded rationality as ecological rationality argue that the fit between these two blades is the basis of rational human decision making, as minds with limited cognitive resources can be successful by exploiting existing structures in their environment. Or in the words of Simon [1956]:

> "a great deal can be learned about rational decision making [...] by taking account of the fact that the environments to which it must adapt possess properties that permit further simplification of its choice mechanisms" (Simon [1956], p.129).

The first component of bounded rationality as ecological rationality is based on the actual decision behavior of human beings. It largely conforms with the research associated to the vision of bounded rationality as cognitive illusions as it is also concerned with the investigation of actual human decision behavior. However, in contrast to the cognitive illusions approach, the central objective of the first blade is not to detect deviations of human behavior from the economic norm of rationality, but to analyze the actual human behavior and to evaluate the usefulness of humans' adaptive methods. That is, the first blade of the scissors asks how human beings cope with the complexity of the real world and whether they are successful in doing so. In principle, humans "must use approximate methods to handle most tasks" (Simon [1990], p. 6) as their cognitive skills are limited. According to Simon [1995], these approximate methods include (see Gigerenzer and Todd [1999a])

a) recognition processes and

b) simple decision rules.

The proponents of bounded rationality as ecological rationality deal with both approximate methods in depth and evaluate their usefulness in the real world (see Gigerenzer and Todd [1999b] for a survey of this research program). For the evaluation of the usefulness of humans' simplification strategies, the advocates of ecological rationality refer to their adaptability to the decision environment, which is the second component of bounded rationality as ecological rationality. The environmental structure is of crucial importance as it explains when and why simple decision methods used in decision processes perform well (see Gigerenzer and Todd [1999a]). Thus, if the approximate method is well adapted to the environmental structure, the application of such simplification strategies is rational in a cognitive sense.

According to Todd et al. [2000], the environmental structure imposes two important constraints on actual human decision behavior. First, because of the fact that the external world is uncertain, the applied mental mechanisms must be robust. The robustness of approximate methods depends crucially on its simplicity. According to Todd et al. [2000], simple approximate methods that use only a few parameters are most likely to be robust. Second, because of the fact that the world is competitive and time is money, decision mechanisms must be fast in general. In order to be able to reach fast decisions, human beings need to minimize the required information. Thus, the external world constrains human beings to be frugal in what they search for (see Todd et al. [2000]). As in many cases important characteristics of an agent's decision environment are created by other subjects it interact with, the social environment of decision makers is of crucial importance for their decision behavior (see Gigerenzer and Todd [1999a]). In this context, Gigerenzer and Todd [1999a] coin the term 'social rationality'. Social rationality can be seen as a special variant of ecological rationality.

Overall, the proponents of bounded rationality as ecological rationality argue that both aspects of human decision making – limited cognitive resources and decision environment – have to be considered when thinking about rational human decision behavior. Studying only one blade of the scissors is not enough as it takes both for the scissors to cut.

IV.2.3 Summary

Overall, models of bounded rationality deal with the question how people make decisions in the real world, where time is short, knowledge lacking, and other resources limited (see Gigerenzer [2000]). The foregoing discussion of different visions of bounded rationality has clarified that at least two elements are, in Herbert Simon's view, essential for the concept of bounded rationality. First, models of bounded rationality ask for an in-depth analysis of the actual human decision making process whereas the cognitive limitations of decision makers are explicitly considered. Furthermore, models of bounded rationality require that the decision environment is explicitly considered. The usefulness of simplification strategies used by human beings can only be evaluated by the adaptability to the real world.

IV.3 Behavioral decision theory: a psychological analysis of judgment and decision

The discussion of bounded rationality as an alternative concept for human decision making has revealed that a sound understanding of human decision making requires a sound understanding of the human decision making process. The decision making process is a major topic in psychological research. Therefore, we discuss in the section IV.3.1 the psychological view on human decision behavior in detail. Within the human decision making process, simple decision rules play a crucial role, as such simple rules allow for an efficient usage of scarce cognitive resources. Simple decision rules will be the subject of section IV.3.2. In this section, we also discuss the relevance of the decision environment, as it is important for evaluating the usefulness of simplification strategies.

IV.3.1 The psychological view of human decision behavior

The concept of bounded rationality highlights the importance of the analysis of the human decision process. Principally, the decision process is composed of three different elements (see Bless et al. [2004]):

a) input from a given situation,

b) input from prior knowledge, and

c) the processes that operate on the given input.

Within the information processing, all three components of the decision process are linked. A central assumption of the psychological approach to human decision making is that human beings possess only limited information processing capacity. The limitations of the human processing capacity force people to use simplifications and shortcuts in decision situations (see Bless et al. [2004]). Thus, people do not process all information when making decisions. Following Fiedler and Bless [2001] and Bless et al. [2004] the sequence of the human decision process can be schematically illustrated as in Figure IV-1. The upper panel of Figure IV-1 represents the psychological view on human decision behavior and the lower panel the economic view.

Figure IV-1: Schematic illustration of the human decision process

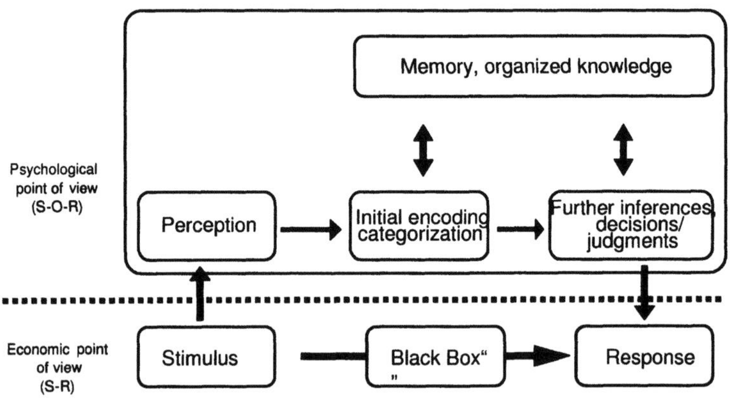

The most important difference between economics and psychology is that economists are mainly interested in the mapping from information ('decision input') to choice ('decision output'). Thereby economic analysis does not illuminate the decision process itself, rather it is assumed that the decision maker acts rationally, i.e. his behavior satisfies the axioms of rational choice so that the decision process can be ignored. Thus, the economic view of the human decision process can be characterized by the stimulus-response-paradigm (S-R-Paradigm). In contrast, the main focus of psychologists is to understand the nature of the different decision elements, how they are established and modified by experience, and how they determine choices by their interaction. Thus, in psychology an explicit analysis of the various decision elements is carried out, which is clearly in line with the concept of Bounded Rationality. This broader analysis of the human decision process is denoted as the stimulus-organism-response-paradigm (S-O-R-Paradigm). The human information processing is thereby usually divided into different cognitive stages as depicted in the upper half of Figure IV-1. First, the individual has to perceive an observed stimulus event; then he needs to encode and interpret his perceptions. This encoding stage is heavily influenced by prior knowledge stored in memory. The encoded perception will be stored in memory and will potentially affect the assessment of future information. Both, the newly encoded input and the old knowledge in memory, will then provide the basis for further processing, leading to inferences and judgments. Sometimes, but not always, the final outcome of this cognitive process is manifested in a visible behavioral response (see Fiedler and Bless [2001]). According to Bless et al. [2004], the human information processing exhibits in a stylized illustration four important elements:[52]

1. Perception

Due to limited cognitive capacities, people need to select which information will enter the information processing. The selection process is in general guided by the attention paid to a specific piece of information. Human beings possess the ability to direct their attention to some aspects of their environmental structure and exclude other aspects (see Bless et al. [2004]). The attention is usually attracted to new information that is distinctive or salient. Salience signifies the distinctiveness of a given stimulus relative to the environmental context (see Fiedler and Bless [2001]). A particular piece of information can be salient in various ways: a stimulus can be salient in relation to a) other stimuli in the environmental context, b) an

[52] The following description of the human information processing draws on the illustration given by Fiedler and Bless [2001] and Bless et al. [2004].

individual's prior knowledge and expectations, and c) a person's current objective that guide the information processing.

The salience of a specific piece of information has an important impact on the subsequent processes. Psychological evidence indicates that the size of a stimulus impact on judgments increases with its salience and that increasing salience of a stimulus exaggerates an already existing judgmental tendency (see Bless et al. [2004]). The perception of stimuli may also be influenced by a person's existing attitudes. In psychology this issue is discussed in the context of cognitive consistency. A central results of the research on cognitive consistency is that individuals try to maintain consistency of their cognitive structure by retrieving new information in line with their existing attitudes and by suppressing new information inconsistent with existing attitudes (see Festinger [1957] and Bohner and Wänke [2002]). From this point of view, an attitude may serve the human mind as a cognitive schema, which on the one hand simplifies reality, and on the other hand may affect the processing of new information. Thus attitudes help to handle the cognitive tasks of human beings.

2. Encoding and interpretation

The next stage of the stylized information processing includes the encoding and interpretation of the perceived information. The encoding of new information relies on prior knowledge by relating new stimuli to information already known. The stimulus is categorized into a meaningful category. A category denotes an elementary knowledge structure of the memory organization, which allows for economical storage and efficient memory search and retrieval. Thus, encoding and interpretation comprises the interplay of new stimuli and prior knowledge. The nature of the interaction of new information and prior knowledge depends on the available processing capacity and the motivation; the less processing capacity and motivation is available, the stronger the impact of prior knowledge on new information will be. In this case the processing is denoted as top-down processing. Conversely, the more processing resources are spent on the new stimulus, the greater is the likelihood that new information will change existing knowledge. This kind of processing is called bottom-up processing. Again, individuals rely on cognitive mechanisms that allow for a simplification of the required process, and possess a high degree of efficiency and adaptability. (see Bless et al. [2004]).

3. Storage and retrieval

When new information has attained sufficient attention and has been encoded, it can enter further cognitive processes such as the storage of information in memory. Thus, some of the new information is not only used for the immediate response of the individual but also for subsequent behavior at a later point in time. The probability that new information is stored in memory and afterwards retrieved for further decisions increases with the attention given to new information. Furthermore, individuals tend to store the encoding of new information rather than the 'raw data' of the new information itself. The advantage of this procedure is that it allows a simplification of the information processing by focusing only on encoded information. However, it may also lead to some drawbacks, as individuals base their decisions only on stored information rather than on the initial information (see Bless et al. [2004]). As in case of the perception of new information, cognitive consistency may also exert a substantial impact on the storage and retrieval of information. In the case of new information consistent with prior knowledge, it is sufficient to store a link to the prior knowledge rather than storing the new information anew. Thus, it is easier to retrieve consistent information (see Fiedler and Bless [2001] and Bless et al. [2004]).

4. Further processes, inferences, judgments and decisions

Individuals base their judgments and decisions on activated information.[53] The activated information comprises prior knowledge that is retrieved from memory as well as encoded stimulus input of the specific decision situation. Thus, judgments reflect the information content that comes to mind when the judgment is formed. The fourth step of information processing is also affected by the limited cognitive processing capacity of human beings. Because of capacity constraints, individuals are unable to consider or even retrieve all relevant information. Instead, they have to base their decisions on a subset of information, which is obtained from a limited search for information. Also the ultimate judgmental task is characterized by simplification strategies. In this context, psychological research refers to the relevance of rules of thumb in the decision making process. In psychology, rules of thumb are described as simple decision heuristics. We will discuss the relevance of decision heuristics in the next section in more detail.

Overall, the short discussion of human information processing has shown that it is characterized by various simplification strategies at each stage. Theses cognitive simplification strategies are necessary to cope with the great deal of information.

[53] The distinction between inferences, judgments and decisions is rather fuzzy and arbitrary. We use these terms in the following as synonyms (see Bless et al. [2004]).

IV.3.2 The relevance of heuristics in human decision making

The psychological analysis of human decision making highlights the importance of simplification mechanisms in information processing. Simple rules of thumb, so-called simple heuristics, play a decisive role in the process of judgment and decision making. In this section, we take a closer look at the relevance of simple heuristics in human decision making. In particular, we discuss the topic of simple heuristics against the background of two interrelated but still different research strands. In addition, we discuss the existence of social heuristics in the context of financial markets.

Principally, a simple heuristic can be characterized as a simple rule of thumb, which allows quick and efficient decisions even under a high degree of complexity and uncertainty (see Fiedler and Bless [2001]). Heuristics normally permit a fast and frugal decision making by reducing "the complex tasks of assessing probabilities and predicting values to simple judgmental operations" (Tversky and Kahneman [1999], p. 3).

In economics the subject of heuristics is usually ascribed to the research of Daniel Kahneman and Amos Tversky. Within the "Heuristics & Biases" research program they initiated enormous research efforts to compare the actual decision behavior with the reference point of probability law. The results of the research related to the Heuristics & Biases research program indicate that simple heuristics are advantageous in many cases, but sometimes lead to severe and systematic distortions (see Mussweiler et al. [2000] and Plous [1993]). The "Heuristics & Biases" research program focuses mainly on the decision biases evolving from the application of simple heuristics. The reason for focusing on decision biases rather than successes is that decision biases usually reveal more information about the underlying processes than do successes. The observed decision biases in the "Heuristics & Biases" research program are always decision biases compared to the concept of economic rationality. Thus, the concept of rationality, although it is not practicable for human beings, serves further on as a norm with which actions is compared.

The most common heuristics related to the "Heuristics & Biases research program are the availability heuristic, the representativeness heuristic and the anchoring and adjustment heuristic.[54] According to Tversky and Kahneman [1974], the availability heuristic is a rule of thumb by which decision makers "assess the frequency of a class or the probability of an event by the ease with which instances or occurrences can be brought to mind" (Tversky and Kahneman [1999], p. 11). The application of the representativeness heuristic in decision making process implies that people tend to evaluate "the probability of an uncertain event by the degree to which it is: (i) similar in essential properties to its parent population; and (ii) reflects the salient features of the process by which it is generated" (Kahneman and Tversky [1999], p. 33). Due to the anchoring and adjustment heuristic people tend to gauge numerical values by starting from an initial value, which is called the anchor, and adjusting it during the further process of judgment and decision making. However, as Tversky and Kahneman [1974] argue, the adjustment of the judgment is usually insufficient so that the judgment is biased in the direction of the initial anchor (see Bless et al. [2004]). This holds true even in cases where the initial anchor is completely irrelevant to the decision problem. A joint attribute of all these heuristics is their inherent familiarity, so that a decision behavior oriented on the usage of these heuristics tends to result in conservative and preserving decisions. That is, human decision behavior leads to an orientation on the already existing.

In addition to the "Heuristics & Biases" research program initiated by Daniel Kahneman and Amos Tversky, a further research strand in psychology also deals with the usefulness of simple heuristics in the context of human decision making. However, the aims of the ABC research group[55] are rather different from that of the "Heuristics & Biases" research program. While the main focus of the "Heuristics & Biases" research program lies on the decision biases compared to the norm of economic rationality, the ABC research program concentrates on the accuracy of simple heuristics in decision situations without using any dubious norm to compare. Their point of reference is rather the adaptability of simple heuristics to the environmental structure. Thus, they evaluate the usefulness of simple heuristics relative to the environmental context. Overall, their results suggest that simple heuristics do not only reduce the required cognitive resources

---

[54] For a detailed illustration of the simple heuristics proposed by the Heuristics & Biases research program we refer to Kahneman et al. [1999], Wärneryd [2001] and Strack and Deutsch [2002].

[55] The Adaptive Behavior and Cognition research group is part of the Max Planck Institute for Human Development in Berlin; http://www.mpib-berlin.mpg.de/ABC/. For a detailed illustration of the ABC Research Group's research results see Gigerenzer and Todd [1999b].

but also represent accurate solution methods for complex decision situations, so that the usage of simple heuristics seems to be very reasonable (see Gigerenzer and Todd [1999b]).

The most prominent heuristics of the ABC research program belong to the classes of ignorance-based decision making heuristics and one-reason decision making heuristics.[56] The recognition heuristic is based on the assumption that if one alternative is recognized and the other alternative is not, then the decision maker can use the recognition as a cue in making his decisions (see Marsh et al. [2004]). The recognition heuristic has been investigated in several different contexts (see e.g. Goldstein and Gigerenzer [1999], Borges et al. [1999] and Goldstein and Gigerenzer [2002]). The results indicate that the recognition heuristic is often used by participants in experiments and that it is successful in many different environmental settings. For example, Borges et al. [1999] investigate the usefulness of the recognition heuristic in a stock market context. Their experimental procedure can be summarized as follows: Borges et al. [1999] asked 480 Americans and Germans to indicate which companies they recognized from those listed on the New York Stock Exchange (NYSE) and several German stock exchanges. The participants were divided into four different groups: American laypeople, American experts, German laypeople, German experts. Laypeople were 360 pedestrians surveyed in Chicago and Munich, experts were graduate students in finance or economics. In order to test the recognition heuristic, they constructed two investment portfolios for each group. The portfolios consisted of highly recognized companies for each of the four groups. The first portfolio contained highly recognized companies (recognized by at least 90% of the group) from the group's home country. The other portfolio comprised the 10 companies that each group recognized most often from the other country. The performance of each portfolio was analyzed for a period of six months starting on December 13, 1996. The returns of the recognition-based portfolios were compared with the performance of a) stocks of unrecognized companies, b) market indices, c) mutual funds, d) chance portfolios and e) individuals' investment choices. The results of the experiment conducted by Borges et al. [1999] are astonishing:

1. Portfolios of highly recognized stocks outperformed the portfolios of unrecognized stocks.

[56] For a detailed illustration of the simple heuristics proposed by the ABC research group see e.g. Gigerenzer and Todd [1999b], Todd and Gigerenzer [2003] and Marsh et al. [2004].

2. In tests of domestic recognition, the results show that the recognition heuristics outperformed the DAX 30 market index for both groups. However, in case of US stocks the recognition heuristic yields lower returns than the Dow market index.

3. In tests of international recognition, the recognition heuristic beat the relevant market index in all four cases. Furthermore, the international recognition led throughout to higher returns than domestic recognition, and recognition of laypeople tends to be slightly more profitable than that of experts. Thus, it seems that the greater the degree of ignorance the better the choice of stocks.

4. The recognition heuristic beat the performance of mutual funds and randomly composed portfolios.

Overall, the results of Borges et al. [1999] suggest that a lack of recognition can contain implicit knowledge that is possibly more powerful than explicit knowledge. According to Borges et al. [1999], "the superiority of international over domestic recognition and the superiority of laypeople over experts in stock picking supports the notion that a certain degree of ignorance can be virtue." (Borges et al. [1999], p. 71). Thus, the corollary of the reported success of applying the recognition heuristic is that an intermediate amount of knowledge, which is needed for recognition, can yield the highest proportion of correct inferences (see Marsh et al. [2004]). Marsh et al. [2004] denote this counterintuitive consequence as the 'less-is-more-effect'. Borges et al. [1999] allude, in this context, to the 'beneficial degree of ignorance'.

If more than one cue is available for guiding decisions, people often base their decisions nevertheless on only one single reason. The ABC research group has proposed various specific one-reason decision heuristics, which differ in their assumed specific search rules. The "take the best" heuristic, for example, implies that people select cues in order of their validity, i.e. how often each cue has indicated the correct option in the past (see Todd and Gigerenzer [2003]). According to the "take the last" heuristic, decision makers look for cues that were used on the preceding occasion. The minimalist heuristic selects cues in a purely random way. The performance of such one-reason decision making heuristics is throughout experimental tests rather good. Despite their simplicity they still made accurate choices in many situations. Todd and Gigerenzer [2000] confirm that such simple heuristics always came close to and often exceeded the proportion of correct inferences achieved by either multiple regression or linear strategies (see Todd and Gigerenzer [2000] and Gigerenzer and Todd [1999b]).

In addition to the above-mentioned heuristics, some researchers put forward the existence of so-called social heuristics. Social heuristics are related to the aspect of social rationality (see section IV.2.2.3) as those heuristics allow a fast and frugal decision making in social contexts by exploiting the information structure of the social environment. Interestingly, although many judgment and decision making heuristics have been proposed and tested to date, only a few researchers pay attention to the issue of how people use heuristics in their everyday social interactions (see e.g. Marsh [2002]).

According to Marsh [2002], candidates for social heuristics can be found by looking for patterns in the way people tend to respond to commonly faced social problems. In this context, Marsh [2002] cites various examples of social heuristics like e.g. focusing on similarity, social comparison and social imitation. In group contexts, which are of particular importance with regard to financial markets, social imitation heuristics play a decisive role. A social imitation heuristic can be interpreted as a fast and frugal decision making strategy that saves a subject having to extract information from the environment anew (see Goldstein et al. [2001]). Thus, social imitation heuristics can be assessed as procedurally rational, as they encompass simplification processes which permit a fast and frugal decision making in complex social decision situations. Imitative behavior can be used instead of selecting new information. Thus, imitating the behavior of others may serve as a way to acquire information. Obviously, mimetic behavior is in that case self-reinforcing, as it transmits information throughout the economy (see Charbit and Fernandez [2001]). The application of an imitation heuristic can be seen as a substitute for a information-based strategy, whereas the usage of imitation heuristics is more likely in situations where relevant information is scarce. Thus, people tend to imitate because there is no information to indicate an optimal choice, and imitation at least permits a choice, even if the decision situation is very complex. In economics, imitative behavior is discussed in the context of herd behavior. However, within the related literature the relevance of imitation as a simple heuristic has been – to our knowledge – largely neglected.

Goldstein et al. [2001] argue that the usefulness of social imitation heuristics depends strongly on the given decision environment. They conclude that only in a relatively stable environment is imitation a reasonable choice. If the environmental conditions change permanently, imitation will fail because a successful strategy at the time of observation may no longer be effective at a later time. Furthermore, the environment must disclose the behavior of others. If the environment disguises the behavior of others, imitation is impossible (see Goldstein et al. [2001]).

In this context, a further kind of social heuristic related to social imitation and the stability of the environment is of particular relevance. In social life, conventions play a decisive role for the actual behavior of human beings. Conventions help people to find their way in everyday decision situations by reducing the uncertainty concerning human interaction. This holds true also for the decision making tasks in financial markets. As Keynes [1936] has argued, the functioning of financial markets can be compared with the functioning of a Beauty Contest in a newspaper. Theoretically, the 'Beauty Contest' can be described by means of game theory. The relevant type of game here is a matching game. A matching game is a pure coordination game in which the participating players get a reward if and only if all choose the same action; and the reward is the same whatever this action may be (see Bacharach [1997]). The formal structure of such a matching game can be exemplarily represented for a two-player case as follows: Player 1 chooses a strategy from a set $\{s_{11}, s_{12},....,s_{1n}\}$, where $n \geq 2$; player 2 chooses a strategy from his set $\{s_{21}, s_{22},....,s_{2n}\}$. Let the chosen strategies be s_{1g} and s_{2h}. If $g = h$ each player receives a prize; if $g \neq h$, each receives zero (see Mehta et al. [1994]). The Figure IV-2 illustrates exemplarily a pure coordination game with 2 players and 2 possible states.

Figure IV-2: Coordination game

	Player 1: s_{11}	Player 1: s_{12}
Player 2: s_{21}	(1,1)	(0,0)
Player 2: s_{22}	(0,0)	(1,1)

As can be easily seen, a pure coordination game has n strict Nash-equilibria and both players are indifferent between all of them. This characteristic of a pure coordination game implies that the standard decision criterion of a Nash-equilibrium does not suffice, as a player cannot find a coordination equilibrium by simply contemplating what a purely rational player or a set of purely rational players would do. Thus, classical game theory is unable to give a coherent account of how a player should play a game like this. However, in reality people are quite successful in solving coordination problems (see Camerer [2003]). The human ability to coordinate behavior stems from the existence of conventions. Conventions denote regularities in individual behaviors that are maintained without any explicit formal sanction. Lewis [1969] gives a basic definition of what is meant by the term 'convention':

> "A regularity R in the behavior of members of a population P when they are agents in a recurrent situation S is a convention if and only if, in any instance of S among members of P,
> (1) everyone conforms to R;
> (2) everyone expects everyone to conform to R;
> (3) everyone prefers to conform to R on condition that others do, since S is a coordination problem and uniform conformity to R is a coordination equilibrium in S."
> (Lewis [1969], p. 42)

Conventions fulfill important functions in everyday human interaction. In particular, conventions help to make decisions by

a) reducing the necessity to search for new clues; thus, conventions allow a fast decision making by designating the adequate choice.

b) Furthermore, conventions reduce the degree of behavioral uncertainty in human interaction. Consequently, conventions reduce the complexity of decision situations where cooperation is needed.

c) Conventions also serve as a basis for the expectation formation of individuals because of their self-reinforcing characteristic. This point is of particular interest in financial markets. The prevailing convention has an essential bearing on the nature of expectations.

The consequence of the role played by conventions is that conventions allow a fast and frugal decision making in social contexts as long as the convention is accepted by large parts of the population. Davis [1998] supports this conclusion by referring to Simon [1982] when he states that

> "people are procedurally or boundedly rational, not substantively so, and thus they employ rules and conventions to economize on scarce computational resources. [...] Thus, conventions and rules are essentially simplifying devices individuals use in decision making" (Davis [1998], p. 83-84).

The issue of the acceptance of conventions leads us directly to the origins of conventions. In principle, there are two different ways to establish conventions: authority and precedents. First, conventions are due to prescriptions of an authority. The form in which an authority manifests itself can vary from prescriptions by law, including punishments in case of disobedience, to the mere advice of a friend or the evaluation of an expert (see Pingle and Day [1996] and Pingle [1997]). In several experiments, Pingle and Day [1996] and Pingle [1997] show that people tend to orientate their decision on the prescription of authorities even if the authority's prescription is far from optimal and there is no penalty for deviating form the prescription. Thus, people are bound to the prescription of authorities by more than penalties for disobedience. In this context, Pingle [1997] refers to three different reasons why people orientate their decision on the prescription of authorities voluntarily: a) the prescription of an authority may serve as a reference point from which to start searching for better choices.; b) adopting the authority's prescription allows for economizing decision costs; and c) deviating from authority's prescription may lead to poor decision performances. This point applies especially in the case of coordination problems.

Second, conventions are the outcome of a steady accumulation of precedents (see Young [1996]). The idea here is that in a repeated coordination game one particular way of interaction emerges successively as a superior way of resolving the game. Thus, it reaches a greater degree of prominence, which in turn entails that more people notice it, which leads to more people using it, and so forth. Consequently, a positive feedback loop is created. In this context, Schelling [1960] concept of focal points takes on particular importance. A focal point indicates a contextual clue that lies outside the pure coordination game, but allows people to coordinate their behavior on a particular equilibrium (see Young [1996]). Thus, it is reasonable for players in a pure coordination game to look for a prominent and unique clue of the game, which helps them to coordinate by serving as a focal point. Obviously the relevant focal point of a game is *a priori* unknown and depends on the existing coordination problem and the game environment.

Additionally, conventions possess the important characteristic of stability. Since everyone conforms to established convention, everyone expects others to conform to it, and everyone has good reason to conform because conforming is in each person's best interest when everyone else plans to conform, established conventions show a high degree of persistence (see Young [1996]). No member of a group has an incentive to change common expectations once established (Duncan and Isaac [2000]).

IV.3.3 Behavioral economics and exchange rate movements

The decision environment in foreign exchange markets is characterized by a high degree of complexity which is due to various factors. Firstly, trading in foreign exchange markets is accompanied by a high degree of uncertainty. Uncertainty in foreign exchange markets has many facets. On the one hand, the future development of exogenous factors, i.e. factors which are mainly independent from exchange trading, is highly uncertain as many studies report difficulties in forecasting macroeconomic variables (see e.g. Fildes and Stekler [2002]). On the other hand, trading in foreign exchange markets is also hampered by 'model uncertainty'. Since there exists no generally accepted exchange rate model, foreign exchange traders cannot be sure of considering all relevant fundamentals in a correct manner. This fact seems to distinguish the foreign exchange market from other asset markets, e.g. the stock market. In stock markets it seems to be pretty clear for a stock market trader that a company's profit warning has a negative impact on the stock price of this company, but in foreign exchange markets it is not that clear for a trader what an interest rate cut means for the future exchange rate development. This point was also recognized by Simon [1987b]:

> "The cognitive limits are not simply limits on specific information. They are almost always limits on the adequacy of the scientific theories that can be used to predict the relevant phenomena. [...] the accuracy of predictions of the economy by computer models is severely limited by lack of knowledge about fundamental economic mechanisms represented in the models' equations." (Simon [1987b], p. 267)

In addition, trading in foreign exchange markets is accompanied by uncertainty about the behavior of other market participants. This kind of uncertainty is primarily due to the speculative nature of foreign exchange markets. It requires that each market participant consider the behavior of other market participants when making his own decisions.

An additional factor boosting the complexity of the decision situation in foreign exchange markets is the plethora of information which arrives during the course of a day. In particular, in foreign exchange markets many new items of information about macroeconomic fundamentals, political developments etc. become known, which need to be processed in a reasonable way. Furthermore, many foreign exchange traders are usually pressed for time. For example, market makers, which account for most trading in foreign exchange markets, often pass most of their positions within a few minutes.

Decision environments which are characterized by such high complexity make high demands on human judgments. As the foregoing discussion about human decision making has clarified, people are forced in reality to apply simplification strategies in such situations, like simple heuristics; this holds true also in foreign exchange markets. The main advantage of using simple decision heuristics is that they allow fast and at the same time frugal decision making. The experimental evidence shows that the application of simple heuristics is normally a good compromise between economic rationality and an efficient use of scare human cognitive resources (see Gigerenzer and Todd [1999b]). However, in some circumstances simple heuristics also lead to systematically biased judgments (see e.g. Kahneman et al. [1999]). An important simple social heuristic in strategic decision situations is convention. Conventions allow decision makers a fast and frugal decision making as long as the prevailing convention is accepted by large parts of the relevant population, primarily by reducing the degree of behavioral uncertainty. In this context, it is important to stress once again that exchange rates are a social fact just like the stock price is also a social fact:

> "The price of a stock is more than an objective, rationally determined number; it is an opinion, an aggregate opinion, the moment-to-moment resultant of the evaluation of the community of investors. As an opinion, stock price is subject to the same set of social pressures and cultural influences as any other opinion, such as the evaluation of a work of art, the preference for a political candidate, or the popularity and spread of a fad." (Wärneryd [2001], p.21)

What does the existence of conventions as simple heuristics mean for trading in foreign exchange markets? In the context of foreign exchange markets, it is likely that existing exchange rate trends reflect prevailing conventions concerning the evaluation of currencies (see Bofinger [2001]). As the simplest form of convention, one can think of a common view of market participants as to which trend the exchange rate will follow in the near future, e.g. the Euro is generally judged a strong currency and consequently will appreciate or, conversely, the US dollar is judged a weak currency and will consequently depreciate in the future. If such a convention has attained a certain degree of acceptance among foreign exchange market participants, it will display a high degree of persistence. Once established, conventions possess validity, due to the reinforcing psychological effects that influence human information processing. A related view is also represented by De Grauwe [2000]. He emphasizes that foreign exchange market participants are confronted with a high degree of uncertainty concerning the connection between macroeconomic fundamentals and exchange rate movements. This uncertainty, in his opinion, can be ascribed to the speculative dynamics of foreign exchange markets. Because of the high uncertainty about the impact of the underlying fundamentals on the exchange rate, the exchange rate movements themselves serve as a clue for the market participants' beliefs. Due to these beliefs the market participants start searching for those fundamentals that can explain the observable exchange rate movements (see De Grauwe [2000]).

The existence of conventions concerning the evaluation of exchange rates suggests that it is reasonable to extrapolate recent trends when making decisions in foreign exchange rates. Thus, a logical consequence of conventions as social heuristics is the application of trend-following trading rules in foreign exchange markets. In this context, trend-following trading rules by themselves can be interpreted as simple heuristics. As long as the current exchange rate trend is intact, it is reasonable for each market participant in foreign exchange markets to orientate their trading decisions on trend heuristics, as they take the prevailing convention into consideration. Thus, against the background of psychological evidence and the characteristic structure of foreign exchange markets, trend heuristics may be a reasonable response of market participants to the complexity of the decision environment in foreign exchange markets. Trend heuristics allow fast and frugal decision making by considering the prevailing conventions.

IV.4 Summary

The objective of behavioral economics is to provide a more realistic view of actual human behavior in economic contexts by underpinning economic analysis with psychological evidence. This task appears to be necessary, as there are many empirical and experimental examples for deviations from the economic rationality paradigm. The alternative concept of bounded rationality, which can be seen as the theoretical basis of behavioral economics, highlights the importance of considering actual human decision behavior. In particular, models of behavioral economics should consider the actual cognitive capabilities of human beings and the relevance of simple heuristics in decision making processes. In the context of foreign exchange markets, conventions and simple trend heuristics may play a decisive role. In the following, we try to asses the relevance of conventions and trend heuristics in foreign exchange markets. Thereby, we follow two different approaches. First, we use laboratory experiments to analyze expectation formation in the context of foreign exchange markets. Second, empirical methods are used to evaluate the nature of expectations. This procedure coincides with the suggestion of Reinhard Selten, who notes that

> "Behavior cannot be invented in the armchair. It has to be observed. Therefore, the development of theories of bounded rationality needs an empirical basis. Laboratory experimentation is an important source of empirical evidence. Of course, also field data are important, but they are more difficult to obtain and harder to interpret." (Selten [1998], p. 414)

Chapter V
Experimental and empirical evidence

In this chapter we deal with human expectation formation in experimental settings. The objective is to find evidence for the relevance of simple decision heuristics in general and evidence for the suggested trend heuristics based on conventions in particular. We assume that trend heuristics are frequently used in the context of foreign exchange markets and thus have an essential influence on expectation formation concerning future exchange rates. In general, the objective of experimental economics is to draw inferences from the observed behavior in controlled experimental settings on consistencies of human behavior in an economic context. Thus, while experimental economics always investigates the actual behavior of people, recourse to economic models or theories is not mandatory. The major advantages of using experimental methods are replicability and control (see Davis and Holt [1993]). Replicapility refers to the possibility of other researchers reproducing the experiments. Thus, experimental findings can be independently verified (see Stramer [1999]). Control is the capacity to manipulate the experimental settings in such a way that the observed behavior can be used to evaluate alternative theories. It should be noted that experimental methods should be seen as complements to empirical evidence rather than as substitutes (see Davis and Holt [1993]).

In the first experiment, we investigate the forecasting performance of novices and compare their forecasting behavior with that of professional exchange rate analysts. The results indicate that professional exchange rate analysts seem to be misled by fundamental considerations when forming their expectations. In contrast, novices orient their expectations on the course of the time series, which leads to better albeit not good results compared to professional forecasts. The environmental structure of the first experiment is characterized by its non-reflexivity, i.e. the expectation formation of individuals has no impact on the behavior of the considered time series. In contrast, the second experiment comprises the analysis of expectation formation in an experimental foreign exchange market. Thus, expectation formation is analyzed within a reflexive environment where the behavior of the other market participants exerts a crucial impact on the individual's behavior. In this context, the results show that market participant use trend extrapolating techniques when forming expectations. Furthermore, market participants show a tendency to coordinate their expectations in a Keynesian sense. As the experiments reveal that trend heuristics may play a decisive role in the process of expectation formation, we investigate afterwards the usefulness of technical analysis in foreign exchange markets. In this context, technical analysis can be seen as the practical implementation of the suggested trend heuristic. Gigerenzer and Todd [1999b] argue that the reliability of simple heuristics should be evaluated against their usefulness in the real world, so we are in particular interested in the profitability of simple technical trading rules in foreign exchange markets. Only if those simple trading rules are profitable on average is it reasonable to choose them.

V.1 A systematic comparison of professional exchange rate expectations with experimental expectations of novices

The first experiment deals with the investigation of human expectation formation in the context of foreign exchange markets. Basically, the literature distinguishes two different approaches with regard to the analysis of expectation formation. On the one hand, expectation formation is analyzed within empirical studies. These studies use survey expectations collected by suppliers of financial data (see e.g. section II.2.2). On the other hand, experimental studies deal with the expectation formation drawing on expectations collected from subjects in a laboratory. In this section, we consider both ways of analyzing human expectation formation and contrast both results against each other.

The experimental analysis of expectation formation goes back to the early 1960s. Fisher [1962] asked undergraduate students to forecast values of deflated wheat prices. Based on past observations of the time series, subjects had to predict its future values, period by period. In the majority of related studies, time series are generated artificially by linear autoregressive processes (see e.g. Becker [1967] and Hey [1994]) or pure random walks (see e.g. Dwyer et al. [1993] and Beckman and Downs [1997]). The main characteristic of these experiments is their experimental procedure: subjects just have to forecast a time series judgmentally, i.e. without relying on any statistical tools; in most studies the only available information is the past values of the time series. However, a few experimental designs include also additional sources of information, e.g. the output of time series analysis models, in order to observe behavior in settings closer to reality. For a detailed discussion of this topic we refer to Webby and O'Connor [1996], who reviewed the literature about judgmental and statistical time series forecasting. In reality, experts often predict future values of a time series judgmentally, when they are pressed for time, or when sufficient data or useful models are not available. Several empirical studies prove that in reality the practice of forecasting is dominated by judgmental approaches. Although statistical methods are widely used, forecasts usually are not solely based on the output of statistical forecast models, but are adjusted by their users judgmentally (see e.g. Dalrymple [1975] and [1987], Sanders and Manrodt [1994], Klassen and Flores [2001]).

A further interesting issue in analyzing expectations is the comparison of experts and novices. In a large number of mostly experimental studies the influence of expertise on the forecasting performance is analyzed. Comparisons of experts and novices repeatedly revealed that novices' forecasts are more accurate than forecasts of experts. Stael von Holstein [1972] compared stock price predictions of statisticians, students, university teachers, market experts and bankers. While the predictions of all subjects were astonishingly poor, bankers' forecasting performance was the worst. This result is confirmed in two related experiments conducted by Yates et al. [1991] and Önkal and Muradoglu [1994]. Their results indicate that students with prior investment experience (i.e. semi-experts) performed worse than inexperienced students in a stock price forecasting task. However, the use of semi-experts may lead to false conclusions. While these two studies were limited to students, Önkal and Muradoglu [1996] asked portfolio managers (experts), bank managers (semi-experts) and business students (novices) for probability forecasts under different task formats. They could not find general support for the inverted expertise effect.

The finding that experts perform worse than novices is usually denoted as the 'inverted expertise' effect. In principal, the inverted expertise effect can be explained as a by-product of experts' cue utilization (see Yates et al. [1991]). Due to the alleged larger background knowledge of experts, the judgment task of experts is more difficult than those of novices. It is assumed that experts use a larger number of cues compared to novices when making their forecasts. Consequently, the more difficult judgment task distorts experts' forecasting accuracy (see Muradoglu [2002]). The existence of an inverted expertise effect can thus be seen as implicit evidence for the 'less-is-more-effect' discussed in section IV.3.2.

In the first experiment, we compare point forecasts of the EUR/USD exchange rate surveyed from professional analysts and experimentally generated point forecasts of students for a simulated exchange rate time series. Our analysis focuses on the aggregated level of exchange rate forecasts, thus we compare average behavior and neglect the behavior of individuals. There exist many studies dealing with forecasting accuracy especially in the context of earnings forecasts of financial analysts (for a concise review we refer to Brown [1993]). However, in the context of foreign exchange rates, studies dealing with the forecasting accuracy are rather rare. The focus of studies related to exchange rate expectations deals rather with the question of whether expectations are rational (see e.g. Cavaglia et al. [1994]).

Overall, we investigate forecasts for three different forecasting horizons: one-step/month, three-step/months and six-step/months ahead forecasts. With our systematic analysis of professional exchange rate forecasts and judgmental forecasts of novices, we try to find similarities and differences in the human expectation formation that allow us to derive possible explanations for the poor forecasting accuracy of the professional exchange rate forecasters.

The remainder of section V.1 is as follows. The next section represents the design of the experiments. Afterwards, we examine the forecasting accuracy of professional exchange rate expectations and experimental expectations of novices. Section V.1.3 deals with the nature of both kinds of expectations. In this context, we evaluate the rational expectations hypothesis in the context of experimental expectations and explore different expectation formation mechanisms for both kinds of expectations. Finally, we discuss our results and provide a possible explanation for the poor forecasting performance of professional exchange rate expectations compared to the experimental expectations of novices.

V.1.1 Experimental design and data

Our comparison of the human forecasting behavior is based on exchange rate expectations of professional analysts and on exchange rate expectations of novices deduced from our experiments.[57] The data on professional exchange rate expectations correspond to the data used in section II.2.2. The experimental exchange rate expectations of novices stem from experiments conducted in 2003 at the Department of Economics, University of Wuerzburg, and at the Department of Statistics and Operations Research, University of Graz. Overall, three experiments were run with a total of 136 undergraduate students. The subjects' task included only the prediction of a time series, one-period (46 subjects), three-periods (45 subjects) and six-periods ahead (45 subjects). The group size is comparable to the samples of professional exchange rate analysts. Subjects were not allowed to participate in more than one experiment. The experimental procedures were identical in all three experiments. Only the forecasting

[57] The evaluation of the experiments introduced in this section is an extended analysis based on Leitner and Schmidt [2004].

horizon varied across the three experiments. Figure V-1 shows an English translation of the computer screen the participants were facing during the experiment. On the screen, the subjects are informed about their own past forecasts and the actual time series up to the time of forecasting. The instructions given to the participants in the experiments are found in Appendix E.

Figure V-1: Screenshot of the first experiment

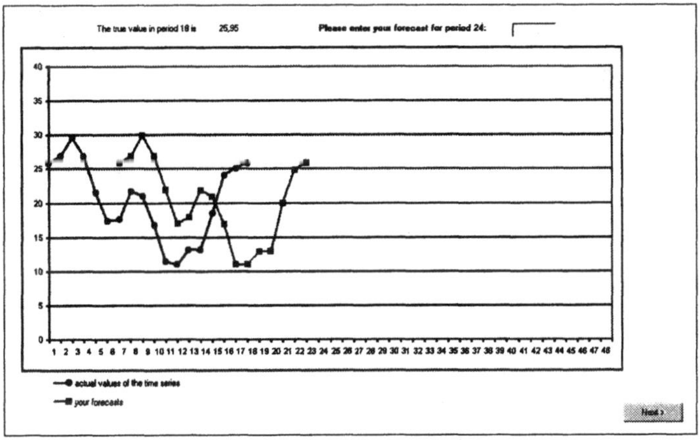

In order to rule out the possibility that the participants in the experiments knew the time series, we decided to simulate an artificial exchange rate time series.[58] We estimate the parameters of an AR(2) process for the actual, monthly EUR/USD exchange rate time series and use the estimated parameters for the simulation. All parameters in the regression are statistically significant and a high value of R^2 indicates that the AR(2) process approximates to the actual exchange rate time series quite well. Thus, the time series x_t presented to the subjects is a realization of an AR(2) process,

$$x_t = \alpha_0 + \alpha_1 x_{t-1} + \alpha_2 x_{t-2} + \varepsilon_t \qquad \text{(V-1)}$$

with the coefficients $\alpha_0 = 0.08$, $\alpha_1 = 1.19$, $\alpha_2 = -0.27$ and the error term ε_t being uniformly distributed in the interval [-5;5]. All values have two decimal places. The first value of the

[58] It should be noted that our results seem to be robust for the applied time series. In a related experiment, we analyze the expectation formation of novices in the context of the actual EUR/USD exchange rate time series. The results are qualitatively identical to the results that we present in this section (see Leitner and Schmidt [2005]).

experimental time series was presented to the subjects before they released their first forecast. No further history of past values was presented. The time series was unlabelled and the subjects were not given any contextual or background information. Overall, the subjects made 41 forecasts. Figure V-2 shows the time series x_t and the average forecasts of the three groups.

Figure V-2: Experimental time series and forecasts

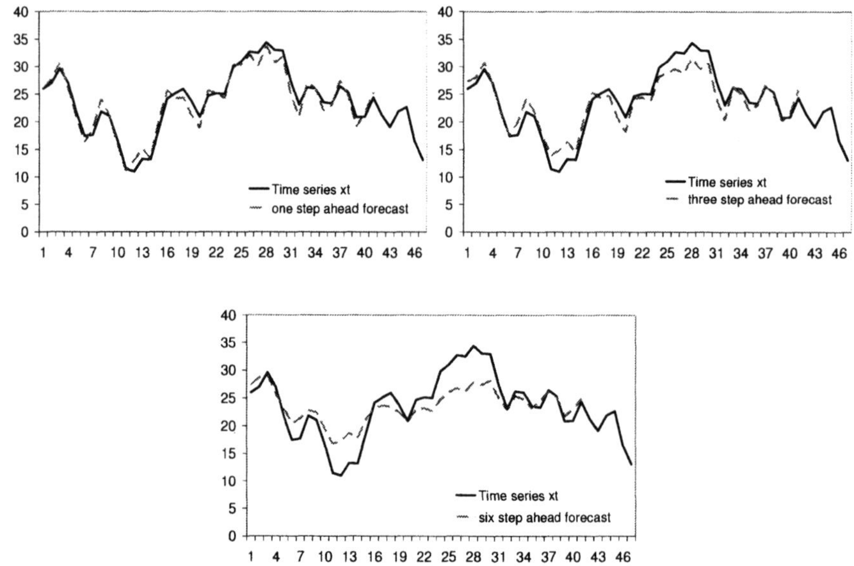

Note: The judgmental forecasts are shifted back to the time of forecast formation.

In order to provide appropriate incentives, participants in the experiments received payments according to their forecasting accuracy. The payments were based on absolute forecast errors, whereby the concrete form is given by

$$\sum_{t=2}^{42} \max\{a - f_t; 0\}, \tag{V-2}$$

where f_t denotes the individual forecast and a is a constant value. The constant a was set to 30 cents in the one-step and six-step task and was set to 40 cents for the three-step ahead forecasts, in order to assure equal payments.[59] The average payment across all three experiments was approximately 3 € for an average duration of about 20 minutes.

V.1.2 Forecasting exchange rates in real world and experiments – a comparison

The first objective of our analysis is to evaluate the forecasting accuracy of professional analysts and novices in the context of foreign exchange markets. The results of the forecasting accuracy serve us as a starting point for the further analysis of human expectation formation behavior.

V.1.2.1 Forecasting accuracy of professional exchange rate expectations

For an evaluation of the forecasting accuracy of professional analysts, we refer to the relative mean error (ME), the relative mean squared error (MSE) and the relative mean absolute error (MAE). In addition we use the Theil's inequality coefficient to directly compare the forecasting performance of professional forecasts with naïve random walk forecasts, i.e. no-change forecasts (see Moosa [2000] and Appendix D).

Table V–1 summarizes the results for the accuracy of professional exchange rate forecasts. As for all market forecasts the mean errors are positive, professional forecasters tend to overestimate the future development of the Euro against the US-dollar in the considered time period. In addition, the comparison of the accuracy of professional forecasts with naïve random walk forecasts reveals that, for all measures, the random walk is superior to professional forecasts. This result is also confirmed by the Theils's inequality coefficients, which are clearly above one for all market forecasts.

---

[59] We knew from the results of pilot studies that the three-step ahead forecasting task was more difficult than the others. The payment scheme had to be modified in order to equalize the financial rewards for all subjects.

Table V-1: Forecasting accuracy of professional exchange rate forecasts

	ME	MSE	MAE	Theil's U
1-month Reuters forecasts	0.0056 (0.0012)	0.0010 (0.0009)	0.0265 (0.0233)	1.0952
3-months Reuters forecasts	0.0219 (0.0021)	0.0047 (0.0034)	0.0591 (0.0494)	1.1710
3-months Consensus forecasts	0.0314 (0.0021)	0.0053 (0.0034)	0.0625 (0.0494)	1.2462
6-months Reuters forecasts	0.0492 (0.0059)	0.0096 (0.0053)	0.0860 (0.0609)	1.3465
6-months ZEW forecasts	0.0325 (0.0059)	0.0071 (0.0053)	0.0718 (0.0609)	1.1611

Note: In parenthesis are the measures for naïve random walk forecasts.

To evaluate whether the differences between the forecasting accuracy of market forecasts and naïve random walk forecasts are statistically significant, we perform three different statistical tests. In particular, we apply an asymptotic test as suggested by Diebold and Mariano [1995], the Wilcoxon's Signed-Rank test and the Morgan-Granger-Newbold test (see for a detailed discussion of these tests Diebold and Mariano [1995]).

Table V-2: Statistical tests for differences in professional exchange rate forecasts

	Asymptotic test	Wilcoxon's signed rank test	Morgan-Granger-Newbold test
1-month Reuters forecasts	1.7128 (0.0867)	-1.878 (0.060)	1.9599 (0.0557)
3-months Reuters forecasts	1.7795 (0.0752)	-2.154 (0.031)	3.600 (0.0008)
3-months Consensus forecasts	1.7143 (0.0865)	-2.434 (0.015)	3.7946 (0.0004)
6-months Reuters forecasts	1.5531 (0.1204)	-3.189 (0.001)	5.0572 (0.0000)
6-months ZEW forecasts	1.2489 (0.2117)	-2.198 (0.028)	3.1304 (0.0031)

Note: p-values are given in parenthesis.

Table V-2 summarizes the results of the statistical tests, comparing the forecasting accuracy of professional exchange rate forecasters and naïve random walk forecasts. The corresponding null hypothesis consists of no differences in the forecasting accuracy of both forecasts. The results indicate that the forecasting performance of professional exchange rate forecasters is statistically significantly worse than those of naïve random walk forecasts. Only for the six month forecasts of Reuters and ZEW does the asymptotic test indicate the same forecasting performance for both types of forecasts.

To investigate the usefulness of professional forecasts as direction of change forecasts we carry out a χ^2-test of independence (see Diebold and Lopez [1996] and Appendix B). The forecasting quality of professional forecasts is compared to a naïve coin flip. Table V-3 presents the results of the χ^2-test of independence. It shows that professional forecasts are poor predictors for the future direction of exchange rate changes. Only the six months forecasts of the ZEW Finanzmarkttest show a hit rate slightly above 50%. However, this result is not statistically significant.[60] For all other market forecasts the hit rate is well below 50%, implying that no result is statistically significant.

Table V-3: Professional exchange rate forecasts as direction-of-change forecasts

	Forecast ↑, Actual↑	Forecast ↑, Actual ↓	Forecast ↓, Actual ↑	Forecast ↓, Actual ↓	Hit rate
1-month Reuters forecasts	13	18	10	9	44.00% [0.5426]
3-months Reuters forecasts	21	25	0	2	47.92% [1.6232]
3-months Consensus forecasts	21	25	0	2	47.92% [1.6232]
6-months Reuters forecasts	21	23	0	1	48.89% [0.8949]
6-months ZEW forecasts	21	22	0	2	51.11% [1.8314]

Note: Test-statistics are given in brackets.

Altogether, the empirical results show that the forecasting accuracy of professional exchange rate forecasts is rather low. None of the professional exchange rate forecasts is able to beat a naïve random walk forecast, whereby this result is on the whole statistically significant. Furthermore, professional market forecasts even fail to predict the future direction of exchange rate changes.

V.1.2.2 Forecasting accuracy of experimental exchange rate expectations

In this section we analyze the forecasting accuracy of experimental exchange rate expectations. To make the experimental forecasts comparable to the professional exchange rate forecasts, we

[60] The 0.90 quantile of the χ^2 -distribution is 2.7055 (df = 1).

aggregated the individual forecasts of novices in each experiment by calculating their arithmetic mean. The accuracy of the experimentally generated average forecasts is analyzed by means of the above applied accuracy measures. Table V-4 presents the results for the forecasting accuracy of experimental forecasts. Whereas professional forecasters overestimate the time series, the negative values for mean errors indicate that the experimental forecasts underestimate the time series in all experiments. The mean squared errors in all experiments are lower than the corresponding values of the naïve random walk forecasts. Consequently, the Theil's inequality coefficient is below the critical value of one for all three forecast horizons. However, the experimental forecasts are not generally superior to naïve random walk forecasts, since the mean absolute errors of one- and three-step ahead forecasts are larger than the naïve benchmark. Only for the six-step ahead horizon do experimental forecasts perform better than the random walk by all error measures.

Table V-4: Accuracy of experimental exchange rate forecasts

	ME	MSE	MAE	Theil's U
1 step ahead forecasts	-0.0106 (-0.0056)	0.0202 (0.0213)	0.1121 (0.1094)	0.9725
3 step ahead forecasts	-0.0135 (0.0186)	0.0737 (0.0872)	0.2103 (0.2051)	0.9195
6 step ahead forecasts	-0.0064 (0.0306)	0.1112 (0.1729)	0.2735 (0.3154)	0.8018

Note: In parenthesis are the measures for naïve random walk forecasts.

To check the results for statistical significance, we also carried out the tests for differences in the forecast errors of experimental forecasts and naïve random walk forecasts. The results reveal that although the performance seems to be better at first glance it is not statistically significant (see Table V-5). Only for the six step ahead forecasts does the Morgan-Granger-Newbold test suggest a statistically significantly better performance of experimental forecasts.

Table V-5: Statistical tests for differences in experimental exchange rate forecasts

	Asymptotic test	Wilcoxon's signed rank test	Morgan-Granger-Newbold test
1 step ahead forecasts	-0.4479 (0.6542)	-0.175 (0.861)	-0.3950 (0.6949)
3 step ahead forecasts	-0.5877 (0.5568)	-1.341 (0.18)	-1.3472 (0.1855)
6 step ahead forecasts	-0.9993 (0.3177)	-0.253 (0.801)	-2.5166 (0.0160)

Note: P-values are given in parenthesis.

A possible explanation for the relatively good performance of experimental forecasts compared to professional forecasts may be found in the correct anticipation of the future direction of the time series. Table V-6 illustrates the quality of experimental forecasts as a direction of change forecasts. However, although the one step and six step ahead forecasts show a hit rate of over 50%, the results are statistically insignificant, so that it is fair to conclude that experimental forecast are not able to predict the future direction of the time series accurately.

Table V-6: Experimental exchange rate forecasts as direction-of-change forecasts

	Forecast ↑, Actual↑	Forecast ↑, Actual ↓	Forecast ↓, Actual ↑	Forecast ↓, Actual ↓	Hit rate
1 step ahead forecasts	13	18	10	9	56.1% [0.563]
3 step ahead forecasts	7	11	14	9	39.0% [1.953]
6 step ahead forecasts	7	10	10	14	51.2% [0.001]

Note: Test statistics are given in brackets.

V.1.2.3 Summary

The results for the forecasting accuracy of exchange rate expectations of professional analysts and experimental exchange rate expectations of novices have shown that professional exchange rate forecasts perform worse than forecasts of novices in an experimental environment. The forecasting accuracy of professional exchange rate forecasts is significantly worse than naïve random walk forecasts, whereas the forecasts of novices in our experimental setting perform at least as well as the naïve forecasts. This outcome is quite astonishing as, on the one hand, novices did not possess any contextual information concerning the evolution of the time series and, on the other hand, the forecasting performance of novices is evaluated over all 41 periods, although the subjects did not knew any history of the time series. Thus, the forecasting task is very difficult in the first periods.

V.1.3 The nature of expectations

An explanation for the differences in the forecasting accuracy of professional analysts and novices may be found in the nature of expectations. Possibly, professional analysts and novices show different characteristics with regard to their expectations that may be responsible for differences in their forecasting performance. With respect to expectations, the economic literature highlights the prominence of the concept of rational expectations. According to the rational expectations hypothesis, rational subjects produce unbiased forecasts by using all available information. In the following, we first evaluate the rational expectation hypothesis. Afterwards, we investigate different expectation formation mechanisms which may also help us to identify important differences between professional exchange rate forecasts and judgmental forecasts of novices.

V.1.3.1 Rationality of experimental expectations

Chapter II has highlighted the importance of the rational expectations hypothesis for the asset approach models to exchange rate determination. However, for the exchange rate expectations of professional analysts, the hypothesis of rational expectations has to be rejected (see the results of section II.2.2). The unbiasedness hypothesis is dismissed for all considered forecasting horizons; the orthogonality hypothesis and the hypothesis of no serial correlation in the expectations errors can only be maintained for the short-run (one month) expectations, but for the three and six months exchange rate expectations of professional analysts both hypotheses have to be rejected as well.

In the following, we analyze the rational expectation hypothesis for the experimental expectations of novices. For the empirical evaluation we use the three above-mentioned aspects of rational expectations (see section II.2.2). In contrast to the professional expectation errors, experimental expectation errors of novices fluctuate much more randomly and show no systematic biases (see Figure V-3). This visual impression is also confirmed by the scatter diagrams for the unbiasedness hypothesis of experimental expectations (see Figure V-4). Unlike the professional exchange rate expectations, the correlation between the expected change and the actual change appears to be clearly positive for the experimental expectations.

Figure V-3: Expectation errors for experimental exchange rate forecasts

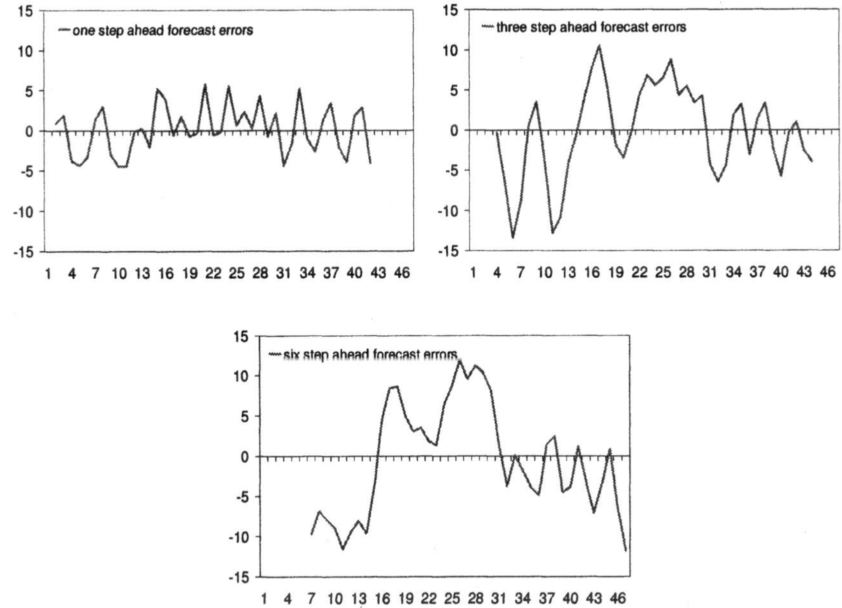

In order to analyze statistically whether experimental expectations are consistent with the unbiasedness hypothesis, we run the regression equation (II-46) for the experimental expectations of novices for all three forecasting horizons, applying the same two estimation approaches as in section II.2.2. The estimation results are summarized in Table V-7.

Figure V-4: Scatter diagrams for the unbiasedness hypothesis of experimental exchange rate forecasts

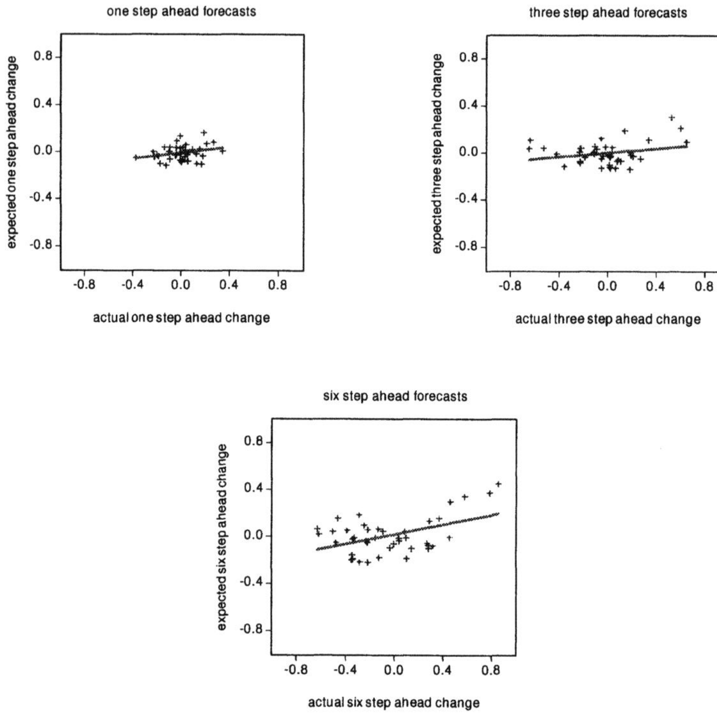

Table V-7: Test of unbiasedness for experimental exchange rate forecasts

	Estimation procedure	Q-statistic	α	H_0: $\alpha = 0$	β	H_0: $\beta = 1$	H_0: $\alpha = 0$, $\beta = 1$
1 step ahead	NW	--	-0.0004 (0.0225)	0.0003 [0.9853]	0.6535 (0.2465)	1.9757 [0.1678]	1.0071 [0.3746]
	ARMA	Q(12) = 0.692 Q(24) = 0.885	-0.0004 (0.0224)	0.0004 [0.9852]	0.6535 (0.3516)	0.9712 [0.3305]	0.4894 [0.6167]
3 step ahead	NW	--	-0.0209 (0.0622)	0.1131 [0.7384]	0.7464 (0.7516)	0.1139 [0.7376]	0.0745 [0.9282]
	ARMA	Q(12) = 0.465 Q(24) = 0.311	-0.0094 (0.0536)	0.0307 [0.8619]	-0.2900 (0.4088)	9.9558 [0.0033]	4.9934 [0.0124]
6 step ahead	NW	--	-0.0513 (0.0857)	0.3588 [0.5526]	1.1173 (0.5128)	0.0523 [0.8202]	0.2474 [0.7820]
	ARMA	Q(12) = 0.556 Q(24) = 0.872	-0.0561 (0.2490)	0.0508 [0.8231]	1.6574 (0.4156)	2.5028 [0.1232]	1.2621 [0.2964]

Notes: Standard errors are given in parentheses, p-values in brackets.
NW denotes the Newey & West estimation procedure, ARMA denotes the ARMA estimation procedure.

Overall, the results indicate that the unbiasedness hypothesis can largely be maintained for the experimental expectations (see Table V-7). All α coefficients do not depart significantly from zero. For the β coefficients the corresponding Wald-tests suggest that solely for the three step ahead experimental expectations must the null hypothesis of $\beta = 1$ be rejected in case of the ARMA estimation procedure. This conclusion is also supported by the F-statistics for the Wald-tests testing the joint hypothesis of , $\alpha = 0, \beta = 1$.

However, the empirical results for the evaluation of the orthogonality hypothesis in the context of experimental expectations reveal that the rational expectations hypothesis is not universally valid. Here, the results are somewhat mixed (see Table V-8). For the one step ahead expectations, the estimation procedure using Newey and West [1987] adjusted standard errors gives rise to a rejection of the orthogonality hypothesis. In contrast, an explicit modeling of the residuals shows that experimental expectations comply with the orthogonoality hypothesis. For the three steps ahead expectations, the results are inverted. Here the result for the Newey and West [1987] estimation procedure suggests that experimental expectations conform with the orthogonality hypothesis, whereas an explicit modeling of residuals leads to a rejection. For the six steps ahead expectations, orthogonality is consistently rejected.[61]

Table V-8: Orthogonality tests for experimental exchange rate forecasts

	Estimation procedure	Q-statistic	α	β_1	β_2	β_3	β_4	$H_0: \alpha = \beta_1 ... \beta_4 = 0$
1 step ahead	NW	--	0.2203 (0.4393)	0.1103 (0.2104)	-0.4173 (0.2922)	0.5240 (0.2201)	-0.2862 (0.1389)	3.4300 [0.0132]
	ARMA	Q(12) = 0.860 Q(24) = 0.917	0.2203 (0.3132)	0.1103 (0.1907)	-0.4173 (0.3118)	0.5240 (0.3137)	-0.2862 (0.1911)	0.6557 [0.6593]
3 step ahead	NW	--	0.7189 (0.8195)	-0.1135 (0.3440)	-0.2480 (0.5063)	0.3497 (0.6009)	-0.2178 (0.2693)	1.1252 [0.3664]
	ARMA	Q(12) = 0.668 Q(24) = 0.797	0.3094 (0.9815)	-0.5350 (0.2410)	0.5075 (0.1971)	0.1834 (0.1895)	-0.2545 (0.2207)	3.8429 [0.0086]
6 step ahead	NW	--	1.2999 (0.5304)	-0.1994 (0.4019)	-0.0833 (0.3869)	0.5674 (0.3678)	-0.7067 (0.3112)	4.0730 [0.0055]
	ARMA	Q(12) = 0.238 Q(24) = 0.432	1.0392 (1.1390)	-0.6655 (0.2127)	0.2537 (0.2324)	0.2049 (0.2313)	-0.1415 (0.2126)	2.9400 [0.0276]

Notes: Standard errors are given in parentheses, p-values in brackets.
NW denotes the Newey & West estimation procedure, ARMA denotes the ARMA estimation procedure.

[61] However, the results for the orthogonality hypothesis are quite sensitive to the size of lags included in the regression. For example, including eight lags in the regression leads to a rejection of the null of orthogonality.

Further evidence against the rational expectation hypothesis in the context of experimental expectations can be obtained from the verification of the hypothesis of serially uncorrelated expectation errors (see Equation II-49 and Table V-9). Although for the one step ahead expectations the F-statistic of the corresponding Wald-test suggests that the hypothesis of serially uncorrelated expectation errors cannot be rejected, the second order autocorrelation appears to be significant. For the three-step and six-step ahead expectations the hypothesis of serially uncorrelated expectation errors is resoundingly rejected.

Table V-9: Test for serial correlation in experimental exchange rate forecasts

	α	β_1	β_2	β_3	β_4	$H_0: \alpha = \beta_1 ... \beta_4 = 0$
1 step ahead	0.0073 (0.0239)	0.1944 (0.1762)	-0.2843 (0.1764)	0.2204 (0.1776)	-0.0769 (0.1790)	0.7804 [0.5712]
3 step ahead	0.0038 (0.0273)	1.1990 (0.1764)	-0.8982 (0.2629)	0.3716 (0.2617)	-0.0528 (0.1679)	11.4333 [0.0000]
6 step ahead	-0.0067 (0.0270)	1.3014 (0.1694)	-0.8943 (0.2642)	0.7394 (0.2807)	-0.3414 (0.1823)	20.7908 [0.0000]

Note: Standard errors are given in parentheses, p-values in brackets.

Overall, the rational expectation hypothesis must also be rejected for the experimental expectations. Although the experimental expectations seem to be unbiased predictors of future exchange rates, the hypothesis of orthogonality and serially uncorrelated expectation errors are largely rejected. Solely for the short-run, one step ahead experimental expectations can the rational expectation hypothesis be approximately maintained. Overall, our results agree with evidence reported in previous experimental studies. Various researchers find little support for the rational expectation hypothesis in the context of experimental data (see e.g. Schmalensee [1976], Garner [1982], Brennscheidt [1993] and Hey [1994]). The inadequacy of rational expectation hypothesis holds true especially for individual expectations.

Table V-10 summarizes the results for the rational expectations hypothesis in the context of experimental forecasts and compares them with the results for the professional exchange rate expectations (see section II.2.2). The results reveal that the rational expectation hypothesis is by and large rejected for both kinds of expectations. However, the results show interesting differences in the characteristics of professional exchange rate forecasts and experimental forecasts of novices. Whereas the unbiasedness hypothesis has to be clearly rejected for the professional exchange rate forecasts, the experimental forecasts of novices seem to be unbiased. According to the results of testing for serial correlation in forecast errors and orthogonality, we find no meaningful differences between professional forecasts and forecasts of novices. Thus, the main difference between the professional and experimental expectations consists in the fact that professional exchange rate expectations appear to be merely a biased predictor of future exchange rates, while experimental expectations of novices seem to be unbiased.

Table V-10: Summary of the results for the rational expectation hypothesis

	Professional exchange rate expectations	**Experimental exchange rate expectations**
Unbiasedness	Rejection	Acceptance
Orthogonality	▪ Short-run: acceptance ▪ Medium/long-run: rejection	▪ Short-run: acceptance ▪ Medium/long-run: rejection
Serially uncorrelated expectations errors	▪ Short-run: acceptance ▪ Medium/long-run: rejection	▪ Short-run: acceptance ▪ Medium/long-run: rejection

V.1.3.2 A common bias in expectation formation

The results of section V.1.3.1 have shown that the rational expectation hypothesis is rejected for professional exchange expectations as well as experimental exchange rate expectations. In our view, an important cause for the rejection of the rational expectation hypothesis is found in a very strong impact of the current exchange rate development on expectations concerning future exchange rates (see Bofinger and Schmidt [2003]). This finding is illustrated by Figure V-5 and Figure V-6 which show that overall expectations move very much in line with the development of the actual exchange rate. Thus, if the current exchange rate depreciates, analysts and participants in the experiments tend to reduce their forecasts for all horizons by about the current depreciation rate. Andres and Spiwoks [1999] denote this regularity as a topically orientated trend adjustment behavior (TOTA) which has the effect that expectations can lose at worst their future-oriented characteristic.

Figure V-5: TOTA behavior of professional exchange rate forecasts

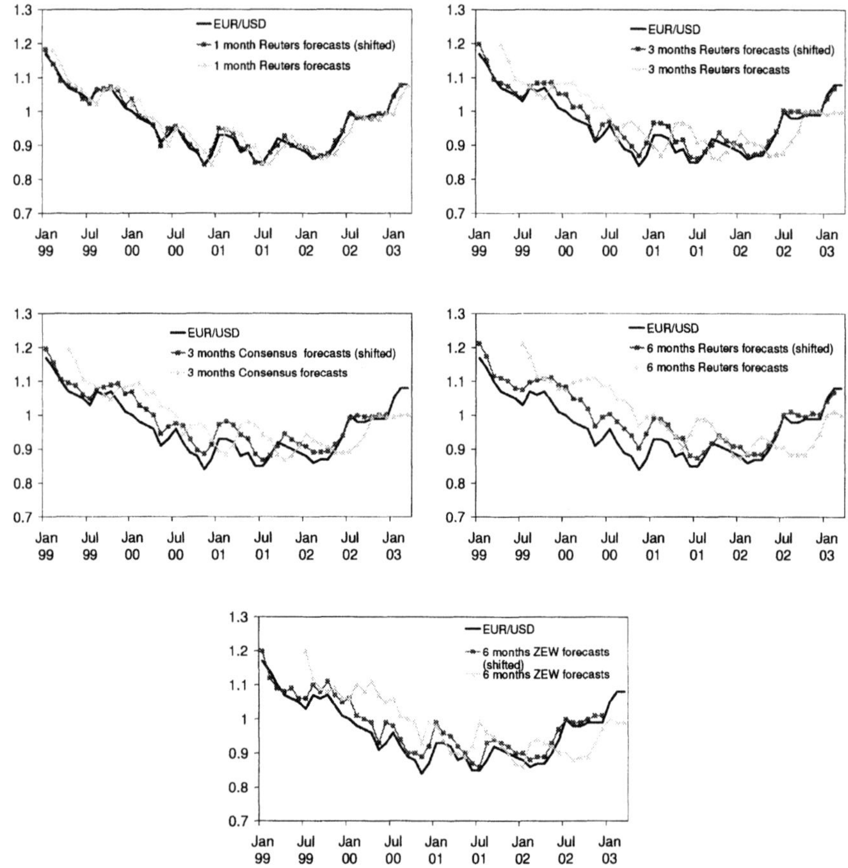

Figure V-6: TOTA behavior of experimental exchange rate forecasts

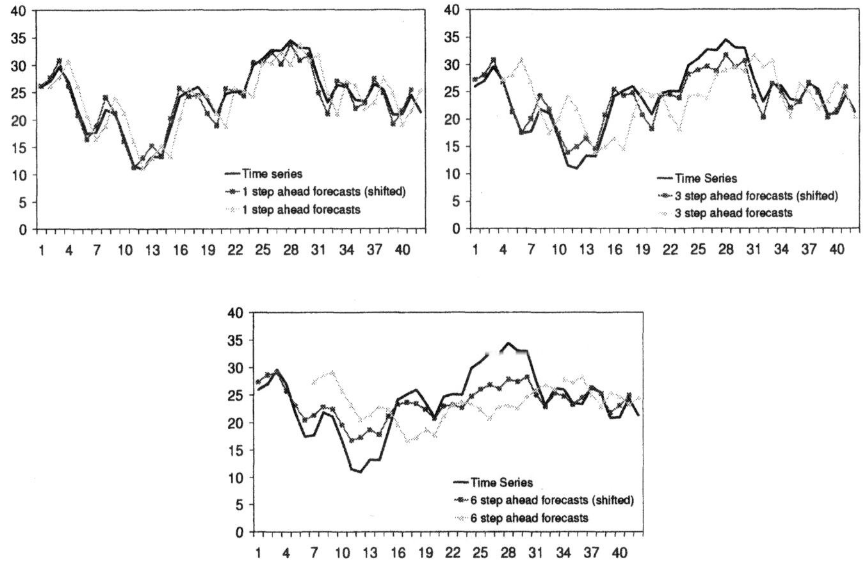

For an evaluation of the TOTA behavior Andres and Spiwoks [1999] recommend the following coefficient:

$$TOTA\text{-}coeffcient = \frac{R^2_{forecast,\ actual}}{R^2_{forecast,\ actual-h}} \qquad \text{(V-3)}$$

where

$$R^2_{forecast;\ actual} = \frac{\left[\frac{1}{T-h}\sum_{t=h+1}^{T}\left(\hat{x}_t - \frac{1}{T-h}\sum_{t=h+1}^{T}\hat{x}_t\right)\left(x_t - \frac{1}{T-h}\sum_{t=h+1}^{T}x_t\right)\right]^2}{\left[\frac{1}{T-h}\sum_{t=h+1}^{T}\left(\hat{x}_t - \frac{1}{T-h}\sum_{t=h+1}^{T}\hat{x}_t\right)^2\right]\left[\frac{1}{T-h}\sum_{t=h+1}^{T}\left(x_t - \frac{1}{T-h}\sum_{t=h+1}^{T}x_t\right)^2\right]}$$

is the coefficient of determination for the actual exchange rate and the corresponding market expectations and

$$R^2_{forecast;\,actual-h} = \frac{\left[\frac{1}{T-h}\sum_{t=h+1}^{T}\left(\hat{x}_t - \frac{1}{T-h}\sum_{t=h+1}^{T}\hat{x}_t\right)\left(x_{t-h} - \frac{1}{T-h}\sum_{t=h+1}^{T}x_{t-h}\right)\right]^2}{\left[\frac{1}{T-h}\sum_{t=h+1}^{T}\left(\hat{x}_t - \frac{1}{T-h}\sum_{t=h+1}^{T}\hat{x}_t\right)^2\right]\left[\frac{1}{T-h}\sum_{t=h+1}^{T}\left(x_{t-h} - \frac{1}{T-h}\sum_{t=h+1}^{T}x_{t-h}\right)^2\right]}$$

is the coefficient of determination for the market expectations and the actual exchange rate at the time of the expectation formation. Values of the TOTA-coefficient smaller than one indicate that the h-months/h-step ahead expectations, shifted back for h months/steps to its creation time, exhibit a higher correlation with the actual exchange rate than the expectations for this time. Table V-11 summarizes the TOTA coefficients for the professional and experimental expectations covering all forecast horizons. Obviously, all TOTA coefficients are well below one, so that the professional and experimental expectations exhibit a higher correlation with the current exchange rate at the time of expectation formation than with the exchange rate for which the expectations were made.

Table V-11: TOTA coefficients

		R^2 (forecast, actual exchange rate)	R^2 (forecast, actual exchange rate – h)	TOTA
Professional exchange rate forecasts	1 month Reuters	0.8639	0.9837	0.8781
	3 months Reuters	0.4694	0.9683	0.4847
	3 months Consensus	0.4386	0.9507	0.4613
	6 months Reuters	0.2196	0.9340	0.2351
	6 months ZEW	0.2593	0.9598	0.2702
Experimental exchange rate forecasts	1 step ahead	0.7345	0.9488	0.7741
	3 step ahead	0.1674	0.9131	0.1833
	6 step ahead	0.0034	0.8498	0.0041

An important explanation for the observed characteristic of professional and experimental expectations can be deduced from the perspective of behavioral economics. Chapter IV has highlighted the human limitations in the acquisition and the processing of information. Particularly in very difficult decision problems, economic agents try to reduce the complexity of the world by using simple rules of thumb or "heuristics", which allow quick and efficient decisions even under high uncertainty. As there is no doubt that forecasting exchange rates is a very complex and difficult task, the relevance of heuristics is beyond all question. On the one hand, no reliable macroeconomic models are available, so that it is unclear which fundamental variables are relevant at all and what concrete impact they have on future exchange rates. On the other hand, the speculative nature of the foreign exchange market requires that an individual forecaster take into account the forecasts of other market participants who are confronted with the same problem. This problem was addressed already by Keynes [1936].

A heuristic, which is, in the context of topically oriented trend adjustment behavior, of particular importance is the anchoring and adjustment heuristic. It implies that quantitative judgments are often biased towards an initial anchor, which has come to the mind of the decision maker implicitly or explicitly but which is often completely irrelevant for the decision problem. The degree of anchoring effects depends on the degree of uncertainty about the decision process. Jacowitz and Kahneman [1995] demonstrate that the more uncertain judges were about their judgments, the more the numeric estimates were assimilated to the provided anchor (see Jacowitz and Kahneman [1995] and Mussweiler and Strack [2000]). In financial markets the current price of an asset can be regarded as such an anchor (see von Nitzsch [2002]). So, foreign exchange market participants tend to use the current exchange rate as a constitutional anchor when forming their expectations and adjust their expectations only minimally due to future expectations about other relevant factors. Interestingly, this result holds true for both kinds of expectation – professional and experimental. Thus it is reasonable to conclude that the topically oriented trend adjustment behavior appears to be a universally valid phenomenon of human expectation formation in financial markets. This conclusion can be confirmed by the results of other empirical analyses related to this topic. Spiwoks [2003b] analyzes the accuracy of German banks interest rate forecasts and finds that all forecasts are characterized by a topically oriented trend adjustment behavior. Furthermore, Spiwoks [2003a] investigated the accuracy of exchange rate, bond and stock market forecasts of the Zentrum für Europäische Wirtschaftsforschung (ZEW). His results indicate that across all three different financial markets the topically oriented trend adjustment behavior is of relevance in the expectation formation. By the way, already Keynes [1936] illustrates a mechanism of human expectation formation in the context of financial markets that is very similar to the above-mentioned anchoring and adjustment heuristics:

> "It would be foolish, in forming our expectations, to attach great weight to matters which are very uncertain. It is reasonable, therefore, to be guided to a considerable degree by the facts about which we feel somewhat confident, even though they may be less decisively relevant to the issue than other facts about which our knowledge is vague and scanty, for this reason the facts of the existing situation enter, in a sense disproportionately, into the formation of our long-term expectations; our usual practice being to take the existing situation and to project it into the future, modified only to the

extent that we have more or less definite reasons for expecting a change." (Keynes [1936], p.148)

Overall, the results of our comparison of professional real world expectations and judgmental expectations in an experimental setting have revealed that topically oriented trend adjustment behavior (TOTA) is a quite robust phenomenon of human expectation formation. This is also confirmed by the related empirical work, which shows that TOTA behavior is a phenomenon common to many financial markets. Thus, the anchoring heuristic, since it provides a reasonable explanation for the TOTA behavior, plays a major role in the human expectation formation process. However, the TOTA behavior cannot serve as a reasonable explanation for the different forecasting performances of professional and experimental expectations, as it seems to be a generally prevailing phenomenon of human expectation formation.

V.1.3.3 Different expectation formation mechanisms?

A possible explanation for the differences in the forecasting performance of professional forecasters and novices in our experimental setting can be found in different expectation formation mechanisms. Frankel and Froot [1987] suggest the following general framework for illustrating different expectation formation mechanisms. Equation (V-4) describes the expected future exchange rate as a weighted average of the current exchange rate (s_t) and some other relevant factor (x_t) that affects the expectation formation of market participants:

$$E_t s_{t+h} = \gamma x_t + (1-\gamma) s_t \,, \qquad \text{(V-4)}$$

where γ represents the weight given to the other relevant factors and $(1-\gamma)$ is the weight of the current exchange rate (see Frankel and Froot [1987]). Usually, in the relevant literature the factor x_t is substituted by either (a) lagged exchange rates, or (b) lagged expectations or (c) some notion of a long-run equilibrium level of the exchange rate. In the first case, the expectations are called extrapolative expectations, as the expected exchange rate movement for the next period is given by the past exchange rate movement. This can be illustrated by substituting x_t with a past realization of the exchange rate (s_{t-h}):

$$E_t s_{t+h} = \gamma s_{t-h} + (1-\gamma) s_t \qquad \text{(V-5)}$$

or

$$E_t s_{t+h} - s_t = \gamma (s_{t-h} - s_t) \,. \qquad \text{(V-6)}$$

Crucial for the interpretation of this expectation formation mechanism is the sign of the coefficient γ. If $\gamma > 0$, expectations are stabilizing in the sense that a recent movement in the exchange rate gives rise to the expectation of a reverse change in the future. Where $\gamma < 0$, expectations are called bandwagon expectations. Here, forecasters expect that current exchange rate movements will recur in the future. For $\gamma = 0$, forecasters have static expectations, i.e. they expect that future exchange rate changes are independent from past exchange rate changes. Thus, they believe exchange rates follow a random walk process.

If the factor x_t is replaced by lagged expectations, the expectations are denoted as adaptive expectations. According to the adaptive expectations scheme, it is assumed that market participants form their expectation of future exchange rates as a weighted average of the current and the lagged expected exchange rate (see Frankel and Froot [1987], p. 142):

$$E_t s_{t+h} = \gamma E_{t-h} s_t + (1-\gamma) s_t \tag{V-7}$$

or

$$E_t s_{t+h} - s_t = \gamma (E_{t-h} s_t - s_t) \tag{V-8}$$

According to this definition of adaptive expectations, values of $\gamma > 0$ imply that exchange rate expectations are stabilizing in the sense that an unanticipated appreciation of the exchange rate leads to an expected depreciation of the exchange rate. If $\gamma < 0$, exchange rate expectations can be interpreted as destabilizing, as an unanticipated appreciation of the exchange rate leads to continued expected appreciation (see Takagi [1991]). For $\gamma = 0$, expectations are static.

Considering long-run equilibrium exchange rates as the relevant factor x_t leads to the regressive expectation mechanism:

$$E_t s_{t+h} = \gamma \bar{s}_t + (1-\gamma) s_t \tag{V-9}$$

or

$$E_t s_{t+h} - s_t = \gamma (\bar{s}_t - s_t) \tag{V-10}$$

where $\bar{s}_t$ denotes some notion of the equilibrium exchange rate. Equation (V-10) shows that according to this expectation scheme the actual exchange rate is assumed to regress toward the equilibrium exchange rate in the case that $\gamma > 0$. If $\gamma < 0$ market participants expect that the deviation of the current exchange rate from its equilibrium value will deepen in the future. Again, $\gamma = 0$ correspond to static expectations.

In the following we evaluate the three different expectation formation mechanisms for the professional exchange rate expectations as well as for the experimental exchange rate expectations. Implicitly our null hypothesis is always that expectations are static, i.e. $\gamma = 0$, so that market participants would believe that exchange rates follow a random walk.

V.1.3.3.1 Extrapolative expectations

According to extrapolative expectations, the expectation formation is solely affected by past realizations of the exchange rate. Thus, the expected future exchange rate change is a function of past exchange rate changes. The regression equation is given as follows:

$$E_t s_{t+h} - s_t = \alpha + \beta\left(s_{t-h} - s_t\right) + \varepsilon_{t+h}\,. \qquad \text{(V-11)}$$

Figure V-7 displays the scatter diagrams of the expected h-month exchange rate change versus the previous h-month change. Obviously, past exchange rate changes have a substantial impact on the expected future exchange rate changes. The positive slope of the regression line indicates that professional exchange rate forecasters usually expect a reversal of past exchange rate movements in the future. Consequently professional exchange rate expectations can be classified as stabilizing in the above mentioned sense.

Figure V-7: Expected versus previous exchange rate changes (professional exchange rate forecasts)

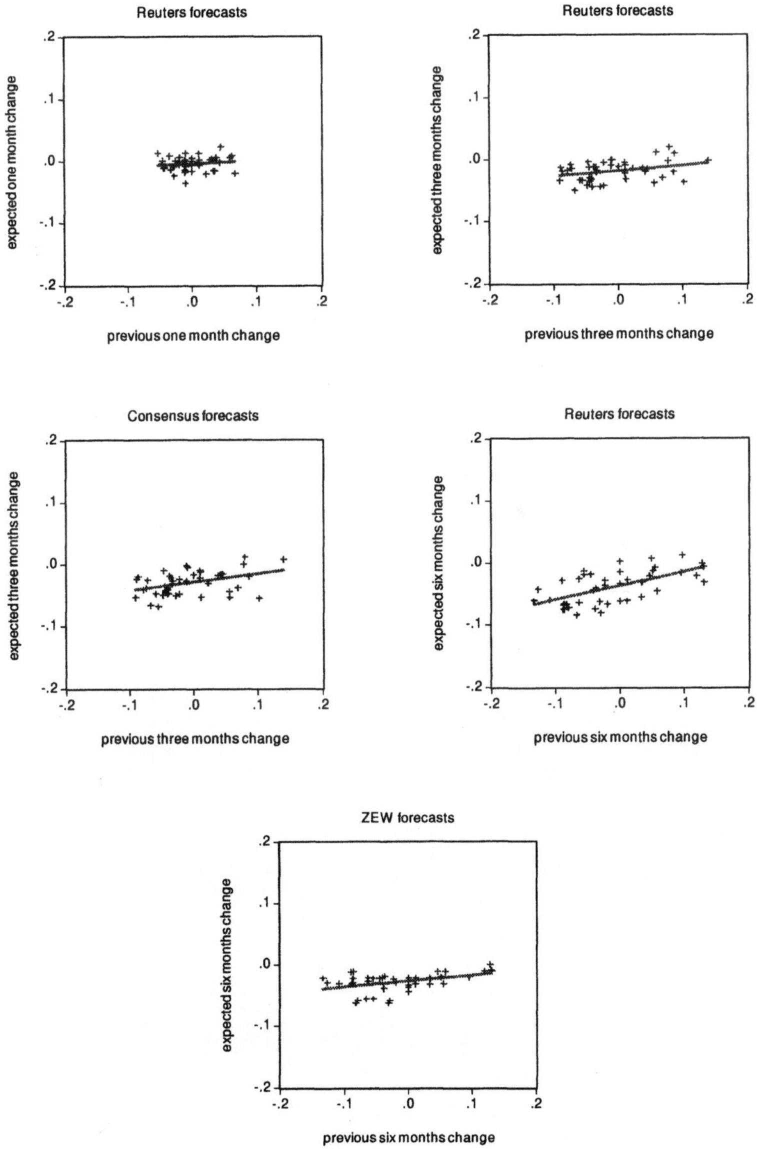

The visual evidence is also confirmed by empirical analysis. For this purpose we run the regression equation (V-11) for all available professional exchange rate forecasts, including previous one month exchange rate changes as well as past exchange rate changes over the applied forecasting horizon. Again, we run all regressions twice, using Newey and West [1987] estimation procedure as well as an explicit modeling of the correlation structure of residuals. The estimation results are summarized in Table V-12. The results show that the professional exchange rate expectations appear to be static for the 1 month forecasting horizon. Both β coefficients do not deviate significantly from zeros. However, the null hypothesis of $\alpha = \beta = 0$ is rejected for the AR regression. For the three and six month forecasting horizon, the estimation results indicate that the extrapolative expectation mechanism is valid. The positive values of the β coefficients suggest that the professional exchange rate expectations are stabilizing in the sense that recent changes in the exchange rate cause expectations of a reverse change in the future. These results are largely in line with the results of other empirical evaluations of survey data. Takagi [1991] summarizes the existing literature up to 1990 and reports that for the long-run horizons the empirical evidence indicates stabilizing exchange rate expectations. Beng and Siong [1993] analyzes survey data on the expectations of the Singapore/US dollar exchange rate and find that expectations for the one month till 12 month forecasting horizon are all stabilizing. Similar results are provided by Cavaglia et al. [1993] who also arrive at positive β coefficients for all considered forecasting horizons for professional exchange rate forecasts.

Table V-12: Tests for extrapolative expectations of professional exchange rate forecasts

Expectation horizon		Estimation procedure	Q-statistic	α	β	H_0: α=β = 0
1 month Reuters	$s_t - s_{t-1}$	NW	--	0.0041 (0.0020)	0.0477 (0.0678)	3.2025 [0.0497]
		ARMA	Q(12) = 0.734 Q(24) = 0.053	0.0047 (0.0023)	0.0428 (0.0540)	2.2697 [0.1156]
3 month Reuters	$s_t - s_{t-3}$	NW	--	0.0183 (0.0035)	0.0889 (0.0512)	20.4610 [0.0000]
		ARMA	Q(12) = 0.499 Q(24) = 0.228	0.0184 (0.0042)	0.0794 (0.0514)	10.4924 [0.0002]
	$s_t - s_{t-1}$	NW	--	0.0187 (0.0033)	0.2311 (0.1072)	31.7053 [0.0000]
		ARMA	Q(12) = 0.416 Q(24) = 0.060	0.0186 (0.0042)	0.1527 (0.0622)	12.5693 [0.0001]
3 month Consensus	$s_t - s_{t-3}$	NW	--	0.0284 (0.0044)	0.1355 (0.0664)	4.1630 [0.0475]
		ARMA	Q(12) = 0.724 Q(24) = 0.454	0.0289 (0.0055)	0.1325 (0.0590)	5.0384 [0.0303]
	$s_t - s_{t-1}$	NW	--	0.0288 (0.0041)	0.3679 (0.1187)	9.6079 [0.0034]
		ARMA	Q(12) = 0.463 Q(24) = 0.147	0.0292 (0.0060)	0.2981 (0.0559)	28.4881 [0.0000]
6 month Reuters	$s_t - s_{t-6}$	NW	--	0.0368 (0.0050)	0.2260 (0.0491)	32.8091 [0.0000]
		ARMA	Q(12) = 0.398 Q(24) = 0.522	0.0336 (0.0153)	0.0844 (0.0613)	2.8902 [0.0672]
	$s_t - s_{t-1}$	NW	--	0.0396 (0.0061)	0.4423 (0.1514)	42.8671 [0.00009
		ARMA	Q(12) = 0.176 Q(24) = 0.067	0.0274 (0.0258)	0.1919 (0.0494)	8.0676 [0.0011]
6 month ZEW	$s_t - s_{t-6}$	NW	--	0.0266 (0.0023)	0.0933 (0.0247)	14.2285 [0.0005]
		ARMA	Q(12) = 0.323 Q(24) = 0.501	0.0266 (0.0022)	0.0933 (0.0312)	8.9678 [0.0047]
	$s_t - s_{t-1}$	NW	--	0.0281 (0.0032)	-0.0608 (0.0890)	0.4665 [0.4985]
		ARMA	Q(12) = 0.180 Q(24) = 0.072	0.0281 (0.0024)	-0.0608 (0.0822)	0.5462 [0.4642]

Notes: Standard errors are given in parentheses, p-values in brackets.
NW denotes the Newey & West estimation procedure, ARMA denotes the ARMA estimation procedure.

In contrast to the professional exchange rate expectations, the results for the experimental expectations of the participants in the experiments are not so clear cut. The scatter diagrams of the expected *h*-step change versus the previous *h*-step change indicate that, for the one step ahead forecasts, a negative slope coefficient is found, so that participants in the experiments form bandwagon expectations over the short forecasting horizon (see Figure V-8). However, for the three-step and six-step ahead forecast the slope coefficients are again positive, which implies that long-run expectations are expected to be stabilizing.

Figure V-8: Expected versus previous change in the experimental time series

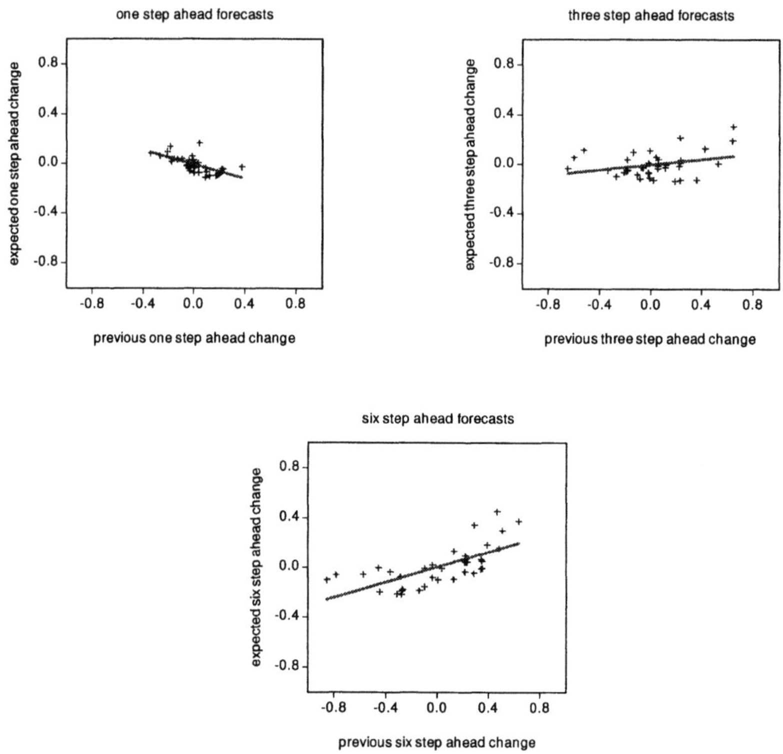

Table V-13 shows the results for estimating equation (V-11) for the experimental expectations. Again, we include previous one–step ahead changes as well as past changes over the applied forecasting horizon in the regression analysis and perform each regression equation twice, using the Newey and West [1987] estimation procedure as well as an explicit modelling of residuals' autocorrelation structure. As expected from the visual evidence, the one-step ahead experimental exchange rate expectations reveal a tendency to extrapolate past trend changes into the future. The related β coefficients are all significantly smaller than zero and the Wald test suggest a rejection of the null hypothesis of static expectations. For the three step ahead expectations the results indicate that they are static. Solely for the ARMA regression considering the previous one step change is the β significantly negative, indicating trend-extrapolative expectations. With regard to the six step ahead experimental exchange rate expectations, the results show a tendency that these expectations are stabilizing, although considering previous one-step ahead changes indicate static expectations for the Newey and West [1987] estimation procedure.

Table V-13: Tests for extrapolative expectations of experimental exchange rate forecasts

		Estimation procedure	Q-statistic	α	β	H_0: α=β = 0
1 step ahead	$s_t - s_{t-1}$	NW	--	-0.0069 (0.0126)	-0.2864 (0.0495)	22.3759 [0.0000]
		ARMA	Q(12) = 0.935 Q(24) = 0.998	-0.0094 (0.0219)	-0.3585 (0.0370)	47.0916 [0.0000]
3 step ahead	$s_t - s_{t-3}$	NW	--	-0.0050 (0.0266)	0.1086 (0.0960)	0.7678 [0.4715]
		ARMA	Q(12) = 0.719 Q(24) = 0.678	0.0037 (0.0439)	0.0683 (0.0603)	0.6428 [0.5325]
	$s_t - s_{t-1}$	NW	--	-0.0025 (0.0287)	-0.1171 (0.1372)	0.3999 [0.6733]
		ARMA	Q(12) = 0.708 Q(24) = 0.844	-0.0055 (0.0457)	-0.2212 (0.0511)	9.3670 [0.0006]
6 step ahead	$s_t - s_{t-6}$	NW	--	0.0035 (0.0375)	0.3055 (0.1105)	3.8264 [0.0320]
		ARMA	Q(12) = 0.359 Q(24) = 0.750	0.0105 (0.0647)	0.2115 (0.0535)	7.8135 [0.0019]
	$s_t - s_{t-1}$	NW	--	0.0076 (0.0518)	0.2036 (0.2262)	0.4048 [0.6704]
		ARMA	Q(12) = 0.835 Q(24) = 0.939	0.0039 (0.0780)	0.1682 (0.0605)	3.8651 [0.0325]

Notes: Standard errors are given in parentheses, p-values in brackets.
NW denotes the Newey & West estimation procedure, ARMA denotes the ARMA estimation procedure.

Overall, we find interesting differences concerning the impact of past realizations on future expected movements between professional and experimental expectations for the extrapolative expectation mechanism (see Table V-14). Whereas professional exchange rate forecasters predominantly expect that current exchange rate movements will be reversed in the future, the experimental expectations of the participants in the experiments exhibit a structure which is consistent with the phenomenon of mean reversion, which is often observed in financial time series (see Cutler et al. [1990]). The results coincide with the results of De Bondt [1993] who studied probabilistic forecasts of students in several experimental settings. He found evidence that novices expect a continuation of past trends, while experts expect a reversal.

Table V-14: Summary of the results for the extrapolative expectations mechanism

	Professional exchange rate expectations	Experimental exchange rate expectations
Short-run	Static expectations	Destabilizing expectations
Medium-run	Stabilizing expectations	Static expectations
Long-run	Stabilizing expectations	Stabilizing expectations

V.1.3.3.2 Adaptive expectations

The next expectation formation mechanism is the adaptive expectations scheme. The corresponding regression equation is given by

$$E_t s_{t+h} - s_t = \alpha + \beta\left(E_{t-h} s_t - s_t\right) + \varepsilon_{t+h}. \tag{V-12}$$

Table V-15 summarizes the results for testing the adaptive expectation scheme for the professional exchange rate expectations. The results reveal that for all regressions the β coefficient is positive, so that the professional exchange rate expectations appear to be stabilizing (i.e. an unanticipated appreciation leads to an expected depreciation). However, the results for the one month professional expectations are statistically insignificant, so that they have to be evaluated as static. For the three and six month expectations all β coefficients are statistically significant. Thus the adaptive expectation formation scheme is accepted. Our results largely conform to those in the literature. Takagi [1991] reports that for the long-run expectations of three to twelve months the sign of β was generally positive. Beng and Siong [1993] also find consistently positive β coefficients for forecasting horizons of one to twelve months. Cavaglia et al. [1993] analyze the various exchange rate expectations over forecasting horizons of three to twelve months and report that almost all expectations coincide with stabilizing adaptive expectations. Similar results are provided by Bénassy-Quéré et al. [1999] by analyzing panel data for DM/USD, YEN/USD and GBP/USD expectations.

Table V-15: Test for adaptive expectations of professional exchange rate forecasts

	Estimation procedure	Q-Statistic	α	β	H_0: α=β = 0
1 month Reuters	NW	--	0.0039 (0.0019)	0.0570 (0.0552)	3.7463 [0.0309]
	ARMA	Q(12) = 0.732 Q(24) = 0.051	0.0045 (0.0022)	0.0448 (0.0539)	2.5630 [0.0888]
3 month Reuters	NW	--	0.0164 (0.0036)	0.0970 (0.0378)	24.1754 [0.0000]
	ARMA	Q(12) = 0.574 Q(24) = 0.343	0.0167 (0.0041)	0.0906 (0.0467)	12.4426 [0.0001]
3 month Consensus	NW	--	0.0240 (0.0047)	0.1448 (0.0437)	10.9586 [0.0019]
	ARMA	Q(12) = 812 Q(24) = 551	0.0246 (0.0054)	0.1423 (0.0567)	6.3057 [0.0161]
6 month Reuters	NW	--	0.0278 (0.0045)	0.2141 (0.0405)	37.4407 [0.0000]
	ARMA	Q(12) = 0.538 Q(24) = 0.784	0.0302 (0.0112)	0.1234 (0.0622)	6.0396 [0.0051]
6 month ZEW	NW	--	0.0245 (0.0023)	0.0824 (0.0257)	10.2976 [0.0026]
	ARMA	Q(12) = 0.195 Q(24) = 0.311	0.0245 (0.0025)	0.0824 (0.0299)	7.5667 [0.0089]

Notes: Standard errors are given in parentheses, p-values in brackets.
NW denotes the Newey & West estimation procedure, ARMA denotes the ARMA estimation procedure.

The estimation results for the experimental expectations of novices are summarized in Table V-16. In contrast to the results for the professional exchange rate expectations, the behavior of experimental expectations seems to change over the different forecasting horizons. For the one step ahead expectations, the results indicate that the β coefficients are significantly negative. Consequently, the short-run expectations can be assessed as destabilizing in the above-mentioned sense. In contrast, the expectations for the six step ahead horizon appear to be stabilizing, as all β coefficients are statistically significantly positive. For the three step ahead experimental expectations the results are mixed. The Newey and West [1987] estimation procedure leads to a significant positive β coefficient, but the explicit modeling of the autocorrelation structure of residuals result in static expectations.

Table V-16: Tests for adaptive expectations of experimental exchange rate forecasts

	Estimation procedure	Q-Statistic	α	β	H_0: α=β = 0
1 step ahead	NW	--	-0.0089 (0.0146)	-0.2298 (0.0446)	15.2727 [0.0000]
	ARMA	Q(12) = 0.094 Q(24) = 0.304	-0.0118 (0.0277)	-0.3282 (0.0352)	43.5141 [0.0000]
3 step ahead	NW	--	-0.0060 (0.0224)	0.1786 (0.0807)	3.0066 [0.0620]
	ARMA	Q(12) = 0.715 Q(24) = 0.679	0.0032 (0.0381)	0.0792 (0.0586)	0.9130 [0.4115]
6 step ahead	NW	--	-0.0013 (0.0179)	0.4790 (0.0614)	30.8015 [0.0000]
	ARMA	Q(12) = 0.482 Q(24) = 0.923	0.0020 (0.0373)	0.3910 (0.0519)	28.5221 [0.0000]

Notes: Standard errors are given in parentheses, p-values in brackets.
NW denotes the Newey & West estimation procedure, ARMA denotes the ARMA estimation procedure.

Overall, the results for the adaptive expectation scheme reveal a pattern quite similar to the results for the extrapolative expectation scheme (see Table V-17). For the professional exchange rate expectations, a clear tendency for stabilizing expectations is found. Thus, professional exchange rate forecasters tend to expect that an unanticipated depreciation of the Euro against the US dollar leads in the future to appreciation of the Euro. This conclusion holds true in particular for the three and six month exchange rate expectations. It is noteworthy that this result agrees with the conclusion drawn from the extrapolative expectations of professionals. For the experimental expectations of novices the results reveal that in the short-run (one step ahead expectations) a tendency for destabilizing expectations is found out. Thus the participants in the experiment expect that unanticipated exchange rate movements will be carried forward in the future. In the medium-run (three step ahead expectations) experimental expectations are static and in the long-run (six step ahead expectations) the expectations appear to be stabilizing, like the professional exchange rate forecasts. Again the pattern of the experimental results for the adaptive expectation scheme corresponds to that of the results for the extrapolative expectation scheme.

Table V-17: Summary of the results for the adaptive expectation mechanism

	Professional exchange rate expectations	Experimental exchange rate expectations
Short-run	Static expectations	Destabilizing expectations
Medium-run	Stabilizing expectations	Static/stabilizing expectations
Long-run	Stabilizing expectations	Stabilizing expectations

V.1.3.3.3 Regressive expectations

The last considered type of expectation formation is the regressive expectation scheme. According to the regressive expectation scheme it is assumed that market participants respond to a deviation of the current spot rate from some notion of an equilibrium exchange rate by expecting a movement towards the supposed equilibrium level. The corresponding regression equation is given by

$$E_t s_{t+h} - s_t = \alpha + \beta(\bar{s}_t - s_t) + \varepsilon_{t+h}. \tag{V-13}$$

In our analyses of the regressive expectation scheme for professional expectations, we decided to use two different kinds of an equilibrium exchange rate. On the one hand, we substitute $\bar{s}_t$ by the purchasing power parity exchange rate. We calculate the PPP exchange rate using consumer price indices. As a starting point for our calculation we choose the actual spot exchange rate in February 1987. This can be justified by the statements of the Louvre Accord in February 1987. The corresponding PPP level is around 1.20 US-$/€ and coincides largely with other estimates for the US-$/€ fundamental equilibrium rate (see Table V-18). On the other hand, we assume that the equilibrium exchange rate ($\bar{s}_t$) is given by a non-linear trend of the actual exchange rate. The non-linear trend is in our analysis defined by a Hodrick-Prescott filter (see Hodrick and Prescott [1997]).[62] Figure V-9 shows both variants of the equilibrium exchange rate.

[62] For the smoothing parameter of the Hodrick-Prescott filter we use the default values of Eviews 4.0 for monthly data. Note that this Hodrick Prescott filter is akin to a medium-term moving average of the actual exchange rate time series.

Table V-18: Selected estimates for the US-$/€ fundamental equilibrium rate

	Reference period	Equilibrium exchange rate (US-$/€)
Wren-Lewis and Driver [1998]	2000	1.19 – 1.45
Borowski and Couharde [2000]	1999 (first half)	1.23 – 1.31
Clostermann and Schnatz [2000]	Winter 1999/2000	Short-run: 1.20 Medium-run: 1.13
Chinn and Alquist [2000]	June 2000	Medium-run: 1.17 – 1.24
Lorenzen and Thygesen [2000]	1999	Long-run: 1.28
Goldman Sachs [2000]	May 2000	1.21

Source: Schneider [2003], European Central Bank [2002]

Figure V-9: Equilibrium exchange rates for the US-$/€ rate

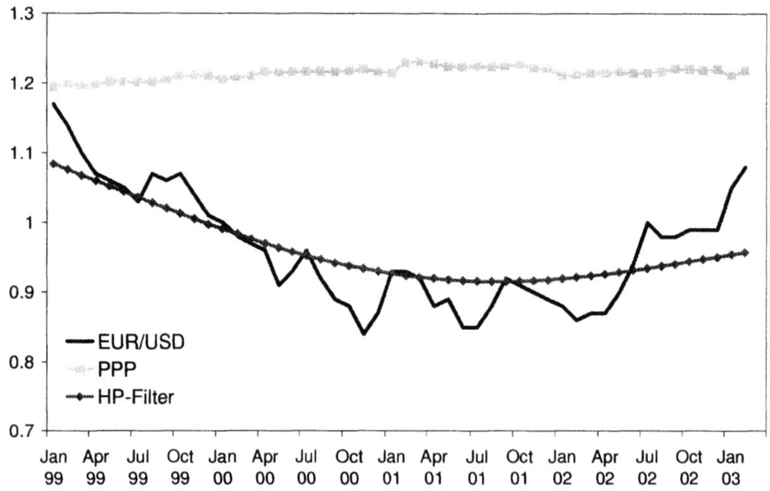

Note: the fundamental exchange rate is calculated according to the purchasing power parity using consumer price indices. As starting point for the calculation of the fundamental exchange rate we use the actual exchange rates at the time of the Louvre Accord in February 1987.

The results of estimating equation (V-13) for the professional exchange rate expectations are illustrated in Table V-19. Considering the purchasing power parity exchange rate as equilibrium exchange rate leads to the following results: except for the six month horizon, all professional exchange rate expectations appear to be unaffected by deviations from the PPP exchange rate. This conclusion can be drawn since all β coefficients – regardless of the applied estimation procedure – are statistically insignificant from zero. For the six month expectations the results vary depending on the applied estimation procedure. Using the Newey and West [1987] estimation procedure one has to conclude that those expectations are static. However, when the autocorrelation structure of residuals is explicitly considered, the six month professional exchange rate expectations appear to be stabilizing in the sense that a reduction of the deviation from the PPP exchange rate is expected. Thus, in total it seems to be fair to conclude that the PPP exchange rate has only very limited impact on the expectation formation of professionals, at least for the considered forecasting horizons. In contrast to our results Beng and Siong [1993] report stabilizing regressive expectations considering the PPP exchange rate as equilibrium rate for all considered forecasting horizons. Similarly, Bénassy-Quéré et al. [1999] use PPP exchange rates as equilibrium rate in a panel analysis of professional expectations and find positive β coefficients for 3 month and twelve months expectations which were almost significant.

Applying the HP-filter as equilibrium exchange rate results in a rather different conclusion: here, the results reveal that professional exchange rate expectations over the three forecasting horizons expect almost consistently a movement of the exchange rate towards the equilibrium value represented by the Hodrick-Prescott filter. Solely for the one month expectations does the ARMA regression indicate that expectations are static. Thus, exchange rate expectations of professional analysts tend to be orientated on a medium-term trend in the EUR/USD exchange rate.

Table V-19: Tests for regressive expectations of professional exchange rate forecasts

		Estimation procedure	Q-statistic	α	β	H_0: α=β = 0
1 month Reuters	PPP	NW	--	-0.0013 (0.0050)	0.0229 (0.0180)	3.7119 [0.0319]
		ARMA	Q(12) = 0.710 Q(24) = 0.060	0.0011 (0.0076)	0.0143 (0.0291)	1.9783 [0.1507]
	HP-Filter	NW	--	0.0040 (0.0019)	0.0437 (0.0248)	5.1448 [0.0095]
		ARMA	Q(12) = 0.735 Q(24) = 0.077	0.0040 (0.0019)	0.0596 (0.0411)	3.8533 [0.0297]
3 months Reuters	PPP	NW	--	0.0092 (0.0113)	0.0389 (0.0407)	14.8411 [0.0000]
		ARMA	Q(12) = 0.520 Q(24) = 0.140	-0.0032 (0.0141)	0.0847 (0.0523)	7.6305 [0.0015]
	HP-Filter	NW	--	0.0182 (0.0035)	0.1100 (0.0561)	17.9187 [0.0000]
		ARMA	Q(12) = 0.547 Q(24) = 0.169	0.0179 (0.0044)	0.1295 (0.0626)	10.6832 [0.0002]
3 months Consensus	PPP	NW	--	0.0138 (0.0121)	0.0629 (0.0428)	2.1614 [0.1488]
		ARMA	Q(12) = 0.929 Q(24) = 0.910	-0.0313 (0.0217)	0.2279 (0.0734)	9.6324 [0.0035]
	HP-Filter	NW	--	0.0277 (0.0045)	0.1771 (0.0602)	8.6393 [0.0053]
		ARMA	Q(12) = 0.807 Q(24) = 0.781	0.0268 (0.0065)	0.2537 (0.0797)	10.1446 [0.0028]
6 months Reuters	PPP	NW	--	0.0239 (0.0240)	0.0599 (0.0860)	15.2351 [0.0000]
		ARMA	Q(12) = 0.342 Q(24) = 0.290	-0.0330 (0.0263)	0.2352 (0.0618)	7.5725 [0.0016]
	HP-Filter	NW	--	0.0376 (0.0066)	0.2400 (0.1020)	18.1787 [0.0000]
		ARMA	Q(12) = 0.372 Q(24) = 0.408	0.0334 (0.0159)	0.2523 (0.0648)	9.0182 [0.0006]
6 months ZEW	PPP	NW	--	0.0236 (0.0105)	0.0168 (0.0381)	0.1940 [0.6619]
		ARMA	Q(12) = 0.263 Q(24) = 0.174	0.0236 (0.0093)	0.0168 (0.0343)	0.2395 [0.6272]
	HP-Filter	NW	--	0.0270 (0.0031)	0.0860 (0.0649)	1.7555 [0.1927]
		ARMA	Q(12) = 0.331 Q(24) = 0.373	0.0270 (0.0024)	0.0860 (0.0551)	2.4315 [0.1268]

Notes: Standard errors are given in parentheses, p-values in brackets.
NW denotes the Newey & West estimation procedure, ARMA denotes the ARMA estimation procedure.

For the evaluation of the regressive expectation scheme for the experimental expectations of novices, we use also a non-linear trend of the actual time series as equilibrium exchange rate. This trend is again derived by applying the Hodrick-Prescott filter for the original time series. Figure V-10 shows the experimental time series and the corresponding Hodrick-Prescott filter. The estimation results for the regressive expectation scheme in the experimental setting are summarized in Table V-20. The results reveal unambiguously that the β coefficients for all experimental expectations are statistically significantly positive. Thus, those expectations are stabilizing in the sense that a deviation of the current rate from the equilibrium rate is expected to be reduced in the future.

Figure V-10: Equilibrium exchange rates for the experimental time series

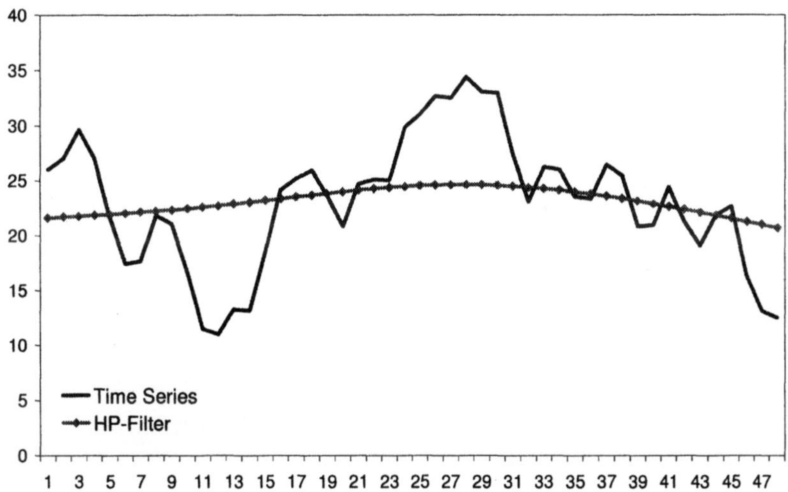

Table V-20: Tests for regressive expectations of experimental exchange rate forecasts

		Estimation procedure	Q-statistic	α	β	H_0: α=β = 0
1 step ahead	**HP Filter**	NW	--	-0.0085 (0.0088)	0.0861 (0.0395)	3.6474 [0.0356]
		ARMA	Q(12) = 0.562 Q(24) = 0.929	-0.0124 (0.0068)	0.1253 (0.0292)	10.1448 [0.0004]
3 step ahead	**HP Filter**	NW	--	-0.0116 (0.0105)	0.3052 (0.0321)	52.1616 [0.0000]
		ARMA	Q(12) = 0.692 Q(24) = 0.928	-0.0140 (0.0087)	0.3357 (0.0366)	42.1789 [0.0000]
6 step ahead	**HP Filter**	NW	--	-0.0124 (0.0113)	0.6127 (0.0173)	827.7123 [0.0000]
		ARMA	Q(12) = 0.747 Q(24) = 0.740	-0.0134 (0.0255)	0.5076 (0.0357)	101.7058 [0.0000]

Notes: Standard errors are given in parentheses, p-values in brackets.
NW denotes the Newey & West estimation procedure, ARMA denotes the ARMA estimation procedure.

Overall, the results for the regressive expectation scheme can be summarized as follows: Using the PPP exchange rate as long-run equilibrium exchange rate leads to the conclusion that those expectations are primarily static. Thus, the PPP exchange rate has no meaningful impact on the expectation formation of professional analysts. On the contrary, using a Hodrick-Prescott filter as approximation for the equilibrium exchange rate leads to the conclusion that professional exchange rate analysts expect on average a movement towards the equilibrium level. Thus, the expectations of professional analysts have to be evaluated as stabilizing expectations. The same result is obtained for the experimental exchange rate expectations using also a Hodrick-Prescott filter as approximation of the equilibrium exchange rate.

Table V-21: Summary of the results for the regressive expectation mechanism

	Professional exchange rate expectations		**Experimental exchange rate expectations**
	PPP	**HP-Filter**	**HP-Filter**
Short-run	Static expectations	Static/stabilizing expectations	Stabilizing expectations
Medium-run	Static expectations	Stabilizing expectations	Stabilizing expectations
Long-run	Static/stabilizing expectations	Stabilizing expectations	Stabilizing expectations

V.1.3.3.4 Discussion of the results

Section V.1.2 has revealed that the accuracy of professional exchange rate forecasts and judgmental forecasts of novices differ significantly from one another. Therefore we decided to analyze the expectations of professional forecasters and novices in more detail to extract important differences in their expectations. Overall, we have found two remarkable differences. First, professional forecasters form predominantly expectations, which correspond to a reversal of the most recent exchange rate movements, whereas novices show a tendency to extrapolate recent trends in the short-run (one step ahead forecasts) and expect a reversal in the long-run (six step ahead forecasts). Second, the tests of unbiasedness show that professional forecasts are over all forecast horizons biased predictors of future exchange rates, whereas judgmental forecasts of novices appear to be unbiased.

These results may serve as an indication for an explanation of the inferior forecasting accuracy of market forecasts compared to judgmental forecasts. Professional exchange rate forecasts seem to be biased by fundamental considerations, as these forecasts are oriented towards the fundamental equilibrium exchange rate. Figure V-11 clearly shows that professional forecasters expected for the whole period that the EUR/USD rate should appreciate towards its fundamental PPP value in the future. Overall, the phenomenon of an expected convergence towards the fundamental exchange rate is more distinctive the longer the forecast horizon is. However, Figure V-11 reveals also that professional forecasters do not expect an immediate adjustment of the actual exchange rate to its fundamental level. Professional analysts rather assume that current exchange rates only move gradually towards the PPP level.[63] The sluggishness in the expected exchange rate movements, although it seems reasonable at first glance, clearly contradicts the predictions of the efficient market hypothesis. According to the efficient market hypothesis, deviations of the actual exchange rate from its fundamental justified level evoke speculative trading activities of rational market participants that bring the actual exchange rate directly towards its fundamental value (see Friedman [1953]).

[63] This sluggishness in the expectation of professional analysts is also responsible for the regression results of section 0. Also professional analysts always expect at least a minor movement towards the long-run PPP level of the EUR/USD exchange rate, the sluggishness of expectations veils the immediate relationship between professional exchange rate expectations and PPP exchange rates.

Figure V-11: Professional exchange rate expectations and PPP exchange rate

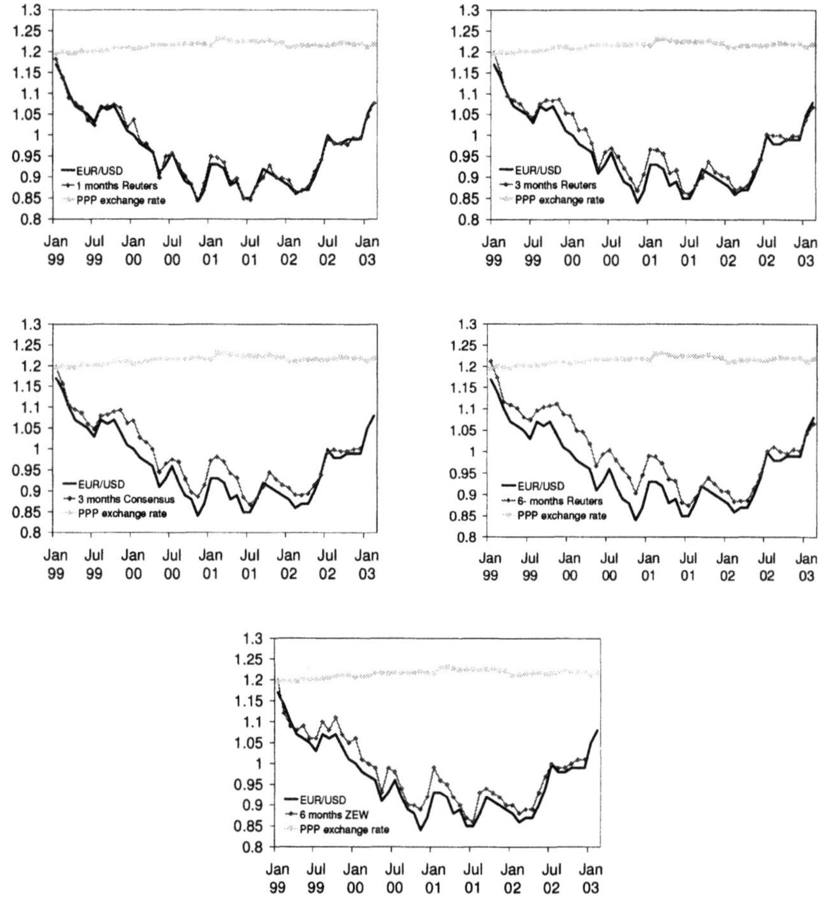

Note: the fundamental exchange rate is calculated according to the purchasing power parity using consumer price indices. As starting point for the calculation of the fundamental exchange rate we use the actual exchange rates at the time of the Louvre Accord in February 1987.

Rationales for expecting a sluggish adjustment to the fundamental rate expectations can be found in the reasons for the rejection of the efficient market hypothesis. Contrary to the efficient market hypothesis, foreign exchange markets are dominated by heterogeneous traders who follow – at least partially – non-fundamental trading practices such as technical analysis, bandwagon expectations and herding (see Menkhoff [1998], Cheung and Chinn [2001] and

Gehrig and Menkhoff [2004]). These trading practices may be responsible for long-lasting deviations of the actual exchange rate from its fundamental level and may cause adjustments towards that level to occur – if at all –only gradually. Thus, it is quite reasonable for professional analysts to expect that the adjustment to the fundamental level does not occur in an abrupt manner but sluggishly. A further explanation for sluggish expectations with respect to the adjustment to PPP levels can be found in the representativeness heuristic (see Kahneman et al. [1999]). According to this heuristic, subjects tend to believe that past movements of exchange rates are representative for the data generating process of the exchange rate itself and it is likely that similar movements will recur in the future. Thus, professional forecasters assume that the speed of adjustment towards the fundamental level is limited by the usually observable exchange rate movements.

To assess the suggestion of fundamental-biased professional exchange rate forecasts, we compare the professional exchange rate forecasts with artificial fundamental-oriented forecasts. We decided to approximate the fundamental value of the €/US-$ exchange rate by the purchasing power parity condition (PPP) as it is an adequate long-run equilibrium exchange rate model (see Sarno and Taylor [2002]). Furthermore, we incorporate an inertia factor that accounts for the sluggishness of expectations. We assume that the artificial fundamental-oriented forecasts predict an appreciation of the €/US-$ rate if the current rate is below its fundamental value, and a depreciation if the current rate is above its fundamental value:

$$E_t^{fund} S_{t+h} = \begin{cases} \text{if } S_t < \bar{S}_t : \ S_t(1+\alpha_h) \\ \text{if } S_t > \bar{S}_t : \ S_t(1-\alpha_h) \end{cases} \qquad \text{(V-14)}$$

where $\bar{S}_t$ is the fundamental equilibrium exchange rate measured by the purchasing power parity and α_h denotes an inertia factor. The values for the inertia factor α_h vary with the forecast horizon and are deduced from the mean absolute exchange rate changes over the three different forecast horizons; i.e. $\alpha_1 = 0.02$, $\alpha_3 = 0.05$ and $\alpha_6 = 0.06$.

Figure V-12 illustrates the professional exchange rate forecasts and the corresponding artificial fundamental-oriented forecasts calculated according to equation (V-14). Both kinds of forecasts show similar characteristics. This visual impression is also confirmed by the correlation between the professional forecasts and the artificial fundamental-oriented forecasts (see Table V-22). It is in our opinion therefore accurate to claim that professional exchange rate forecasts are biased towards a fundamental value. This finding is also supported by the results of a recent survey conducted by the Zentrum für Europäische Wirtschaftsforschung (ZEW). According to this survey, the interviewed financial analysts state that they base their forecasts to about 60% on fundamental considerations (see Zentrum für Europäische Wirtschaftsforschung (ZEW) [2004]).

Figure V-12: Artificial fundamental exchange rate forecasts and professional expectations

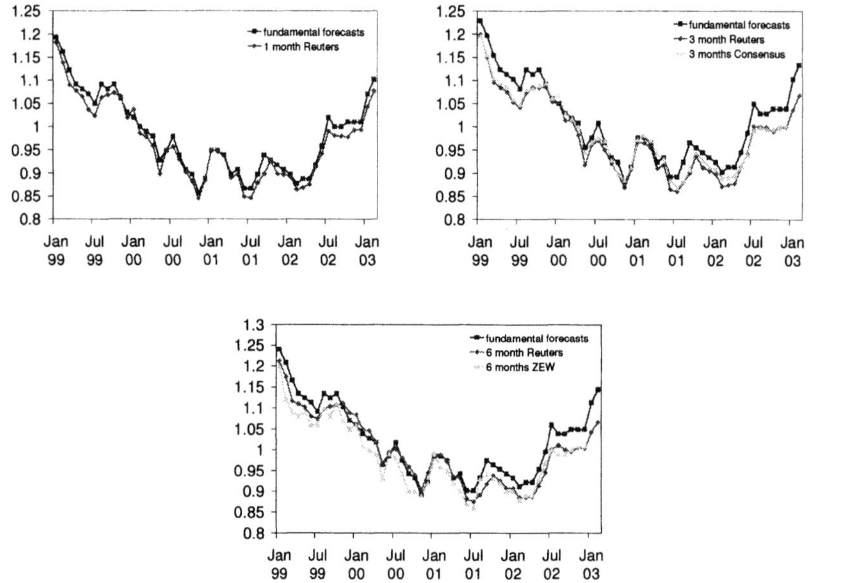

Table V-22: Correlation between professional and artificial expectations

	1 month Reuters forecasts	3 months Reuters forecasts	3 months Consensus forecasts	6 months Reuters forecasts	6 months ZEW forecasts
Correlation coefficient	0.9918	0.9821	0.975	0.9566	0.9795

The strict orientation of professional exchange rate forecasts on the fundamental level of the EUR/USD rate, however, is in our view an unwise decision. Due to the speculative nature of foreign exchange markets, macroeconomic factors are judged to be more or less unimportant in the short and medium run. Cheung and Wong [2000] and Cheung and Chinn [2001] report that dealers believe that the poor performance of fundamental exchange rate models is due to excessive speculation in foreign exchange markets (see also section III.2.3).

In contrast, speculative markets tend to cause exchange rates to move in long trends. This can be explained with the widespread usage of technical analysis in foreign exchange markets which can be interpreted as a kind of trend heuristic. Taylor and Allen [1992] report that a large proportion of foreign exchange traders bases expectation formation upon technical analysis, at least in the short and medium run. More recently, Cheung et al. [2000], Cheung and Wong [2000] and Cheung and Chinn [2001] systematically analyze the British, Asian and American foreign exchange markets by using questionnaires. Their results also suggest that technical analysis is a widely used tool in foreign exchange markets. The survey of Gehrig and Menkhoff [2004] even shows that the importance of technical analysis in foreign exchange markets has increased in recent times. Furthermore, trend extrapolative expectations are a reasonable choice in foreign exchange markets. Many empirical studies reveal that technical analysis, which is primarily based on trend extrapolation, is a useful and profitable tool in foreign exchange markets. Okunev and White [2003] analyze the profitability of momentum-based strategies in various foreign exchange markets. Their results indicate that the potential exists for investors to generate excess returns by adapting a simple moving average rule. This finding is robust for the time periods under consideration, the base currency of reference and the benchmark of comparison. Similar results for the profitability of technical analysis in foreign exchange markets are also reported by e.g. Neely [1997] Chang and Osler [1999], LeBaron [1999] and Neely [2002] (see also section V.3).

Thomson et al. [2003] arrive at a very similar conclusion by comparing the judgmental forecasting accuracy of experts and novices using a simulated currency series. Their results indicate that novices perform better than experts throughout all experiments. They explain their results by the reluctance of experts to recognize strong trends. According to the authors, experts' behavior is due to their "academic leaning towards random walk theory" that may result "in an explicit search for randomness in the face of contradictory evidence" (Thomson et al. [2003], p. 248). A similar conclusion is also reached by Van Hoek [1992] who states that "... analysts appear to expect some reversal in recent exchange rate movements or a return to some long-run 'normal' value" (Van Hoek [1992], p. 467). De Bondt [1993] as well provides further evidence that novices and experts forecast trended time series differently. Whereas experts tend to expect a trend reversal, novices forecast a trend continuation.

Overall, our results concerning the forecasting accuracy of professional exchange rate analysts and novices may rely on the beneficial impact of the 'less-is-more-effect' discussed by Marsh et al. [2004]. According to this phenomenon, considering only one or a few cues allows people to arrive at better decisions. However, professional exchange rate analysts pursue a detailed analysis of macroeconomic fundamentals when making their exchange rate forecasts. Furthermore they are usually well-trained in economics and have a concise vision about the efficient functioning of foreign exchange markets. All these factors imply that professional exchange rate analysts have large background knowledge, which may result in the use of a large number of cues, so that the decision task is rather complicated. In contrast, novices are rather unversed in making forecasts. Furthermore, novices cannot pursue a detailed analysis of the decision environment, as they were given no contextual information. Thus, the only information novices can use when making their forecasts is past exchange rate realizations. Consequently, the decision task of novices in our experimental settings is a lot easier compared to the decision situation of professional exchange rate analysts. However, as the results reveal, using only a little information is obviously a reasonable choice due to a "beneficial degree of ignorance" (see Borges et al. [1999]).

V.1.4 Summary

The aim of our first series of experiments was to investigate the relevance of psychological effects, in particular decision heuristics, in the context of expectation formation. Moreover, we intended to compare the forecasting accuracy and expectation formation of professional exchange rate analysts with that of novices to identify meaningful differences between the two groups. Our results can be summarized as follows: with regard to the forecasting accuracy, the forecasts of professional exchange rate analysts perform worse than those of novices in the experimental settings. Whereas the forecasting accuracy of professional exchange rate forecasts is significantly worse than naïve random walk forecasts, the forecasts of novices in our experimental settings perform at least as well as the naïve forecasts. An important issue in traditional exchange rate economics is the assumption of rational expectations. Here, our results show that both professional exchange rate analysts and novices do not generate rational expectations. However, in contrast to the professional exchange rate forecasts, novices' forecasts appear to be unbiased. A common phenomenon, which is found in both groups, is the topically oriented trend adjustment behavior of exchange rate forecasts. Thus, forecasts of professional exchange rate analysts and novices move very much in line with the actual exchange rate instead of predicting future exchange rate developments. Interesting differences between the forecasting behavior of professional exchange rate analysts and novices are found in connection with the nature of expectations. Whereas professional exchange rate analysts mainly expect a reversal of the most recent exchange rate movement over all forecasting horizons, novices tend to extrapolate the most recent trend in the short-run and expect reversal only in the long-run. Furthermore, as section V.1.3.3.4 has shown, professional exchange rate forecasts are biased towards the presumed fundamental equilibrium value of the EUR/USD exchange rate. Overall, we interpret our results as a first indication of the relevance and usefulness of trend heuristics in the context of foreign exchange markets. Obviously, people tend to extrapolate trends in decision situations characterized by a high degree of ignorance – at least in the short run. The results reveal that, at least in the short-run, trend extrapolating trading behaviors are a reasonable choice, as they allow for better decisions than a fully-fledged analysis by considering only one cue, namely the recent trend.

V.2 Expectation formation in an experimental foreign exchange market

V.2.1 Introduction

A review of the literature on experimental studies of expectation formation reveals that the related research can be divided into two sections: on the one hand there are forecasting experiments in the context of time series (see e.g. section V.1), on the other hand there exist studies dealing with experimental markets. Although there are a vast number of studies on experimental asset markets in general, only a few of them focus on foreign exchange markets in particular. Noussair et al. [1997] deal with the experimental verification of exchange rate models. Their results indicate that the purchasing power parity is not confirmed in an experimental setting. Fisher and Kelly [2000] explore the occurrence of speculative bubbles in a foreign exchange market with two almost identical dividend-paying assets, where the exchange rate represents their relative prices. Although all of these experiments include a dynamic feedback component, a pure analysis of expectations hypotheses is not possible. The observed market behavior also includes other behavioral features that may for example be due to trading activities.

In contrast to the first series of experiments, we now explicitly consider expectations feedback, as individuals' expectations directly influence the actual realization of the time series. In our view, this is an important feature of the experimental design, which accurately reproduces the actual decision-making situation in foreign exchange markets in the laboratory. Furthermore, we decide to focus solely on the expectations of subjects to exclude potential undesirable effects, e.g. trading decisions. To date, there exist only a few related studies. Gerber et al. [2002] investigate forecasting behavior in a beauty contest experiment. According to their experimental setting, participants are only able to sell and to buy an asset whose price is determined by aggregated orders and a noise component. Although the framework is quite similar to our experimental setting, it is rather abstract and expectations are not explicitly analyzed. In contrast, Hommes et al. [2002] and [2003] explore expectation formation in an experimental asset market with expectations feedback. In their experimental setting, participants have to forecast the future price of an asset. The market clearing price is given as a function of the average forecasts of all subjects, a noise component and (in a few treatments) some computer traders who always forecast the fundamental value of the asset. Hommes et al. [2002] and [2003] report that in many of the experiments speculative bubbles arise as the realized asset prices differ significantly from the fundamental value. This result is quite astonishing, since all participants possess perfect knowledge of dividends and interest rates so that the fundamental value could be easily computed. They also find that individuals in experimental markets coordinate their expectations on a common prediction strategy such as naïve, adaptive or autoregressive expectations.

The remainder of the section V.2 is as follows: In the next section we describe the experimental design. Afterwards, we analyze the human expectation formation in an experimental foreign exchange market. We first analyze the aggregated market behavior; subsequently, the individual expectation formation behavior in experimental foreign exchange markets is examined. In the last section we discuss our main results.

V.2.2 Design of the experimental foreign exchange market

The experimental design of the foreign exchange market focuses on the exploration of the expectation formation of the subjects. Consequently, the only task of the subjects is to forecast the exchange rate development. The subjects do not actually trade in the market. Each subject acts as a professional forecaster employed by a bank, who gives advices to the corresponding foreign exchange traders of the bank. The foreign exchange traders (represented by the computer) base their trading decisions on the forecast of the participant in the experiment. Given the predictions of all subjects, the computer derives the exchange rate from the aggregate demand for the currencies. Thus, the price reactions solely reflect the forecasts of the subjects.

The experiment is presented to the subjects as follows. The subjects are trading floor economists in different leading European banks. They watch the EUR/USD exchange rate and inform the currency dealers of the bank about the expected development of the exchange rate at the beginning of each period. The participants are told that the trading decisions of the dealers and consequently the demand for Euros and US Dollars are exclusively based on their forecasts. Thus, the profits from foreign exchange trading activities realized by the bank depend only on the quality of the individual forecasts and therefore the payoffs for the subjects in the experiment are inversely proportional to their forecast errors. Besides this information about the experimental task, the subjects are given background information about the exchange rate market. They know that the exchange rate is influenced by the forecasts of the other participants in the experiment and slightly influenced by the demand of private investors. However, the subjects do not know the exact market equilibrium equation. They also know values of domestic and foreign interest rates and expected inflation rates, which give them the possibility of calculating the fundamental values of the EUR/USD exchange rate. An English translation of the instructions given to the participants is presented in Appendix F. The price reaction function generating the experimental exchange rate (S) is given by

$$S_{t+1} = S_t + \Delta E_t^{avg} S_{t+1} + \xi_{t+1} \qquad \text{(V-15)}$$

where $\Delta E_t^{avg} S_{t+1} = \frac{1}{N}\sum_{n=1}^{N} E_t^n S_{t+1} - S_t$ denotes the average forecasted change by N subjects made in period t for the exchange rate in the period $t+1$. ξ_{t+1} is an independently normally distributed error term with $\xi_{t+1} \sim N(0,1)$ and represents random demand and supply shocks from private investors. The initial value of the exchange rate S_1 equals 50. The fundamental value S^f is given by the standard Fisher relation

$$S_{t+1}^f = S_t + S_t \cdot \left(i_t - i_t^*\right) = S_t + S_t \cdot \left(\pi_t - \pi_t^*\right) \qquad \text{(V-16)}$$

where i (i^*) denotes the domestic (foreign) interest rate and π (π^*) denotes the expected domestic (foreign) inflation rate. The values of these variables were chosen so that a rather stable fundamental value around 50 is ensured. The values of the four variables were presented to the subjects in each period.

In every period t, the task of the subjects is to forecast the value of the exchange rate in period $t+1$. The information set of subject n consists of the realizations of the exchange rate S_t, S_{t-1}, ... , S_1 and his/her own past forecasts $E_{t-1}^n S_t, E_{t-2}^n S_{t-1}, \ldots, E_1^n S_2$. After all participants have completed their forecast for period $t+1$, the actual exchange rate of period $t+1$ is presented on the screen and subjects are asked for the next forecast. This procedure is repeated for 49 periods. The subjects are told that their forecasts have to be between 0 and 100. Figure V-13 shows an English translation of the experimental computer screen. All past values of the exchange rate and the participant's own forecasts are graphed in a different color and are additionally presented in a tabular format. Furthermore, the information about the expected domestic and foreign inflation rates and interest rates are presented on the screen.

Figure V-13: Screenshot of the second experiment

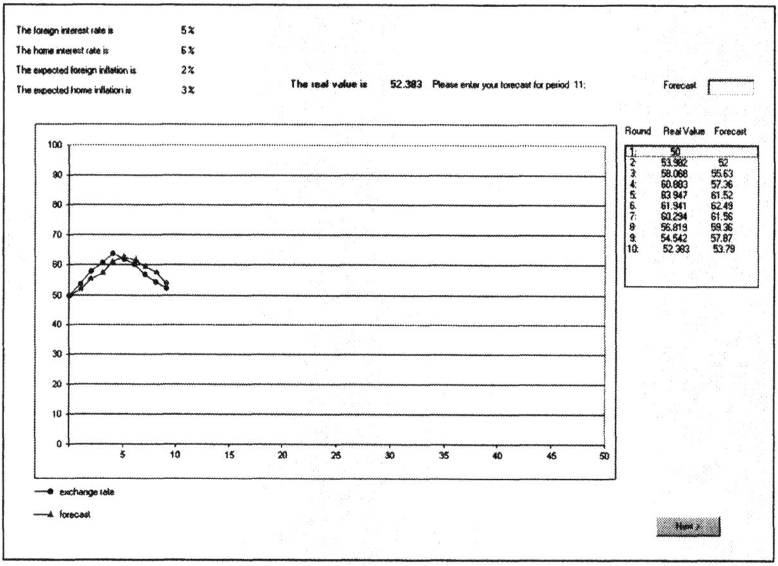

The participants were recruited from a course in game theory at the Department of Statistics and Operations Research, University of Graz. All subjects were undergraduate students of business administration without special education in financial markets. None of the subjects had participated in a similar experiment before. They participated voluntarily. The payment scheme of the subjects is solely related to their performance in the experiment and does not include any fixed show-up fee. The payoff p_t^n of subject n in period t is given by

$$p_t^n = \max\left\{30 - 10\left|S_t - E_{t-1}^n S_t\right|; 0\right\} \qquad \text{(V-17)}$$

where the unit of p_t is cents. For a perfect forecast, the subjects are paid 30 Cents, for a deviation of more than 3 units, the payment equals 0. The average payoffs were 6.94 Euros for an average duration of about 45 minutes. Each market consists of six subjects. Altogether, 36 students participated in the experiment.

V.2.3 Experimental results

Our analysis of the results is divided into two subsections. We first examine the aggregated behavior of the experimental exchange rate. In this context, we are particularly interested in the observable exchange rate developments. Furthermore, we evaluate the efficiency of the experimental exchange rate market. In the second subsection, we analyze in depth the individual behavior of the market participants. Here, we are interested in the nature of experimental expectations.

V.2.3.1 Aggregated behavior of exchange rates in experimental foreign exchange markets

V.2.3.1.1 Similarity of experimental exchange rates

Figure V-14 shows the realized exchange rates of the six experimental groups and the development of the fundamental value. The most striking feature of the results is the obvious similarity of the group behaviors. The course of the exchange rate starts with an upswing, falls in period 5 and stabilizes around periods 12 to 21. The exchange rate time series continues its downward trend until period 30 and turns upwards for the final 20 periods. This applies for almost all groups, only group 2 is inconsistent with this pattern. However, this is due to several extreme forecasts of one subject in the periods 7, 14, 31 and 33. This can be seen from the charts in Figure V-17. To underline these findings, the correlation of the exchange rates is presented in Table V-23. The correlation coefficients are highly significant and indicate a very strong similarity between all groups. The correlations with group 2 are comparatively weaker, but still significant and at a minimum level of 0.614.

Figure V-14: Realized exchange rates and fundamental value

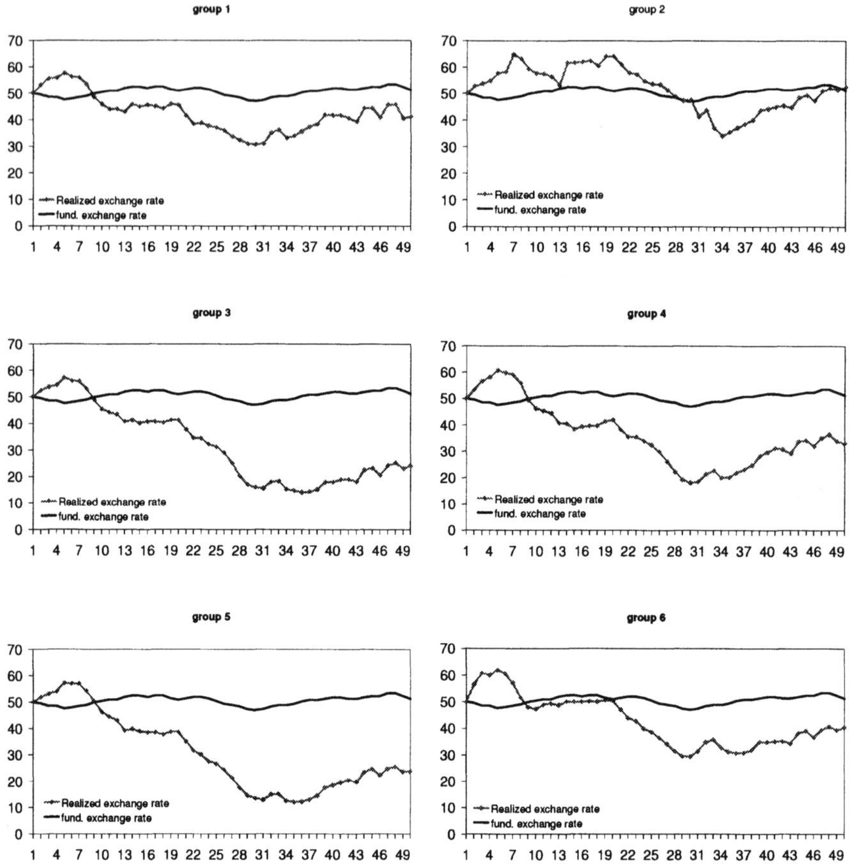

Table V-23: Correlation between aggregated group forecasts

Group	1	2	3	4	5
2	0.614**	-	-	-	-
3	0.846**	0.823**	-	-	-
4	0.953**	0.739**	0.952**	-	-
5	0.891**	0.803**	0.992**	0.977**	-
6	0.901**	0.777**	0.968**	0.955**	0.968**

Note: ** denotes that correlation is significant at the 0.01 level (two tailed)

The reason for this astonishing result can be found in the structure of the random shocks ξ of equation (V-15). We calculate the average changes of the predictions $\Delta E_t^{avg} S_{t+1} = E_t^{avg} S_{t+1} - E_{t-1}^{avg} S_t$ and compare them to the random shocks ξ_t. These values are highly correlated at a 99% level of significance. The corresponding correlation coefficients are reported in Table V-24. Again, only group 2 shows a weaker association.

Table V-24: Correlation between forecasted changes and shocks

Group	1	2	3	4	5	6
Correlation coefficient	0.881**	0.653**	0.962**	0.937**	0.969**	0.900**

Note: ** denotes that correlation is significant at the 0.01 level (two tailed)

The development of the exchange rate is obviously driven to a high degree by the random shocks. Thus, the occurrence of local extrema and longer trends can be ascribed to the course of random shocks. The periods 12 to 21 are very representative for this phenomenon. The random shocks are very small in five periods successively. They amount to absolute values of about 0.5. In periods 21 and 22, random shocks of -3.33 and -2.06 occur respectively and start a downtrend that lasts for about ten periods. Between the periods 21 and 31 the random shocks are negative in nine cases, and a large positive shock stops the trend. The exchange rates have many characteristic local minima and maxima in common, due to the same random shocks in all experiments. This is especially noticeable in the final periods e.g. periods 43, 45 and 46. In Figure V-15, $\Delta E_t^{avg} S_{t+1}$ of each group and ξ_t are compared graphically. The changes of average forecasts correspond to the sign of the shocks in almost all periods. Only in group 2 can larger deviations be observed, due to the reasons discussed above.

Overall, we have to conclude that subjects extrapolate trends that are mainly caused by random shocks. The influence of the shocks is remarkably stable for all experiments. Furthermore, our findings of mainly shock-driven aggregated forecasts imply that the fundamental value of the exchange rate does not have a noticeable influence on the realized prices in all groups.

Figure V-15: Forecasted changes and random shocks

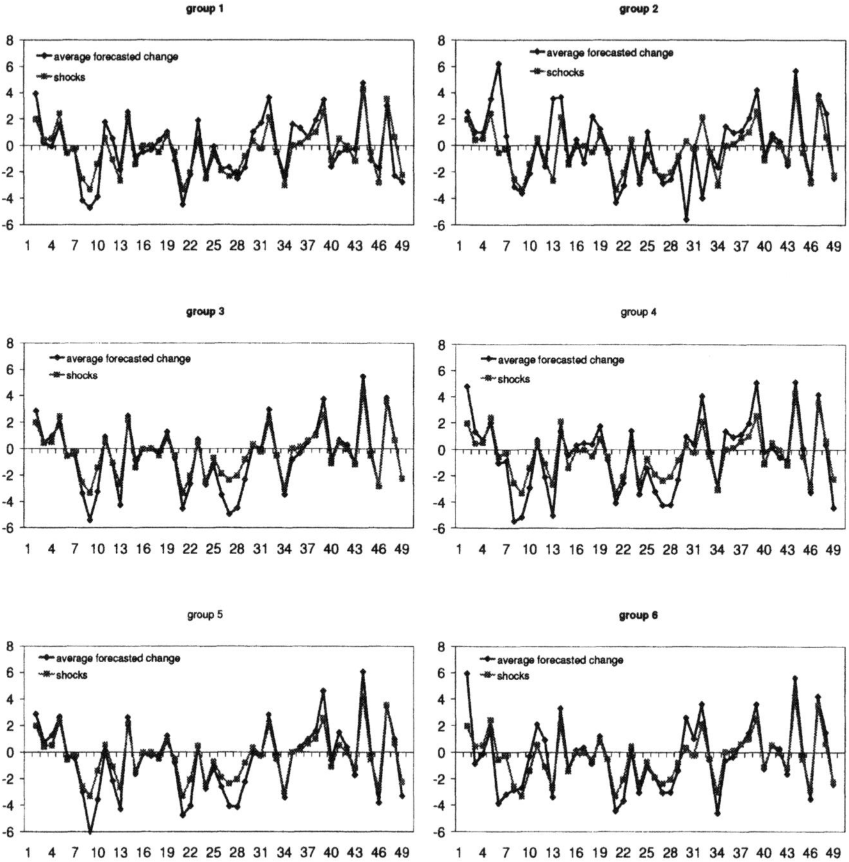

V.2.3.1.2 Efficiency of experimental foreign exchange markets

A central building block of traditional exchange rate models is the assumption that exchange rates are determined in efficient markets (see section II.1.3). A testable implication of the efficient market hypothesis is that excess returns defined as $x_t = \ln S_t - \ln S_{t-1}$ should be serially uncorrelated with any excess return in the past or future. To analyze the autocorrelation of excess returns we again carry out the variance ratio test proposed by Lo and MacKinlay [1988] (see section II.2.4).

The results of the variance ratio test for each experimental exchange rate are summarized in Table V-25. Almost all *VR(q)*s are larger than one, indicating a tendency for trend behavior in the experimental exchange rates. However, the *VR(q)*s for group 1 and group 2 are on the whole not statistically significant, so we have to conclude that those experimental exchange rate time series do not exhibit an autocorrelation pattern which can be exploited for abnormal trading profits. In contrast, the results for the *VR(q)*s of the experimental exchange rates in group 3 to 6 show distinct evidence for positive autocorrelation in the excess returns. All *VR(q)*s are statistically significantly above one and thus indicate a strong trend behavior in those exchange rates. Skeptics might suspect that the positive serial correlation in the excess returns is due to the chosen shock sequences. We therefore also analyze the autocorrelation of the exchange rate, which is only determined by the shock sequence. The results indicate that this 'shock-driven' exchange rate exhibits no tendency for significant autocorrelation pattern in excess returns. Thus, the positive autocorrelation in most of the experiments is, without much doubt, caused by the behavior of the participants in the experiment.

Overall, we have to reject the hypothesis of efficient markets in the context of our experimental analysis in 4 of 6 cases. The rejection of the efficient market hypothesis is always due to positive autocorrelation in the excess returns, suggesting trend extrapolating trading behaviors. Furthermore, the rejection of the efficient market hypothesis cannot be linked to the shock sequence.

Table V-25: Variance ratio tests

Group	VR(2)	T-stat (hom)	T-stat (het)	VR(3)	T-stat (hom)	T-stat (het)	VR(4)	T-stat (hom)	T-stat (het)	VR(5)	T-stat (hom)	T-stat (het)
1	1.154	1.077 (0.282)	1.342 (0.180)	1.099	0.459 (0.646)	0.531 (0.595)	1.213	0.797 (0.426)	0.881 (0.378)	1.290	0.925 (0.355)	1.009 (0.313)
2	1.060	0.417 (0.677)	0.414 (0.679)	1.201	0.945 (0.345)	0.888 (0.374)	1.429	1.606 (0.108)	1.486 (0.137)	1.561	1.793 (0.073)	1.674 (0.094)
3	1.314	2.199 (0.028)	2.046 (0.041)	1.496	2.328 (0.020)	2.171 (0.030)	1.760	2.843 (0.005)	2.643 (0.008)	1.874	2.791 (0.005)	2.602 (0.009)
4	1.493	3.452 (0.001)	3.112 (0.002)	1.765	3.592 (0.000)	3.288 (0.001)	2.058	3.960 (0.000)	3.671 (0.000)	2.289	4.119 (0.000)	3.855 (0.000)
5	1.481	3.365 (0.001)	3.014 (0.003)	1.829	3.891 (0.000)	3.483 (0.001)	2.211	4.530 (0.000)	4.077 (0.000)	2.490	4.759 (0.000)	4.325 (0.000)
6	1.406	2.844 (0.005)	2.760 (0.006)	1.550	2.583 (0.010)	2.594 (0.010)	1.691	2.585 (0.010)	2.661 (0.008)	1.679	2.170 (0.030)	2.275 (0.023)
Schock	1.005	0.033 (0.974)	0.038 (0.970)	0.942	-0.273 (0.785)	-0.302 (0.763)	1.123	0.465 (0.642)	0.491 (0.623)	1.137	0.439 (0.661)	0.454 (0.650)

Notes: P-values are given in parenthesis; hom denotes the standard normal test statistic under homoscedasticity; het denotes the heteroscedasticity-consistent test statistic.

V.2.3.1.3 Summary

The analysis of the aggregated market behavior in experimental foreign exchange markets has revealed two main results. First, in our experimental setting the aggregated behavior of experimental exchange rates is similar across all experiments. The reason for the similarity of the course of experimental exchange rates is due to the considered shock sequence. The finding of shock-driven aggregated exchange rates implies that fundamental consideration have no meaningful impact on the expectation formation of market participants. Second, the analysis of the efficient markets hypothesis for the experimental foreign exchange markets has shown that, for most of the experimental exchange rates, the efficient markets hypothesis is rejected. In the case of rejection of the efficient market hypothesis, the rejection is due to positive autocorrelation in the experimental exchange rate returns, suggesting a trend behavior in those exchange rates. It should be borne in mind that the positive autocorrelation cannot be related to the considered shock sequence.

V.2.3.2 Individual behavior in experimental foreign exchange markets – the nature of expectations

V.2.3.2.1 Rationality of Individual Expectations

In this section we analyze the rationality of expectations in experimental foreign exchange markets. The rationality of expectations is evaluated on the basis of the implications of rational expectations hypothesis introduced in Chapter II. In particular, we test the unbiasedness hypothesis, the orthogonality hypothesis and the hypothesis of no serial correlation in the expectation errors (see section II.2.2). As before, we run each regression equation twice (Newey and West [1987] and ARMA estimation procedure). The results for testing the rational expectations hypothesis are summarized in Table V-26. The detailed regression results are presented in Appendix G. The results reveal that, although forecasts anticipate the future direction of change rather well (almost all β coefficients are larger than zero), the hypothesis of unbiased forecast is rejected for most of the participants in the experiments. Furthermore, the participants tend to make only inefficient use of past information, as the orthogonality hypothesis must be rejected in most cases. We reach a similar conclusion for the hypothesis of uncorrelated forecast errors. Nearly all participants form expectations concerning future exchange rates such that the forecast errors are serially correlated. Consequently, we have to reject the hypothesis of serially uncorrelated forecast errors.

Table V-26: Tests for rational expectations

Group	No. of Participants	Unbiased forecasts	$\beta > 0$	Efficient use of information	Uncorrelated forecast errors
1	6	1 (1)	6 (6)	2 (2)	1
2	6	1 (1)	5 (5)	1 (4)	4
3	6	3 (3)	5 (5)	0 (3)	0
4	6	2 (3)	6 (6)	1 (3)	2
5	6	3 (2)	6 (5)	0 (3)	3
6	6	0 (1)	5 (6)	1 (2)	1

Notes: the figures are based on the results of the corresponding F-tests; the considered significance level is 10%. Results for the ARMA modeling are given in parenthesis.

V.2.3.2.2 Overreaction

Overreaction is a frequently observed phenomenon in asset markets (see e.g. De Bondt and Thaler [1990]). Hommes et al. [2003] suggest a comparison of the following two measures to evaluate the degree of overreaction in experimental settings. The first measure represents the average absolute change in expectations of participant *i* and is marked as a single point (▪) in Figure V-16:

$$\Delta_i^e = \frac{1}{N-1}\sum_{t=2}^{N}\left|S_{i,t}^e - S_{i,t-1}^e\right|. \tag{V-18}$$

The second measure accounts for the average absolute change in the exchange rate and is represented by the straight line in Figure V-16:

$$\Delta = \frac{1}{N-1}\sum_{t=2}^{N}\left|S_t - S_{t-1}\right|. \tag{V-19}$$

According to Hommes et al. [2003], overreaction occurs if the individual absolute change in expectations exceeds the average absolute change in the exchange rates ($\Delta_i^e > \Delta$), and underreaction occurs if the individual absolute change in expectations is smaller than the average absolute change in the exchange rates ($\Delta_i^e < \Delta$). Figure V-16 illustrates the degree of overreaction in each group. Obviously, almost all market participants in the experiment tend to overreact in the above defined sense. To evaluate whether the degree of overreaction is significant, we carry out the Wilcoxon signed rank test to test for differences in the change of expectations and exchange rates. The results are summarized in Table V-27. In each experimental group at least one market participant tends to overreact significantly. However, the phenomenon of overreaction appears to be more pronounced in the groups 4 to 6. Here, approximately half of the market participants show a significant tendency to overreact.

Figure V-16: Average absolute changes in expectations and exchange rates

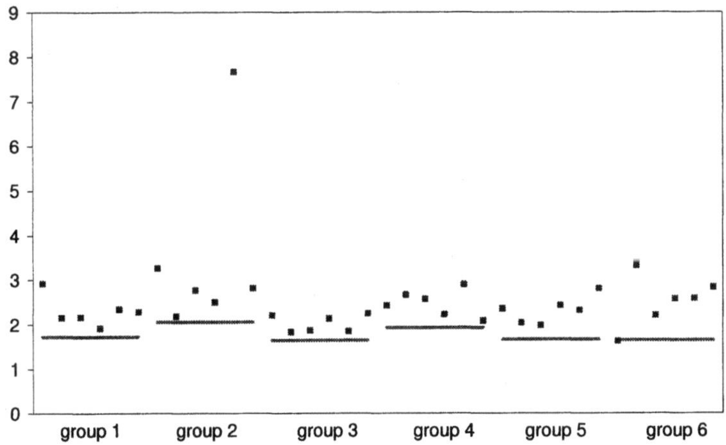

Table V-27: Results of the Wilcoxon signed rank test

Group \ Subject	1	2	3	4	5	6
1	-2.985 (0.003)	-1.128 (0.259)	-0.574 (0.566)	-0.605 (0.545)	-1.569 (0.117)	-1.385 (0.166)
2	-0.667 (0.505)	-0.277 (0.782)	-0.533 (0.594)	-1.108 (0.268)	-3.087 (0.002)	-0.646 (0.518)
3	-1.569 (0.117)	-0.615 (0.538)	-0.554 (0.580)	-0.903 (0.367)	-0.410 (0.682)	-1.887 (0.059)
4	-1.436 (0.151)	-1.826 (0.068)	-2.128 (0.033)	-0.503 (0.615)	-2.062 (0.039)	-0.328 (0.743)
5	-1.538 (0.124)	-0.964 (0.335)	-1.026 (0.305)	-1.831 (0.067)	-1.836 (0.066)	-2.913 (0.004)
6	-0.010 (0.992)	-2.954 (0.003)	-1.923 (0.054)	-2.421 (0.015)	-2.903 (0.004)	-2.903 (0.004)

Note: p-values are given in parenthesis.

The phenomenon of overreaction can be well explained by the representativeness heuristic. According to the representativeness heuristic, subjects tend to give certain developments more importance or a higher degree of probability than they really deserve (see e.g. Barberis and Thaler [2003]). The consequence of such behavior is that people tend to assign too much importance to most recent experiences, so that they neglect the sample size. In situations in which the data-generating process is unknown, neglecting the sample size leads to the tendency to perceive regularities in the data-generating process too quickly. For instance, a short sequence of equal exchange rate movements will enforce the belief in the existence of a persistent trend. According to Tversky and Kahneman [1999] "people view a sample randomly drawn from a population as highly representative, that is, similar to the population in all essential characteristics." (Tversky and Kahneman [1999], p. 24). The belief that even small samples reflect the properties of the parent population is often called the "law of small numbers" (see Rabin [2002]).

V.2.3.2.3 Individual expectation formation mechanisms

In this section, we analyze the individual expectation formation mechanisms. We therefore revert to the expectation mechanisms introduced in section V.1.3.3. Table V-28 presents the summarized results of the tests for various expectation formation mechanisms. The detailed regression results are given in Appendix G. Our results indicate that for group one and group two the majority of individuals show static expectations. However, some individuals depart significantly from the static expectation formation mechanism, especially in group one. Here, at least three participants form trend-extrapolative expectations. For groups 3 to 6 we can conclude that trend-extrapolative, destabilizing expectations play a decisive role. In all of these groups, most participants generate expectations consistent with the extrapolative expectation model. As most β coefficients are larger than zero, those expectations can be characterized as bandwagon expectations. Conforming to our findings for the extrapolative expectation scheme, the results for the adaptive expectations scheme indicate that individuals either possess static expectations or form destabilizing expectations in the sense that they expect a continued appreciation of the exchange rate due to an unanticipated appreciation. The results for the regressive expectation scheme demonstrate that the fundamental value of the exchange rate has only a minor influence on the expectation formation of individuals in our experimental setting. Thus, the regressive expectation hypothesis has to be rejected for the majority of the subjects.

Table V-28: Individual expectation formation mechanisms

Group	Extrapolative			Adaptive			Regressive		
	β<0	β=0	β>0	β<0	β=0	β>0	β<0	β=0	β>0
1	3 (4)	2 (1)	1 (1)	1 (1)	4 (4)	1 (1)	0 (0)	4 (4)	2 (2)
2	1 (2)	5 (5)	0 (1)	1 (2)	5 (4)	0 (0)	0 (0)	3 (4)	3 (2)
3	6 (6)	0 (0)	0 (0)	2 (4)	4 (2)	0 (0)	0 (0)	6 (6)	0 (0)
4	6 (6)	0 (0)	0 (0)	4 (6)	2 (0)	0 (0)	0 (0)	5 (6)	1 (0)
5	6 (6)	0 (0)	0 (0)	6 (6)	0 (0)	0 (0)	0 (0)	6 (6)	0 (0)
6	5 (5)	1 (1)	0 (0)	4 (5)	2 (1)	0 (0)	0 (0)	6 (6)	0 (0)

Notes: the considered significance level is 10%. Results for the ARMA modeling are given in parenthesis.

Overall, the results for the individual expectation formation correspond with the aggregated behavior of the market participants discussed above. The subjects extrapolate the trends initiated by random shocks and therefore show a high degree of similarity between the groups. The fundamental value is obviously not considered in the expectation formation process of the market participants. In our opinion, the previous results inevitably raise the question of coordinated expectations as suggested by Keynes [1936].

V.2.3.3 Keynes Beauty Contest – Coordinated Expectations?

Keynes [1936] metaphor of the beauty contest suggests that market participants tend to coordinate their expectations concerning future asset prices in speculative markets. As Figure V-17 shows, an eye-catching characteristic of individuals' expectations is actually that different participants within one group tend to coordinate their expectations in our experimental setting.

Figure V-17: Individual expectations for each group

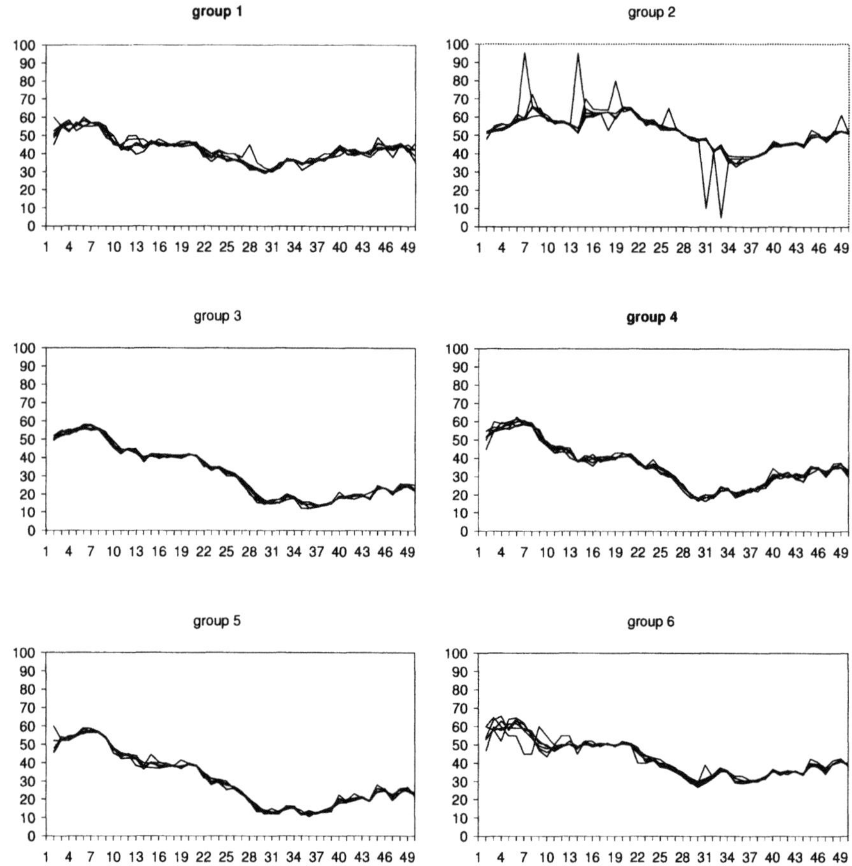

To analyze the suggested coordination of expectations in more detail we carry out the procedure used by Hommes et al. [2003]. They recommend considering for each group the average individual squared forecast error, which corresponds to the individual squared forecast error averaged over time and over participants within a group:

$$AISE = \frac{1}{N(T-1)} \sum_{n=1}^{N} \sum_{t=2}^{T} \left(E_{t-1}^{n} S_t - S_t \right)^2 , \qquad \text{(V-20)}$$

where N is the number of participants in each group and T represents the number of periods. According to Hommes et al. [2003], the *AISE* can be divided into two separate terms

$$AISE = \frac{1}{N(T-1)}\sum_{n=1}^{N}\sum_{t=2}^{T}\left(E_{t-1}^{n}S_t - E_{t-1}^{avg}S_t\right)^2 + \frac{1}{T-1}\sum_{t=2}^{T}\left(E_{t-1}^{avg}S_t - S_t\right)^2 , \qquad \text{(V-21)}$$

where $E_{t-1}^{avg}S_t$ is defined as $\frac{1}{N}\sum_{n=1}^{N}E_{t-1}^{n}S_t$. The first term on the right-hand side of equation (V-21) measures the dispersion between the individual expectations. Thus, it can be denoted as average dispersion error (*ADE*). The *ADE* is composed of the distance between the individual expectation and the average expectation within a group, averaged over time and participants. If all participants within a group form the same expectations about the future exchange rate, the *ADE* equals zero. By contrast, if the expectation formation of participants differs within a group, the *ADE* is expected to increase. Thus, *ADE* measures the degree of deviation from coordinated expectations. The second term on the right-hand side of equation (V-21) measures the average distance between the mean expectations, $E_{t-1}^{avg}S_t$, and the realized exchange rate, S_t. Thus, it can be denoted as the average common error (*ACE*). Hommes et al. [2003] highlight that the *ACE* is expected to be relatively small under the null hypothesis of rational expectations.

Table V-29: Coordination measure

Group	AISE	ADE	ACE
1	6.28	3.14 (50%)	3.14 (50%)
2	23.64	20.50 (87%)	3.14 (13%)
3	3.84	0.70 (18%)	3.14 (82%)
4	4.71	1.58 (33%)	3.14 (67%)
5	4.54	1.40 (31%)	3.14 (69%)
6	7.19	4.06 (56%)	3.14 (44%)

Overall, Table V-29 shows that the expectations of participants within a group are coordinated on a common expectation formation to a great extent. The average dispersion error is predominately smaller than the average common error. This holds true in particular for groups 3 to 5. For group 2 only the *ADE* is substantially greater than the *ACE*. However, group 2 must be evaluated with care, since one participant of group 2 formed irreproducible expectations concerning the future exchange rates in many periods. Hommes et al. [2003] report similar results with regard to the coordination of expectations in an experimental asset market.

According to their findings, on average 75% of the AISE can be attributed to the average common error (*ACE*).

A further way to empirically evaluate the coordination of expectations within an experimental foreign exchange market can be found in a test for heterogeneous expectations of market participants. Elliott and Ito [1999] propose the following regression approach to analyze heterogeneous expectations by testing the null hypothesis of nonsystematic deviations in expectations

$$E_t^n s_{t+1} - E_t^{avg} s_{t+1} = c_n + \varepsilon_{t+1} \tag{V-22}$$

where $E_t^n s_{t+1}$ are the individual (log) expectations for s_{t+1} and $E_t^{avg} s_{t+1}$ is defined as $\frac{1}{N}\sum_{n=1}^{N} E_t^n s_{t+1}$. Under the null hypothesis of nonsystematic deviations in expectations, which consequently corresponds to homogeneous expectations, it is expected that the mean c_n should be zero. Table V-30 summarizes the results of estimating equation (V-22) using the corresponding expectations of participants in each group. The detailed regression results are given in Appendix G. All in all, the results indicate that the expectations of participants in each group do not deviate systematically from the average group expectations. Thus, the results of testing for heterogeneous expectations provide further evidence for homogenous, coordinated expectations in each group.

Table V-30: Test for heterogeneous expectations

Group	No. of participants	No. of heterogeneous expectations
1	6	0
2	6	1
3	6	0
4	6	1
5	6	0
6	6	1

A logical consequence of coordinated expectations is that market participants can anticipate the direction of future exchange rate changes rather well.[64] To evaluate the performance of

[64] However, it should be noted that this holds true only for cases in which market participants do not coordinate their expectation formation on naïve expectations.

participants' expectations as direction-of-change forecasts, we carry out a simple χ^2 –test of independence (see Diebold and Lopez [1996] and Appendix D). Using the χ^2 –test of independence, the forecasting quality of expectations is compared to a naïve coin flip. Table V-31 summarizes the results for the χ^2 –test of independence. The detailed results are given in Appendix G. In almost all cases the hit rate of the individual predictions exceeds 50%. Furthermore, the results often appear to be statistically significant.

Table V-31: Individual predictions as direction-of-change forecasts

Group	No. of participants	Hit rate > 50%	Thereof significant
1	6	6	5
2	6	5	4
3	6	6	1
4	6	6	6
5	6	6	3
6	6	4	3

V.2.4 Discussion of the experimental results

The foreign exchange market experiment in section V.2 deals with the expectation formation of subjects. We are particularly interested in whether subjects tend to coordinate their expectations as suggested by Keynes [1936]. Furthermore, we are curious as to whether market participants tend to base their expectations on trends heuristics.

Since our experimental setting is closely related to that of Hommes et al. [2002] and [2003], our results are similar. The market participants show a strong tendency to coordinate their expectations on a common expectation formation mechanism. According to our findings, the most common expectation formation mechanism is described as trend-extrapolative. Hommes et al. [2002] and [2003] also find strong evidence for trend-chasing expectations, which they refer to as "positive feedback expectations". In contrast to their results, we find that the behavior is mainly influenced by the small random demand shocks in the price reaction function. Besides these two main results, we provide further evidence against the rationality of experimental expectations. Although the forecasts appear to be unbiased, the subjects tend to make only inefficiently use of available information. In addition, subjects in the experiments tend to overreact.

A central result of our experiment is that participants do indeed tend to coordinate their expectations on a common prediction strategy. This finding is consistently supported by our corresponding analyses. The tests for heterogeneous expectations reveal that only a minor number of participants show expectations that deviate significantly from the average expectations. In addition, at least for groups 3, 4 and 5, the average individual squared forecast error is mainly due to average common expectation errors. Consequently, within these groups expectations are clearly coordinated. Thus, it is reasonable to conclude that Keynes [1936] description of how asset markets influence the individual expectation formation is quite accurate. In this context Lawson [1985] states that the Keynesian "conventional judgment" is not irrational, as it allows for an efficient use of scarce cognitive resources (see Lawson [1985]). Thus, the relevance of simple decision heuristics is again highlighted. Our findings are in line with that of Hommes et al. [2002], [2003] and Gerber et al. [2002]. Hommes et al. [2002], [2003] report evidence for coordination in all of their experiments. Gerber et al. [2002] find that experimental asset prices exhibit short-term momentum and long-term reversal due to unpredictable switches in the coordination of the market participants.

Akerlof [2002] characterizes Keynes as the progenitor of the modern Behavioral Economics view of asset markets. According to the new research field of Behavioral Economics, market participants use simple heuristics instead calculating exact rational solutions. In Chapter IV we argue that it might be rather reasonable for market participants to use a simple trend heuristic. This suggestion is also confirmed in our experimental setting. For most of the participants in the experiment we find that a trend-extrapolative, destabilizing expectation formation mechanism is an accurate description of their prediction strategy. This is especially true for the groups that show a high tendency for coordinated expectations. Also Hommes et al. [2003] report strong evidence for trend extrapolation of the market participants. They show that, for a large majority of participants, a simple linear autoregressive forecasting rule best describes the individual prediction strategies.

However, our results are affected by the random shock sequence in the price reaction function. In contrast to Hommes et al. [2003], who observe coordination within the groups, but find clear differences between the groups, our results for the aggregated market exchange rate show quite similar behaviors across all groups. This finding can be ascribed to the influence of random shock that mainly causes deviations from coordination results. In the experiments of Gerber et al. [2002] the effects of random shocks on the collective forecasts are very similar. However, the random shocks differ between the experimental series and therefore the realizations of the different markets cannot be compared directly, as is possible with the experiments of Hommes et al. [2003]. We relate our findings to the concept of focal points. It is suggested that subjects do not have any incentive to deviate from a common forecasting strategy, once a common strategy of expectation formation has been established. This is exactly what we observe.

In consideration of our results, we need to pay more attention to the findings of Hommes et al. [2002], [2003]. Most of the realized asset prices in their experiments show strong oscillations, whereas some were persistent over the whole duration of the experiment and some were converging to the fundamental value. Only in a few groups were asset prices fairly stable and thus more consistent with our results. The different results in our experiments and the experiments of Hommes et al. [2002], [2003] occur, despite the experimental designs being alike in most features. The price generating function is mainly determined by average forecasts and random shocks. We also acquired undergraduate students as market participants. Furthermore, the payment schemes and the experimental context are similar. The remarkably oscillating aggregated behavior was observed in both of their studies. The realized experimental asset prices differ notably from our experimental exchange rates. In the first series of experiments (see Hommes et al. [2002]) the participants predict asset prices up to 1000 while the fundamental value of the asset corresponds to 60. Only the artificially set upper bound of 1000 stops the participants from forecasting even higher asset prices. In the later settings (see Hommes et al. [2003]) the asset price developments mostly reveal the same oscillating characteristics. However, as the range of possible forecasts is reduced to 0 to 100, the oscillation is lower. Unfortunately, we are unable to explain the differences between the results of Hommes et al. [2002], [2003] and our experimental results. Therefore, it has to be explored in future research why subjects in our experiments were rather unwilling to change their forecasts and extrapolate random trends, and why the expectations of subjects in Hommes et al. [2002], [2003] cause large fluctuations in experimental asset prices.

V.3 Technical analysis as a simple heuristic

So far, we dealt with the topic of human expectation formation in different experimental settings. Now, we are going to investigate the human expectation formation in an empirical analysis by using field data. Chapter IV and the foregoing discussion highlighted the relevance and importance of psychological effects in the context of experimental foreign exchange markets. In particular, the expectation formation is considerably influenced by cognitive limitations of human beings. The experimental evidence has revealed that market participants in experimental foreign exchange markets apply simple trend heuristics, when forming their expectations about future exchange rates. In this context, Gigerenzer and Todd [1999b] argue that the reliability of simple heuristics can only be evaluated against their usefulness in the real world. Thus, for evaluating the usefulness of simple trend heuristics in the context of foreign exchange markets, one has to evaluate their profitability in this specific environment. Therefore, section V.3 deals with the profitability of technical trading rules in foreign exchange markets. Principally, the technical trading approach can be interpreted as a practical implementation of simple trend heuristics. The next section summarizes the main objectives of technical trading and evaluates their profitability in foreign exchange markets. In case of profitable technical trading rules, the application of simple trend heuristics must be regarded as a reasonable choice in the context of foreign exchange markets. It allows for a quick decision making and is easy to implement, so that cognitive resources are economized. Additionally, the application of technical trading is profitable and thus ensures that the technically oriented trader survives in the market.

V.3.1 Objectives and functioning of technical analysis

Among academic circles, technical analysis is known as 'voodoo finance'. In his influential book 'A Random Walk down Wall Street' Malkiel [1999] concludes that "[u]nder scientific scrutiny, chart-reading must share a pedestal with alchemy." A similar assessment is given in the book of Campbell et al. [1997]:

> "Historically, technical analysis has been the 'black sheep' of the academic finance community. Regarded by many academics as a pursuit that lies somewhere between astrology and voodoo, technical analysis has never enjoyed the same degree of acceptance that, for example, fundamental analysis has received. This state of affairs persists today, even though the distinction between technical and fundamental analysis is becoming progressively fuzzier." (Campbell et al. [1997], p. 43)

In contrast, practitioners possess a more pragmatic view on technical analysis. They are interested in the profitability of technical analysis and "beating the market" by means of technical analysis. Economists, however, are mainly engaged in the analysis of technical trading rule because its success raises serious doubt on the efficiency of asset markets and may imply that exchange rates are disconnected from their fundamental value for longer periods (see Neely [1997]).

Chapter III has shown that in foreign exchange markets technical analysis can be seen as a tool used by many practitioners when forming expectations about future exchange rates. Table V-32 summarizes again the relative importance of technical analysis according to the studies of Menkhoff [1998], Cheung and Chinn [2001] and Gehrig and Menkhoff [2003]. All three studies show that technical analysis is a prominent tool for the expectation formation of foreign exchange market participants.

Table V-32: The importance of technical analysis in foreign exchange markets

	Technical analysis	Fundamental analysis	Order flow	Other
Menkhoff [1998]	37.2%	44.9%	17.9%	--
Cheung and Chinn [2001]	30%	25%	22%	23%
Gehrig and Menkhoff [2003]	35.8%	29.4%	17.4%	17.4%

In the following, we first identify the main objective of technical analysis. Afterwards, we illustrate some important tools of technical analysis. The last part of this section deals with the profitability of technical trading rules. In particular, we evaluate the profitability of different moving average trading rules for daily DM/USD and YEN/USD exchange rates in the time period from 1975 to 2003. Using moving average trading rules, a specific technical trading rule is in our context a reasonable choice, as such trading rules are very easy to implement and thus correspond rather well to the ideal of a simple decision rule.

V.3.1.1 Philosophy of technical analysis

According to Murphy [1999] the aim of technical analysis is "the study of market action, primarily through the use of charts, for the purpose of forecasting trends" (Murphy [1999], p. 1). By using technical analysis, investors attempt to exploit recurring and predictable patterns in asset prices to generate abnormal trading profits. Or in the words of Pring [2003]:

> "[T]he technical approach to investment is essentially a reflection of the idea that the stock market moves in trends which are determined by the changing attitudes of

> investors to a variety of economic, monetary, political, and psychological forces. The art of technical analysis, for it is an art, is to identify changes in such trends in an early stage and to maintain an investment posture until a reversal of that trend is indicated." (Pring [2003], p. 2)

According to the technical approach to analyzing asset prices, three different principles guide the behavior of technical analysts (see e.g. Murphy [1999]):

a) The market discounts all relevant factors affecting exchange rates:

   Technical analysis rests on the assumption that all factors affecting exchange rates are discounted. Consequently, all relevant factors about the exchange rate are reflected in its price history. Thus, it is completely sufficient to analyze the price movements themselves. However, in contrast to the traditional economic approach, technical analysis explicitly includes, in addition to economic factors, also political and psychological factors.

b) Exchange rates tend to move in persistent trends:

   According to the technical analysis approach, exchange rates tend to move in persistent trends and the main purpose of technical analysis is to detect such trends in an early stage in order to trade in line with those trends. In this context, practitioners often refer to Newton's law of motion to explain the existence and persistence of trends. According to Newton's law of motion, trends tend to continue as long as no other force acts on them. Thus, it is more likely that a trend in motion is continued in the future than that it be reversed. This suggestion clearly corresponds to our statement on the relevance of simple social heuristics and the importance of conventions in financial markets (see Chapter IV).

c) Exchange rate history repeats itself:

   The advocates of technical analysis argue that, due to the human nature, people tend to react to similar situations in a consistent manner. Thus, technical analysts are concerned with the analysis of the recurrence of similar characteristics in exchange rate time series to identify major peaks and troughs.

Obviously, all three principles that guide – according to the technical analysis approach – the behavior of investors are closely related to behavioral economics and psychology. This view is also endorsed by Goldberg [1997]. In his view the technical analysis approach constitutes the instrument of a behavioral analysis of financial markets. The main difference between the traditional fundamental oriented trading approach and technical analysis is very well summarized by Day and Huang [1990]:

> "In the present theory [fundamental; RS] investors are sophisticated and base their behavior on an assessment of the chance of a market response to a spread between price and carefully estimated future economic values. Such behavior is expensive: It takes time, costly information and a substantial investment in intellectual and computational capital. Most participants cannot afford to pursue behavior of this kind *and they do not*. The great majority instead use relatively simple rules and relatively low cost advice." (Day and Huang [1990], p. 304)

In our view, the technical analysis approach can be interpreted as a set of simple trading heuristics. Due to limited cognitive resources, market participants are forced to use such simple heuristics to reduce the complexity of the decision situation. In the context of foreign exchange markets, technical analysis can be interpreted as a set of simple trend heuristics that allow each individual market participant to easily reach an investment decision (see Goldberg [1997], Goldberg and von Nitzsch [2001]).

V.3.1.2 Examples of technical analysis

To distinguish trends from shorter-run stochastic fluctuations in foreign exchange rates, technical analysis primarily suggests two different types of analysis tools: chartism and quantitative technical trading rules. Chartism includes the analysis of records or charts of past exchange rates with the aim of finding patterns that can be exploited to make profits. Prominent patterns in this context are, for example, support and resistance levels and head and shoulders pattern. Quantitative trading rules or technical indicators are applied to assess the prospects for future up- and downswings in the exchange rate. In the following we discuss some examples of each type of technical analysis tool to illustrate the principle functioning of technical analysis.

A very simple but often used graphical tool of technical analysis is support and resistance levels. Support and resistance levels are used for analyzing trend continuation pattern by comparing local peaks and troughs. Peaks represent price levels at which the selling pressure exceeds the buying pressure and are usually called resistance levels. In contrast, troughs describe levels at which the selling pressure is exceeded by the buying pressure and are therefore denoted as support levels (see Figure V-18). Typically, in an upward trend, the consecutive support and resistance levels must exceed each other respectively. The reverse holds true for a downward trend. According to technical analysis, a substantial break of an existing support level in an upward trend indicates a trend reversal while a break of a resistance level announces a further progress of the existing trend (see Luca [2000]). Empirical research on support and resistance levels in foreign exchange markets also suggests that such levels are always at round numbers such as 10, 15, 20, and so on. In this context, such numbers act as psychological levels at which current movements come to an end (see Moosa [2000]). De Grauwe and Decupere [1992] analyze the relevance of psychological barriers in foreign exchange markets and find evidence in favor of such psychological barriers. Numbers like 130 or 140 Yen/USD for example tend to influence the market behavior such that exchange rates tend to resist movements towards these numbers. Furthermore, the results of De Grauwe and Decupere [1992] indicate that, once these barriers have been crossed, there appears to be an acceleration away from these numbers.

Figure V-18: Diagram of a typical support and resistance pattern

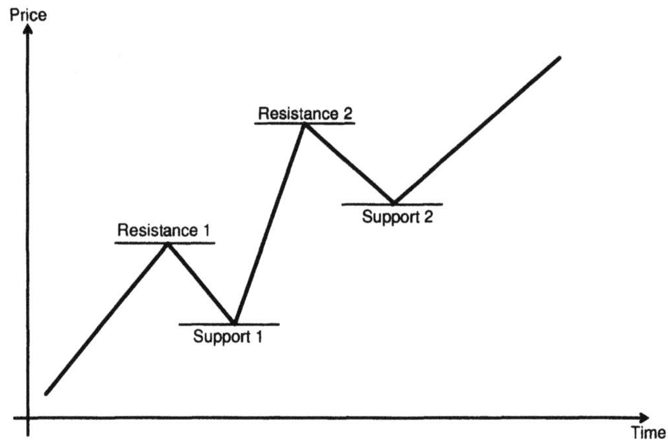

Figure V-19: Diagram of a typical head-and-shoulders pattern

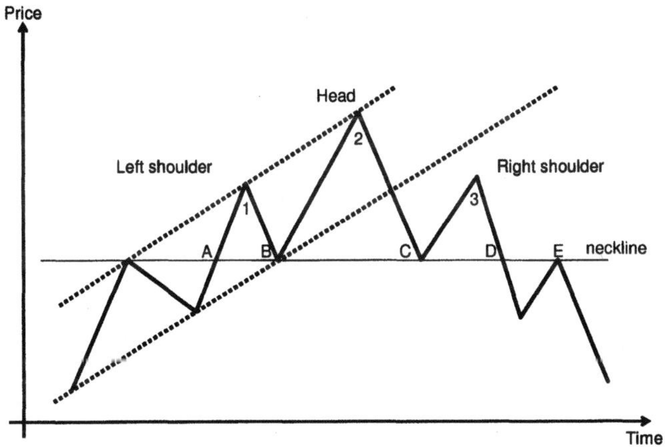

One of the most prominent trend reversal patterns is the head-and-shoulders formation (see Figure V-19). The head-and-shoulders pattern is made up of three local maxima, whereby the first local maximum (point 1) and third local maximum (point 3) should have approximately the same level. The second local maximum (point 2) should exceed both other maxima. Between the bottoms of the left and right shoulder usually a neckline is drawn. According to the head-and-shoulders formation, a trend reversal is indicated when the exchange rate breaks through the neckline. An inverse head-and-shoulders pattern indicates a trend reversal from downwards to upwards.

Among many other quantitative technical trading rules, two technical trading rules are salient as they are often used in both practice and academic research: the filter rule and the moving average trading rule. According to the filter rule, a currency is bought when it appreciates by a certain percentage (x%) from its most recent trough and is sold when it depreciates by a certain percentage (x%) from its most recent peak. Figure V-20 illustrates how a typical x% filter rule works. The justification for the filter rule can be found in the second premise of the technical trading approach. When a currency appreciates by x%, then it is, according to the technical approach to investing, likely that further appreciations will follow and consequently the currency should be bought.

Figure V-20: Diagram of a typical filter rule

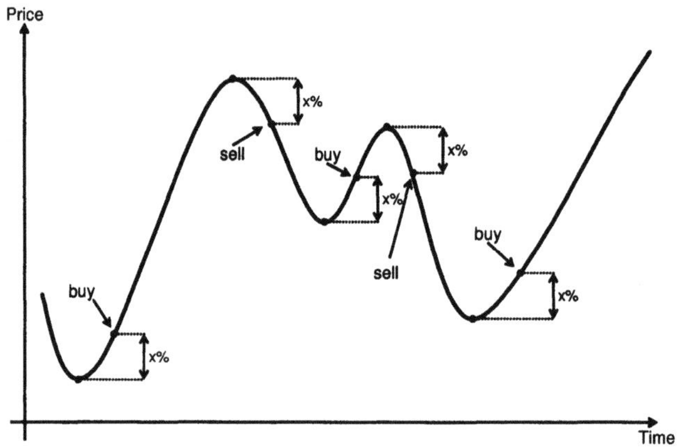

The second important quantitative technical trading rule, which we consider, is the moving average trading rule. According to the moving average trading rule, trading signals are derived from the behavior of the exchange rate relative to one or more moving averages of a certain length. A moving average of length m at time t is given by

$$MA_t = \frac{1}{m}\sum_{i=0}^{m-1} S_{t-1} \qquad \text{(V-23)}$$

where m is the length of the moving average and S denotes the spot exchange rate. Equation (V-23) shows that a moving average is in essence a moving arithmetic mean of the exchange rate. Moosa [2000] states that this specification of a moving average is most widely used by technical analysts because of its easy calculation and at the same time proper effectiveness. According to the moving average trading rule, buying or selling signals are indicated by the intersection of the time paths of the exchange rate and a moving average. Figure V-21 illustrates the functioning of a typical moving average trading rule. Prior to t_1 the moving average is above the exchange rate, i.e. $S < MA$. After the intersection of the exchange rate and the moving average at t_1 the relationship is reversed. According to the moving average trading rule, such situations, in which the moving average cuts the exchange rate from above, indicates a buying signal. In contrast, when the exchange rate cuts the moving average from below (see at t_2), a selling signal is indicated by the moving average trading rule. Obviously, this trading practice is profitable since the sell exchange rate is higher than the buy exchange rate.

Figure V-21: Illustration of a moving average trading rule

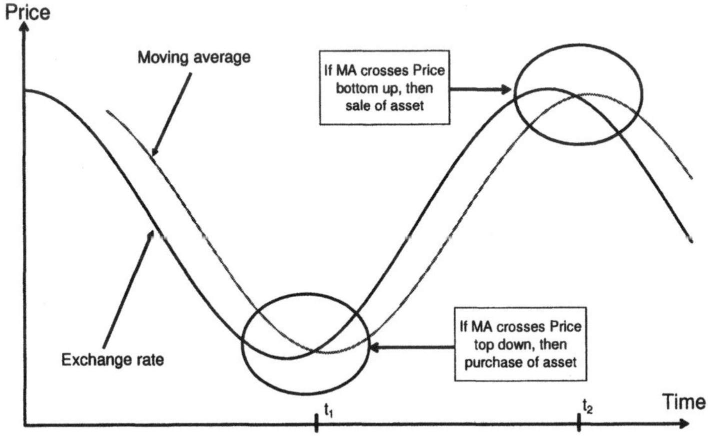

V.3.2 Profitability of technical trading rules

In section V.3.1 we have argued that technical analysis can be interpreted as a set of simple trend heuristics used in financial decision situations. According to Gigerenzer and Todd [1999b], a main characteristic of simple heuristics is their reliability in the real world. Therefore, in this section we are concerned with the profitability of technical trading rules in foreign exchange markets. We first review in brief the existing literature on the profitability of technical analysis in the context of foreign exchange markets. Afterwards, we evaluate the profitability of technical trading rules for the DM/USD and YEN/USD exchange rate by applying various moving average trading rules for the time period of 1975 to 2003.

V.3.2.1 A selective survey of the existing literature

So far only a limited number of empirical studies exists with regard to chartism. A main reason for this is the fact that trading rules based on chartism are largely subjective and thus rather difficult to express algebraically. Consequently, a computer based analysis of such rules is difficult to implement. However, most recently Lo et al. [2000] tried to formalize different chart patterns like head-and-shoulders so that they can be identified by computer based algorithms.

Overall, the empirical studies related to chartism suggest that those trading rules are at least to some extent profitable. Osler [2000] examines the predictive power of support and resistance levels for intraday exchange rates. Her results show that exchange rate trends were substantially more often interrupted at published support and resistance levels than would have occurred if the levels were chosen arbitrarily (see Osler [2000]). Overall, her results appear to be statistically significant and robust to alternative parameterizations. Chang and Osler [1999] analyze the profitability of technical trading signals with regard to head-and-shoulders patterns. Their results indicate that trading signals based on head-and-shoulders pattern lead to significant profits for the DM/USD and YEN/USD exchange rate. However, Chang and Osler [1999] state that trading in accordance with the head-and-shoulders pattern is not efficient since it is dominated by simpler technical trading rules like moving average trading rules or momentum rules. Negative results for the profitability of technical trading based on head-and-shoulders patterns are reported by Lucke [2003]. He analyses various daily exchange rates vis-à-vis the US dollar[65] and finds that head-and-shoulder trading rules do not lead to significantly positive returns. Moreover, if there is evidence for non-zero returns at all, the results show negative returns.

In contrast to technical trading based on chartism, quantitative technical trading rules can be easily evaluated by means of computer algorithms that automatically generate buy and sell trading signals. Hence, the advices of quantitative technical trading rules do not depend on any subjective perceptions of charts, but are clear cut. The empirical analysis of quantitative technical trading rules has been largely concentrated on the profitability of filter rules and moving average trading rules. Dooley and Shafer [1983] analyze various filter rules and report evidence of substantial profits to almost all applied rules over the period 1973-1981 for the Deutsche Mark, the Japanese Yen and the British Pound. Sweeney [1986] also investigates the profitability of filter rules in foreign exchange markets. His results suggest that filter rules are significantly profitable. These results are confirmed within an update of the earlier study in Surajaras and Sweeney [1992] for the period of July 1974 to May 1986. In contrast, Curcio et al. [1997] provide evidence that applying filter rules to high-frequency exchange rates does not lead on average to substantial profits. Levich and Thomas [1993] analyze the profitability of filter rules and moving average trading rules for various exchange rates, using currency future

[65] In particular, Lucke [2003] considers the German Mark, the British Pound, the Swiss Franken and the Japanese Yen against the US Dollar.

contracts. They find that both trading rules lead to positive profits in the time period of 1975 to 1990. Szakmary and Mathur [1997] utilize moving average trading rules to show that significant positive transaction cost adjusted profits can be earned by applying technical trading strategies. More recently, LeBaron [1999] investigates the predictability of technical trading rules for the DM/USD and YEN/USD exchange rates. The results show that it is possible to earn substantial profits by applying a simple moving average trading rule. Further confirmation for the profitability of moving average trading rules is given by Neely [2002]. He analyses the profitability of a simple moving average trading rule for the DM/USD, SFR/USD and AUD/USD exchange rate and concludes that moving average trading rules are profitable. Okunev and White [2003] examine the performance of moving average trading rules in foreign exchange markets and find that the profitability of such trading rules has continued throughout the 1990s. The results suggest that the potential exists for investors to generate excess returns by adopting a momentum strategy. Furthermore, according to the evaluation of Okunev and White [2003] it is not at all apparent that foreign exchange markets operate in an efficient manner and that returns are determined entirely by fundamentals. The results of Okunev and White [2003] seem to be robust for the time-period of analysis, the base currency of reference and the benchmark of comparison. Moreover, there exists only little evidence that the performance is due to risk, as it is not sufficient to generate the levels of returns witnessed in the paper. Recently, Dewachter and Lyrio [2002] analyse the economic value of technical trading rules by the means of a nonparametric utility-based approach. According to this approach, they determine the optimal portfolio choice of a risk-averse foreign exchange investor who uses moving average trading signals as the information instrument for investment opportunities. The results show that the estimated optimal trading rules represent a significant economic value for the investor.

Overall, the existing literature on the profitability of technical analysis in foreign exchange markets suggests that those trading rules are profitable. However, some researches ascribe the profitability of technical analysis merely to central bank interventions in foreign exchange markets (see e.g. LeBaron [1999]). They argue that monetary authorities are willing to take losses on their trading as their objective is to maintain orderly market conditions rather than making profits. Thus, the profitability of technical analysis may represent a transfer from central banks to technical traders (see Szakmary and Mathur [1997]). In this context, Neely [1998] shows that central bank interventions are generally against the position taken by technical traders who guess the sign of excess return right, so that interventions seems to be unprofitable at least in the short-run. However, this argumentation appears to be more than equivocal. On the one hand, trading rules also generate excess profits in other asset markets such as e.g. stock markets, where no official interventions occur (see e.g. Jegadeesh and Titman [1993] and [2001]). On the other hand, the empirical results of Neely [2002] show that central bank interventions respond to exchange rate trends which are responsible for the profitability of technical trading rules. Furthermore, empirical studies on the profitability of central bank interventions reveal that in the long run interventions generate substantial profits for monetary authorities (see e.g. Leahy [1995], Sweeney [2000], Saacke [2002], Ito [2003], Goldberg and von Nitzsch [2001], LeBaron [1999], Rosser [2003]). Thus, it would be reasonable for investors to trade in accordance with central banks instead of taking the opposite position.[66]

V.3.2.2 Empirical results for the DM/USD and Yen/USD exchange rate

Section V.3.2.2 deals with the profitability of technical trading rules for the DM/USD and YEN/USD exchange rates. In particular, we investigate the profitability of several moving average trading rules. We consider various lengths of the moving average to safeguard against the results being only due the specific length of the chosen moving average. The main objective of this section is to answer the question whether such trend heuristics are a reliable rule of thumb in foreign exchange markets. If technical trading rules are profitable in foreign exchange markets, the application of trend heuristics is a reasonable choice for each market participant, as it allows for a fast and frugal decision making in a rather complex decision situation.

V.3.2.2.1 Data

For our evaluation of the profitability of moving average trading rules in foreign exchange markets we use daily exchange rates for the German Deutsch Mark (DM) and the Japanese Yen

[66] The crucial point in the context of intervention effectiveness is the considered time horizon. If the objective of central bank interventions is to break existing trends it may take longer to realize this change. This suggestion is supported by the empirical findings of Saacke [2002] who shows that profitability only occurs in the longer-run (after 26 days positive impact, statistically significant after 330 days), meaning that in the short-run the response of exchange rates to interventions is either insignificant or has the wrong sign. However, in the longer-run his results indicate that exchange rates tend to move in a manner consistent with the central bank's intentions. This result is in line with previous findings suggesting that in the longer-run central bank interventions affect exchange rates in the desired direction, but that in the short-run the central bank is likely to experience losses (see e.g. Goodhart and Hesse [1993]).

(YEN) against the US Dollar (USD).[67] The sample runs from January 1, 1975 to June 30 2003. Figure V-22 and Figure V-23 show the frequency distributions and some summary statistics of the daily DM/USD and Yen/USD exchange rate changes. The exchange rate changes are defined as $r_t = (\ln S_t - \ln S_{t-1}) * 100$. Overall, both time series of exchange rate changes seem to have little drift and there appears to be some evidence for skewness but strong evidence for excess kurtosis. The Jarque-Bera test indicates that for both time series the null hypothesis of normality of returns must be rejected.

Figure V-22: Frequency distribution and summary statistics of daily DM/USD exchange rate returns

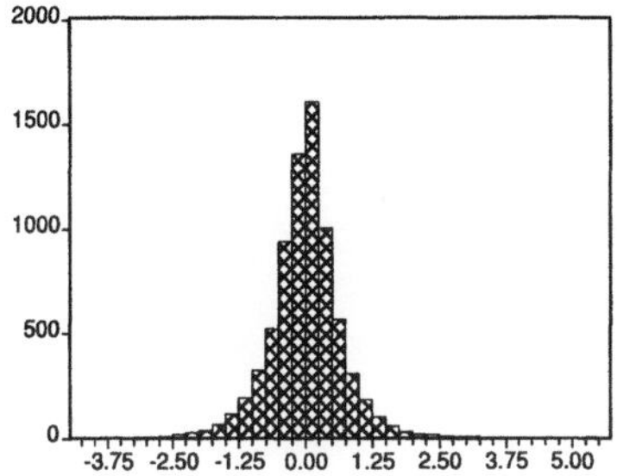

Series: D_DMUSD	
Sample 1/02/1975 6/30/2003	
Observations 7433	
Mean	-0.004662
Median	0.000000
Maximum	5.263204
Minimum	-4.011732
Std. Dev.	0.641380
Skewness	-0.088914
Kurtosis	5.829658
Jarque-Bera	2489.617
Probability	0.000000

Figure V-23: Frequency distribution and summary statistics of daily Yen/USD exchange rate returns

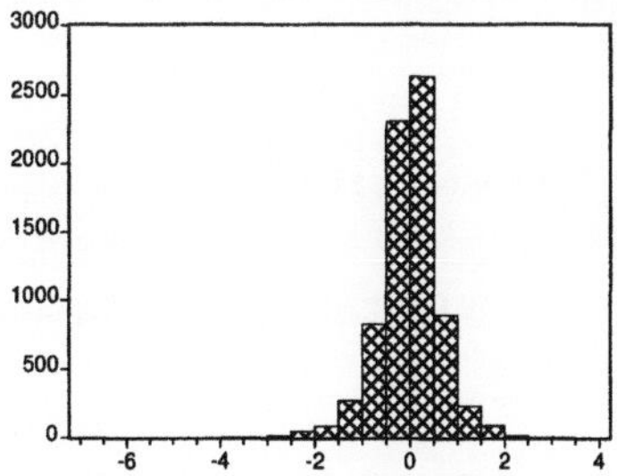

Series: D_YENUSD	
Sample 1/02/1975 6/30/2003	
Observations 7433	
Mean	-0.012338
Median	0.000000
Maximum	3.571055
Minimum	-6.581770
Std. Dev.	0.659733
Skewness	-0.566345
Kurtosis	8.186338
Jarque-Bera	8727.917
Probability	0.000000

67 The exchange rate data were taken from the Datastream of Thomson Financial. As no continuous exchange rate series exists for DM/USD and YEN/USD exchange rates for the time period of 1975 to 2003, we refer to the corresponding cross rates via the British Pound. The mnemonics are DMARKER, USDOLLR and JAPAYEN.

V.3.2.2.2 Implementation of the moving average trading rule

According to moving average trading rules, a buy of USD is indicated when the exchange rate exceeds the moving average. Conversely, when the exchange rate is below the moving average the trading rule recommends a sell of USD. Thus, the trading signal (y_t) of a moving average trading rule can be defined as

$$y_t = \begin{cases} 1 & \text{if} \quad S_t \geq MA_t \\ -1 & \text{if} \quad S_t < MA_t \end{cases} . \tag{V-24}$$

In our analysis of the profitability of technical trading rules, we evaluate various moving average trading rules using different length of the moving average. The main reason for choosing several lengths of moving average is to ensure that our results are not biased by the impact of data snooping. In particular, we apply the technical trading rule for moving averages of a length of 200, 150, 100, 50 and 36 days. The choice of the length of the moving averages is somewhat arbitrary, but coincides largely with those often used in practice.

The estimated raw return according to the moving average trading rule on each day in the observation period is given by

$$r_t^{raw} = y_t \cdot r_t . \tag{V-25}$$

The raw return describes the profit or loss on each trading day in the sample, which is associated with the application of the moving average trading rule. However, trading in the spot foreign exchange market requires also a consideration of interest rates when evaluating the trading performance of moving average strategies. Thus, we also compute interest-rate-adjusted augmented returns:

$$r_t^{aug} = \left[\ln S_{t+1} - \ln S_t - \ln(1+i_t) + \ln(1+i_t^*)\right] \tag{V-26}$$

where i_t denotes the US interest rate and i_t^* the German respectively Japanese interest rate.[68]

[68] The interest rates for the USA are daily Federal Fund Rates provided by the Board of Governor, the German interest rates are daily overnight money market rates provided by the Deutsche Bundesbank and the Japanese interest rates are monthly overnight interbank rates. Here, we assume that the daily interest rates are equal for the whole month.

Table V-33: Technical trading profits for the DM/USD exchange rate

	MA 36	MA 50	MA 100	MA 150	MA 200	RW
Mean of raw returns	8.33	7.89	7.05	5.27	5.25	0.00
Mean of aug. returns	8.09	7.65	6.88	5.16	5.13	-1.83
Trade fraction (in %)	6.64	5.27	3.63	2.92	2.42	1.52
Avg. trades per year	16.59	13.17	9.07	7.31	6.05	3.8
Mean of net returns*	7.58	7.26	6.61	4.95	4.95	-1.95
Sign predictions (in %)**	52.11 (13.60)	52.03 (12.51)	51.91 (12.32)	51.87 (11.83)	52.39 (18.32)	51.51 (1.55)
IPM	0.0672	0.0636	0.0570	0.0428	0.0423	-0.0160
Sharpe Ratio	0.7677	0.7273	0.6557	0.4950	0.4914	-0.1818
t-Statistic	4.18	3.95	3.55	2.67	2.64	-0.99

Notes: Return measures are annualized percentage returns.
* It is assumed that the transaction costs equal 0.03%.
** Sign predictions are evaluated according to the χ^2-test of independence (see Appendix); t-statistics are given in parenthesis.

Table V-34: Technical trading profits for the Yen/USD exchange rate

	MA 36	MA 50	MA 100	MA 150	MA 200	RW
Mean of raw returns	5.56	6.92	8.62	7.05	5.56	-0.42
Mean of aug. returns	5.20	6.54	8.14	6.58	5.20	-2.70
Trade fraction (in %)	7.80	6.30	3.53	2.42	2.25	1.12
Avg. trades per year	19.50	15.74	8.83	6.04	5.63	2.79
Mean of net returns	4.6	6.06	7.87	6.40	5.02	-2.79
Sign predictions (in %)**	50.74 (1.68)	51.16 (4.19)	51.83 (10.75)	51.77 (10.90)	51.33 (7.89)	51.53 (0.42)
IPM	0.0440	0.0549	0.0673	0.0545	0.0430	-0.0238
Sharpe Ratio	0.4854	0.6072	0.7480	0.6079	0.4820	-0.2168
t-stat	2.64	3.30	4.05	3.28	2.59	-1.43

Notes: Return measures are annualized percentage returns.
* It is assumed that the transaction costs equal 0.03%.
** Sign predictions are evaluated according to the χ^2-test of independence (see Appendix); t-statistics are given in parenthesis.

The results for the average annualized raw and augmented returns according to the different moving average trading rule are summarized in the Table V-33 and Table V-34. It becomes apparent that for both exchange rate time series all analyzed moving average trading rules lead to substantial positive returns so that technical trading rules appear to be profitable at first glance. This conclusion is also confirmed by comparing the returns of moving average trading rules with those of a naïve investment strategy. The naïve investment strategy is in this context defined as an exclusive orientation on the interest rate differential. The investor always chooses to put his money in the currency which offers the higher interest yield. Implicitly, such a naïve trading strategy coincides with the idea that exchange rates follow a random walk process and thus any kind of exchange rate forecasting is futile. Consequently, this naïve investment strategy is denoted as random walk investment strategy (RW). However, the results indicate that the performance of the naïve investment strategy is below that of all moving average trading rules. To assess the significance of these results, we compute the Student t-statistic. The considered null hypothesis in this context is that the augmented returns of the moving average trading strategy are equal to zero. The t-statistic is defined as

$$t = \sqrt{N}\frac{\mu_{r_{aug}}}{\sigma_{r_{aug}}} \qquad \text{(V-27)}$$

where N is the number of observations (see Lequeux [1998]).[69] If t exceeds 1.645, the returns are said to be significantly positive at the critical threshold of 5%. The t-statistics indicate that for all moving average trading rules the profits are statistically significantly positive. In contrast, for the naïve investment strategy, the t-statistics show that the profits are statistically not different from zero.

Table V-35 summarizes the previous results for the profitability of the different moving average trading rules and sorts these trading rules according to their profitability, starting with the most profitable trading rule. For the DM/USD exchange rate the results suggest that the profitability of moving average trading rules increase with shorter moving averages. In contrast, for the YEN/USD exchange rate course of profitability, moving average trading rules show a humped shape. The most profitable trading rule is the rule with a moving average of length 100. With regard to the profitability of the naïve investment strategy, we can conclude that this strategy is basically unprofitable and leads to the worst results.

---

[69] However, t-tests may not be the proper way to test for the significance of moving average profitability because of deviations from normality in the foreign exchange returns (see LeBaron [1999]).

Table V-35: Ranking of moving average trading rules

Ranking	DM/USD	YEN/USD
1	MA 36	MA 100
2	MA 50	MA 150
3	MA 100	MA50
4	MA 150	MA 36 / MA 200
5	MA 200	
6	RW	RW

V.3.2.2.3 Profitability indicators for technical trading rule profits

The results for the raw and augmented returns have shown that moving average trading rules are profitable in the investigated period. This holds true for both exchange rate time series. However, we have not evaluated the profitability of this technical trading rule sufficiently accurately. Therefore, we are in this section concerned with a deeper analysis of the profitability of technical trading rules. We evaluate a set of profitability indicators suggested by the relevant literature (see Sosvilla-Rivero et al. [2002] for a brief survey).

First, we deal with transaction costs associated with dealing according to the moving average trading rule. Thus, we analyze whether our results of positive returns withstands the inclusion of transaction costs. Every change in the trading position is associated with trading costs so that the returns of the technical trading rules should be adjusted for such transaction costs. A possibility to account for transaction costs directly is to adjust the augmented returns by the costs for round trip trades[70]:

$$R_T^{net} = \sum_{t=T+1}^{N} y_t \cdot r_t^{aug} + nrt\left[\ln(1-c) - \ln(1+c)\right] \qquad \text{(V-28)}$$

where R_T^{net} is the total net return for a period of length N, nrt is the number of round trip trades and c denotes the transaction costs. Usually, it is suggested that the transaction costs

[70] A round trip trade consists of a long position taking at time t and short position taking at time t+k.

are round about 0.03% per transaction. This value corresponds largely with the realities in foreign exchange trading (see Lequeux and Acar [1998], LeBaron [1999] and Sosvilla-Rivero et al. [2002]). In addition to this direct consideration of transaction costs, Lequeux [1998] proposes a second way of considering transaction costs. The advantage of this approach is that it provides a more general impression of the relevance and development of transaction costs for various moving average trading rules. Lequeux [1998] shows that under the assumption that the underlying time series S_t follows a centered iid normal distribution, the expected number of trades per year generated by a moving average trading rule of order m is approximated by

$$E(N) = 1 + (T-2)\left[\frac{1}{2} - \frac{1}{\pi}\arcsin(\rho_F)\right] \tag{V-29}$$

where T is the assumed number trading days per year and ρ_F is defined as

$$\rho_F = \frac{\sum_{i=0}^{m-2}(m-i-1)(m-i-2)}{\sum_{i=0}^{m-2}(m-i-1)^2} \quad \text{if } m \geq 2. \tag{V-30}$$

Subsequently, the expected transaction costs related to a moving average trading rule is given by

$$E(TC) = -cE(N) \tag{V-31}$$

where c is the trading cost per round turn. Figure V-24 illustrates the development of the expected number of trades and transaction costs subject to the length of the moving average. Obviously, the number of expected trades decreases rather fast with increasing lengths of the moving average and, associated with decreasing number of expected trades, the transaction costs diminish.

Figure V-24: Expected number of transactions and cost under the random walk assumption

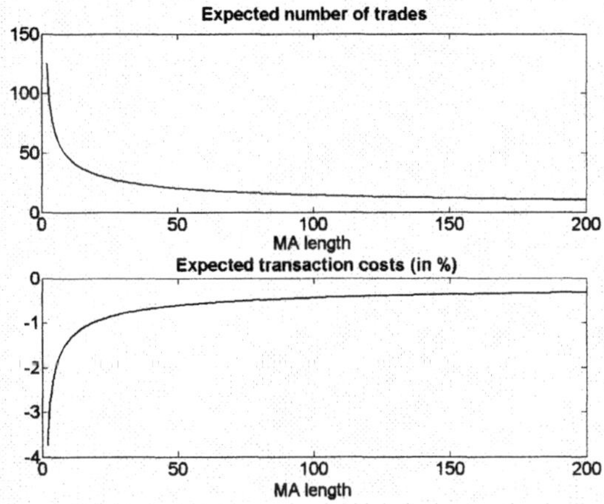

Table V-36 summarizes the transaction costs associated with each moving average trading rule considering both the expected costs according to Lequeux [1998] and the actual costs calculated via equation (V-28). Interestingly, the expected number of trades and correspondingly the expected costs always exceed the actual figures. The reason for this finding may be seen in the assumed random walk behavior of foreign exchange rates on which the calculation of expected trades rests (see Lequeux [1998]).

Table V-36: Moving average trading rules and transaction costs

	Lequeux [1998] method		Actual observations		
				DM/USD	YEN/USD
MA 36	Expected number of trades	24	Actual Number of trades	17	20
	Expected costs (in %)	-0.72	Actual costs (in %)	-0.51	-0.60
MA 50	Expected number of trades	20	Actual Number of trades	13	16
	Expected costs (in %)	-0.61	Actual costs (in %)	-0.39	-0.48
MA 100	Expected number of trades	15	Actual Number of trades	9	9
	Expected costs (in %)	-0.44	Actual costs (in %)	-0.27	-0.27
MA 150	Expected number of trades	12	Actual Number of trades	7	6
	Expected costs (in %)	-0.37	Actual costs (in %)	-0.21	-0.18
MA 200	Expected number of trades	11	Actual Number of trades	6	6
	Expected costs (in %)	-0.32	Actual costs (in %)	-0.18	-0.18

Note: Transaction costs are assumed to be 0.03% (see e.g. Levich and Thomas [1993], Osler and Chang [1995] and Sosvilla-Rivero et al. [2002])

Overall the discussion on the relevance of transaction costs and the values for the net returns (see Table V-33 and Table V-34) show that in our empirical evaluation transaction cost plays only a minor role. All transaction-cost-adjusted returns are positive and the ranking of the various moving average trading rules is almost the same for both exchange rate time series.

A further measure for the profitability of moving average trading rules is the number of correctly anticipated changes in the exchange rate time series. If the sign prediction of the moving average trading rule exceeds 50%, it allows better forecasts than a naïve random walk forecast. To evaluate the significance of the direction-of-change forecasts we perform a simple χ^2-test of independence. The corresponding test statistics are also reported in Table V-33 and Table V-34. The hit rates for the considered moving average trading rules reflect the fact that those trading rules tend to anticipate the direction of future exchange rate changes somewhat better than a naïve coin flip. The test-statistics of the χ^2-test of independence for evaluating the significance of the sign predictions suggest that except for the MA 36 trading rule for the YEN/USD all hit rates are significantly different from 50%. In contrast, for the naïve investment strategy the hit rates are also above 50%, but the test statistics indicate that the results are not significant.

A related measure for the profitability of technical trading rules is the ideal profit measure (IPM). The IPM measures the returns of the moving average trading rule against a perfect predictor and is defined as

$$IPM = \frac{\sum_{t=T+1}^{N} y_t \cdot r_t^{aug}}{\sum_{t=T+1}^{N} \left| r_t^{aug} \right|}. \qquad \text{(V-32)}$$

According to equation (V-32), the IPM corresponds to 1 if the trading signal y_t takes the correct trading position for all observations in the sample. In case that all trading signals y_t are wrong the value of IPM equals −1. An IPM = 0, which corresponds to the random walk prediction, is considered as a benchmark to evaluate the performance of the technical trading rule (see Sosvilla-Rivero et al. [2002]). The results for the ideal profit measures are summarized in Table V-33 and Table V-34. For both exchange rate time series the ideal profit measure for all moving average trading rules indicates that using technical analysis tools leads to better forecasts than naive random walk forecasts.

To adjust the technical trading returns for risk, we calculate the Sharpe ratio for each moving average trading rule. The Sharpe ratio (Sharpe [1966]) describes a measure for risk-adjusted returns from the technical trading rule. It is defined as the ratio of mean returns in excess of the risk free-rate of interest and the standard deviation of returns. Given the mean and standard deviation of daily returns ($\mu_{r^{aug}}; \sigma_{r^{aug}}$), the annual Sharpe ratio can be approximated as follows (see Sosvilla-Rivero et al. [2002]):

$$SR = \frac{250\mu_{r^{aug}}}{\sqrt{250\sigma_{r^{aug}}^2}} = \sqrt{250}\frac{\mu_{r^{aug}}}{\sigma_{r^{aug}}}. \qquad \text{(V-33)}$$

Equation (V-33) clarifies that the higher the Sharpe ratio, the higher the return of the trading strategy and the lower the volatility of the returns. To interpret the values of the Sharpe ratio for the technical trading rules, one usually compares it with the Sharpe ratios for buy and hold strategies on aggregate stock portfolios. The annual Sharpe ratio for aggregate stock portfolios is around 0.3 or 0.4 (see LeBaron [1999]). As Table V-33 and Table V-34 illustrate, the values of Sharpe ratio for both exchange rate time series and all moving average trading rules are larger than the comparative value for aggregate stock portfolios. In addition the moving average rules with the highest returns possess also the highest value of Sharpe ratio.

To examine the robustness of our findings we calculate the performance of moving average trading rules on a rolling basis so that we analyze the profitability for a great deal of moving average trading rules (see Table V-37 and Table V-38). Furthermore, this approach can be used to evaluate on a broad basis how reliable the application of trend heuristics is in foreign exchange markets. Overall, the results show that the application of moving average trading rules is a reasonable choice in foreign exchange markets. The results also indicate that in case of the DM/USD exchange rate the fraction of negative returns increases with the length of the moving average. This result coincides with the ranking for the moving average trading rules for the DM/USD exchange rate (see Table V-35). Furthermore, the fraction of negative returns decreases with increasing time horizons. For the YEN/USD exchange rate the fraction of negative returns coincides also with the ranking presented in Table V-35 as the hump shaped course of returns is also found in the fraction of negative returns. As for the DM/USD exchange rate, the fraction of negative returns tends to decrease with increasing time horizons. Only for the three years time horizon is this finding not true. With regard to the naïve investment strategy, which is based on the belief in the random walk behavior, the results for the fraction of negative returns indicate that the application of this trading rule is rather uncertain as every second return for the considered time horizons is negative.

Table V-37: Fraction of negative augmented returns for various rolling time periods, DM/USD exchange rate

Length of MA		**36d**	**50d**	**100d**	**150d**	**200d**	**RW**
Fraction of negative augmented returns	**1 year**	14.56%	13.90%	19.00%	32.31%	27.71%	51.27%
	2 year	3.06%	4.89%	7.11%	24.21%	22.64%	49.99%
	3 year	7.70%	1.51%	6.00%	16.08%	17.27%	52.18%

Table V-38: Fraction of negative augmented returns for various rolling time periods, Yen/USD exchange rate

Length of MA		**36d**	**50d**	**100d**	**150d**	**200d**	**RW**
Fraction of negative augmented returns	**1 year**	28.39%	22.16%	14.55%	22.75%	31.71%	49.53%
	2 year	22.55%	13.68%	6.64%	10.80%	22.08%	55.65%
	3 year	24.20%	6.10%	3.02%	9.33%	18.98%	64.58%

V.4 Summary

Overall, both conducted experiments provide in our view evidence for the relevance of psychological effects in experimental foreign exchange markets. In particular, the results reveal that it is likely that in the short run trend heuristics play a decisive role. In the first experiment, we found that in the short run participants just extrapolate the most recent exchange rate trends. Thereby, the forecasting performance of novices is better than that of professional exchange rate analysts. Thus, it is fair to conclude that orientating on recent trends is a reasonable choice at least in the short run. In contrast, our results for the professional exchange rate forecasts reveal that orientating on macroeconomic fundamentals when forming expectations about future exchange rates is rather futile, at least for the considered time horizons. The second experiment provides additional evidence for the existence of trend heuristics in experimental foreign exchange markets. The results reveal that more or less all participants base their expectations concerning future exchange rates on the most recent trend in the experimental exchange rate time series. Furthermore, the relevance of coordinating the expectations in speculative markets is also analyzed and confirmed in our experimental foreign exchange market. On our results we have to conclude that the implications of the Keynesian beauty context metaphor are highly relevant in an environment characterized by a high degree of behavioral uncertainty. The results show that most of the participants in an experimental market use the same expectation formation strategy, so that the expectations concerning future exchange rates are coordinated. The expectation formation strategy can be interpreted as a convention with regard to the future development of the exchange rate.

In our view, technical analysis can be interpreted as a concrete implementation of trend heuristics in the context of foreign exchange markets. Thus, the importance and relevance of technical analysis in foreign exchange markets must be seen as the result of the human search for ways to cope with the complexity of the decision situation within foreign exchange markets. As Gigerenzer and Todd [1999b] stress, the usefulness of applying simplification strategies like trend heuristics can only be evaluated against their usefulness in real world decision situation. Thus, applying trend heuristics is only a reasonable choice if they lead to profits on average. The literature on the profitability of technical trading rules and our investigation of the profitability of different moving average trading rules suggest that in foreign exchange markets technical analysis is profitable on average. Consequently, applying technical analysis and thus trend heuristics is a reasonable behavior as it allows each market participant to come to fast and by the same time frugal decisions in the complex decision environment of foreign exchange markets.

Chapter VI
Concluding remarks

VI.1 Summary

This study has dealt with psychological factors in the human expectation formation. Our particular interest was on the human expectation formation in the context of foreign exchange markets. The aim was to find a reasonable explanation for the mysterious development of the EUR/USD exchange rate. At the beginning of this study, we have illustrated the exchange rate disconnect puzzle for the EUR/USD exchange rate. Our results indicated that macroeconomic fundamentals can not explain the development of the EUR/USD exchange rate sufficiently. Furthermore, our empirical evaluation revealed that important implications of the asset market theory (e.g. rational expectations, the impact of news, efficient market hypothesis etc.) are not supported by the data for the EUR/USD exchange rate. Thus, the exchange rate disconnect puzzle is still valid.

In Chapter III we have addressed the relevance of trends and speculation in foreign exchange markets. Instead of looking at macroeconomic fundamentals, our analysis showed that exchange rates rather move in long and persistent trends disconnected from macroeconomic developments. In our view, these trends can be mainly ascribed to the speculative trading behaviors of many foreign exchange market participants. The overview of the empirical evidence suggested that in the short- and medium-run the actual trading behavior of most foreign exchange market participants is dominated by non-fundamental, destabilizing factors like e.g. technical analysis and bandwagon effects. In this context, the Keynesian view of the functioning of asset markets is of particular relevance. Keynes argued that people instead of calculating an optimal decision rather base their decisions on a 'conventional judgment'. Thereby, psychological phenomena play a decisive role. We have explored these psychological factors in Chapter IV in more detail.

According to the psychological evidence presented in Chapter IV, human beings tend to use simplification mechanisms when making their decisions to cope with the complexity of the decision situation. Important types of simplification mechanisms are simple decision heuristics.

Simple heuristics are rules of thumbs, which allow individuals quick and efficient decision making even under a high degree of uncertainty. In the context of foreign exchange markets, the 'conventional judgment' can be interpreted as a simple heuristics. Thereby it is likely that the existing exchange rate trend reflects the prevailing 'conventional judgment' concerning the evaluation of a specific currency. The existence of a convention concerning the evaluation of an exchange rate suggests that it is reasonable to simply extrapolate the recent trend when making decisions in foreign exchange markets. Thus, the application of trend-following trading rules is a logical consequence of conventions as simple heuristics.

In Chapter V we presented experimental and empirical investigations related to the human expectation formation in the context of foreign exchange markets. Our results largely confirmed the idea of the existence of a simple trend heuristic in foreign exchange markets. People seem to show a strong tendency to extrapolate at least in the short-run recent exchange rate movements in the future.

The first experiment has revealed remarkable differences between the forecasting behavior of professional analysts and novices. Whereas professional analysts usually expected a reversal of the recent exchange rate movements novices tended to extrapolate the most recent trend in the short-run. Only in the long-run novices also expected a reversal of the most recent exchange rate trend. In this context, it should be noticed that the forecasting accuracy of novices was more accurate than that of professional analysts. Thus, trend-extrapolating expectation formation mechanisms appear to be a reasonable choice as they allow for better decisions than the fully-fledged analysis of professional analysts. In our view this surprising result can be ascribed to the beneficial impact of the 'less is more effect' (see Marsh et al. [2004]). According to this phenomenon considering only one or a few cues allows people to arrive at better decisions than considering all relevant factors.

The second experiment included the analysis of human expectation formation in an experimental foreign exchange market. Our results also provided evidence for a trend-extrapolating behavior of experimental foreign exchange market participants. The most common expectation formation mechanism in our experimental setting can be described as trend-extrapolating. Furthermore, the second experiment also provided evidence for the Keynesian view that the expectations of market participants are guided by a 'conventional judgment'. We found that the participants in the experiment tend to coordinate their expectations on a common trend-extrapolating prediction strategy. Thus, the results of the second experiment also provided evidence for the relevance of the suggested simple trend heuristic in foreign exchange markets.

As Gigerenzer and Todd [1999b] argue, the reliability of simple heuristics can only be evaluated against their usefulness in the real world. So, we analyzed in our empirical part of Chapter V the profitability of a specific simple trend heuristic – a moving average trading rule – in the context of foreign exchange markets. Our results revealed that using moving average trading rules leads on average to substantial profits. This conclusion appears to be also in line with the evidence of the profitability of technical analysis in foreign exchange markets reported in the literature.

Thus, it is fair to conclude that using simple trend heuristics in foreign exchange markets is a reasonable choice as it allows a quick and efficient decision making while generating substantial profits.

VI.2 Outlook

Our study, of course, should not be seen as a closing paper to the issue of human expectation formation in the context of foreign exchange markets. It rather represents a first attempt to solve the existing exchange rate disconnect puzzle by referring to psychological insights.

At least three important issues are on the agenda for further research in this area. First, it is clearly necessary to expand the experimental evidence on the expectation formation of professional exchange rate analysts and novices. In particular, we need more research that pays attention to a direct comparison of the forecasting behaviors of professional analysts and novices. In this context, one can – for example – think of experiments in which novices should predict the course of the actual EUR/USD exchange rate so that we can directly compare the forecasting performance of both groups. However, in experiments with real exchange rate time series there always exists the risk that the participants in the experiments know the time series to be forecasted.

Second, we need more experimental research conducted in a simulated market environment. Additional market experiments should allow us to verify whether the observed trend-extrapolating expectation formation gives a solid result and can be seen as a general property of human expectation formation in the context of foreign exchange markets. Furthermore, new foreign exchange market experiments enable us to check the robustness of the coordination of expectations in a market environment. However, further experiments should be modified in such a way that the dominating impact of the random shock is eliminated.

Third, the presented study has in our view important implications for economic policy making. Future research should analyze these implications. Here, we only want to outline the most compelling issue very briefly. Where do the conventions come from? Who or what is responsible for changes in the prevailing conventions? In our view, central banks play a pivotal role in foreign exchange markets. The major turning points in free floating exchange rates are always accompanied by central banks' foreign exchange market interventions. Figure VI-1 shows – as an example – the course of the DM/USD exchange rate and the intervention activities of the Deutsche Bundesbank and the Federal Reserve Bank. All major turning points of the DM/USD exchange rate coincide with heavy foreign exchange market interventions of the related central banks. This point was already mentioned by Catte et al. [1994] who stated that

> "... eight of nine major turning points of the dollar between 1985 and 1991 coincided with an episode of concerted intervention. At the very least, concerted interventions appear to have determined the exact timing of the turning points, within the broad trends set by the development of fundamentals." (Catte et al. [1994], p. 217)

Figure VI-1: Intervention activities in the DM/USD market

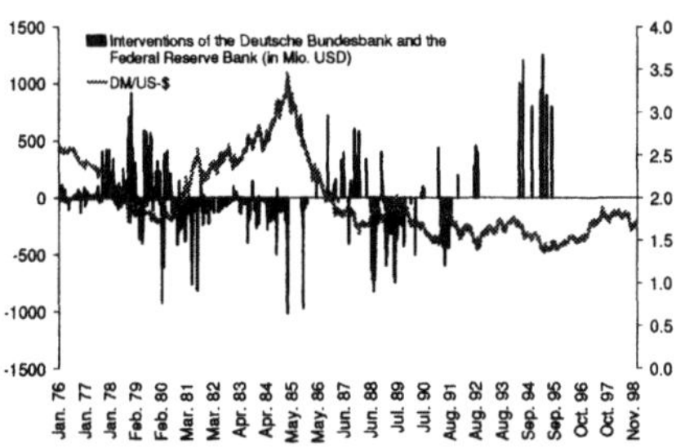

Figure VI-2: Intervention activities in the EUR/USD market

Also in the EUR/USD foreign exchange market, central banks' intervention activities seem to be responsible for breaking the downward trend of the Euro. On September 22, 2000 the European Central Bank (ECB) intervened in concert with the Federal Reserve Bank and the monetary authorities of Japan, France, England and Canada in support of the Euro. Afterwards, at the beginning of November 2000 the ECB intervened again on occasion, but alone (see Figure VI-2).

As Figure VI-1 and Figure VI-2 show, virtually all major turning points of free floating exchange rates are accompanied by foreign exchange market interventions. Market participants seem to be unable to change existing trends in foreign exchange markets by themselves. As these trends are the results of conventions, market participants seem to adhere on the prevailing conventions. According to the results of psychological research, this behaviour is very comprehensible. Conventions serve foreign exchange market participants as simple heuristics which allow them fast and frugal decision making in a complex environment.

In principle, conventions can be established in at least two different ways (see Chapter IV.3.2): first, convention can be established by authority and, second, by the gradual accretion of precedent. The second opportunity would imply that conventions change gradually, i.e. more and more market participants change their evaluation in the direction of the new convention. Since no turning point exists without intervention activity of central banks this opportunity seems to be less important than the first one. We argue that central banks may affect the exchange rates by altering the prevailing convention with foreign exchange market interventions. Through interventions central banks explicate their own assessment concerning the future exchange rate development. Because of their special role in foreign exchange markets, central banks can be seen as opinion leaders with regard to the assessment of exchange rates. Because of their opinion leadership central banks influence the decision behavior of all other market participants. Pingle [1997] emphasizes that individual decision makers tend to rely on authority's prescription as it helps them to avoid needless decision costs associated with comparing alternative choices. Within the scope of foreign exchange markets, central bank interventions can be interpreted as a prescription of central banks concerning the future exchange rate development. Thus, central bank interventions may provide a guideline for the market participants and consequently help to alter prevailing conventions in foreign exchange markets, i.e. central banks provide a coordination mechanism with the aid of interventions.

This point of view concerning the way central bank interventions works is rather uncommon in the literature on foreign exchange interventions. One of the first who indirectly mentioned a coordination function of interventions are Frankel and Dominguez [1993]:

> "Our own inclination is to believe that expectations only tend to be extrapolative in occasional periods: speculative bubble environments, when the foreign exchange market loses its moorings and forecasters forget about fundamentals. Of course, these are precisely the periods in which central bankers might be most interested in using the tool of intervention." (Frankel and Dominguez [1993], p. 343)

A very similar point of view is shared by Sarno and Taylor [2001]. They propose a new channel of how intervention may affect the exchange rate through its role in eliminating a coordination failure in the foreign exchange market. The coordination failure is attributed to the suggestion that foreign exchange rate may be subject to irrational speculative bubbles so that the exchange rate is driven away from a level consistent with the underlying fundamentals. If the exchange rate movements are dominated by trend behavior for a long time, "it takes a great deal of courage for an individual trader to attempt to buck the market" (Sarno and Taylor [2001], p. 863). In this context, Sarno and Taylor [2001] interpret foreign exchange market intervention as "fulfilling a coordinating role in that they may organize the "smart money" to enter the market in the same time." Also De Grauwe [2000] states that central bank interventions may work through affecting prevailing beliefs. However, he suggests that central bank interventions are scarcely able to affect the beliefs of the other market participants so that it is unlikely that central bank interventions have much effect. With reference to the ECB interventions he concludes that the best possible attitude of the ECB is one of benign neglect, as the prevailing beliefs will change sooner or later and bring about a turnaround in the exchange rate. Nevertheless, in situations where the divergence between prevailing beliefs and economic reality becomes too great De Grauwe [2000] advocates that central bank interventions may work through altering the prevailing beliefs. He refers in this context to the large misevaluation of the dollar in the mid 1980s. The concerted interventions of the FED, the Bundesbank and the Bank of Japan led to a decline of the dollar and convinced the market participants that the high dollar value was fundamentally unjustified.

The concept of a 'coordination channel' can explain two essential empirical regularities with regard to the effectiveness of foreign exchange market interventions. First, numerous empirical studies reach the conclusion that foreign exchange market intervention are ineffective (see e.g. Frenkel et al. [2001]). These studies usually analyze the direct response of the exchange rate to central bank interventions, i.e. the analysis is limited to a day-to-day perspective. However, the psychological characteristics of conventions would suggest that a change in the prevailing convention is only possible in a longer time span. For this, empirical support can be found by Saacke [2002]. His empirical analysis related to the effectiveness of central bank interventions suggests that the short-term response of exchange rates to interventions is largely consistent with the existing literature, i.e. econometric estimates of the influence of interventions on the level of the exchange rate is either statistically insignificant or has the wrong sign. However, in the longer-run the results of Saacke [2002] suggest that the exchange rates tend to move in a manner consistent with the central banks intentions. Second, according to many empirical studies central bank interventions increase the volatility of exchange rates (see e.g. Bonser-Neal and Tanner [1996], Baillie and Osterberg [1997] and Dominguez [1998]). This empirical regularity can also be explained by the 'coordination channel'. In connection with the intervention activity of central banks the existing uncertainty in foreign exchange markets increases due to the fact that the present convention, which serves traders as a coordination mechanism, is queried by central bank's interventions.

A first attempt to deal with the 'coordination channel' on a theoretical basis can be found in Schmidt and Wollmershäuser [2005]. This paper analyzes the effectiveness of central bank interventions within a chartist-fundamentalist-model. The results show that sterilized interventions lead to a reduction of existing exchange rate misalignments and, in particular, to an earlier occurrence of turning points.

Chapter VII
Appendices

Appendix A: Estimation procedures

Hansen and Hodrick [1980] demonstrate that, when the forecast horizon is larger than the observational frequency, the forecast error ε_{t+k} will be serially correlated. We decide to account for the autocorrelation in the residuals on the one hand by using the Newey and West [1987] estimation procedure (see Cavaglia et al. [1994]) and on the other hand by explicitly modeling the autocorrelation structure of residuals by ARMA methods.

The Newey and West [1987] estimation procedure provides a covariance estimator that is consistent in the presence of heteroscedasticity and autocorrelation of unknown form. Thus, the standard errors are adjusted by taking into account heteroscedasticity and autocorrelation in the residuals (see Verbeek [2000]). In our context, the advantage of using the Newey and West [1987] estimation procedure is that it allows a direct testing of the relationship between exchange rates and expectations in a bivariate regression approach. Thus, the supposed correlation can be easily evaluated by means of regression analysis. However, the Newey and West [1987] estimation procedure involves also some drawbacks. First, the bivariate approach may entail that we disregard variables that are important to explain the development of the depending variable. Thus, we may have an omitted variable problem. Furthermore, the Newey and West [1987] estimation procedure may imply that the Test statistics of the F-Test are biased, as the standard assumptions with respect to the F-test are rather demanding. Thus, it must be noted that the results of the Wald Tests should be interpreted with caution.

An opportunity to avoid the above-mentioned problems is to model the autocorrelation structure of the residuals explicitly by either autoregressive processes or moving average processes. In this case the appropriate regression equation is given by

$$y_t = \alpha + \beta_t x_t + \varepsilon_t \qquad \text{(VII-1)}$$

where y_t and x_r denote observed time series (e.g. actual and expected exchange rate changes) and the error term ε_t is explicitly modeled by either autoregressive (AR) terms

$$\varepsilon_t = \gamma_1\varepsilon_{t-1} + \gamma_2\varepsilon_{t-2} + .. + \gamma_p\varepsilon_{t-p} + u_t \tag{VII-2}$$

or moving average (MA) terms

$$u_t = \phi_1 u_{t-1} + \phi_2 u_{t-2} + ... + \phi_q u_{t-q} \, . \tag{VII-3}$$

In the second regression approach we choose the order of autoregressive and moving averages terms so that the error terms ε_t do not indicate any significant autocorrelation measured by the Ljung-Box test statistic. In our view the second regression approach possesses the advantage that the standard assumption of the Wald tests are normally fulfilled and thus the test statistics appear to be unbiased. Furthermore, the explicit modeling of the autocorrelation structure of the residuals has the advantage that it accounts implicitly for the problem of omitted variables.

Appendix B: Asymmetric and time-varying impact of macroeconomic news on exchange rate movements

The principal topic of our study is the relevance of trend heuristics in foreign exchange markets. The experimental and empirical evidence suggest that market participants in foreign exchange markets use trend heuristics to form their expectations about future exchange rates. The experimental evidence demonstrates a trend-extrapolative expectation formation in the context of foreign exchange markets. The empirical evidence reveals that the application of trend heuristics in foreign exchange markets is a reasonable choice, as simple trend extrapolating trading rules generate substantial profits over the recent years of floating exchange rates.

The application of trend heuristics when forming expectations may also have impact on the perception and processing of new incoming information about macroeconomic fundamentals. In this context, the psychological effects related to the theory of social hypothesis testing and the theory of cognitive dissonance are of major importance. In principle, expectations can be interpreted as subjective hypotheses concerning the arrival or non-arrival of a certain event or situation. Furthermore, expectations are closely connected to the psychological concept of attitudes, as expectations reflect to some degree the personal evaluation of e.g. an exchange rate. The concept of attitude is defined as a "psychological tendency that is expressed by evaluating a particular entity with some degree of favour or disfavour" (Eagly and Chaiken [1998], p. 269).

Psychological research has long investigated the impact of hypotheses and attitudes on the human decision process. The results suggest that they both have a noticeable impact on the individual's decision behavior. As theoretical foundations for these findings, psychologists have developed the theory of social hypothesis testing and the theory of cognitive dissonance.[71] The basic message of both theories is that the human information processing is driven by subjective hypotheses or attitudes. Their impact on human behavior is based on the notion that people tend to organize newly received information (stimulus) into a pattern with other previously encountered stimuli (see Chapter IV). Consequently the mind acts as an intermediary between stimulus and response. If a new stimulus does not fit the pattern or is inconsistent with prior beliefs, people will feel discomfort. To remove this situation of inconsistency or discomfort, people usually behave in such a way that the new information (stimulus) and the existing

---

[71] For an overview concerning the theory of social hypothesis testing see Trope and Liberman [1996]; a review concerning the theory of cognitive dissonance is given by Baron et al. [1998].

pattern become consistent. In this adjustment process, subjective hypotheses and attitudes play a crucial role. Both the impact of subjective hypotheses and attitudes on the perception of new information and their impact on the subsequent information processing and judgment need to be considered. Corresponding to the theory of social hypothesis testing and the theory of cognitive dissonance, people tend to perceive information selectively. This means that people tend to look actively for information which corresponds with their subjective hypotheses or attitudes. In addition, people tend to regard only congruent information, and to ignore information which is inconsistent with their existing subjective hypotheses or attitudes. At the level of information processing and judgment, existing subjective hypotheses and attitudes cause people to tend to interpret information in such a way that it becomes consistent with their subjective hypotheses or attitudes. In consequence, the considered theories of social hypothesis testing and cognitive dissonance suggest that people hang on to their subjective hypotheses and attitudes with unwarranted tenacity and confidence, so that the human information processing at large can be characterized as a conservative process (See Klayman [1995] and Fiedler and Bless [2001]). In the psychological literature this tendency is often denoted as 'confirmation bias'. Following Klayman [1995] the term 'confirmation bias' includes two different, but interrelated elements. First, the term 'confirmation bias' means, "looking for the presence of what you expect" (Klayman [1995], pp.385). This part is obviously related to human information perception. Second, the term 'confirmation bias' refers also "to an inclination to retain, or a disinclination to abandon, a currently favored hypothesis" (Klayman [1995], p. 386). This part can be associated with the levels of information processing and judgment. Rabin and Schrag [1999] specify different underlying roots for the 'confirmation bias'. First, people seem to succumb to confirmation bias if they must interpret ambiguous evidence. This is surely the case for decision situations of foreign exchange traders. In the foreign exchange markets the existing model uncertainty does not allow the individual trader to be sure of considering the right parameters. Second, a 'confirmation bias' can arise when decision makers must interpret statistical evidence to assess the correlation between phenomena that are separated by time. The inability to accurately identify correlation between phenomena seems to be one of the most robust shortcomings in human reasoning. People often imagine correlation between events when no such correlation exists. Third, confirmation bias occurs when decision makers selectively collect or scrutinize evidence. In this context confirmation bias corresponds to a so-called 'hypothesis-based filtering'. While it is sensible to interpret ambiguous data according to current hypotheses, people tend to use the 'filtered' evidence inappropriately as further evidence for existing hypotheses. This sort of error is especially likely when the complexity and ambiguity of evidence requires the use of prior theories when interpreting data and deciding what data should be examined (see Rabin and Schrag [1999]). All things considered, the human tendency to incline to a 'confirmation bias' leads to the implication that "people create for themselves a world in which hypotheses become self-conforming hypotheses and beliefs become self-perpetuating beliefs" (Snyder and Swann [1978], p. 1211).

> Even if one were to develop sufficient doubt about the accuracy of [...] beliefs to proceed to test them actively, one nevertheless might be likely to "find" all the evidence one needs to confirm and retain these beliefs. And, in the end, one may be left with the secure (but totally unwarranted) feeling that these beliefs must be correct because they have survived (what may seem to the individual) perfectly appropriate and even rigorous procedures for assessing their accuracy." (Snyder and Swann [1978], p. 1212)

Moreover, the existence of a 'confirmation bias' in human decision behavior may be responsible for another generally known psychological effect - overconfidence. Rabin and Schrag [1999] show in a model of confirmation bias and belief formation that confirmation bias leads to overconfidence. Overconfidence means that people tend to be excessively confident about their own judgment. This bias of overconfidence seems to persist even if people do learn substantially in circumstances when the consequences of their errors are repeatedly presented to them (see Shiller [1998]). With regard to asset markets, overconfidence is often used as an explanation for the observable over- and underreaction of market participants to new information.

Psychological evidence on the impact of hypotheses and attitudes suggests that individuals react to new information depending on their prior beliefs. In the context of foreign exchange markets, this implies that the impact of newly incoming information about macroeconomic fundamentals should vary across individuals and time. First, each individual may possess a slightly different perception of what factors drive exchange rates. However, this point seems to be of little importance, as experimental evidence suggests that market participants coordinate their expectations rather well. Second, the impact of news may vary across time due to different trend phases of exchange rates. That is, if a currency is in an appreciation phase it is perceived as a strong currency and market participants actively search for information that supports this perception. Conversely, if a currency depreciates continuously, market participants tend to assess this currency as a weak currency and restrict their information search and perception to negative information for that currency. Thus, according to psychological considerations, the impact of macroeconomic news should vary across different trend phases. In the next section, we deal with the assumed asymmetric, time-varying impact of macroeconomic news in detail. Therefore, we refer again to the data used in the analysis of the impact of macroeconomic news on exchange rates (see section II.2.3).

A) Asymmetric response to macroeconomic news?

- **Sign effects – Are good and bad news different?**

In Chapter II, we assume that exchange rates react symmetrically to positive and negative news, i.e. in opposite direction but to the same extent. However, exchange rates may exhibit asymmetries according to the nature of 'news'. Regression equation (VII-4) considers the possibility of asymmetries according to positive and negative news:

$$\Delta s_t = \alpha + \sum_{k=1}^{K} \beta_{1,k} X_{k,t}^{Good} + \sum_{k=1}^{K} \beta_{2,k} X_{k,t}^{Bad} + \varepsilon_t \, . \qquad \text{(VII-4)}$$

The results for estimating equation (VII-4) are summarized in Table VII-1. To test for symmetric reactions of exchange rates to positive and negative news, we carried out Wald tests. The corresponding null hypothesis consists of H_0: $\beta_{1,k}^{GOOD} = -\beta_{2,k}^{BAD}$ for each news variable k. The results are also summarized in Table VII-1.

Overall, for the half of all news variables an asymmetric response to positive and negative news is found in the data. The asymmetric response to positive and negative news can be normally ascribed to the fact that either purely positive or purely negative news for a specific macroeconomic variable produces a significant impact on exchange rate movements. Thus, some macroeconomic variables seem to have an impact on exchange rate movements only in the case of positive surprises, while other macroeconomic news is only relevant for exchange rate movements in the case of negative surprises.

Table VII-1: Sign effects: Differences in the response to good and bad news

		Coefficient	t-Statistic	p-value	Wald test (p-values)
US announcement					
Consumer price index	**Good**	0.2586	1.5751	0.1155	0.0447
	Bad	0.2888	1.3208	0.1868	
Durable orders	**Good**	0.0078	0.0662	0.9472	0.0643
	Bad	-0.4099	-2.2431	0.0251	
GDP	**Good**	-0.2158	-2.4267	0.0154	0.4606
	Bad	0.0271	0.1134	0.9097	
Industrial production	**Good**	-0.0530	-0.5343	0.5933	0.1250
	Bad	-0.2043	-1.4676	0.1425	
ISM index	**Good**	-0.2318	-1.1928	0.2332	0.0034
	Bad	-0.3887	-4.2940	0.0000	
Non-farm payrolls	**Good**	-0.4969	-4.3696	0.0000	0.0001
	Bad	0.0186	0.2570	0.7972	
Producer price index	**Good**	0.0837	0.6170	0.5374	0.6715
	Bad	-0.1511	-1.8619	0.0629	
Retail sales	**Good**	-0.0540	-0.6322	0.5274	0.8075
	Bad	0.1300	0.4301	0.6672	
Trade balance	**Good**	0.1071	1.4300	0.1530	0.1202
	Bad	-0.3118	-2.8034	0.0051	
Unemployment rate	**Good**	0.6245	3.8735	0.0001	0.0002
	Bad	0.0110	0.1310	0.8958	
German announcement					
Consumer price index	**Good**	-00122	-0.1159	0.9078	0.0775
	Bad	-0.2868	-2.0865	0.0372	
GDP	**Good**	0.3342	0.5770	0.5640	0.2596
	Bad	0.3267	2.6903	0.0072	
Ifo-Index	**Good**	0.2132	1.3381	0.1811	0.0038
	Bad	0.3254	3.4074	0.0007	
Industrial production	**Good**	0.1269	1.3952	0.1632	0.0823
	Bad	0.0662	0.9467	0.3440	
Manufacturing orders	**Good**	0.0317	0.2294	0.8186	0.7654
	Bad	0.0145	0.1882	0.8508	
Producer price index	**Good**	0.0328	0.4834	0.6289	0.0794
	Bad	0.1520	1.8043	0.0715	
Retail sales	**Good**	-0.1533	-1.2723	0.2035	0.2935
	Bad	0.0032	0.0392	0.9687	
Unemployment	**Good**	0.0593	0.5595	0.5760	0.3381
	Bad	-0.2179	-1.6560	0.0980	

$R^2 = 0.07$
adjusted $R^2 = 0.04$
D.W. = 1.94

- **Geographical effects – Is US and Euro area news different?**

A second cause for asymmetric reactions of exchange rates to news announcements can be seen in their geographical origins. Galati and Ho [2003] postulate that in principle news from both related countries should matter for exchange rates, as the exchange rate is solely the relative price of two currencies. However, the impact of news may vary according to its origins. For example, Edison [1997] reports that news from the US economy statistically has an impact on exchange rates, while news from Germany does not.

To estimate the aggregate impact of news and to evaluate the geographical asymmetries empirically, we modify our basic approach by substituting the surprises about the individual announcements with a dummy for geographic news. The dummy variable for the US news (D^{USA}) is composed of the sorted and aggregated dummy variables D_k for the US news. The same holds for the dummy variable for the German news (D^{GER}). The appropriate regression equation is given by

$$\Delta s_t = \alpha + \beta_1 D_t^{USA} + \beta_2 D_t^{GER} + \varepsilon_t . \qquad \text{(VII-5)}$$

The results for estimating equation (VII-5) are summarized in Table VII-2. The results reveal that aggregated US and German news have significant impact on the EUR/USD exchange rate. Furthermore, the estimated coefficients have the expected signs, since positive US news result in an appreciation of the US dollar and positive German news lead to an appreciation of the Euro. However, the hypothesis of asymmetric reactions to news from different countries is rejected by the data. The Wald test indicates that the null hypothesis H₀: $\beta_1^{USA} = -\beta_2^{GER}$ cannot be rejected.

Table VII-2: Geographical differences in the response to macroeconomic 'news', I

	Coefficient	t-Statistic	p-value
US news	- 0.1109	- 3.0590	0.0023
German news	0.0938	3.0379	0.0024
R^2 = 0.02 adjusted R^2 = 0.01 D.W. = 1.94			
Wald test	**Null hypothesis**		**p-value**
	$\beta_1^{USA} = -\beta_2^{GER}$		0.7135

A further way to analyze asymmetric reaction of exchange rates to news due to geographical origins is presented by equation (VII-6). In addition, this approach allows also for asymmetries due to the nature of news. The appropriate regression equation is given by

$$\Delta s_t = \alpha + \beta_1 D_t^{USA,GOOD} + \beta_2 D_t^{USA,BAD} + \beta_3 D_t^{GER,GOOD} + \beta_4 D_t^{GER,BAD} + \varepsilon_t , \qquad \text{(VII-6)}$$

where $D^{USA,GOOD}$ and $D^{USA,BAD}$ represent dummies containing good and bad US news and $D^{GER,GOOD}$ and $D^{GER,BAD}$ denotes positive and negative German news announcements. The estimation results are given in Table VII-3. It can be seen that US good and bad news as well as German good and bad news have a significant impact on the EUR/USD exchange rate. In addition, all coefficients show the expected sign, as higher economic activity implies an appreciation of the domestic currency. However, the hypothesis of asymmetries due to geographical considerations is rejected again. The impact of good US and German news on the EUR/USD exchange rate seem to have the same magnitude. The same applies to the bad US and German news.

Interestingly, the results further indicate that the impact of news varies with the nature of news, as the results for testing the null hypothesis $\beta_1^{USA,GOOD} = -\beta_2^{USA,BAD}$ and $\beta_3^{GER,GOOD} = -\beta_4^{GER,BAD}$ show that the impact of positive and negative news varies within each country, whereby the magnitude of negative news appear to be large to some extent.

Table VII-3: Geographical differences in the response to macroeconomic 'news', II

	Coefficient	t-Statistic	p-value
US good news	- 0.0825	- 1.6434	0.1006
US bad news	- 0.1406	- 2.4028	0.0164
GER good news	0.0872	1.6485	0.0995
GER bad news	0.0971	1.9311	0.0537
R^2 = 0.02 adjusted R^2 = 0.01 D.W. = 1.94			
Wald test	**Null hypothesis**		**p-value**
	$\beta_1^{USA,GOOD} = -\beta_2^{USA,BAD}$		0.0022
	$\beta_1^{USA,GOOD} = -\beta_3^{GER,GOOD}$		0.9479
	$\beta_2^{USA,BAD} = -\beta_4^{GER,BAD}$		0.5713
	$\beta_3^{GER,GOOD} = -\beta_4^{GER,BAD}$		0.0030

Overall, the results indicate that the EUR/USD exchange rate reacts in part asymmetrically to news about macroeconomic fundamentals. The asymmetry is due to the nature of news. Thus, positive and negative news about macroeconomic fundamentals has a different impact on exchange rate movements. The hypothesis of asymmetric response of exchange rates to news due to different geographical origins is rejected.

B) Time-varying impact of macroeconomic news on exchange rates

In this section we deal with the time-varying impact of macroeconomic news on the EUR/USD exchange rate. According to the theory of social hypothesis testing and the theory of cognitive dissonance, we expect that exchange rates respond to news about macroeconomic fundamentals depending on the prevailing trend in exchange rates. Consequently, we investigate the impact of news on the EUR/USD exchange rate for various sub-periods. The considered sub-periods are deduced from the different trend phases the Euro has gone through since its launch as the new single currency in the European Monetary Union (EMU) at the beginning of 1999. Since then, the EUR/USD exchange rate has gone through three different phases (see Figure VII-1): at first, the Euro depreciated strongly against the US-$ for nearly two years until October 2000; subsequently, the Euro moved sideways against the US-$ in a range between 0.85 and 0.95 US-$ per Euro; since February 2002 the Euro has entered an appreciation trend against the US-$.

Figure VII-1: Three stages of the EUR/USD exchange rate

To test for time-varying impact of macroeconomic news on exchange rates during the different sub-periods, we run regression equation (II-52) from Chapter II for the various sub-periods. Overall the results provide no support for the hypothesis of time-varying impact of macroeconomic news due to different exchange rate trends. Rather, the results indicate again that the correlation between exchange rate changes and news appears to be in general very weak. For much macroeconomic news the regression analysis results in the conclusion that the considered macroeconomic news has no statistically meaningful impact at all on exchange rate movements. Only for the US GDP and trade news and for the German retail sales news can a significant impact of news on EUR/USD exchange rate development be observed. For the US GDP news we can conclude that in the first trend phase from January 1999 to October 2000 positive surprises for the GDP growth led to depreciation of the Euro against the US dollar. However, in the recent trend phase from February 2002 to June 2003 positive US GDP news led to appreciation of the Euro against the US dollar. A similar result is obtained for US trade news where, in the period from January 1999 to October 2000, larger than expected trade deficits led to an appreciation of the US dollar and, in the trend phase from November 2000 to January 2002, to a depreciation. Also for the German retail sales news we found a significant change of the sign of impact for different trend phases. Whereas in the trend phase from January 1999 to October 2000 positive news about the retail sales development led astonishingly to a depreciation of the Euro against the US dollar, positive German retail news led in the time period from February 2002 to June 2003 to an appreciation of the Euro, which is in line with the idea that higher economic activity leads to an appreciation of the currency.

The results are also confirmed by a rolling regression approach (see Figure VII-2). We estimate equation (VII-6) based on a rolling regression using a time window of 120 days, which corresponds to about half a year. Overall, the rolling regression approach does not provide systematic evidence for time-varying impact of news on exchange rate development due to different trend phases.

Figure VII-2: Results for rolling regressions of equation

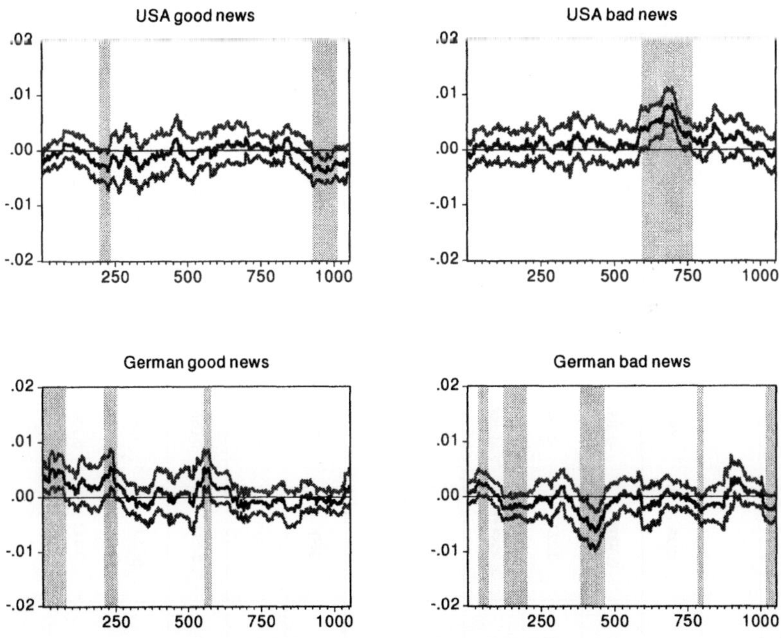

Note: shaded areas indicate phases in which a significant impact is found. The blue line represents the estimated coefficient; grey lines above and below the blue lines specify the 20% significance level.

Table VII-4: News impact of macroeconomic fundamentals in various sub-periods

	United States									
	CPI	DO	GDP	IP	ISM	NP	PPI	RS	Trade	UN
1/1999 – 10/2000	0.343*	-0.301	-0.300**	-0.106	-0.162	-0.054	0.076	-0.061	-0.476***	0.462***
11/2000 – 6/2003	0.190	-0.034	0.027	-0.142	-0.345**	-0.160**	0.051	-0.012	-0.018	0.169*
11/2000 – 1/2002	0.553**	-0.034	-0.435***	-0.257	-0.596***	-0.147	0.059	-0.008	0.133**	0.028
2/2002 – 6/2003	-0.019	-0.003	0.292**	-0.088	-0.242**	-0.109	-0.006	-0.045	-0.1427	0.237**

	Germany							
	CPI	GDP	IFO	IP	MO	PPI	RS	UN
1/1999 – 10/2000	-0.066	0.629	0.456***	0.079	0.134	0.118	-0.143**	-0.042
11/2000 – 6/2003	-0.181*	0.095	0.133	0.056	-0.027	0.094	0.124	-0.082
11/2000 – 1/2002	-0.296	-0.065	0.357*	-0.086	-0.025	0.189*	-0.019	-0.027
2/2002 – 6/2003	-0.109	0.146	-0.012	0.148	-0.046	0.021	0.176***	-0.097

Note: * denotes 10% significance level
** denotes 5 % significance level
*** denotes 1% significance level

Overall, the results for asymmetric and time-varying impact of macroeconomic news on exchange rates movements have revealed that

a) to some extent an asymmetric response of exchange rates to macroeconomic news can be found. The existing asymmetry is thereby due to the nature of news. Thus, exchange rates seem to react differently to positive and negative news.

b) we do not find systematic evidence for time-varying impact of macroeconomic news on exchange rates due to different trend phases.

Appendix C: The special role of private information in foreign exchange trading

The fact that foreign exchange market traders assess knowledge about customer orders as valuable cannot be explained within the traditional economic exchange rate theories. According to the asset approach of exchange rate determination, all information relevant for pricing exchange rates is publicly known. Furthermore, the asset approach assumes that the group of market participants is homogenous, i.e. they all share the same rational expectations about exchange rates. Thus, new information is immediately incorporated into prices (see upper section of Figure VII-3). In contrast, in the literature on foreign exchange market microstructure, the pivotal role of private information is extensively discussed (see for a comprehensive summary Lyons [2001b]).[72] In general, it is assumed that – at least – not all information is publicly known and that private information affects trading in currency markets. The transmission of private information is realized by order flow.[73] As a consequence, order flows in foreign exchange markets may convey important private information about market-clearing prices (see middle section of Figure VII-3).

According to Ito et al. [1998], private information is defined as "information that satisfies two criteria: (1) it is not common knowledge and (2) it is price relevant" (Ito et al. [1998], p. 1114). Due to the low transparency in foreign exchange markets, the first requiremeent is obviously fulfilled. Order flow is not observed by all market makers and customers do not observe any order flow in the interdealer market. With regard to the second requirement, market makers report that their most important source of information is trading with customers, and that this information is exclusive (see Lyons [1995], Yao [1998b] and [1998a]).

---

[72] The microstructure approach differs from the traditional asset approach in at least three aspects including the information set, the role of different market participants and institutions (see Lyons [2001b]). First, according to the microstructure approach some information relevant to exchange rate determination are not publicly available. Second, within the microstructure approach market participants need not to be homogenous, rather the potential heterogeneity of market participants is considered. Third, microstructure models recognize that the specific trading mechanism affect prices.

[73] Order flow is a measure of buying/selling pressure. It is the net of buyer-initiated orders and seller-initiated orders. In a dealer market, it is the dealers who absorb this order flow, and they are compensated for doing so (see Evans and Lyons [1999]).

Figure VII-3: Macro-fundamental analysis versus order flow analysis

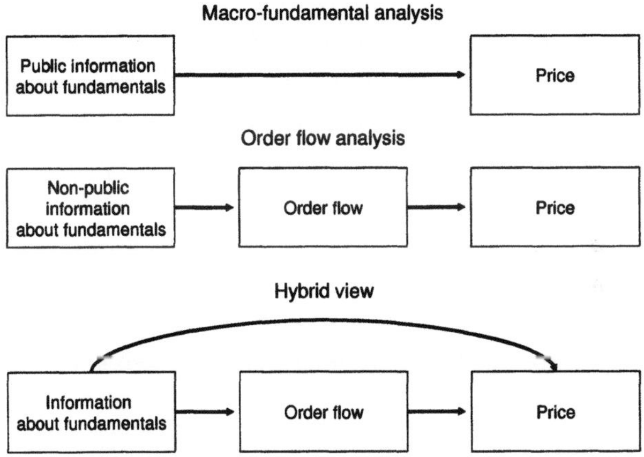

Source: Lyons [2001a]

What kind of private information exists in foreign exchange markets? According to Lyons [2001b] one can distinguish several different sources for private information. To illustrate this point Lyons [2001b] refers to the determination of assets in general:

$$P_t = \frac{E\left[V_{t+1} \middle| \Omega_t\right]}{1+d} \qquad \text{(VII-7)}$$

where P_t is the price at time t, $E\left[V_{t+1} \middle| \Omega_t\right]$ the expected value of the risky asset's pay-off in t+1 conditional upon the available information set in t (Ω_t), and d is the discount rate. If the market maker has information about future payoffs ($E\left[V_{t+1} \middle| \Omega_t\right]$) or discount rates (d), he may be able to predict future exchange rates. Accordingly, Lyons [2001b] labels the first as pay-off information and the second as discount rate information. Payoff information in the context of foreign exchange markets is, for example, secret central bank interventions which may signal future interest rate changes. Moreover, by observing order flows market makers may learn about future trade balance changes (see Lyons [1997]). Discount rate information is related to a risk premium and thus to the discount rate. Lyons [2001b] distinguishes here between two different effects: inventory effects and portfolio balance effects (see for more details Lyons [2001b]).

Beside these two information types, Lyons [2001b] points also to a third information type which may potentially be assigned to either of these two information types. However, this kind of information is, especially against the background of our study's objective, most interesting as it deals with the expectations of market participants and should be treated separately. Payoff or discount rate information may also include information about the different expectations of value of the asset's payoff or discount rate. Here, the microstructure approach explicitly refers to the heterogeneity of market participants. The relevance of this kind of information applies also in cases where all information about fundamentals is publicly known but the mapping from information to exchange rates is not common knowledge. As the standard macroeconomic exchange rate models have failed to explain exchange rate movements, this seems to be very likely. Thus, private information conveyed in order flow can be interpreted as a measure of the different beliefs of market participants concerning future fundamentals or exchange rates.

In principle, market makers can receive private information conveyed by order flow from two different sources. On the one hand, market makers state that customer trades are an important source of information (see Chapter III). On the other hand, private information is received in the interdelaer market by trading with other dealers. It is important for market makers to observe interdealer order flows, as the reality of the foreign exchange market is that market makers can observe some order flow from interdealer trades in which they are not involved (e.g. from brokered trades). Customer-dealer trades, on the other hand, are not observable except by the bank that receives them. Dealers therefore learn about other dealers' customer orders as best they can by observing other dealers' interdealer trades, and they set market prices accordingly. Although this learning from interdealer orders is consistent with the empirical results, the ultimate driver of that interdealer order flow is customer flow." (see Lyons [2001b]). Rime [2000] supports this view, as he found that the strongest effects on weekly foreign exchange rate changes comes from the trading of customers.

Portfolio shifts model of Evans and Lyons [2002b]

In a stylized model of the functioning of foreign exchange markets, Evans and Lyons [2002b] describe the decisive role of private information and interdealer trading for price discovery in foreign exchange markets. The model can be interpreted as a hybrid approach, as it highlights both the role of macro components and microstructure components (see lower panel of Figure VII-3). The basic structure of the hybrid model is as follows:

$$\Delta P_t = f(Z) + g(X) + \varepsilon_t \qquad \text{(VII-8)}$$

where Z describes macroeconomic determinants and X is the order flow. An advantage of a hybrid approach is that an empirical analysis of the model allows am assessment of the relative importance of both components. The process of price discovery can thereby be understood as a complex dynamic interaction between a heterogeneous group of customers and market makers. Within the model, the trading day is divided into three different trading rounds. In round 1, the market makers trade with the public. In round 2, the market makers trade among themselves to share the resulting inventory risk and in round 3 market makers trade again with the public.

Figure VII-4: Daily timing in the model of Evans and Lyons [2002b]

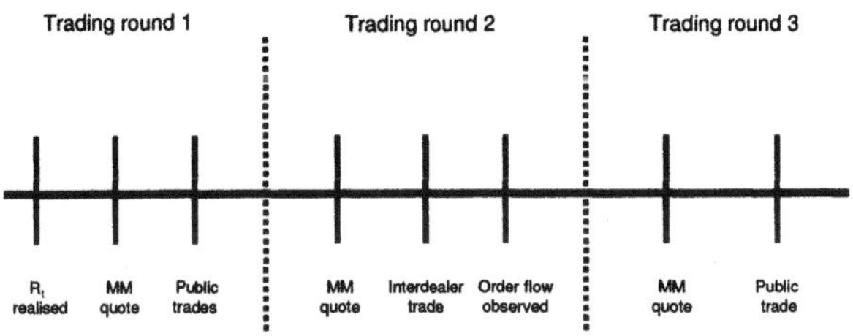

Trading round 1

At the beginning of each trading day, all market makers observe the payoff to holding foreign exchange (R_t). R_t is composed of a series of increments ΔR_t, so that

$$R_t = \sum_{\tau=1}^{t} \Delta R_\tau \,. \tag{VII-9}$$

The payoff increments are i.i.d. $\text{normal}(0,\sigma_R^2)$ and represent the flow of public macroeconomic information. This part of the model reflects the macro component of equation (VII-8). According to the observed payoff and other available information, each market maker sets simultaneously and independently his quote for public customers. Subsequently, each market maker receives a customer-order realization (C_{it}^1) that is executed at his announced quotes. These orders are, according to Evans and Lyons [2002b], labeled as "portfolio shifts" of the non-dealer public. [74] It is assumed that each of the customer orders is distributed normal$\left(0,\sigma_R^2\right)$ and not correlated across market makers. In addition, the model assumes that the customer-order realizations are not observable. The aggregate public demand corresponds to

$$C_t^1 = \sum_{I=1}^{N} C_{It}^1 . \tag{VII-10}$$

Trading round 2

In trading round 2 the interdealer-trading takes place. At first, each market maker simultaneously and independently fixes his quotes at which he agrees to buy and sell any amount. These interdealer quotes are assumed to be observable and available for all market makers in the market. Now, each market maker trades on other market makers' quotes, whereby T_{It} denotes the interdealer trade initiated by market maker I in round 2 at day t. At the end of round 2, all market makers observe the net interdealer order flow from interdelaer trading that day:

$$X_t = \sum_{I=1}^{N} T_{It} . \tag{VII-11}$$

This order flow information is important within the portfolio shifts model, as it conveys the size and sign of customer order flow in trading round 1. The rationale for this can be found in the interdealer trading rule derived by Evans and Lyons [1999].

$$T_{It} = \alpha C_{It}^1 \tag{VII-12}$$

where α is a constant model parameter. According to this rule, the optimal trading strategy for each individual market maker is to realize an interdelaer trading volume that is proportional to the customer orders he has received in trading round 1. Thus, when market makers observe the interdealer order flow they can infer the aggregate customer order flow C_t^1 in trading round 1, as the following relationship shows:

---

[74] The considered portfolio shifts are assumed to have two important features: first, they are not common knowledge so that they are a source of private information in foreign exchange markets, and, second, portfolio shifts are assumed to be large enough to move prices. Therefore, public's demand for foreign currency assets need to be less than perfectly elastic (see Evans and Lyons [1999]).

$$X_t = \sum_{i=1}^{N} T_{it} = \alpha C_t^1 . \qquad \text{(VII-13)}$$

This relationship clarifies a crucial point of the portfolio shifts model. The information which is conveyed in the unobservable customer orders in trading round 1 become gradually known within trading round 2 by interdealer trading and is subsequently incorporated into exchange rates (trading round 3).

Trading round 3

By the end of the day (trading round 3), market makers trade again with the public to share overnight risks. At the beginning of this trading round, each market maker again fixes his quotes simultaneously and independently. These quotes are observable and available to all customers. It is assumed within the portfolio shifts model that market makers set their quotes in trading round 3 such that the public is willing to absorb all market maker inventory imbalances (see Evans and Lyons [2002b]). Thus, each market maker ends with no net position.[75] The logical consequence of this assumption is that $C_t^3 = -C_t^1$.

The quotes of market makers in trading round 3 that induce the public to absorb the inventory imbalances depend on the observable interdealer order flow (X_t), as this informs the market maker about the size of the total position the public needs to absorb ($X_t = \alpha C_t^1$). However, market makers also need information about the public's risk bearing capacity. Within the model of Evans and Lyons [2002b] it is assumed that the public's risk-bearing capacity is limited, that is, foreign and domestic assets are regarded as imperfect substitutes (see Lyons [2002a]). According to Lyons [2002a] the total demand for foreign exchange of the public in trading round 3 is then given by a linear function of its expected return conditional on public information (including all past R_t and X_t):

$$C_t^3 = \gamma E\left[\Delta P_{t+1}^3 + R_{t+1} \middle| \Omega_t^3\right], \qquad \text{(VII-14)}$$

where $\gamma > 0$ captures the aggregate risk-bearing capacity of the public.

---

[75] This assumption is quite reasonable as it is common practice for foreign exchange market makers to end the day with no net position (see Lyons [1995], Yao [1998a]).

Empirical evaluation of the portfolio shifts model

Evans and Lyons [2002b] test the portfolio shifts model empirically by analyzing daily data for the DM/USD and the YEN/USD exchange rates. In the portfolio shifts model, exchange rate changes from the end of trading day t-1 to the end of trading day t are determined as follows (see for a detailed derivation Evans and Lyons [1999]):

$$\Delta P_t = \beta_1 \Delta R_t + \beta_2 X_t \qquad \text{(VII-15)}$$

where β_2 is a positive model parameter which depends on γ and α (see Lyons [2001b]). For an empirical implementation of equation (VII-15), Evans and Lyons [2002b] decide to specify the macro component of the portfolio shifts model as the changes in the nominal interest differential ($\Delta R_t = \Delta(i_t - i_t^*)$). Thus, the estimation equation is given by

$$\Delta p_t = \beta_1 \Delta(i_t - i_t^*) + \beta_2 X_t + \varepsilon_t, \qquad \text{(VII-16)}$$

where Δp_t is the change in the log spot exchange rate from the end of day t-1 to the end of day t, $\Delta(i_t - i_t^*)$ is the change in the overnight interest rate differential, and X_t denotes the interdealer order flow from the end of day t-1 to the end of day t. The results suggest that the portfolio shifts model is quite successful in describing the actual exchange rate changes: it accounts for 64 per cent of the daily change in the DM/USD rate and 45 per cent in the YEN/USD rate (this result is also confirmed in other empirical studies, see e.g. Lyons [2001a]). Furthermore, the coefficient of order flow (β_2) is correctly signed and statistically significant. The size of the order flow coefficient is 2.1 for the DM/USD rate, implying that 1 billion of net USD purchases increases the deutsche mark by 0.54 percent (see Evans and Lyons [2002b]). Another paper of Evans and Lyons [2002a] focuses on informational integration, specifically, the importance of information conveyed by order flow in major currencies for pricing minor currencies. Therefore, Evans and Lyons [2002a] develop a further variant of the portfolio shifts model covering a number of currencies. Their empirical results related to this variant of the model suggest that the model can explain 45 to 78 per cent of daily returns in all nine currencies. In addition, it can be seen that the specification of equation (VII-16) allows for reasonable short-term forecasts. In the spirit of the results of Meese and Rogoff [1983a] and Meese and Rogoff [1983b], Evans and Lyons [1999] compare the forecasting accuracy of the portfolio shifts model with that of a naïve random walk model. The results clearly reveal that the portfolio shifts model produces better forecasts than the random walk model measured by root mean squared errors.

The results of Evans and Lyons [1999] and Evans and Lyons [2002b] are confirmed by a number of studies. Payne [1999], for example, reports that according to his estimation 40 per cent of the permanent return variance is attributable to order flow. Rime [2000] finds that order flow is an important variable for explaining exchange rate changes. His model fits the data well with unusually high adjusted R^2 (up to 33 per cent) and flow variables which significantly enter the regression with the correct sign. In a further study Rime [2001] shows that order flow is important for changes in various currency pairs (e.g. DM/USD, GBP/USD and CHF/USD).

Beside these studies which are concerned with the relevance of interdealer-order flow for exchange rate movements, other empirical studies related to the microstructure approach deal with the importance of customer order flows. Bjønnes and Rime [2000] evaluate the hypothesis of private information using observations on customer trades. Their results suggest that customer orders influence the trading decisions of market makers. In particular, market makers use their private information about customer orders in the formation of order placement strategies. After a customer's purchase of currency, the market makers tend to buy currency in the interdealer market, which can be described as speculative position taking. In this context, Bjønnes and Rime [2000] refer to the trading behavior of market makers as "dealers ride herd on the customers" (Bjønnes and Rime [2000], p. 33). Rime [2000] reports similar results. According to his analysis, order flow is an important variable for explaining weekly exchange rate changes, with the customer order flow variable being the one that is most often significant. In this context, Rime [2000] suggests that customer order flow captures the portfolio shifts and the information and sentiment of the public most accurately. Evans [2001] states that a central empirical result from his empirical model is that customer orders have both temporary and permanent effects on the level of exchange rates. Using regression analysis Lyons [2001b] finds that aggregate customer order flow has a significant influence on US-$/€ and Yen/US-$ exchange rate changes. The corresponding values of R^2 are 0.16 respective 0.15 which is at least clearly more than that of traditional macro models (almost under 0.10).

However, one major point of criticism is that the order flow approach does not explain the origin of order flow. In this context, Lyons [2002b] states:

> "only when one has uncovered what is driving transacted order flow will this approach be complete. (order flow is a proximate cause, not the underlying cause, of exchange rate movements.) Uncovering the drivers would also resolve the narrow puzzle of macro variables' inability to account for exchange rates." (Lyons [2002b], p. 3)

Therefore, the search for the underlying trading motives of the different market participants and the nature of expectations in foreign exchange markets are the main topic of our study.

Appendix D: Measures for the forecasting accuracy

The applied measures of forecasting accuracy used for the evaluation of professional and experimental expectations are defined as follows:

The mean error (ME) is given by

$$ME = \frac{1}{T}\sum_{t=1}^{T}(\hat{x}_t - x_t) \qquad \text{(VII-17)}$$

where

$$\hat{x}_t = \frac{E_{t-h}S_t - S_{t-h}}{S_{t-h}} \quad \text{and} \quad x_t = \frac{S_t - S_{t-h}}{S_{t-h}}.$$

The mean squared error (MSE) is given by

$$MSE = \frac{1}{T}\sum_{t=1}^{T}(\hat{x}_t - x_t)^2. \qquad \text{(VII-18)}$$

The mean absolute error (MAE) is given by

$$MAE = \frac{1}{T}\sum_{t=1}^{T}\left|\hat{x}_t - x_t\right|. \qquad \text{(VII-19)}$$

The Theil's inequality coefficient (Theil's U) is given by

$$\text{Theil's U} = \frac{\sqrt{\frac{1}{T}\sum_{t=1}^{T}(\hat{x}_t - x_t)^2}}{\sqrt{\frac{1}{T}\sum_{t=1}^{T}(x_t)^2}}. \qquad \text{(VII-20)}$$

Table VII-5 provides a summary of the implications of the numerical values of Theil's U.

Table VII-5: Implications of the value of the Theil's inequality coefficient

Theil's U	Implication
Theil's U = 0	Expectations are perfect forecasts
0 < Theil's U <1	Expectations provide less than perfect forecast but outperforms naïve random walk forecasts
Theil's U = 1	Expectations are as good as naïve random walk forecasts
Theil's U > 1	Expectations are worse than naïve random walk forecasts

Direction of change forecast

To investigate the usefulness of professional forecasts as direction of change forecasts, we carry out a simple χ^2-test of independence (see Diebold and Lopez [1996]). The forecasting quality of professional forecasts is compared to a naïve coin flip. The test is based on a 2 x 2 contingency table (see Table VII-6). The hit rate of the direction-of-change forecasts is given by the quotient $(N_{11} + N_{22})/N$. The actual exchange rate changes are defined as "up" if $\Delta S_{t+h} \geq 0$ and as "down" if $\Delta S_{t+h} < 0$. Accordingly, expected exchange rate changes are defined as "up" if $E_t\Delta S_{t+h} \geq 0$ and as "down" if $E_t\Delta S_{t+h} < 0$. $N_{.1}$ and $N_{.2}$ denote the total frequency of "actual change up" and "actual change down". Correspondingly, $N_{1.}$ and $N_{2.}$ denote the total frequency of "expected change up", respectively, "expected change down". The null hypothesis of the test is that the entries in the contingency table are completely random, so that the hit rate is close to 50 %. According to Diebold and Lopez [1996], the corresponding test statistic is given by

$$C = \sum_{i,j=1}^{2} \frac{\left(N_{ij} - \hat{E}_{ij}\right)^2}{\hat{E}_{ij}} \quad \text{with } \hat{E}_{ij} = N_{i.} \cdot N_{.j} / N \qquad \text{(VII-21)}$$

whereby C is under the null hypothesis $C \to \chi_1^2$.

Table VII-6: 2x2 contingency table of the χ^2-test

	Actual change "up"	Actual change "down"	
Expected change "up	N_{11}	N_{12}	$N_{1.}$
Expected change "down"	N_{21}	N_{22}	$N_{2.}$
	$N_{.1}$	$N_{.2}$	N

Appendix E: Instructions of the first experiment

Your task is to forecast a time series. This time series could be the course of temperature, the price of an asset, the inflation rate of a country, sales figures of a company or anything similar. The exact background of the time series remains unknown to you. The only valuable information that could be used for forecasting is the "gestalt" of the time series itself, which you will discern better and better during course of the experiment.

Keep in mind that the time series can only take values between 0 and 40. All values of the time series are rounded up to two decimal places. Thus, you can produce forecasts with two decimal places.

In the first period you get the initial value of the time series. Then you are asked to produce your forecast for period 2. Subsequently, the true value of the time series in period 2 is disclosed. This procedure is repeated for all forecasting periods. Your forecasts will not affect the course of the time series!

You should forecast the time series as good as possible. For each correct forecast you obtain a reward at the end of the experiment. The payment depends on the following scheme:

$$\sum_{t=2}^{42} \max\{a - f_t; 0\},$$

where a is a constant set to 30 or 40 cents and f denotes your forecast.

Appendix F: Instructions of the second experiment

General information

You are a trading floor economist concerned with the foreign exchange dealings of a leading European bank. You watch the exchange rate between Euros (EUR) and US Dollars (USD). The EUR/USD exchange rate specifies how many Euros have to be paid for one US Dollar. Thus, a rise of the EUR/USD exchange rate implies a devaluation of the Euro compared to the US Dollar and vice versa. At the beginning of each period you inform the currency dealers of your bank about the expected development of the EUR/USD exchange rate. The information you provide is considered by the currency dealers when making decisions on buying and selling Euros or US Dollars. In every period, the main information you provide is a forecast of the development of the EUR/USD exchange rate. Depending on your evaluation of the future development of the exchange rate, the currency dealers will either buy or sell Euros or US dollars. Thus, the currency dealers base their transactions exclusively on your forecast. The trading profit of your bank depends crucially on the quality of your forecasts. Therefore, the management decided to implement a strict performance-related remuneration scheme. Consequently, your earnings in the experiment depend on your forecasting accuracy. The smaller your forecast errors, the higher your payment will be.

Information about the foreign exchange market

The current EUR/USD exchange rate in each period is determined by the balance of supply and demand for Euros and US Dollars. The supply of Euros and US Dollars is constant during the whole experiment. The total demand for Euros and US Dollars is formed predominantly from the aggregated demand of all currency dealers of the various banks that also employ trading floor economists, who determine the trading strategy of their particular bank (these are the other participants in the experiment). Furthermore, there exists a small demand for Euros and US Dollars from private investors, which influences the exchange rate slightly.

Economic background information about the Euro area and the United States

Within the experiment, you obtain information about several economic variables related to the currencies in the experiment. On the one hand, the return of European and US American assets is published in each period. On the other hand, you receive information about the expected inflation rates of the coming period in Europe and the USA.

The task of the trading floor economist

Your only task as a trading floor economist in the experiment is forecasting the EUR/USD exchange rate as well as possible. The EUR/USD exchange rate will always be between 0 and 100. You have to forecast the exchange rate of the next period. After all participants of the experiment have finished their forecast, the EUR/USD exchange rate will be calculated from demand and supply: Subsequently, the EUR/USD exchange rate will be presented to all participants. You have to make 49 forecasts altogether.

Earnings

The earnings only depend on your forecasting accuracy. The better you predict the EUR/USD exchange rate, the higher your earnings. The payments in each period correspond to the following function:

$$\textit{Payment per period} = \max\{30\ \textit{Cents} - 10|e_t - f_t|;0\} \qquad \text{(VII-22)}$$

where e_t is the true realization of the exchange rate and f_t denotes your forecast. The maximum earnings per period are 30 Cents, the minimum is 0 Cents. Your absolute forecast error is multiplied by the factor 10 and is subtracted from the maximum earnings of 30 Cents. The concrete payoffs are presented in the following earnings table (see Table VII-7):

Table VII-7: Payoff scheme

Forecast error	payment	Forecast error	payment	Forecast error	payment
0	30	**1.05**	19.5	**2.1**	9
0.05	29.5	**1.1**	19	**2.15**	8.5
0.1	29	**1.15**	18.5	**2.2**	8
0.15	28.5	**1.2**	18	**2.25**	7.5
0.2	28	**1.25**	17.5	**2.3**	7
0.25	27.5	**1.3**	17	**2.35**	6.5
0.3	27	**1.35**	16.5	**2.4**	6
0.35	26.5	**1.4**	16	**2.45**	5.5
0.4	26	**1.45**	15.5	**2.5**	5
0.45	25.5	**1.5**	15	**2.55**	4.5
0.5	25	**1.55**	14.5	**2.6**	4
0.55	24.5	**1.6**	14	**2.65**	3.5
0.6	24	**1.65**	13.5	**2.7**	3
0.65	23.5	**1.7**	13	**2.75**	2.5
0.7	23	**1.75**	12.5	**2.8**	2
0.75	22.5	**1.8**	12	**2.85**	1.5
0.8	22	**1.85**	11.5	**2.9**	1
0.85	21.5	**1.9**	11	**2.95**	0.5
0.9	21	**1.95**	10.5	**≥ 3**	0
0.95	20.5	**2**	10		
1	20	**2.05**	9.5		

Appendix G: Regression results of the second experiment

Table VII-8: Unbiasedness test for each individual, group 1 to group 3

Experiment	Subject	Estimation procedure	Q-Statistic	α	$H_0: \alpha = 0$	β	$H_0: \beta = 1$	$H_0: \alpha = 0. \beta = 1$
Group 1	1	NW	--	-0.0031 (0.0063)	0.2426 [0.6239]	0.5034 (0.1133)	19.2054 [0.0001]	9.9725 [0.0002]
		ARMA	Q(12) = 0.055 Q(24) = 0.193	-0.0044 (0.0055)	0.6480 [0.4251]	0.6283 (0.1492)	6.2054 [0.0165]	3.3840 [0.0427]
	2	NW	--	-0.0044 (0.0085)	0.2713 [0.6049]	0.3754 (0.2199)	8.0661 [0.0066]	4.0376 [0.0241]
		ARMA	Q(12) = 0.137 Q(24) = 0.269	-0.0044 (0.0076)	0.3416 [0.5617]	0.3754 (0.1920)	10.5820 [0.0021]	5.5348 [0.0069]
	3	NW	--	-0.0065 (0.0090)	0.5308 [0.4699]	0.1222 (0.1812)	23.4672 [0.0000]	13.4540 [0.0000]
		ARMA	Q(12) = 0.221 Q(24) = 0.557	-0.0065 (0.0083)	0.6226 [0.4340]	0.1222 (0.1279)	47.0764 [0.0000]	28.7809 [0.0000]
	4	NW	--	-0.0064 (0.0063)	1.0403 [0.3130]	0.8338 (0.2054)	0.6549 [0.4224]	0.8812 [0.4210]
		ARMA	Q(12) = 0.263 Q(24) = 0.420	-0.0088 (0.0048)	3.4134 [0.0717]	1.0989 (0.1853)	0.2845 [0.5966]	1.7840 [0.1805]
	5	NW	--	-0.0043 (0.0067)	0.4193 [0.5204]	0.4234 (0.1099)	27.5496 [0.0000]	19.6973 [0.0000]
		ARMA	Q(12) = 0.199 Q(24) = 0.404	-0.0043 (0.0073)	0.3523 [0.5556]	0.4234 (0.1443)	15.9594 [0.0002]	8.2016 [0.0009]
	6	NW	--	-0.0011 (0.0074)	0.0238 [0.8780]	0.5261 (0.1568)	9.1380 [0.0040]	4.7676 [0.0130]
		ARMA	Q(12) = 0.248 Q(24) = 0.434	-0.0011 (0.0070)	0.0268 [0.8707]	0.5261 (0.1453)	10.6321 [0.0021]	5.3347 [0.0082]
Group 2	1	NW	--	-0.0024 (0.0104)	0.0514 [0.8216]	0.1497 (0.1075)	65.5938 [0.0000]	58.4388 [0.0000]
		ARMA	Q(12) = 0.393 Q(24) = 0.141	-0.0024 (0.0088)	0.0716 [0.7902]	0.1497 (0.1597)	28.3675 [0.0000]	17.7171 [0.0000]
	2	NW	--	0.0004 (0.0085)	0.0027 [0.9586]	0.4435 (0.2938)	3.5881 [0.0644]	2.6919 [0.0782]
		ARMA	Q(12) = 0.340 Q(24) = 0.093	0.0004 (0.0080)	0.0031 [0.9560]	0.4435 (0.3429)	2.6342 [0.1113]	1.3176 [0.2775]
	3	NW	--	-0.0006 (0.0098)	0.0037 [0.9516]	0.1086 (0.1049)	72.2916 [0.0000]	42.7798 [0.0000]
		ARMA	Q(12) = 0.617 Q(24) = 0.267	-0.0006 (0.0087)	0.0047 [0.9457]	0.1086 (0.2158)	17.0635 [0.0001]	9.9521 [0.0002]
	4	NW	--	0.0010 (0.0094)	0.0105 [0.9188]	-0.0278 (0.7889)	1.8837 [0.1764]	1.0582 [0.3552]
		ARMA	Q(12) = 0.574 Q(24) = 0.272	0.0010 (0.0082)	0.0140 [0.9063]	-0.0278 (0.5813)	3.1257 [0.0836]	1.5962 [0.2135]
	5	NW	--	0.0063 (0.0069)	0.8277 [0.3676]	0.0954 (0.0135)	4508.133 [0.0000]	2414.138 [0.0000]
		ARMA	Q(12) = 0.267 Q(24) = 0.331	0.0063 (0.0061)	1.0651 [0.3073]	0.0954 (0.0153)	3499.567 [0.0000]	1793.509 [0.0000]
	6	NW	--	-0.0015 (0.0096)	0.0230 [0.8801]	0.3863 (0.3639)	2.8435 [0.0984]	2.8327 [0.0689]
		ARMA	Q(12) = 0.515 Q(24) = 0.337	-0.0015 (0.0082)	0.0314 [0.8601]	0.3863 (0.2920)	4.4163 [0.0410]	2.4320 [0.0988]
Group 3	1	NW	--	-0.0105 (0.0102)	1.0686 [0.3066]	0.8567 (0.4575)	0.0981 [0.7555]	0.6723 [0.5154]
		ARMA	Q(12) = 0.462 Q(24) = 0.635	-0.0140 (0.0103)	1.8516 [0.1823]	0.7904 (0.3584)	0.3421 [0.5624]	0.9744 [0.3874]
	2	NW	--	-0.0086 (0.0105)	0.6764 [0.4150]	0.8838 (0.2892)	0.1614 [0.6897]	0.5673 [0.5709]
		ARMA	Q(12) = 0.106 Q(24) = 0.345	-0.0086 (0.0102)	0.7099 [0.4038]	0.8838 (0.2011)	0.3337 [0.5662]	0.4640 [0.6316]
	3	NW	--	-0.0074 (0.0106)	0.4872 [0.4886]	0.8073 (0.3264)	0.3484 [0.5578]	0.4304 [0.6528]
		ARMA	Q(12) = 0.102 Q(24) = 0.222	-0.0056 (0.0097)	0.3281 [0.5697]	1.0128 (0.3014)	0.0018 [0.9664]	0.1982 [0.8210]
	4	NW	--	-0.0037 (0.0103)	0.1265 [0.7237]	0.4403 (0.1722)	10.5704 [0.0021]	5.6461 [0.0063]
		ARMA	Q(12) = 0.056 Q(24) = 0.491	-0.0049 (0.0170)	0.0843 [0.7730]	0.5092 (0.1792)	7.4989 [0.0091]	3.9066 [0.0280]
	5	NW	--	-0.0153 (0.0150)	1.0539 [0.3099]	-0.3291 (0.7883)	2.8434 [0.0984]	3.3311 [0.0444]
		ARMA	Q(12) = 0.239 Q(24) = 0.545	-0.0198 (0.0163)	1.4707 [0.2336]	-1.0685 (0.6582)	9.8753 [0.0035]	5.5164 [0.0084]
	6	NW	--	-0.0122 (0.0115)	1.1409 [0.2909]	0.5659 (0.1454)	8.9122 [0.0045]	7.0515 [0.0021]
		ARMA	Q(12) = 0.076 Q(24) = 0.308	-0.0138 (0.0165)	0.6990 [0.4077]	0.5316 (0.1457)	10.3352 [0.0025]	5.3439 [0.0085]

Notes: Standard errors are given in parentheses, p-values in brackets.
NW denotes the Newey & West estimation procedure, ARMA denotes the ARMA estimation procedure.

Table VII-9: Unbiasedness test for each individual, group 5 to group 6

Experiment	Subject	Estimation procedure	Q-Statistic	α	H_0: $\alpha = 0$	β	H_0: $\beta = 1$	H_0: $\alpha = 0, \beta = 1$
Group 4	1	NW	--	-0.0113 (0.0104)	1.1827 [0.2824]	0.7630 (0.1398)	2.8729 [0.0967]	2.5217 [0.0911]
		ARMA	Q(12) = 0.208 Q(24) = 0.468	-0.0113 (0.0093)	1.4755 [0.2305]	0.7630 (0.2011)	1.3887 [0.2446]	1.5557 [0.2217]
	2	NW	--	-0.0020 (0.0087)	0.0528 [0.8193]	0.7113 (0.2392)	1.4565 [0.2335]	0.9191 [0.4059]
		ARMA	Q(12) = 0.154 Q(24) = 0.436	-0.0020 (0.0096)	0.0437 [0.8353]	0.7113 (0.1979)	2.1272 [0.1514]	1.0659 [0.3526]
	3	NW	--	-0.0090 (0.0079)	1.2906 [0.2617]	0.7343 (0.0829)	10.2638 [0.0024]	5.3491 [0.0081]
		ARMA	Q(12) = 0.922 Q(24) = 0.890	-0.0099 (0.0142)	0.4848 [0.4900]	0.7532 (0.0900)	7.5296 [0.0088]	3.9068 [0.0276]
	4	NW	--	-0.0051 (0.0126)	0.1630 [0.6882]	0.6037 (0.2393)	2.7418 [0.1044]	1.9293 [0.1566]
		ARMA	Q(12) = 0.178 Q(24) = 0.484	-0.0072 (0.0144)	0.2475 [0.6212]	0.1855 (0.2255)	13.0483 [0.0007]	6.5363 [0.0032]
	5	NW	--	-0.0088 (0.0105)	0.7018 [0.4064]	0.5402 (0.1887)	5.9370 [0.0187]	5.5064 [0.0071]
		ARMA	Q(12) = 0.052 Q(24) = 0.183	-0.0088 (0.0096)	0.8336 [0.3659]	0.5402 (0.1718)	7.1659 [0.0102]	4.0245 [0.0244]
	6	NW	--	-0.0138 (0.0106)	1.6954 [0.1992]	0.8208 (0.0972)	3.4000 [0.0715]	4.3606 [0.0183]
		ARMA	Q(12) = 0.553 Q(24) = 0.474	-0.0138 (0.0086)	2.5893 [0.1143]	0.8208 (0.1610)	1.2392 [0.2713]	2.1628 [0.1263]
Group 5	1	NW	--	-0.0102 (0.0131)	0.5994 [0.4427]	0.4065 (0.2212)	7.2021 [0.0100]	3.6693 [0.0331]
		ARMA	Q(12) = 0.092 Q(24) = 0.412	-0.0102 (0.0118)	0.7435 [0.3929]	0.4065 (0.1755)	11.4326 [0.0015]	5.7474 [0.0058]
	2	NW	--	-0.0127 (0.0157)	0.6559 [0.4221]	0.6080 (0.3045)	1.6569 [0.2043]	1.3176 [0.2775]
		ARMA	Q(12) = 0.514 Q(24) = 0.742	-0.0184 (0.0169)	1.1884 [0.2833]	-0.4307 (0.2404)	35.4074 [0.0000]	17.9873 [0.0000]
	3	NW	--	-0.0131 (0.0120)	1.1993 [0.2790]	0.9872 (0.3202)	0.0016 [0.9682]	0.6680 [0.5175]
		ARMA	Q(12) = 0.195 Q(24) = 0.534	-0.0166 (0.0099)	2.8052 [0.1029]	0.8995 (0.3122)	0.1036 [0.7494]	1.4221 [0.2548]
	4	NW	--	-0.0088 [0.0124]	0.5007 [0.4827]	0.6330 [0.2418]	2.3043 [0.1357]	1.1853 [0.3146]
		ARMA	Q(12) = 0.124 Q(24) = 0.473	-0.0088 (0.0114)	0.5947 [0.4445]	0.6330 (0.2088)	3.0906 [0.0853]	1.6486 [0.2032]
	5	NW	--	-0.0081 (0.0136)	0.3575 [0.5528]	0.5900 (0.1820)	5.0734 [0.0290]	2.5951 [0.0853]
		ARMA	Q(12) = 0.146 Q(24) = 0.640	-0.0157 (0.0152)	1.0725 [0.3077]	0.2506 (0.2411)	9.6593 [0.0038]	4.8916 [0.0136]
	6	NW	--	-0.0138 (0.0144)	0.8480 [0.3618]	0.2355 (0.1600)	22.8193 [0.0000]	22.3005 [0.0000]
		ARMA	Q(12) = 0.306 Q(24) = 0.801	-0.0173 (0.0173)	0.9962 [0.3255]	0.1852 (0.1223)	44.3808 [0.0000]	22.3380 [0.0000]
Group 6	1	NW	--	-0.0105 (0.0096)	1.1923 [0.2804]	0.5327 (0.1890)	6.1151 [0.0171]	4.0585 [0.0237]
		ARMA	Q(12) = 0.105 Q(24) = 0.285	-0.0089 (0.0117)	0.5832 [0.4490]	0.1038 (0.3224)	7.7296 [0.0079]	4.6099 [0.0151]
	2	NW	--	-0.0048 (0.0082]	0.3467 [0.5588]	0.2471 (0.0781)	93.0396 [0.0000]	50.1263 [0.0000]
		ARMA	Q(12) = 0.276 Q(24) = 0.238	-0.0048 (0.0070)	0.4753 [0.4939]	0.2471 (0.0779)	93.4933 [0.0000]	47.1528 [0.0000]
	3	NW	--	-0.0046 (0.0099)	0.2105 [0.6485]	-0.2290 (0.3581)	11.7788 [0.0013]	6.3112 [0.0037]
		ARMA	Q(12) = 0.091 Q(24) = 0.256	-0.0084 (0.0115)	0.5384 [0.4669]	0.0434 (0.3150)	9.2226 [0.0040]	4.9111 [0.0118]
	4	NW	--	-0.0030 (0.0068)	0.1991 [0.6575]	0.6407 (0.1696)	4.4906 [0.0394]	2.5042 [0.0926]
		ARMA	Q(12) = 0.503 Q(24) = 0.761	-0.0030 (0.0068)	0.2002 [0.6566]	0.6407 (0.1703)	4.4548 [0.0401]	2.2849 [0.1130]
	5	NW	--	-0.0071 (0.0081)	0.7656 [0.3860]	0.4711 (0.1660)	10.1481 [0.0026]	7.1269 [0.0020]
		ARMA	Q(12) = 0.445 Q(24) = 0.527	-0.0071 (0.0071)	1.0192 [0.3179]	0.4711 (0.1472)	12.9048 [0.0008]	7.5212 [0.0015]
	6	NW	--	-0.0019 (0.0090)	0.0427 [0.8372]	0.4210 (0.1237)	21.8920 [0.0000]	11.2754 [0.0001]
		ARMA	Q(12) = 0.069 Q(24) = 0.193	-0.0065 (0.0107)	0.3734 [0.5442]	0.2013 (0.1570)	25.8908 [0.0000]	12.9523 [0.0000]

Notes: Standard errors are given in parentheses, p-values in brackets.
NW denotes the Newey & West estimation procedure, ARMA denotes the ARMA estimation procedure.

Table VII-10: Orthogonality test for each individual, group 1 to group 3

Experiment	Subject	Estimation procedure	Q-Statistic	α	β_1	β_2	β_3	β_4	H_0: $\alpha = \beta_1 ... \beta_4 = 0$
Group 1	1	NW	--	0.2784 (0.1615)	-0.4616 (0.1090)	0.4181 (0.2166)	0.1946 (0.2636)	-0.2274 (0.1671)	5.5049 [0.0006]
		ARMA	Q(12) = 0.254 Q(24) = 0.398	0.2784 (01748.)	-0.4616 (0.1434)	0.4181 (0.2156)	0.1946 (0.2214)	-0.2274 (0.1438)	2.9882 [0.0217]
	2	NW	--	0.3505 (0.1547)	0.1485 (0.1350)	-0.3314 (0.2251)	0.5717 (0.2293)	-0.4846 (0.1099)	5.2447 [0.0008]
		ARMA	Q(12) = 0.484 Q(24) = 0.449	0.3505 (0.1866)	0.1485 (0.1530)	-0.3314 (0.2302)	0.5717 (0.2363)	-0.4846 (0.1535)	2.8968 [0.0249]
	3	NW	--	-0.1011 (0.2629)	0.5424 (0.2044)	-0.5466 (0.1497)	0.5170 (0.1738)	-0.4931 (0.1274)	11.0588 [0.0000]
		ARMA	Q(12) = 0.121 Q(24) = 0.163	-0.1011 (0.2295)	0.5424 (0.1883)	-0.5466 (0.2832)	0.5170 (0.2910)	-0.4931 (0.1888)	4.9906 [0.0012]
	4	NW	--	0.18743 (0.2025)	-0.0126 (0.1091)	-0.2097 (0.1558)	0.3629 (0.1767)	-0.1918 (0.1269)	1.0426 [0.4059]
		ARMA	Q(12) = 0.362 Q(24) = 0.405	0.4263 (0.2707)	-0.2314 (0.2061)	-0.1064 (0.1799)	0.3332 (0.1704)	-0.1131 (0.1447)	1.5718 [0.1908]
	5	NW	--	0.1469 (0.1531)	-0.0888 (0.1305)	-0.2883 (0.1776)	0.4301 (0.2396)	-0.0936 (0.1985)	2.5878 [0.0400]
		ARMA	Q(12) = 0.955 Q(24) = 0.984	0.1469 (0.1982)	-0.0888 (0.1626)	-0.2883 (0.2445)	0.4301 (0.2510)	-0.0936 (0.1630)	1.1599 [0.3452]
	6	NW	--	-0.0116 (0.1458)	-0.1724 (0.1088)	-0.0114 (0.1525)	0.5064 (0.1879)	-0.3201 (0.1662)	1.7152 [0.1528]
		ARMA	Q(12) = 0.988 Q(24) = 0.853	0.1964 (0.3489)	-0.4050 (0.1877)	0.0992 (0.1720)	0.5467 (0.1733)	-0.2948 (0.1654)	3.8865 [0.0059]
Group 2	1	NW	--	0.1352 (0.2178)	-0.1696 (0.2221)	0.3239 (0.2556)	0.1598 (0.1869)	-0.3546 (0.1261)	3.0133 [0.0209]
		ARMA	Q(12) = 0.443 Q(24) = 0.537	0.1352 (0.2464)	-0.1696 (0.1869)	0.3239 (0.2603)	0.1598 (0.2602)	-0.3546 (0.1852)	2.0657 [0.0894]
	2	NW	--	0.0132 (0.1415)	-0.1002 (0.1290)	0.2636 (0.2538)	0.1789 (0.1388)	-0.3462 (0.1155)	2.0435 [0.0925]
		ARMA	Q(12) = 0.821 Q(24) = 0.791	0.0132 (0.1985)	-0.1002 (0.1506)	0.2636 (0.2097)	0.1789 (0.2096)	-0.3462 (0.1492)	1.4265 [0.2352]
	3	NW	--	0.2201 (0.1696)	-0.0652 (0.2619)	0.2524 (0.2619)	0.0935 (0.2583)	-0.3410 (0.1310)	2.8285 [0.0277]
		ARMA	Q(12) = 0.542 Q(24) = 0.352	0.2201 (0.2285)	-0.0652 (0.1734)	0.2524 (0.2414)	0.0935 (0.2413)	-0.3410 (0.1717)	1.8539 [0.1237]
	4	NW	--	0.1881 (0.1556)	-0.1034 (0.1115)	0.2142 (0.2310)	0.1032 (0.1427)	-0.2617 (0.1231)	2.6733 [0.0351]
		ARMA	Q(12) = 0.971 Q(24) = 0.804	0.1881 (0.2101)	-0.1034 (0.1594)	0.2142 (0.2219)	0.1032 (0.2218)	-0.2617 (0.1579)	0.7973 [0.5580]
	5	NW	--	1.3954 (1.0300)	0.7935 (0.7116)	-3.3311 (2.2204)	2.0000 (1.3222)	0.2011 (0.5361)	0.6150 [0.6889]
		ARMA	Q(12) = 0.692 Q(24) = 0.939	1.3954 (1.2467)	0.7935 (0.9460)	-3.3311 (1.3172)	2.0000 (1.3166)	0.2011 (0.9370)	2.0598 [0.0903]
	6	NW	--	0.2361 (0.1664)	-0.3642 (0.1293)	0.4189 (0.1719)	0.0823 (0.1477)	-0.1988 (0.1252)	2.9401 [0.0233]
		ARMA	Q(12) = 0.986 Q(24) = 0.978	0.2361 (0.2023)	-0.3642 (0.1535)	0.4189 (0.2138)	0.0823 (0.2137)	-0.1988 (0.1521)	1.5583 [0.1934]
Group 3	1	NW	--	0.1419 (0.0816)	-0.0960 (0.1644)	-0.0965 (0.1655)	0.4465 (0.2581)	-0.2994 (0.1836)	2.5160 [0.0447]
		ARMA	Q(12) = 0.056 Q(24) = 0.373	0.1419 (0.0864)	-0.0960 (0.1455)	-0.0965 (0.2361)	0.4465 (0.2392)	-0.2994 (0.1444)	1.6795 [0.1612]
	2	NW	--	0.1135 (0.0928)	0.0824 (0.1492)	-0.3943 (0.2015)	0.5442 (0.1685)	-0.2688 (0.1387)	3.9038 [0.0055]
		ARMA	Q(12) = 0.381 Q(24) = 0.490	0.1135 (0.0762)	0.0824 (0.1282)	-0.3943 (0.2081)	0.5442 (0.2108)	-0.2688 (0.1273)	2.0598 [0.0903]
	3	NW	--	0.1256 (0.0867)	0.0611 (0.1195)	-0.4217 (0.1696)	0.5484 (0.2688)	-0.2274 (0.1745)	2.4727 [0.0478]
		ARMA	Q(12) = 0.156 Q(24) = 0.485	0.1256 (0.0850)	0.0611 (0.1431)	-0.4217 (0.2322)	0.5484 (0.2353)	-0.2274 (0.1420)	1.6893 [0.1589]
	4	NW	--	0.2980 (0.0769)	-0.3472 (0.1239)	-0.0666 (0.1546)	0.5582 (0.1832)	-0.2328 (0.1140)	5.2617 [0.0008]
		ARMA	Q(12) = 0.603 Q(24) = 0.919	0.2980 (0.0821)	-0.3472 (0.1382)	-0.0666 (0.2242)	0.5582 (0.2272)	-0.2328 (0.1371)	5.3918 [0.0007]
	5	NW	--	0.1348 (0.0886)	0.1229 (0.1976)	-0.3483 (0.1864)	0.4894 (0.2810)	-0.3078 (0.2178)	2.6950 [0.0340]
		ARMA	Q(12) = 0.238 Q(24) = 0.733	0.1965 (0.1318)	-0.4658 (0.2244)	0.3901 (0.2488)	0.5349 (0.2122)	-0.5238 (0.1969)	3.1499 [0.0181]
	6	NW	--	0.0655 (0.1184)	-0.1984 (0.1303)	0.0046 (0.1691)	0.4815 (0.2418)	-0.3109 (0.1747)	2.2433 [0.0680]
		ARMA	Q(12) = 0.615 Q(24) = 0.598	0.0655 (0.0887)	-0.1984 (0.1491)	0.0046 (0.2419)	0.4815 (0.2451)	-0.3109 (0.1480)	1.6821 [0.1606]

Notes: Standard errors are given in parentheses, p-values in brackets.
NW denotes the Newey & West estimation procedure, ARMA denotes the ARMA estimation procedure.

Table VII-11: Orthogonality test for each individual, group 4 to group 6

Experiment	Subject	Estimation Procedure	Q-Statistic	α	β_1	β_2	β_3	β_4	H_0: $\alpha = \beta_1 ... \beta_4 = 0$
Group 4	1	NW	--	0.1802 (0.1156)	0.0395 (0.1485)	-0.3350 (0.2196)	0.5605 (0.2199)	-0.3198 (0.1562)	3.7623 [0.0068]
		ARMA	Q(12) = 0.501 Q(24) = 0.835	0.2302 (0.1618)	-0.1002 (0.1398)	-0.2240 (0.2323)	0.7456 (0.2296)	-0.4902 (0.1336)	2.9922 [0.0246]
	2	NW	--	0.1519 (0.0911)	0.0056 (0.1732)	-0.2947 (0.2262)	0.4201 (0.3184)	-0.1740 (0.1990)	1.1033 [0.3735]
		ARMA	Q(12) = 0.359 Q(24) = 0.579	0.1519 (0.1083)	0.0056 (0.1554)	-0.2947 (0.2708)	0.4201 (0.2737)	-0.1740 (0.1528)	0.9052 [0.4871]
	3	NW	--	0.0222 (0.0850)	-0.0775 (0.0706)	-0.1080 (0.1409)	0.5137 (0.1196)	-0.3371 (0.0974)	4.6226 [0.0020]
		ARMA	Q(12) = 0.732 Q(24) = 0.495	0.0222 (0.0880)	-0.0775 (0.1262)	-0.1080 (0.2199)	0.5137 (0.2223)	-0.3371 (0.1241)	1.9393 [0.1086]
	4	NW	--	0.1683 (0.1064)	0.2939 (0.1048)	-0.5171 (0.1895)	0.4031 (0.2573)	-0.2289 (0.1611)	2.8950 [0.0250]
		ARMA	Q(12) = 0.191 Q(24) = 0.410	0.1683 (0.1036)	0.2939 (0.1486)	-0.5171 (0.2590)	0.4031 (0.2618)	-0.2289 (0.1461)	2.1988 [0.0729]
	5	NW	--	0.1456 (0.0970)	-0.2092 (0.1805)	-0.0862 (0.2316)	0.6168 (0.2573)	-0.3666 (0.1614)	3.4791 [0.0103]
		ARMA	Q(12) = 0.151 Q(24) = 0.491	0.1480 (0.0978)	-0.1600 (0.1587)	-0.1782 (0.2856)	0.7186 (0.3014)	-0.4269 (0.1634)	2.9236 [0.0258]
	6	NW	--	0.0023 (0.0972)	0.2003 (0.1312)	-0.3608 (0.1903)	0.3879 (0.1692)	-0.2319 (0.1137)	2.7162 [0.0359]
		ARMA	Q(12) = 0.700 Q(24) = 0.634	0.0023 (0.0979)	0.2003 (0.1405)	-0.3608 (0.2448)	0.3879 (0.2475)	-0.2319 (0.1381)	1.0117 [0.1785]
Group 5	1	NW	--	0.1046 (0.0925)	-0.1399 (0.1941)	-0.1986 (0.2689)	0.5092 (0.2531)	-0.2037 (0.1750)	2.0426 [0.0927]
		ARMA	Q(12) = 0.119 Q(24) = 0.549	0.1046 (0.0897)	-0.1399 (0.1710)	-0.1986 (0.2929)	0.5092 (0.2957)	-0.2037 (0.1692)	1.2459 [0.3056]
	2	NW	--	0.1375 (0.0911)	0.1337 (0.1243)	-0.1577 (0.1952)	0.2350 (0.2835)	-0.2552 (0.1602)	3.2255 [0.0151]
		ARMA	Q(12) = 0.088 Q(24) = 0.154	0.1374 (0.0595)	0.1410 (0.1501)	-0.1669 (0.2688)	0.3602 (0.2800)	-0.3784 (0.1536)	5.6647 [0.0006]
	3	NW	--	0.1138 (0.0707)	0.0054 (0.1474)	-0.1430 (0.1801)	0.3929 (0.2299)	-0.2933 (0.1595)	2.8512 [0.0267]
		ARMA	Q(12) = 0.058 Q(24) = 0.377	0.0916 (0.0613)	0.0820 (0.1496)	-0.2629 (0.02704)	0.5887 (0.2896)	-0.4384 (0.1591)	3.3573 [0.0137]
	4	NW	--	0.0718 (0.0804)	-0.1186 (0.1654)	-0.0689 (0.2450)	0.4426 (0.2328)	-0.2795 (0.1295)	2.3869 [0.0546]
		ARMA	Q(12) = 0.625 Q(24) = 0.581	0.1886 (0.1368)	-0.1717 (0.1526)	-0.0922 (0.2513)	0.7351 (0.2543)	-0.5343 (0.1526)	2.7153 [0.0367]
	5	NW	--	0.13357 (0.0785)	-0.0572 (0.1215)	-0.1836 (0.1963)	0.5259 (0.2800)	-0.3271 (0.1622)	2.2602 [0.0663]
		ARMA	Q(12) = 0.079 Q(24) = 0.258	0.13357 (0.0826)	-0.0572 (0.1576)	-0.1836 (0.2700)	0.5259 (0.2725)	-0.3271 (0.1560)	1.4238 [0.2361]
	6	NW	--	0.1140 (0.1191)	-0.0997 (0.3226)	-0.1919 (0.5195)	0.5531 (0.3787)	-0.2996 (0.2703)	2.1509 [0.0785]
		ARMA	Q(12) = 0.795 Q(24) = 0.743	0.1140 (0.1103)	-0.0997 (0.2105)	-0.1919 (0.3606)	0.5531 (0.3639)	-0.2996 (0.2083)	0.8571 [0.5180]
Group 6	1	NW	--	0.0934 (0.1362)	0.4806 (0.1576)	-0.6974 (0.1940)	0.4460 (0.2222)	-0.2577 (0.1858)	6.8642 [0.0000]
		ARMA	Q(12) = 0.431 Q(24) = 0.562	0.0934 (0.1299)	0.4806 (0.1673)	-0.6974 (0.2876)	0.4460 (0.2857)	-0.2577 (0.1551)	3.6385 [0.0071]
	2	NW	--	-0.0012 (0.2869)	0.1657 (0.2163)	0.1262 (0.3212)	0.6669 (0.3164)	-0.6278 (0.1637)	3.5608 [0.0091]
		ARMA	Q(12) = 0.471 Q(24) = 0.811	-0.0012 (0.2200)	0.1657 (0.2835	0.1262 (0.4872)	0.6669 (0.4840)	-0.6278 (0.2627)	1.5879 [0.1850]
	3	NW	--	0.2771 (0.1244)	0.3143 (0.1859)	-0.6042 (0.2414)	0.4073 (0.2342)	-0.1936 (0.1826)	4.5702 [0.0021]
		ARMA	Q(12) = 0.225 Q(24) = 0.590	0.2099 (0.1119)	0.4137 (0.1811)	-0.7591 (0.3322)	0.5923 (0.3599)	-0.3047 (0.1970)	3.2275 [0.0165]
	4	NW	--	0.3105 (0.1177)	-0.1853 (0.1356)	-0.0856 (0.1886)	0.4468 (0.2291)	-0.2600 (0.1782)	1.8026 [0.1338]
		ARMA	Q(12) = 0.603 Q(24) = 0.716	0.3105 (0.1200)	-0.1853 (0.1546)	-0.0856 (0.2657)	0.4468 (0.2640)	-0.2600 (0.1433)	2.1135 [0.0831]
	5	NW	--	0.0866 (0.1399)	0.0431 (0.1434)	-0.1962 (0.2366)	0.4359 (0.2710)	-0.3091 (0.1919)	2.7331 [0.0320]
		ARMA	Q(12) = 0.380 Q(24) = 0.420	0.0866 (0.1465)	0.0431 (0.1887)	-0.1962 (0.3244)	0.4359 (0.3223)	-0.3091 (0.1749)	1.1297 [0.3601]
	6	NW	--	0.4020 (0.1314)	-0.1547 (0.1503)	-0.3063 (0.2046)	0.6194 (0.1424)	-0.2680 (0.1295)	5.7613 [0.0004]
		ARMA	Q(12) = 0.422 Q(24) = 0.458	0.4020 (0.1239)	-0.1547 (0.1596)	-0.3063 (0.2743)	0.6194 (0.2725)	-0.2680 (0.1479)	3.5249 [0.0096]

Notes: Standard errors are given in parentheses, p-values in brackets.
NW denotes the Newey & West estimation procedure, ARMA denotes the ARMA estimation procedure.

Table VII-12: Serial correlation test for each individual

Experiment	Subject	α	β_1	β_2	β_3	β_4	H_0: $\alpha = \beta_1 ... \beta_4 = 0$
Group 1	1	-0.0077	-0.3744	-0.0938	0.1424	-0.1864	2.0312
		(0.0082)	(0.1674)	(0.1770)	(0.1770)	(0.1679)	[0.0949]
	2	-0.0064	0.1176	-0.0423	0.3914	-0.0707	1.6478
		(0.0086)	(0.1581)	(0.1494)	(0.1507)	(0.1629)	[0.1697]
	3	-0.0169	0.4877	-0.0727	0.0911	0.0169	4.8905
		(0.0113)	(0.1582)	(0.1763)	(0.1746)	(0.1489)	[0.0014]
	4	-0.0132	0.0953	-0.3069	0.0816	-0.4157	2.6932
		(0.0067)	(0.1392)	(0.1402)	(0.1405)	(0.1405)	[0.0344]
	5	-0.0041	-0.0359	-0.1615	0.0137	-0.0779	0.2634
		(0.0090)	(0.1654)	(0.1637)	(0.1640)	(0.1798)	[0.9304]
	6	-0.0013	0.2065	-0.1817	0.4060	-0.3344	2.0363
		(0.0076)	(0.1601)	(0.1563)	(0.1565)	(0.1601)	[0.0941]
Group 2	1	-0.0198	-0.1236	0.0827	0.1791	0.0699	1.5084
		(0.0135)	(0.1569)	(0.1551)	(0.1570)	(0.1583)	[0.2089]
	2	-0.0026	-0.1322	0.0979	0.3626	0.0115	1.4085
		(0.0085)	(0.1571)	(0.1473)	(0.1472)	(0.1584)	[0.2420]
	3	-0.0149	-0.0388	0.2390	0.1932	-0.1080	1.4381
		(0.0106)	(0.1561)	(0.1663)	(0.1629)	(0.1685)	[0.2317]
	4	-0.0004	-0.0709	0.0750	0.2447	0.0189	0.5734
		(0.0091)	(0.1579)	(0.1535)	(0.1531)	(0.1604)	[0.7199]
	5	0.0439	0.0063	0.5730	-0.0327	-0.2766	3.1483
		(0.0526)	(0.1519)	(0.1519)	(0.1518)	(0.1520)	[0.0173]
	6	-0.0091	-0.2739	0.0275	0.1384	-0.0353	1.0366
		(0.0092)	(0.1564)	(0.1598)	(0.1593)	(0.1596)	[0.4096]
Group 3	1	-0.0142	0.0039	-0.2172	0.2787	-0.1984	1.6997
		(0.0122)	(0.1550)	(0.1504)	(0.1520)	(0.1689)	[0.1570]
	2	-0.0114	0.2001	-0.1854	0.3477	-0.3471	2.1369
		(0.0106)	(0.1511)	(0.1500)	(0.1508)	(0.1578)	[0.0807]
	3	-0.0086	0.1114	-0.2973	0.2436	-0.2041	1.4012
		(0.0118)	(0.1552)	(0.1522)	(0.1575)	(0.1679)	[0.2446]
	4	0.0054	0.0452	-0.0916	0.4228	-0.0693	1.8827
		(0.0132)	(0.1578)	(0.1456)	(0.1463)	(0.1637)	[0.1190]
	5	-0.0170	0.2222	-0.1863	0.3218	-0.2812	1.8711
		(0.0135)	(0.1525)	(0.1510)	(0.1523)	(0.1634)	[0.1211]
	6	-0.0153	0.0298	-0.0687	0.2140	-0.3192	1.5218
		(0.0127)	(0.1514)	(0.1490)	(0.1506)	(0.1589)	[0.2048]
Group 4	1	-0.0161	0.0871	-0.1390	0.1115	-0.1371	0.7885
		(0.0111)	(0.1559)	(0.1576)	(0.1578)	(0.1652)	[0.5642]
	2	0.0013	0.0293	-0.2514	0.0699	-0.0080	0.5488
		(0.0103)	(0.1582)	(0.1589)	(0.1596)	(0.1666)	[0.7382]
	3	-0.0082	0.0029	-0.1425	0.4535	-0.1391	2.8617
		(0.0086)	(0.1595)	(0.1461)	(0.1466)	(0.1641)	[0.0266]
	4	-0.0064	0.2288	0.0332	0.2024	-0.2476	1.3436
		(0.0102)	(0.1530)	(0.1546)	(0.1546)	(0.1462)	[0.2660]
	5	-0.0215	-0.0640	-0.3811	0.1380	-0.3394	2.8027
		(0.0107)	(0.1471)	(0.1454)	(0.1470)	(0.1527)	[0.0292]
	6	-0.0176	0.0752	0.0985	0.1317	-0.2314	1.5411
		(0.0100)	(0.1500)	(0.1496)	(0.1509)	(0.1530)	[0.1990]
Group 5	1	-0.0037	-0.0784	-0.4027	0.0075	-0.4169	2.5859
		(0.0123)	(0.1447)	(0.1456)	(0.1477)	(0.1476)	[0.0406]
	2	-0.0118	0.1821	0.1734	0.2062	-0.2429	1.7339
		(0.0126)	(0.1533)	(0.1554)	(0.1546)	(0.1563)	[0.1491]
	3	-0.0130	0.1718	-0.0925	0.2934	-0.1785	1.3773
		(0.0122)	(0.1555)	(0.1529)	(0.1527)	(0.1653)	[0.2533]
	4	-0.0136	-0.1489	-0.2364	0.0576	-0.2112	1.2121
		(0.0121)	(0.1541)	(0.1560)	(0.1566)	(0.1540)	[0.3212]
	5	-0.0060	0.0756	-0.1791	0.3125	-0.1362	1.2382
		(0.0124)	(0.1566)	(0.1500)	(0.1527)	(0.1624)	[0.3095]
	6	-0.0147	0.0274	-0.3435	0.3035	-0.2713	2.6526
		(0.0154)	(0.1536)	(0.1474)	(0.1513)	(0.1638)	[0.0366]
Group 6	1	-0.0146	0.4193	-0.1583	0.2100	-0.2435	3.2387
		(0.0084)	(0.1531)	(0.1672)	(0.1640)	(0.1532)	[0.0151]
	2	-0.0075	0.4014	-0.3940	0.3713	-0.4563	3.8296
		(0.0110)	(0.1377)	(0.1432)	(0.1430)	(0.1382)	[0.0063]
	3	-0.0062	0.4589	-0.3178	0.3445	-0.2897	2.9079
		(0.0075)	(0.1518)	(0.1619)	(0.1634)	(0.1355)	[0.0248]
	4	-0.0022	-0.0316	-0.1754	0.1966	-0.0808	0.8186
		(0.0072)	(0.1564)	(0.1479)	(0.1474)	(0.1660)	[0.5437]
	5	-0.0126	-0.2533	-0.0927	0.3227	0.1202	2.3715
		(0.0090)	(0.1561)	(0.1523)	(0.1508)	(0.1591)	[0.0563]
	6	-0.0031	0.0564	-0.1738	-0.0024	-0.2920	1.1867
		(0.0078)	(0.1520)	(0.1401)	(0.1420)	(0.1449)	[0.3329]

Notes: Standard errors are given in parentheses, p-values in brackets.
NW denotes the Newey & West estimation procedure, ARMA denotes the ARMA estimation procedure.

Table VII-13: Extrapolative expectations for each individual, group 1 to group 3

Experiment	Subject	Estimation procedure	Q-Statistic	α	β	H_0: α = β = 0
Group 1	1	NW	--	0.0007 (0.0052)	-0.5381 (0.0909)	19.9431 [0.0000]
		ARMA	Q(12) = 0.559 Q(24) = 0.498	0.0015 (0.0031)	-0.5319 (0.0835)	20.4971 [0.0000]
	2	NW	--	0.0008 (0.0058)	0.0486 (0.1146)	0.0985 [0.9064]
		ARMA	Q(12) = 0.641 Q(24) = 0.783	0.0008 (0.0059)	0.0486 (0.1074)	0.1167 [08902]
	3	NW	--	0.0225 (0.0097)	0.3543 (0.1758)	3.1990 [0.0500]
		ARMA	Q(12) = 0.949 Q(24) = 0.541	0.0211 (0.0115)	0.3780 (0.1548)	5.1999 [0.0094]
	4	NW	--	0.0027 (0.0046)	-0.1564 (0.0766)	2.7295 [0.0785]
		ARMA	Q(12) = 0.827 Q(24) = 0.993	0.0027 (0.0049)	-0.1564 (0.0898)	1.6002 [0.2129]
	5	NW	--	-0.0019 (0.0076)	-0.2229 (0.1766)	0.8870 [0.4188]
		ARMA	Q(12) = 0.329 Q(24) = 0.833	-0.0019 (0.0062)	-0.2229 (0.1124)	2.0749 [0.1372]
	6	NW	--	-0.0035 (0.0074)	-0.3421 (0.0918)	7.3314 [0.0017]
		ARMA	Q(12) = 0.507 Q(24) = 0.144	-0.0035 (0.0066)	-0.3421 (0.1208)	4.2897 [0.0196]
Group 2	1	NW	--	0.0237 (0.0076)	-0.1246 (0.1677)	7.7116 [0.0013]
		ARMA	Q(12) = 0.626 Q(24) = 0.509	0.0237 (0.0073)	-0.1246 (0.1301)	5.7109 [0.0061]
	2	NW	--	0.0008 (0.0046)	-0.0664 (0.0791)	0.4188 [0.6603]
		ARMA	Q(12) = 0.581 Q(24) = 0.957	0.0006 (0.0051)	-0.0598 (0.0562)	0.5731 [0.5679]
	3	NW	--	0.0146 (0.0054)	0.0111 (0.0493)	3.7848 [0.0301]
		ARMA	Q(12) = 0.977 Q(24) = 0.829	0.0146 (0.0056)	0.0111 (0.0995)	3.3896 [0.0423]
	4	NW	--	-0.0016 (0.0027)	-0.0565 (0.0459)	1.0192 [0.3689]
		ARMA	Q(12) = 0.497 Q(24) = 0.145	-0.0014 (0.0029)	-0.0672 (0.0326)	2.2658 [0.1157]
	5	NW	--	-0.0568 (0.0744)	0.8136 (0.6892)	0.7845 [0.4624]
		ARMA	Q(12) = 0.954 Q(24) = 0.967	-0.0693 (0.0812)	1.5642 (0.8455)	2.0294 [0.1447]
	6	NW	--	0.0055 (0.0028)	-0.3141 (0.0990)	6.3656 [0.0036]
		ARMA	Q(12) = 0.915 Q(24) = 0.867	0.0055 (0.0031)	-0.3141 (0.0542)	18.5012 [0.0000]
Group 3	1	NW	--	0.0007 (0.0022)	-0.3540 (0.0324)	59.6410 [0.0000]
		ARMA	Q(12) = 0.463 Q(24) = 0.251	0.0007 (0.0026)	-0.3540 (0.0310)	67.1274 [0.0000]
	2	NW	--	-0.0041 (0.0071)	-0.2128 (0.0899)	2.8338 [0.0691]
		ARMA	Q(12) = 0.239 Q(24) = 0.768	-0.0041 (0.0071)	-0.2128 (0.0847)	3.7237 [0.0317]
	3	NW	--	-0.0054 (0.0043)	-0.2560 (0.1263)	2.3819 [0.1037]
		ARMA	Q(12) = 0.774 Q(24) = 0.744	-0.0054 (0.0051)	-0.2560 (0.0603)	10.8671 [0.0001]
	4	NW	--	-0.0160 (0.0101)	-0.6047 (0.1437)	9.0163 [0.0005]
		ARMA	Q(12) = 0.481 Q(24) = 0.675	-0.0175 (0.0161)	-0.4005 (0.0905)	11.0395 [0.0001]
	5	NW	--	0.0006 (0.0023)	-0.1381 (0.0225)	23.6781 [0.0000]
		ARMA	Q(12) = 0.913 Q(24) = 0.989	0.0006 (0.0021)	-0.1381 (0.0254)	15.0551 [0.0000]
	6	NW	--	0.0025 (0.0080)	-0.4840 (0.1716)	4.2105 [0.0209]
		ARMA	Q(12) = 0.924 Q(24) = 0.967	-0.0001 (0.0116)	-0.3867 (0.1021)	7.4023 [0.0017]

Notes: Standard errors are given in parentheses, p-values in brackets.
NW denotes the Newey & West estimation procedure, ARMA denotes the ARMA estimation procedure.

Table VII-14: Extrapolative expectations for each individual, group 4 to 6

Experiment	Subject	Estimation procedure	Q-Statistic	α	β	$H_0: \alpha = \beta = 0$
Group 4	1	NW	--	0.0062 (0.0054)	-0.4071 (0.0924)	10.7693 [0.0001]
		ARMA	Q(12) = 0.079 Q(24) = 0.142	0.0062 (0.0052)	-0.4071 (0.0711)	16.5453 [0.0000]
	2	NW	--	-0.0053 (0.0049)	-0.5002 (0.0519)	56.7645 [0.0000]
		ARMA	Q(12) = 0.508 Q(24) = 0.504	-0.0053 (0.0046)	-0.5002 (0.0619)	34.7862 [0.0000]
	3	NW	--	0.0031 (0.0082)	-0.5377 (0.1157)	14.2701 [0.0000]
		ARMA	Q(12) = 0.853 Q(24) = 0.731	0.0031 (0.0084)	-0.5377 (0.1140)	11.1348 [0.0001]
	4	NW	--	-0.0024 (0.0048)	-0.1427 (0.0846)	1.4941 [0.2351]
		ARMA	Q(12) = 0.518 Q(24) = 0.769	-0.0024 (0.0052)	-0.1427 (0.0705)	2.2882 [0.1129]
	5	NW	--	0.0052 (0.0060)	-0.6364 (0.0907)	34.5311 [0.0000]
		ARMA	Q(12) = 0.859 Q(24) = 0.730	0.0075 (0.0044)	-0.6447 (0.0593)	59.1629 [0.0000]
	6	NW	--	0.0067 (0.0067)	-0.2649 (0.0940)	5.2423 [0.0089]
		ARMA	Q(12) = 0.753 Q(24) = 0.190	0.0105 (0.0108)	-0.3057 (0.0923)	5.6279 [0.0069]
Group 5	1	NW	--	-0.0067 (0.0047)	-0.6146 (0.0664)	51.5245 [0.0000]
		ARMA	Q(12) = 0.960 Q(24) = 0.731	-0.0084 (0.0075)	-0.5350 (0.0570)	46.9850 [0.0000]
	2	NW	--	-0.0005 (0.0051)	-0.1744 (0.0618)	3.9825 [0.0254]
		ARMA	Q(12) = 0.614 Q(24) = 0.502	0.0006 (0.0038)	-0.1676 (0.0499)	5.9723 [0.0055]
	3	NW	--	0.0027 (0.0046)	-0.3562 (0.0375)	56.4232 [0.0000]
		ARMA	Q(12) = 0.716 Q(24) = 0.803	0.0027 (0.0041)	-0.3562 (0.0478)	28.0831 [0.0000]
	4	NW	--	-0.0001 (0.0033)	-0.5272 (0.0460)	102.5590 [0.0000]
		ARMA	Q(12) = 0.664 Q(24) = 0.709	-0.0001 (0.0040)	-0.5520 (0.0414)	92.3078 [0.0000]
	5	NW	--	-0.0042 (0.0045)	-0.4516 (0.0924)	20.1855 [0.0000]
		ARMA	Q(12) = 0.695 Q(24) = 0.640	-0.0042 (0.0054)	-0.4516 (0.0622)	28.6265 [0.0000]
	6	NW	--	0.0019 (0.0088)	-0.5287 (0.2072)	3.2674 [0.0471]
		ARMA	Q(12) = 0.821 Q(24) = 0.904	0.0019 (0.0112)	-0.5287 (0.1305)	8.3674 [0.0008]
Group 6	1	NW	--	0.0077 (0.0039)	0.0363 (0.0576)	3.3890 [0.0424]
		ARMA	Q(12) = 0.498 Q(24) = 0.685	0.0077 (0.0030)	0.0363 (0.0563)	3.6707 [0.0332]
	2	NW	--	0.0012 (0.0148)	-0.6027 (0.2019)	5.3069 [0.0084]
		ARMA	Q(12) = 0.723 Q(24) = 0.820	0.0020 (0.0154)	-0.5930 (0.2383)	3.1238 [0.0544]
	3	NW	--	0.0008 (0.0021)	-0.0925 (0.0454)	2.2101 [0.1212]
		ARMA	Q(12) = 0.669 Q(24) = 0.707	0.0008 (0.0025)	-0.0925 (0.0473)	1.9173 [0.1586]
	4	NW	--	-0.0005 (0.0029)	-0.6335 (0.0675)	59.7684 [0.00009
		ARMA	Q(12) = 0.676 Q(24) = 0.934	-0.0005 (0.0027)	-0.6335 (0.0511)	77.6934 [0.0000]
	5	NW	--	0.0066 (0.0060)	-0.3518 (0.0488)	28.1143 [0.0000]
		ARMA	Q(12) = 0.998 Q(24) = 0.996	0.0066 (0.0065)	-0.3518 (0.1205)	4.5438 [0.0158]
	6	NW	--	-0.0052 (0.0047)	-0.4198 (0.1452)	8.2223 [0.0009]
		ARMA	Q(12) = 0.581 Q(24) = 0.678	-0.0022 (0.0031)	-0.5066 (0.0756)	25.3353 [0.0000]

Notes: Standard errors are given in parentheses, p-values in brackets.
NW denotes the Newey & West estimation procedure, ARMA denotes the ARMA estimation procedure.

Table VII-15: Adaptive expectations for each individual, group 1 to group 3

Experiment	Subject	Estimation procedure	Q-Statistic	α	β	H_0: α = β = 0
Group 1	1	NW	--	0.0005 (0.0077)	-0.4057 (0.0977)	9.6210 [0.0003]
		ARMA	Q(12) = 0.125 Q(24) = 0.165	-0.0000 (0.0076)	-0.4617 (0.0764)	18.3537 [0.0000]
	2	NW	--	0.0007 (0.0054)	0.0624 (0.1035)	0.1839 [0.8326]
		ARMA	Q(12) = 0.573 Q(24) = 0.745	0.0007 (0.0059)	0.0624 (0.1006)	0.2067 [0.8140]
	3	NW	--	0.0155 (0.0067)	0.3366 (0.0993)	8.7897 [0.0006]
		ARMA	Q(12) = 0.991 Q(24) = 0.774	0.0155 (0.0082)	0.3366 (0.1019)	10.1885 [0.0002]
	4	NW	--	0.0025 (0.0053)	-0.0557 (0.1004)	0.2811 [0.7562]
		ARMA	Q(12) = 0.690 Q(24) = 0.983	0.0025 (0.0051)	-0.0557 (0.1113)	0.2042 [0.8160]
	5	NW	--	-0.0029 (0.0085)	-0.0037 (0.0865)	0.0560 [0.9456]
		ARMA	Q(12) = 0.811 Q(24) = 0.992	-0.0024 (0.0104)	-0.1417 (0.1049)	0.9405 [0.3981]
	6	NW	--	-0.0049 (0.0088)	-0.0315 (0.1183)	0.1567 [0.8554]
		ARMA	Q(12) = 0.419 Q(24) = 0.273	-0.0073 (0.0132)	-0.1302 (0.1307)	0.9001 [0.4115]
Group 2	1	NW	--	0.0250 (0.0077)	-0.0537 (0.1225)	5.3388 [0.0082]
		ARMA	Q(12) = 0.476 Q(24) = 0.362	0.0250 (0.0077)	-0.0537 (0.1045)	5.3111 [0.0084]
	2	NW	--	0.0009 (0.0047)	-0.0047 (0.0724)	0.0173 [0.9829]
		ARMA	Q(12) = 0.569 Q(24) = 0.959	0.0006 (0.0056)	-0.0598 (0.0524)	0.6564 [0.5237]
	3	NW	--	0.0148 (0.0058)	-0.0142 (0.0528)	3.6028 [0.0352]
		ARMA	Q(12) = 0.982 Q(24) = 0.843	0.0148 (0.0057)	-0.0142 (0.0856)	3.3981 [0.0420]
	4	NW	--	-0.0016 (0.0028)	-0.0371 (0.0488)	0.5862 [0.5605]
		ARMA	Q(12) = 0.493 Q(24) = 0.145	-0.0015 (0.0032)	-0.0679 (0.0305)	2.5835 [0.0869]
	5	NW	--	-0.0564 (0.0712)	0.0153 (0.0409)	2.8325 [0.0692]
		ARMA	Q(12) = 0.937 Q(24) = 0.984	-0.0594 (0.0998)	0.0481 (0.1681)	0.2372 [0.7899]
	6	NW	--	0.0073 (0.0039)	-0.2870 (0.0683)	8.9191 [0.0005]
		ARMA	Q(12) = 0.783 Q(24) = 0.815	0.0073 (0.0032)	-0.2870 (0.0551)	15.1390 [0.0000]
Group 3	1	NW	--	-0.0013 (0.0037)	-0.3343 (0.0434)	58.6979 [0.0000]
		ARMA	Q(12) = 0.565 Q(24) = 0.129	-0.0020 (0.0055)	-0.2847 (0.0354)	33.0471 [0.0000]
	2	NW	--	-0.0060 (0.0086)	-0.1504 (0.0994)	1.1451 [0.3271]
		ARMA	Q(12) = 0.164 Q(24) = 0.432	-0.0060 (0.0074)	-0.1504 (0.1062)	1.5272 [0.2279]
	3	NW	--	-0.0087 (0.0068)	-0.1691 (0.1190)	1.1817 [0.3159]
		ARMA	Q(12) = 0.974 Q(24) = 0.850	-0.0084 (0.0104)	-0.0864 (0.0601)	1.4492 [0.2458]
	4	NW	--	-0.0266 (0.0169)	-0.0947 (0.1018)	1.7756 [0.1808]
		ARMA	Q(12) = 0.247 Q(24) = 0.555	-0.0288 (0.0231)	-0.2598 (0.0716)	7.2836 [0.0019]
	5	NW	--	0.0002 (0.0026)	-0.1243 (0.0195)	26.9077 [0.0000]
		ARMA	Q(12) = 0.847 Q(24) = 0.977	0.0002 (0.0022)	-0.1243 (0.0255)	12.1632 [0.0001]
	6	NW	--	-0.0028 (0.0121)	-0.1994 (0.1216)	1.3559 [0.2678]
		ARMA	Q(12) = 0.893 Q(24) = 0.978	-0.0021 (0.0128)	-0.2851 (0.0760)	7.1660 [0.0021]

Notes: Standard errors are given in parentheses, p-values in brackets.
NW denotes the Newey & West estimation procedure, ARMA denotes the ARMA estimation procedure.

Table VII-16: Adaptive expectations for each individual, group 4 to group 6

Experiment	Subject	Estimation procedure	Q-Statistic	α	β	H_0: α = β = 0
Group 4	1	NW	--	0.0074 (0.0075)	-0.3463 (0.0929)	9.1406 [0.0005]
		ARMA	Q(12) = 0.071 Q(24) = 0.203	0.0064 (0.0099)	-0.3482 (0.0822)	8.9716 [0.0005]
	2	NW	--	-0.0097 (0.0090)	-0.3842 (0.0880)	10.3363 [0.0002]
		ARMA	Q(12) = 0.367 Q(24) = 0.548	-0.0140 (0.0106)	-0.3482 (0.0615)	16.9220 [0.0000]
	3	NW	--	0.0017 (0.0136)	-0.2618 (0.1097)	2.8682 [0.0670]
		ARMA	Q(12) = 0.811 Q(24) = 0.907	-0.0031 (0.0184)	-0.3463 (0.1425)	3.0077 [0.0597]
	4	NW	--	-0.0031 (0.0053)	-0.1373 (0.0882)	1.2164 [0.3056]
		ARMA	Q(12) = 0.512 Q(24) = 0.810	-0.0031 (0.0052)	-0.1373 (0.0732)	1.9949 [0.1476]
	5	NW	--	0.0046 (0.0100)	-0.4280 (0.0869)	12.1540 [0.0001]
		ARMA	Q(12) = 0.253 Q(24) = 0.575	0.0042 (0.0112)	-0.4286 (0.0685)	19.5775 [0.0000]
	6	NW	--	0.0077 (0.0082)	-0.1971 (0.1665)	1.1263 [0.3330]
		ARMA	Q(12) = 0.617 Q(24) = 0.196	0.0108 (0.0167)	-0.2299 (0.1141)	2.0874 [0.1373]
Group 5	1	NW	--	-0.0150 (0.0133)	-0.2725 (0.0859)	6.4814 [0.0033]
		ARMA	Q(12) = 0.527 Q(24) = 0.503	-0.0213 (0.0198)	-0.2841 (0.0553)	13.6094 [0.0000]
	2	NW	--	-0.0014 (0.0057)	-0.1572 (0.0585)	3.7736 [0.0304]
		ARMA	Q(12) = 0.220 Q(24) = 0.172	-0.0004 (0.0073)	-0.2159 (0.0613)	6.3423 [0.0038]
	3	NW	--	0.0024 (0.0065)	-0.3627 (0.0764)	14.2757 [0.0000]
		ARMA	Q(12) = 0.445 Q(24) = 0.683	0.0012 (0.0071)	-0.3319 (0.0577)	16.6551 [0.0000]
	4	NW	--	-0.0057 (0.0079)	-0.4446 (0.0883)	14.3991 [0.0000]
		ARMA	Q(12) = 0.238 Q(24) = 0.103	-0.0045 (0.0095)	-0.3941 (0.0609)	21.5264 [0.0000]
	5	NW	--	-0.0098 (0.0064)	-0.3821 (0.1077)	7.7231 [0.0013]
		ARMA	Q(12) = 0.139 Q(24) = 0.338	-0.0098 (0.0063)	-0.3982 (0.0748)	16.0150 [0.0000]
	6	NW	--	-0.0037 (0.0138)	-0.2743 (0.1141)	3.0515 [0.0570]
		ARMA	Q(12) = 0.903 Q(24) = 0.881	-0.0039 (0.0163)	-0.3201 (0.1347)	2.9429 [0.0632]
Group 6	1	NW	--	0.0064 (0.0043)	0.0930 (0.0645)	9.7051 [0.0003]
		ARMA	Q(12) = 0.574 Q(24) = 0.683	0.0064 (0.0031)	0.0930 (0.0558)	5.0311 [0.0106]
	2	NW	--	-0.0040 (0.0143)	0.2998 (0.2104)	1.2438 [0.2978]
		ARMA	Q(12) = 0.563 Q(24) = 0.487	0.0022 (0.0120)	-0.3703 (0.1613)	2.6360 [0.0847]
	3	NW	--	0.0008 (0.0023)	-0.1156 (0.0465)	3.3963 [0.0421]
		ARMA	Q(12) = 0.885 Q(24) = 0.890	0.0008 (0.0024)	-0.1156 (0.0416)	3.8635 [0.0281]
	4	NW	--	-0.0025 (0.0061)	-0.4506 (0.0803)	15.8372 [0.0000]
		ARMA	Q(12) = 0.849 Q(24) = 0.539	-0.0065 (0.0043)	-0.4158 (0.0573)	28.1474 [0.0000]
	5	NW	--	0.0075 (0.0068)	-0.2396 (0.1005)	6.0698 [0.0046]
		ARMA	Q(12) = 0.973 Q(24) = 0.978	0.0083 (0.0094)	-0.3096 (0.1248)	3.1766 [0.0514]
	6	NW	--	-0.0075 (0.0055)	-0.3183 (0.0651)	12.2330 [0.0001]
		ARMA	Q(12) = 0.870 Q(24) = 0.879	-0.0045 (0.0045)	-0.4508 (0.0894)	13.5494 [0.0000]

Notes: Standard errors are given in parentheses, p-values in brackets.
NW denotes the Newey & West estimation procedure, ARMA denotes the ARMA estimation procedure.

Table VII-17: Regressive expectations for each individual, group 1 to group 3

Experiment	Subject	Estimation procedure	Q-Statistic	α	β	H_0: $\alpha = \beta = 0$
Group 1	1	NW	--	-0.0012 (0.0088)	-0.0023 (0.0442)	0.0219 [0.9783]
		ARMA	Q(12) = 0.198 Q(24) = 0.251	-0.0012 (0.0106)	-0.0023 (0.0430)	0.0283 [0.9721]
	2	NW	--	-0.0051 (0.0084)	0.0353 (0.0282)	0.8904 [0.4173]
		ARMA	Q(12) = 0.537 Q(24) = 0.714	-0.0051 (0.0086)	0.0353 (0.0347)	0.5480 [0.5818]
	3	NW	--	-0.0061 (0.0122)	0.1493 (0.0561)	4.8348 [0.0123]
		ARMA	Q(12) = 0.936 Q(24) = 0.904	-0.0061 (0.0123)	0.1493 (0.0496)	7.9547 [0.0011]
	4	NW	--	0.0006 (0.0075)	0.0127 (0.0362)	0.1635 [0.8496]
		ARMA	Q(12) = 0.882 Q(24) = 0.994	-0.0050 (0.0110)	0.0319 (0.0435)	0.2844 [0.7538]
	5	NW	--	0.0013 (0.0126)	-0.0021 (0.0481)	0.0058 [0.9943]
		ARMA	Q(12) = 0.570 Q(24) = 0.936	-0.0118 (0.0137)	0.0445 (0.0551)	0.3968 [0.6748]
	6	NW	--	-0.0206 (0.0094)	0.0831 (0.0424)	2.6517 [0.0811]
		ARMA	Q(12) = 0.703 Q(24) = 0.698	-0.0256 (0.0129)	0.1031 (0.0508)	2.2632 [0.1163]
Group 2	1	NW	--	0.0231 (0.0071)	0.0504 (0.0448)	7.5171 [0.0015]
		ARMA	Q(12) = 0.666 Q(24) = 0.644	0.0231 (0.0073)	0.0504 (0.0442)	5.4129 [0.0077]
	2	NW	--	0.0023 (0.0023)	0.0855 0.0180)	11.4128 [0.0001]
		ARMA	Q(12) = 0.394 Q(24) = 0.852	0.0023 (0.0027)	0.0855 (0.0165)	13.4943 [0.0000]
	3	NW	--	0.0152 (0.0050)	0.0433 (0.0215)	5.4587 [0.0074]
		ARMA	Q(12) = 0.964 Q(24) = 0.782	0.0152 (0.0054)	0.0433 (0.0328)	4.5848 [0.0152]
	4	NW	--	-0.0007 (0.0022)	0.0288 (0.0118)	4.1095 [0.0227]
		ARMA	Q(12) = 0.512 Q(24) = 0.516	-0.0007 (0.0019)	0.0288 (0.0117)	3.2094 [0.0494]
	5	NW	--	-0.0584 (0.0676)	-0.2388 (0.2203)	0.6134 [0.5458]
		ARMA	Q(12) = 0.921 Q(24) = 0.975	-0.0556 (0.1119)	0.5080 (0.6950)	0.4093 [0.6666]
	6	NW	--	0.0063 (0.0042)	-0.0029 (0.0315)	1.1167 [0.3359]
		ARMA	Q(12) = 0.983 Q(24) = 0.975	0.0063 (0.0040)	-0.0029 (0.0243)	1.2704 [0.2902]
Group 3	1	NW	--	-0.0029 (0.0075)	-0.0038 (0.0112)	0.3023 [0.7406]
		ARMA	Q(12) = 0.259 Q(24) = 0.347	0.0003 (0.0119)	-0.0094 (0.0163)	0.3974 [0.6744]
	2	NW	--	-0.0100 (0.0061)	0.0056 (0.0193)	1.5375 [0.2255]
		ARMA	Q(12) = 0.782 Q(24) = 0.962	-0.0135 (0.0164)	0.0096 (0.0225)	0.3972 [0.6746]
	3	NW	--	-0.0091 (0.0062)	-0.0001 (0.0130)	1.1926 [0.3124]
		ARMA	Q(12) = 0.965 Q(24) = 0.872	-0.0071 (0.0178)	-0.0011 (0.0241)	0.2401 [0.7876]
	4	NW	--	-0.0034 (0.0115)	-0.0395 (0.0302)	1.3118 [0.2790]
		ARMA	Q(12) = 0.057 Q(24) = 0.432	0.0128 (0.0363)	-0.0652 (0.0478)	1.5610 [0.2211]
	5	NW	--	-0.0034 (0.0027)	0.0029 (0.0070)	0.8729 [0.4244]
		ARMA	Q(12) = 0.595 Q(24) = 0.723	-0.0034 (0.0041)	0.0029 (0.0058)	0.3639 [0.6991]
	6	NW	--	-0.0126 (0.0089)	0.0149 (0.0202)	1.0613 [0.3542]
		ARMA	Q(12) = 0.384 Q(24) = 0.667	-0.0140 (0.0263)	0.0122 (0.0354)	0.1478 [0.8630]

Notes: Standard errors are given in parentheses, p-values in brackets.
NW denotes the Newey & West estimation procedure, ARMA denotes the ARMA estimation procedure.

Table VII-18: Regressive expectations for each individual, group 4 to group 6

Experiment	Subject	Estimation procedure	Q-Statistic	α	β	H_0: α = β = 0
Group 4	1	NW	--	0.0042 (0.0076)	-0.0013 (0.0286)	0.2215 [0.8022]
		ARMA	Q(12) = 0.222 Q(24) = 0.412	0.0080 (0.0141)	-0.0101 (0.0272)	0.2039 [0.8165]
	2	NW	--	-0.0079 (0.0158)	-0.0031 (0.0325)	0.4216 [0.6584]
		ARMA	Q(12) = 0.186 Q(24) = 0.377	-0.0098 (0.0337)	-0.0011 (0.0553)	1.6329 [0.2072]
	3	NW	--	-0.0147 (0.0163)	0.0401 (0.0375)	0.6070 [0.5492]
		ARMA	Q(12) = 0.421 Q(24) = 0.539	-0.0298 (0.0270)	0.0621 (0.0514)	0.7575 [0.4747]
	4	NW	--	-0.0105 (0.0075)	0.0126 (0.0223)	1.2600 [0.2930]
		ARMA	Q(12) = 0.484 Q(24) = 0.647	-0.0105 (0.0086)	0.0126 (0.0170)	0.7784 [0.4650]
	5	NW	--	-0.0062 (0.0070)	0.0174 (0.0262)	0.4830 [0.6200]
		ARMA	Q(12) = 0.914 Q(24) = 0.888	-0.0065 (0.0147)	0.0146 (0.0290)	0.1987 [0.8207]
	6	NW	--	-0.0104 (0.0099)	0.0437 (0.0253)	1.5039 [0.2328]
		ARMA	Q(12) = 0.578 Q(24) = 0.451	-0.0125 (0.0357)	0.0443 (0.0505)	0.6730 [0.5163]
Group 5	1	NW	--	-0.0097 (0.0167)	-0.0042 (0.0293)	0.4042 [0.6698]
		ARMA	Q(12) = 0.633 Q(24) = 0.860	-0.0182 (0.0256)	-0.0062 (0.0314)	1.0104 [0.3722]
	2	NW	--	-0.0062 (0.0072)	0.0037 (0.0125)	0.4534 [0.6382]
		ARMA	Q(12) = 0.665 Q(24) = 0.107	-0.0062 (0.0082)	0.0037 (0.0105)	0.3565 [0.7020]
	3	NW	--	-0.0035 (0.0083)	0.0024 (0.0166)	0.1015 [0.9037]
		ARMA	Q(12) = 0.104 Q(24) = 0.310	-0.0056 (0.0144)	0.0026 (0.0181)	0.1115 [0.8947]
	4	NW	--	-0.0220 (0.0116)	0.0199 (0.0188)	1.8002 [0.1765]
		ARMA	Q(12) = 0.239 Q(24) = 0.277	-0.0135 (0.0172)	0.0092 (0.0217)	0.3539 [0.7039]
	5	NW	--	-0.0123 (0.0056)	0.0019 (0.0166)	3.4261 [0.0408]
		ARMA	Q(12) = 0.362 Q(24) = 0.830	-0.0096 (0.0517)	-0.0056 (0.0444)	0.1337 [0.8753]
	6	NW	--	-0.0125 (0.0110)	0.0075 (0.0217)	0.6425 [0.5306]
		ARMA	Q(12) = 0.937 Q(24) = 0.971	-0.0125 (0.0200)	0.0075 (0.0257)	0.2375 [0.7895]
Group 6	1	NW	--	0.0070 (0.0084)	0.0235 (0.0250)	5.8288 [0.0055]
		ARMA	Q(12) = 0.856 Q(24) = 0.956	0.0070 (0.0061)	0.0235 (0.0210)	3.7449 [0.0310]
	2	NW	--	-0.0107 (0.0320)	0.0663 (0.1003)	0.4771 [0.6236]
		ARMA	Q(12) = 0.579 Q(24) = 0.846	-0.0105 (0.0141)	0.0421 (0.0488)	0.3861 [0.6822]
	3	NW	--	-0.0006 (0.0032)	-0.0014 (0.0126)	0.0855 [0.9182]
		ARMA	Q(12) = 0.617 Q(24) = 0. 816	0.0009 (0.0025)	-0.0041 (0.0085)	0.1149 [0.8917]
	4	NW	--	0.0062 (0.0109)	-0.0429 (0.0351)	0.9130 [0.4083]
		ARMA	Q(12) = 0.826 Q(24) = 0.776	0.0054 (0.0122)	-0.0504 (0.0405)	0.9141 [0.4082]
	5	NW	--	0.0008 (0.0075)	0.0268 (0.0380)	0.4082 [0.6672]
		ARMA	Q(12) = 0.870 Q(24) = 0.914	0.0008 (0.0092)	0.0268 (0.0315)	0.7288 [0.4878]
	6	NW	--	-0.0031 (0.0079)	-0.0150 (0.0277)	0.7051 [0.4992]
		ARMA	Q(12) = 0.871 Q(24) = 0.759	0.0015 (0.0084)	-0.0324 (0.0284)	1.0327 [0.3649]

Notes: Standard errors are given in parentheses, p-values in brackets.
NW denotes the Newey & West estimation procedure, ARMA denotes the ARMA estimation procedure.

Table VII-19: Test for heterogeneous expectations

Experiment	Subject	α	H_0: α = 0
Group 1	1	-0.0049 (0.0051)	0.9181 [0.3428]
	2	-0.0019 (0.0051)	0.1408 [0.7092]
	3	0.0181 (0.0083)	4.8170 [0.0330]
	4	-0.0003 (0.0037)	0.0082 [0.9283]
	5	-0.0024 (0.0066)	0.1317 [0.7183]
	6	-0.0086 (0.0054)	2.4925 [0.1210]
Group 2	1	0.0244 (0.0112)	4.7338 [0.0345]
	2	0.0032 (0.0103)	0.0971 [0.7567]
	3	0.0166 (0.0106)	2.4820 [0.1217]
	4	0.0008 (0.0099)	0.0072 [0.9326]
	5	-0.0534 (0.0475)	1.2637 [0.2665]
	6	0.0083 (0.0097)	0.7356 [0.3954]
Group 3	1	0.0038 (0.0034)	1.2158 [0.2757]
	2	0.0018 (0.0055)	0.1087 [0.7431]
	3	-0.0004 (0.0035)	0.0125 [0.9114]
	4	-0.0165 (0.0069)	5.6798 [0.0212]
	5	0.0069 (0.0043)	2.5760 [0.1151]
	6	0.0043 (0.0063)	0.4721 [0.4953]
Group 4	1	0.0042 (0.0040)	1.1361 [0.2918]
	2	-0.0086 (0.0051)	2.7745 [0.1023]
	3	0.0013 (0.0058)	0.0486 [0.8265]
	4	-0.0051 (0.0053)	0.9369 [0.3379]
	5	0.0011 (0.0051)	0.0484 (0.8267)
	6	0.0070 (0.0051)	1.8804 [0.1767]
Group 5	1	-0.0042 (0.0063)	0.4510 [0.5051]
	2	0.0040 (0.0057)	0.5045 [0.4810]
	3	0.0060 (0.0042)	2.0040 [0.1633]
	4	-0.0020 (0.0045)	0.2036 [0.6539]
	5	-0.0038 (0.0045)	0.7413 [0.3935]
	6	0.0001 (0.0093)	0.0001 [0.9911]
Group 6	1	0.0097 (0.0045)	4.7808 [0.0337]
	2	0.0002 (0.0099)	0.0006 [0.9813]
	3	-0.0027 (0.0044)	0.3569 [0.5530]
	4	-0.0038 (0.0042)	0.8090 [0.3729]
	5	0.0042 (0.0050)	0.6782 [0.4143]
	6	-0.0077 (0.0057)	1.7998 [0.1861]

Note: Newey & West adjusted standard errors are given in parenthesis, p-values are given in brackets

Table VII-20: Individual expectations as direction of change forecasts

Experiment	Subject	Forecast ↑ Actual↑	Forecast ↑ Actual ↓	Forecast ↓ Actual ↑	Forecast ↓ Actual ↓	Hit rate
Group 1	1	5	9	17	18	67.35% [5.8911]
	2	16	11	6	16	65.31% [5.0134]
	3	17	17	5	10	55.10% [1.1686]
	4	18	11	4	16	69.39% [8.4676]
	5	15	9	7	18	67.35% [5.8911]
	6	16	10	6	17	67.35% [6.1998]
Group 2	1	21	13	5	10	63.27% [3.3780]
	2	16	8	10	15	63.27% [3.4961]
	3	22	15	4	8	61.22% [2.4833]
	4	14	13	12	10	48.98% [0.0353]
	5	17	9	9	14	63.27% [3.3775]
	6	20	10	6	13	67.35% [5.7502]
Group 3	1	11	14	9	15	53.06% [0.2142]
	2	11	12	9	17	57.14% [0.8817]
	3	15	10	5	19	69.39% [7.7759]
	4	11	12	9	17	57.14% [0.8817]
	5	11	13	9	16	55.10% [0.4901]
	6	12	12	8	17	59.18% [1.6423]
Group 4	1	20	10	3	16	73.47% [12.0897]
	2	17	6	6	20	75.51% [12.6631]
	3	22	4	1	22	89.80% [31.5701]
	4	16	11	7	15	63.27% [3.6651]
	5	17	9	6	17	69.39% [7.5671]
	6	18	10	5	16	69.39% [7.8935]
Group 5	1	13	6	7	23	73.47% [9.7895]
	2	12	11	8	18	61.22% [2.3147]
	3	16	9	4	20	73.47% [11.3567]
	4	12	9	8	20	65.31% [4.0552]
	5	9	10	11	19	57.14% [0.5515]
	6	9	12	11	17	53.06% [0.0634]
Group 6	1	17	21	5	6	46.94% [0.0018]
	2	14	16	8	11	51.02% [0.0978]
	3	11	16	11	11	44.90% [0.4201]
	4	15	12	7	15	61.22% [2.7610]
	5	15	12	7	15	61.22% [2.7610]
	6	15	12	7	15	61.22% [2.7610]

Note: Test statistics are given in brackets.

Reference List

Ahn, Changmo, Eung-Baek Lee, and Euy-Hoon Suh (2002), Noise Trading in the Korean Foreign Exchange Market: Some Questionnaire Evidence, in: Economic Papers, Vol. 5, 133-155.

Ajayi, Richard A. and David Karemera (1996), A Variance Ratio Test of Random Walks in Exchange Rates: Evidence from Pacific Basin Economies, in: Pacific-Basin Finance Journal, Vol. 4, 77-91.

Akerlof, George A. (2002), Behavioral Macroeconomics and Macroeconomic Behavior, in: American Economic Review, Vol. 92, 411-433.

Akram, Q. Farooq, Kari-Mette Brunvatne, and Raymond Lokshall (2003), Real Equilibrium Exchange Rates, in: Øyvind Eitrheim and Kristin Gulbrandsen (eds.), Explaining Movements in the Norwegian Exchange Rate - Norges Bank Occasional Papers No. 32, Oslo, 31-52.

Alberola, Enrique, Susana G. Cervero, Humberto Lopez, and Angel Ubide (1999), Global Equilibrium Exchange Rates: Euro, Dollar, Yen, 'Ins', 'Outs', and Other Major Currencies in a Panel Cointegration Framework, IMF Working Paper No. 99/175.

Allais, Maurice (1953), Le comportement de l'homme rationnel devant le risque, critique des postulats et axiomes de l'école Américane, in: Econometrica, Vol. 21, 503-546.

Allen, Franklin, Stephen Morris, and Hyun Song Shin (2003), Beauty Contests, Bubbles and Iterated Expectations in Asset Markets, Cowles Foundation Discussion Paper No. 1406, Yale University.

Almeida, Alvaro, Charles Goodhart, and Richard Payne (1998), The Effects of Macroeconomic News on High Frequency Exchange Rate Behavior, in: Journal of Financial and Quantitative Analysis, Vol. 33, 383-408.

Andersen, Torben G., Tim Bollerslev, Francis X. Diebold, and Clara Vega (2003), Micro Effects of Macro Announcements: Real-Time Price Discovery in Foreign Exchange, in: American Economic Review, Vol. 93, 38-62.

Andres, Peter and Markus Spiwoks (1999), Prognosequalitätsmatrix, Ein methodologischer Beitrag zur Beurteilung der Güte von Kapitalmarktprognosen, in: Jahrbücher für Nationalökonomie und Statistik, Vol. 219, 513-542.

Arestis, Philip (1996), Post-Keynesian Economics: Towards Coherence, in: Cambridge Journal of Economics, Vol. 20, 111-135.

Arestis, Philip, Andrew Brown, Kostas Mouratidis, and Malcolm Sawyer (2002), The Euro: Reflections on the First Three Years, in: International Review of Applied Economics, Vol. 16, 1-17.

Arrow, Kenneth J. (1978), The Future and the Present in Economic Life, in: Economic Inquiry, Vol. 16, 157-169.

Arrow, Kenneth J. (1987), Rationality of Self and Others in an Economic System, in: Robin M. Hogarth and Melvin W. Reder (eds.), Rational Choice: The Contrast Between Economics and Psychology, Chicago, 200-216.

Aschinger, Gerhard (1995), Börsenkrach und Spekulation: eine ökonomische Analyse, München.

Augier, Mie (2001), Sublime Simon: The Consistent Vision of Economic Psychology's Nobel Laureate, in: Journal of Economic Psychology, Vol. 22, 307-334.

Bacharach, Michael O. L. (1997), The Variable Frame Theory of Focal Points: An Experimental Study, in: Games and Economic Behavior, Vol. 19, 1-45.

Baillie, Richard T. and Patrick C. McMahon (1990), The Foreign Exchange Market: Theory and Econometric Evidence, Cambridge.

Baillie, Richard T. and William P. Osterberg (1997), Why do Central Banks Intervene?, in: Journal of International Money and Finance, Vol. 16, 909-919.

Bank for International Settlements (2002), Triennial Central Bank Survey: Foreign Exchange and Derivatives Market Activity in 2001, Basel.

Barberis, Nicholas and Richard Thaler (2003), A Survey of Behavioral Finance, in: George M. Constantinides (ed.), Handbook of the Economics of Finance, Amsterdam, 1053-1123.

Baron, Robert A., Donn Byrne, and Blair T. Johnson (1998), Exploring Social Psychology, Boston.

Baum, Christopher F., John T. Barkoulas, and Mustafa Caglayan (1999), Long Memory or Structural Breaks: Can Either Explain Nonlinearity Real Exchange Rates under the Current Float?, in: Journal of International Financial Markets, Institutions and Money, Vol. 9, 359-376.

Baumol, William J. (1957), Speculation, Profitability, and Stability, in: Review of Economics and Statistics, Vol. 38, 263-271.

Baxter, Marianne and Alan C. Stockman (1989), Business Cycles and the Exchange Rate Regime: Some International Evidence, in: Journal of Monetary Economics, Vol. 23, 377-400.

Becker, Otwin (1967), Experimentelle Untersuchung der Erwartungsbildung für eine Zeitreihe, in: Heinz Sauermann (ed.), Beiträge zur experimentellen Wirtschaftsforschung, Tübingen, 226-254.

Beckman, Steven R. and David H. Downs (1997), Forecasters as Imperfect Information Processors: Experimental and Survey Evidence, in: Journal of Economic Behavior & Organization, Vol. 32, 89-100.

Beng, Gan Wee and Wong Keng Siong (1993), Exchange Rate Expectations and Risk Premium in the Singapore/US Dollar Exchange Rate: Evidence from Survey Data, in: Applied Financial Economics, Vol. 3, 365-373.

Berkowitz, Jeremy and Lorenzo Giorgianni (2001), Long-Horizon Exchange Rate Predictability?, in: Review of Economics and Statistics, Vol. 83, 81-91.

Bénassy-Quéré, Agnès, Sophie Larribeau, and Ronald MacDonald (1999), Models of Exchange Rate Expectations: Heterogeneous Evidence form Panel Data, CEPII Working Paper No. 99-03.

Bibow, Jörg, Paul Lewis, and Jochen Runde (2004), Uncertainty, Conventional Behavior, and Economic Sociology, in: American Journal of Economics and Sciology, forthcoming.

Bjønnes, Geir Høidal and Dagfinn Rime (2000), Customer Trading and Information in Foreign Exchange Markets, University of Oslo, Department of Economics Working Paper No. 30/2000.

Black, Fischer (1986), Noise, in: Journal of Finance, Vol. XLI, 529-543.

Bless, Herbert, Klaus Fiedler, and Fritz Strack (2004), Social Cognition: How Individuals Construct Social Reality, Hove.

Bofinger, Peter (2001), Kann die Einführung des Euro-Bargeldes die europäische Währung stabilisieren? Gedanken aus der Sicht der "Behavioral Finance", in: ifo-Schnelldienst, Nr. 13, 3-6.

Bofinger, Peter and Robert Schmidt (2003), On the Reliability of Professional Exchange Rate Forecasts: An Empirical Analysis for the €/US-$ Rate, in: Financial Markets and Portfolio Management, Vol. 17, 437-449.

Bohner, Gerd and Michaela Wänke (2002), Attitudes and Attitude Change, Hove.

Bonser-Neal, Catherine and Glenn Tanner (1996), Central Bank Intervention and the Volatility of Foreign Exchange Rates: Evidence from the Options Market, in: Journal of International Money and Finance, Vol. 15, 853-878.

Borges, Bernhard, Daniel G. Goldstein, Andreas Ortmann, and Gerd Gigerenzer (1999), Can Ignorance Beat the Stock Market? , in: Gerd Gigerenzer and Peter M. Todd (eds.), Simple Heuristics That Make Us Smart, Cambridge, 59-72.

Borowski, Didier and Cecile Couharde (2000), Euro, Dollar, Yen: Pour une Approche Multilaterale des Taux de Change D'equilibre, in: Revue Economique, Vol. 51, 671-681.

Brennscheidt, Gunnar (1993), Predictive Behavior - An Experimental Study, Berlin.

Brown, Lawrence D. (1993), Earning Forecast Research: Its Implications for Capital Markets Research, in: International Journal of Forecasting, Vol. 9, 295-320.

Brunnermeier, Markus K. (2001), Asset Pricing under Asymmetric Information: Bubbles, Crashes, Technical Analysis, and Herding, Oxford.

Bruns, Christoph (1994), Bubbles und Excess Volatility auf dem deutschen Aktienmarkt, Wiesbaden.

Burnham, James B. (1991), Current Structure and Recent Developments in Foreign Exchange Markets, in: Sarkis J. Khoury (ed.), Recent Developments in International Banking and Finance, Chicago, 123-153.

Camerer, Colin (1995), Individual Decision Making, in: John H. Kagel and Alvin E. Roth (eds.), The Handbook of Experimental Economics, New Jersey, 587-703.

Camerer, Colin (1998), Bounded Rationality in Individual Decision Making, in: Experimental Economics, Vol. 1, 163-183.

Camerer, Colin F. (2003), Behavioral Game Theory: Experiments in Strategic Interaction, Princeton.

Camerer, Colin F. and George Loewenstein (2004), Behavioral Economics: Past, Present, Future, in: Colin F. Camerer, George Loewenstein, and Matthew Rabin (eds.), Advances in Behavioral Economics, New York.

Campbell, John Y., Andrew W. Lo, and A. Craig MacKinlay (1997), The Econometrics of Financial Markets, New Jersey.

Carabelli, Anna M. (1988), On Keynes's Method, Basingstoke.

Catte, Pietro, Giampaolo Galli, and Salvatore Rebecchini (1994), Concerted Interventions and the Dollar: An Analysis of Daily Data, in: Peter B. Kenen, Francesco Papadia, and Fabrizio Saccomanni (eds.), The International Monetary System, Cambridge, 201-239.

Cavaglia, Stefano M. F. G., Willem F. C. Verschoor, and Christian C. P. Wolff (1994), On the Biasedness of Forward Foreign Exchange Rates: Irrationality or Risk Premia?, in: Journal of Business, Vol. 67, 321-343.

Cavaglia, Stefano, Willem F. C. Verschoor, and Christian C. P. Wolff (1993), Further Evidence on Exchange Rate Expectations, in: Journal of International Money and Finance, Vol. 12, 78-98.

Chang, Kuo-Ping and Kuo-Shiuan Ting (2000), A Variance Ratio Test of the Random Walk Hypothesis for Taiwan's Stock Market, in: Applied Financial Economics, Vol. 10, 525-532.

Chang, P. H. Kevin and Carol L. Osler (1999), Methodical Madness: Technical Analysis and the Irrationality of Exchange-Rate Forecasts, in: Economic Journal, Vol. 109, 636-661.

Charbit, Claire and Valérie Fernandez (2001), "Simon says ..." What? Rationality of Imitation in a Simonian Perspective, in: Alan Kirman and Jean-Benoit Zimmermann (eds.), Economics with Heterogeneous Interacting Agents, Berlin, 267-286.

Chase, Valerie M., Ralph Hertwig, and Gerd Gigerenzer (1998), Visions of Rationality, in: Trends in Cognitive Sciences, Vol. 2, 206-214.

Cheung, Yin-Wong and Menzie D. Chinn (2001), Currency Traders and Exchange Rate Dynamics: A Survey of the US Market, in: Journal of International Money and Finance, Vol. 20, 439-471.

Cheung, Yin-Wong, Menzie D. Chinn, and Ian W. Marsh (2000), How Do UK-Based Foreign Exchange Dealers Think Their Market Operates?, NBER Working Paper Series No. 7524.

Cheung, Yin-Wong, Menzie D. Chinn, and Antonio G. Pascual (2002), Empirical Exchange Rate Models of the Nineties: are Any Fit to Survive?, NBER Working Paper Series No. 9393.

Cheung, Yin-Wong, Menzie D. Chinn, and Antonio G. Pascual (2003), What Do We Know About Recent Exchange Rate Models? In-Sample Fit and Out-of-Sample Performance Evaluated, CESifo Working Paper No. 902.

Cheung, Yin-Wong and Clement Yuk-Pang Wong (2000), A Survey of Market Practitioners' Views on Exchange Rate Dynamics, in: Journal of International Economics, Vol. 51, 401-419.

Chinn, Menzie D. and Ron Alquist (2000), Tracking the Euro's Progress, in: International Finance, Vol. 3, 357-373.

Chinn, Menzie D. and Richard A. Meese (1995), Banking on Currency Forecasts: How Predictable is Change in Money?, in: Journal of International Economics, Vol. 38, 161-178.

Clostermann, Jörg and Bernd Schnatz (2000), The Determinants of the Euro-Dollar Exchange Rate: Synthetic Fundamentals and a Non-Existing Currency, Discussion Paper No. 2/00, Economic Research Group of the Deutsche Bundesbank.

Cochrane, John H. (1988), How Big Is the Random walk in GNP?, in: Journal of Political Economy, Vol. 96, 893-920.

Conlisk, John (1996), Why Bounded Rationality?, in: Journal of Economic Literature, Vol. 34, 669-700.

Cross, Sam Y. (1998), The Foreign Exchange Market in the United States, Federal Reserve Bank of New York, http://www.ny.frb.org/pihome/addpub/usfxm/.

Curcio, Riccardo, Charles Goodhart , Dominique Guilaume, and Richard Payne (1997), Do Technical Trading Rules Generate Profits? Conclusions from the Intra-Day Foreign Exchange Market, in: International Journal of Finance and Economics, Vol. 2, 267-280.

Cuthbertson, Keith (1996), Quantitative Financial Economics: Stocks, Bonds and Foreign Exchange, Chichester.

Cutler, David M., James M. Poterba , and Lawrence H. Summers (1990), Speculative Dynamics and the Role of Feedback Traders, in: American Economic Review, Papers & Proceedings, Vol. 80, 63-68.

Cutler, David M., James M. Poterba , and Lawrence H. Summers (1991), Speculative Dynamics, in: Review of Economic Studies, Vol. 58, 529-546.

Dalrymple, Douglas J. (1975), Sales Forecasting Methods and Accuracy, in: Business Horizons, Vol. 18, 69-73.

Dalrymple, Douglas J. (1987), Sales Forecasting Practices: Results from a United States Survey, in: International Journal of Forecasting, Vol. 3, 379-391.

Davis, Douglas D. and Charles A. Holt (1993), Experimental Economics, Princeton.

Davis, John B. (1998), Conventions , in: John B. Davis, D. Wade Hands, and Uskali Mäki (eds.), The Handbook of Economic Methodology, Cheltenham, 83-86.

Davis, John Bryan (1994), Keynes's Philosophical Development, Cambridge.

Day, Richard H. and Weihong Huang (1990), Bulls, Bears and Market Sheep, in: Journal of Economic Behavior and Organization, Vol. 14, 299-329.

De Bondt, Werner P. (1993), Betting on Trends: Intuitive Forecasts of Financial Risk and Return, in: International Journal of Forecasting, Vol. 9, 355-371.

De Bondt, Werner P. and Richard H. Thaler (1990), Do Security Analysts Overreact?, in: American Economic Review, Papers & Proceedings, Vol. 80, 52-57.

De Bruijin, Bart Jan (1999), Foundations of Demographic Theory: Choice, Process, Context, Amsterdam, http://www.ub.rug.nl/eldoc/dis/rw/b.j.de.bruijn/

De Grauwe, Paul (2000), Exchange Rates in Serch of Fundamentals: The Case of the Euro-Dollar Rate, in: International Finance, Vol. 3, 329-356.

De Grauwe, Paul and Danny Decupere (1992), Psychological Barriers in the Foreign Exchange Markets, in: Journal of International and Comparative Economics, Vol. 1, 87-101.

De Grauwe, Paul and Marianna Grimaldi (2001), The Mystery of the Decline of the Euro, in: Aussenwirtschaft, Vol. 56, 459-476.

De Grauwe, Paul and Isabel Vansteenkiste (2001), Exchange Rates and Fundamentals: A Non-Linear Relationship?, CESifo Working Paper No. 577.

De Long, J. Bradford (1992), Noise Trading, in: Peter Newman, Murray Milgate, and John Eatwell (eds.), The New Palgrave Dictionary of Money & Finance, Vol. 3, London, 34-35.

De Long, J. Bradford, Andrei Shleifer, Lawrence H. Summers, and Robert J. Waldmann (1989), Positive Feedback Investment Strategies and Destabilizing Rational Speculation, NBER Working Paper Series No. 2880.

De Long, J. Bradford, Andrei Shleifer, Lawrence H. Summers, and Robert J. Waldmann (1990a), Noise Trader Risk in Financial Markets, in: Journal of Political Economy, Vol. 98, 703-738.

De Long, J. Bradford, Andrei Shleifer, Lawrence H. Summers, and Robert J. Waldmann (1990b), Positive Feedback Investment Strategies and Destabilizing Rational Speculation, in: Journal of Finance, Vol. XLV, 379-395.

Destler, Irving M. and C. Randall Henning (1989), Dollar Politics: Exchange Rate Policymaking in the United States, Washington.

Dewachter, Hans (1997), Sign Predictions of Exchange Rate Changes: Charts as Proxies for Bayesian Inferences, in: Weltwirtschaftliches Archiv, Vol. 133, 39-55.

Dewachter, Hans and Marco Lyrio (2002), The Economic Value of Technical Trading Rules: A Nonparametric Utility-based Approach, mimeo.

Dickey, David and Wayne A. Fuller (1979), Distribution of the Estimators for Autoregressive Time Series with a Unit Root, in: Journal of American Statistics Association, Vol. 74, 427-431.

Dickey, David and Wayne A. Fuller (1981), Likelihood Ratio Statistics for Autoregressive Time Series with a Unit Root, in: Econometrica, Vol. 79, 1057-1072.

Diebold, Francis X., Steve Husted, and Mark Rush (1991), Real Exchange Rates under the Gold Standard, in: Journal of Political Economy, Vol. 99, 1252-1271.

Diebold, Francis X. and Jose A. Lopez (1996), Forecast Evaluation and Combination, in: G. S. Maddala and C. R. Rao (eds.), Handbook of Statistics, Vol. 14, Amsterdam, 241-268.

Diebold, Francis X. and Roberto S. Mariano (1995), Comparing Predictive Accuracy, in: Journal of Business & Economic Statistics, Vol. 13, 253-263.

Dominguez, Kathryn M. (1992), Are Foreign Exchange Forecasts Rational? New Evidence From Survey Data, in: Kathryn M. Dominguez (ed.), Exchange Rate Efficiency and the Behavior of International Asset Markets, New York, 3-39.

Dominguez, Kathryn M. (1998), Central Bank Intervention and Exchange Rate Volatility, in: Journal of International Money and Finance, Vol. 17, 161-190.

Dooley, Michael P. and Jeffrey R. Shafer (1983), Analysis of Short-Run Exchnage Rate Behavior: March 1973 to November 1981, in: David Bigman (ed.), Exchange Rate and Trade Instability: Causes, Consequences, and Remedies, Cambridge, 43-69.

Dornbusch, Rüdiger (1976a), Exchange Rate Expectations and Monetary Policy, in: Journal of International Economics, Vol. 6, 231-244.

Dornbusch, Rüdiger (1976b), Expectations and Exchange Rate Dynamics, in: Journal of Political Economy, Vol. 84, 1161-1176.

Dudey, Thomas and Peter M. Todd (2001), Making Good Decisions with Minimal Information: Simultaneous and Sequential Choice, in: Journal of Bioeconomics, Vol. 3, 195-215.

Duncan, James and R. Mark Isaac (2000), Asset Markets: How They Are Affected by Tournament Incentives for Individuals, in: American Economic Review, Vol. 90, 995-1004.

Dwyer, Gerald P., Arlington W. Williams, Raymond C. Battalio, and Timothy I. Mason (1993), Tests of Rational Expectations in a Stark Setting, in: Economic Journal, Vol. 103, 586-601.

Eagly, Alice H and Shelly Chaiken (1998), Attitude Structure and Function, in: Daniel T. Gilbert, Susan T. Fiske, and Gardner Lindzey (eds.), The Handbook of Social Psychology - Volume 1, New York, 269-322.

Edison, Hali J. (1987), Purchasing Power Parity in the Long Run: A Test of the Dollar/Pound Exchange Rate (1890-1978), in: Journal of Money, Credit and Banking, Vol. 19, 376-387.

Edison, Hali J. (1997), The Reaction of Exchange Rates and Interest Rates to News Releases, in: International Journal of Finance and Economics, Vol. 2, 87-100.

Edwards, Sebastian (1983), Floating Exchange Rates, Expectations and New Information, in: Journal of Monetary Economics, Vol. 11, 321-336.

Ehrmann, Michael and Marcel Fratzscher (2004), Exchange Rates and Fundamentals: New Evidence from Real-Time Data, mimeo.

Elliott, Graham and Takatoshi Ito (1999), Heterogeneous Expectations and Tests of Efficiency in the Yen/Dollar Forward Exchange Rate Market, in: Journal of Monetary Economics, Vol. 43, 435-456.

Engel, Charles (1994), Can the Markov Switching Model Forecast Exchange Rates?, in: Journal of International Economics, Vol. 36, 151-165.

Engel, Charles (2000), Long-Run PPP May Not Hold After All, in: Journal of International Economics, Vol. 51, 273.

Engel, Charles and James D. Hamilton (1990), Long Swings in the Dollar: Are They in the Data and Do Markets Know It?, in: American Economic Review, Vol. 80, 689-713.

Engel, Charles and James C. Morley (2001), The Adjustment of Prices and the Adjustment of the Exchange Rate, NBER Working Paper Series No. 8550.

European Central Bank (2002), ECB Monthly Bulletin January 2002, Frankfurt a.M.

European Central Bank (2003), Review of the Foreign Exchange Market Structure, March 2003, http://www.ecb.int/pub/pdf/fxmarketstructure200303.pdf.

European Economic Advisory Group at the CESifo (2002), Report on the European Economy 2002, Munich.

Evans, Martin D. D. (2001), FX Trading and Exchange Rate Dynamics, NBER Working Paper No. 8116.

Evans, Martin D. D. and Richard K. Lyons (1999), Order Flow and Exchange Rate Dynamics, NBER Working Paper No. 7317.

Evans, Martin D. D. and Richard K. Lyons (2002a), Informational Integration and FX Trading, in: Journal of International Money and Finance, Vol. 21, 807-831.

Evans, Martin D. D. and Richard K. Lyons (2002b), Order Flow and Exchange Rate Dynamics , in: Journal of Political Economy, Vol. 110, 170-180.

Fama, Eugene F. (1965a), Random Walks in Stock Market Prices, in: Financial Analysts Journal, Vol. 21, 55-59.

Fama, Eugene F. (1965b), The Behaviour of Stock Market Prices, in: Journal of Business, Vol. 38, 34-105.

Fama, Eugene F. (1970), Efficient Capital Markets: A Review of Theory and Empirical Work, in: Journal of Finance, Vol. 25, 383-417.

Fatum, Rasmus and Michael M. Hutchison (2002), ECB Foreign Exchange Intervention and the EURO: Institutional Framework, News, and Intervention, in: Open Economies Review, Vol. 13, 413-425.

Faust, Jon, John H. Rogers, and Jonathan H. Wright (2003), Exchange Rate Forecasting: The Errors We've Really Made, in: Journal of International Economics, Vol. 60, 35-59.

Fehr, Ernst and Simon Gächter (2004), Fairness and Retaliation: The Economics of Reciprocity, in: Colin F. Camerer, George Loewenstein, and Matthew Rabin (eds.), Advances in Behavioral Economics, Princeton, 510-532.

Festinger, Leon (1957), A Theory of Cognitive Dissonance, Stanford.

Fiedler, Klaus and Herbert Bless (2001), Social Cognition, in: Miles Hewstone and Wolfgang Stroebe (eds.), Introduction to Social Psychology, Oxford, 115-149.

Fildes, Robert and Herman Stekler (2002), The Stae of Macroeconomic Forecasting, in: Journal of Macroeconomics, Vol. 24, 435-468.

Fisher, Eric O'N. and Frank S. Kelly (2000), Experimental Foreign Exchange Markets, in: Pacific Economic Review, Vol. 5 , 365-387.

Fisher, Franklin M. (1962), A priori Information and Time Series Analysis, Amsterdam.

Fleming, J. Marcus (1962), Domestic Financial Policies Under Fixed and Flexible Exchange Rates, in: IMF Staff Papers, Vol. 9, 369-379.

Flood, Robert P. and Andrew K. Rose (1995), Fixing the Exchange Rate Regime: A Virtual Quest for Fundamentals, in: Journal of Monetary Economics, Vol. 36, 3-37.

Flood, Robert P. and Andrew K. Rose (1999), Understanding Exchange Rate Volatility Without the Contrivance of Macroeconomics, in: Economic Journal, Vol. 109, F660-F672.

Flood, Robert P. and Mark P. Taylor (1994), Exchange Rate Economics: What's Wrong with the Conventional Macro Approach?, in: Jeffrey A. Frankel, Giampaolo Galli, and Alberto Giovannini (eds.), The Microstructure of Foreign Exchange Markets, London, 261-301.

Frankel, Jeffrey A. (1986), International Capital Mobility and Crowding Out in the US Economy: Imperfect Integration of Financial Markets or Goods Markets?, in: Rik W. Hafer (ed.), How Open is the US Economy, Lexington, 33-67.

Frankel, Jeffrey A. (1990), Zen and the Art of Modern Macroeconomics: A Commentary, in: William S. Haraf and Thomas D. Willett (eds.), Monetary Policy for a Volatile Global Economy, Washington, 117-123.

Frankel, Jeffrey A. and Kathryn M. Dominguez (1993), Foreign Exchange Intervention: An Empirical Assessment, in: J. Frankel (ed.), On Exchange Rates, Cambridge, 327-345.

Frankel, Jeffrey A. and Kenneth A. Froot (1987), Using Survey Data to Test Standard Propositions Regarding Exchange Rate Expectations, in: American Economic Review, Vol. 17, 133-152.

Frankel, Jeffrey A. and Kenneth A. Froot (1990), Chartists, Fundamentalists and the Demand for Dollars, in: Anthony S. Courakis and Mark P. Taylor (eds.), Private Behaviour and Government Policy in Interdependent Economies, Oxford, 73-126.

Frankel, Jeffrey A. and Andrew K. Rose (1996), A Panel Project on Purchasing Power Parity: Mean Reversion Within and Between Countries, in: Journal of International Economics, Vol. 40, 209-224.

Franses, Philip Hans and Dick van Dijk (2000), Non-linear Time Series Models in Empirical Finance, Cambridge.

Frenkel, Jacob A. (1976), A Monetary Approach to the Exchange Rate: Doctrinal Aspects and Empirical Evidence, in: Scandinavian Journal of Economics, Vol. 78, 200-224.

Frenkel, Jacob A. (1981), Flexible Exchange Rates, Prices, and the Role of "News": Lessons from the 1970s, in: Journal of Political Economy, Vol. 89, 665-705.

Frenkel, Jacob A. and Michael Mussa (1980), The Efficiency of Foreign Exchange Markets and Measures of Turbulence, in: American Economic Review, Papers & Proceedings, Vol. 70, 374-381.

Frenkel, M., C. Pierdzioch, and G. Stadtmann (2001), The Foreign Exchange Market Interventions of the European Central Bank, in: Banca Nazionale Del Lavoro Quarterly Review, Vo. LIV, 249-287.

Frenkel, Michael, Christian Pierdzioch, and Georg Stadtmann (2004), Spekulative Übertreibungen auf Finanzmärkten - Ein Beispiel zum Zusammenwirken von rationalen und irrationalen Spekulanten, in: WiSt, Vol. 33, 140-145.

Frennberg, Per and Bjoern Hansson (1993), Testing the Random Walk Hypothesis on Swedish Stock Prices: 1919 - 1990, in: Journal of Banking & Finance, Vol. 17, 175-191.

Friedman, Milton (1953), The Case for Flexible Exchange Rates, in: Milton Friedman (ed.), Essays in Positive Economics, Chicago, 157-203.

Froot, Kenneth A. and Jeffrey A. Frankel (1989), Forward Discount Bias: Is It an Exchange Risk Premium?, in: Quarterly Journal of Economics, Vol. 104, 139-161.

Froot, Kenneth A., Paul G. J. O'Connell, and Mark S. Seasholes (2001), The Portfolio Flows of International Investors, in: Journal of Financial Economcis, Vol. 59, 151-193.

Froot, Kenneth A. and Tarun Ramadorai (2002), Currency Returns, Institutional Investor Flows, and Exchange Rate Fundamentals, NBER Working Paper No. 9101.

Froot, Kenneth A. and Kenneth Rogoff (1995), Perspectives on PPP and Long-Run Real Exchange Rates, in: Ronald W. Jones and Gene M. Grossman (eds.), Handbook of International Economics, Vol. III, Amsterdam, 1647-1688.

Galati, Gabriele (2001), Why Has Global FX Turnover Declined? Explaining the 2001 Triennial Survey, in: BIS Quarterly Review, December 2001, 39-47.

Galati, Gabriele and Corrinne Ho (2001), Macroeconomic news and the euro/dollar exchange rate, BIS Working Paper No. 105, Bank for International Settlements.

Galati, Gabriele and Corrinne Ho (2003), Macroeconomic News and the Euro/Dollar Exchange Rate, in: Economic Notes by Banca Monte dei Paschi di Siena SpA, Vol. 32, 371-398.

Garner, C. Alan (1982), Experimental Evidence on the Rationality of Intuitive Forecasters, in: Vernon L. Smith (ed.), Research in Experimental Economics, Greenwich, 113-128.

Gehrig, Thomas and Lukas Menkhoff (2003), The Use of Flow Analysis in Foreign Exchange: Exploratory Evidence, Discussion Paper No. 276, Department of Economics, University of Hannover.

Gehrig, Thomas and Lukas Menkhoff (2004), Extended Evidence on the Use of Technical Analysis in Foreign Exchange, in: International Journal of Finance and Economics, forthcoming.

Gerber, Anke, Thorsten Hens, and Bodo Vogt (2002), Rational Investor Sentiment, Working Paper No. 126, Institute for Empirical Research in Economics, University of Zurich.

Gern, Klaus-Juergen, Christophe Kamps, Carsten-Patrick Meier, and Scheide Joachim (2000), Euroland: Peak of the Upswing -Little Evidence of a New Economy, Kieler Diskussionsbeträge No. 369, Institut für Weltwirtschaft.

Gerrard, Bill (1993), Beyond the Logical Theory of Rational Choice, in: Bill Gerrard (ed.), The Economics of Rationality, London, 52-67.

Gigerenzer, Gerd (2000), Adaptive Thinking: Rationality in the Real World, Oxford.

Gigerenzer, Gerd (2004a), Fast and Frugal Heuristics: The Tools of Bounded Rationality, Conference Paper, 12th Annual WZB Conference on Markets and Political Economy, Economics and Psychology: Applications to Industrial Organization, Public Finance, and

Finance, to appear in Koehler, Derek and Harvey, Nigel (eds.) Blackwell Handbook of Judgment and Decision Making, forthcoming .

Gigerenzer, Gerd (2004b), Striking a Blow for Sanity in Theories of Rationality, in: Mie Augier and James G. March (eds.), Essays in Honor of Herbert Simon, Cambridge, 389-410.

Gigerenzer, Gerd and Reinhard Selten (2001), Rethinking Rationality, in: Gerd Gigerenzer and Reinhard Selten (eds.), Bounded Rationality: The Adaptive Toolbox, Cambridge, 1-12.

Gigerenzer, Gerd and Peter M. Todd (1999a), Fast and Frugal Heuristics, in: Gerd Gigerenzer and Peter M. Todd (eds.), Simple Heuristics That Make Us Smart, Oxford, 3-34.

Gigerenzer, Gerd and Peter M. Todd (1999b), Simple Heuristics That Make Us Smart, Oxford.

Gneezy, Uri and Aldo Rustichini (2004), Incentives, Punishment, and Behavior, in: Colin F. Camerer, George Loewenstein, and Matthew Rabin (eds.), Advances in Behavioral Economics, Princeton, 572-589.

Goldberg, Joachim (1997), Behavioral Finance begründet technische Analyse, Börsen-Zeitung, Nr. 229, 28.11.1997, Page 21.

Goldberg, Joachim and Rüdiger von Nitzsch (2001), Behavioral Finance, Chichester.

Goldberg, Michael D. and Roman Frydman (2001), Macroeconomic Fundamentals and the DM/$ Exchange Rate: Temporal Instability and the Monetary Model, in: International Journal of Finance and Economics, Vol. 6, 421-435.

Goldstein, Daniel G. and Gerd Gigerenzer (1999), The Recognition Heuristic: How Ignorance Makes Us Smart, in: Gerd Gigerenzer and Peter M. Todd (eds.), Simple Heuristics That Make Us Smart, Cambridge, 37-58.

Goldstein, Daniel G. and Gerd Gigerenzer (2002), Models of Ecological Rationality: The Recognition Heuristic, in: Psychological Review, Vol. 109, 75-90.

Goldstein, Daniel G., Gerd Gigerenzer, Robin M. Hogarth, Alex Kacelnik, Yaakov Kareev, Gary Klein, Laura Martignon, John W. Payne, and Karl H. Schlag (2001), Group Report: Why and When Do Simple Heuristics Work?, in: Gerd Gigerenzer and Reinhard Selten (eds.), Bounded Rationality: The Adaptive Toolbox, Cambridge, 173-190.

Goldstein, William M. and Robin M. Hogarth (1997), Judgment and Decision Research: Some Historical Context, in: William M. Goldstein and Robin M. Hogarth (eds.), Research on Judgment and Decision Making: Currents, Connections, and Controversies, Cambridge, 3-65.

Goodhart, Charles and Thomas Hesse (1993), Central Bank Forex Intervention Assessed in Continuous Time, in: Journal of International Money and Finance, Vol. 12, 368-389.

Hamilton, James D. (1988), Rational-Expectations Econometric Analysis of Changes in Regime. An Investigation of the Term Structure of Interest Rates, in: Journal of Economic Dynamics and Control, Vol. 12, 385-423.

Hamilton, James D. (1989), A New Approach to the Economic Analysis of Nonstationary Time Series and the Business Cycle, in: Econometrica, Vol. 57 , 357-384.

Hamilton, James D. (1994), Time Series Analysis, Princeton.

Hamilton, James D. (1996), Specification Testing in Markov-Switching Time-Series Models, in: Journal of Econometrics, Vol. 70, 127-157.

Hansen, Lars P. and Robert J. Hodrick (1980), Forward Exchange Rates as Optimal Predictors of Future Spot Exchange Rates: An Econometric Analysis, in: Journal of Political Economy, Vol. 88, 829-853.

Hardouvelis, Gikas A. (1988), Economic News, Exchange Rates and Interest Rates, in: Journal of International Money and Finance, Vol. 7, 23-35.

Harvey, John T. (1999), The Nature of Expectations in the Foreign Exchange Market: A Test of Competing Theories, in: Journal of Post Keynesian Economics, Vol. 21, 181-200.

Hayakawa, Hiroaki (2000), Bounded Rationality, Social and Cultural Norms, and Interdependence via Reference Groups , in: Journal of Economic Behavior & Organization, Vol. 43, 1-34.

Hegwood, Natalie D. and David H. Papell (1998), Quasi Purchasing Power Parity, in: International Journal of Finance and Economics, Vol. 3, 279-289.

Hey, John D. (1994), Expectations Formation: Rational or Adaptive or ...?, in: Journal of Economic Behavior & Organization, Vol. 25, 329-349.

Hodrick, Robert J. and Edward C. Prescott (1997), Postwar US Business Cycles: An Empirical Investigation, in: Journal of Money, Credit and Banking, Vol. 29, 1-16.

Holden, Kenneth, David A. Peel, and John L. Thompson (1985), Expectations: Theory and Evidence, Basingstoke.

Hommes, Cars H., Joep Sonnemans, Jan Tuinstra, and Henk van de Velden (2002), Expectations and Bubbles in Asset Pricing Experiments, CeNDEF Working Paper Series, WP-02-05, Center for Nonlinear Dynamics in Economics and Finance, University of Amsterdam.

Hommes, Cars H., Joep Sonnemans, Jan Tuinstra, and Henk van de Velden (2003), Coordination of Expectations in Asset Pricing Experiments, CeNDEF Working Paper Series, WP-02-07 (revised June 2003), Center for Nonlinear Dynamics in Economics and Finance, University of Amsterdam.

International Monetary Fund (2000), Staff Report on the Monetary and Exchange Rate Policies of the Euro Area, Staff Country Report No. 00/146, Washington D.C.

International Monetary Fund (2004), International Financial Statistics CD-Rom.

Isard, Peter (1995), Exchange Rate Economics, Cambridge.

Ito, Takatoshi (2003), Is Foreign Exchange Intervention Effective? The Japanese Experiences in the 1990s, in: Paul Mizen (ed.), Monetary History, Exchange Rates and Financial Markets: Essays in Honour of Charles Goodhart, Volume 2, Cheltenham, 126-153.

Ito, Takatoshi, Richard K. Lyons, and Michael T. Melvin (1998), Is There Private Information in the FX Market? The Tokyo Experiment, in: Journal of Finance, Vol. LIII, 1111-1130.

Jacowitz, Karen E. and Daniel Kahneman (1995), Measures of Anchoring in Estimation Tasks, in: Personality and Social Psychology Bulletin, Vol. 21, 1161-1166.

Jansen, David-Jan and Jakob De Haan (2003), Statements of ECB Officials and Their Effect on the Level and Volatility of the Euro-Dollar Exchange Rate, CESifo Working Paper No. 927.

Jegadeesh, Narasimhan and Sheridan Titman (1993), Returns to Buying Winners and Selling Loosers: Implications for Stock Market Efficiency, in: Journal of Finance, Vol. 48, 65-91.

Jegadeesh, Narasimhan and Sheridan Titman (2001), Profitability of Momentum Strategies: An Evaluation of Alternative Explanations, in: Journal of Finance, Vol. 56, 699-720.

Jensen, Michael C. (1978), Some Anomalous Evidence Regarding Market Efficiency, in: Journal of Financial Economics, Vol. 6, 95-101.

Johnson, Harry G. (1976), Destabilizing Speculation: A General Equilibrium Approach, in: Journal of Political Economy, Vol. 84, 101-108.

Kahneman, Daniel, Paul Slovic, and Amos Tversky (1999), Judgment Under Uncertainty: Heuristics and Biases, Cambridge.

Kahneman, Daniel and Amos Tversky (1979), Prospect Theory: An Analysis of Decision Under Risk, in: Econometrica, Vol. 47 , 263-291.

Kahneman, Daniel and Amos Tversky (1999), Subjective Probability: A Judgment of Representativeness, in: Daniel Kahneman, Paul Slovic, and Amos Tversky (eds.), Judgment Under Uncertainty: Heuristics and Biases, Cambridge, 32-47.

Kaldor, Nicholas (1939), Speculation and Economic Stability, in: Review of Economic Studies, Vol. 6, 1-27.

Kaminsky, Graciela L. (1993), Is There a Peso Problem? Evidence from the Dollar/Pound Exchange Rate, 1976-1987, in: American Economic Review, Vol. 83, 450-472.

Kettell, Brian (2000), What Drives Currency Markets, London.

Keynes, John M. (1936), The Genral Theory of Employment, Interest, and Money, London.

Keynes, John M. (1973), The General Theory of Employment, in: Donald Moggridge (ed.), The Collected Writings of John Maynard Keynes - Volume XIV, Cambridge, 109-123.

Kilian, Lutz (1999), Exchange Rates and Monetary Fundamentals: What Do We Learn from Long-Horizon Regressions?, in: Journal of Applied Econometrics, Vol. 14, 491-510.

Kilian, Lutz and Mark P. Taylor (2003), Why is it so Difficult to Beat the Random Walk Forecast of Exchange Rates?, in: Journal of International Economics, Vol. 60, 85-107.

Kim, Chang-Jin and Charles R. Nelson (1999), State-Space Models with Regime Switching: Classical and Gibbs-Sampling Approaches with Applications, Cambridge.

Kim, Suk-Joong (1997), Testing the Rationality of Exchange Rate and Interest Rate Expectations: An Empirical Study of Australian Survey-based Expectations, in: Applied Economics, Vol. 29, 1011-1022.

Kirman, Alan (1995), The Behaviour of the Foreign Exchange Market, in: Bank of England Quarterly Bulletin 286-293.

Klaassen, Franc (2001), Long Swings in Exchange Rates: Are They Really in the Data, mimeo, Amsterdam.

Klaes, Matthias and Esther-Mirjam Sent (2002), A Conceptual History of the Emergence of Bounded Rationality, mimeo.

Klassen, Robert D. and Benito E. Flores (2001), Forecasting Practices of Canadian Firms: Survey Results and Comparisons, in: International Journal of Production Economics, Vol. 70, 163-174.

Klayman, Joshua (1995), Varieties of Confirmation Bias, in: The Psychology of Learning and Motivation, Vol. 32, 385-418.

Knight, Frank H. (1921), Risk, Uncertainty, and Profit, New York.

Koen, Vincent, Laurence Boone, Alain de Serres, and Nicola Fuchs (2001), Tracking the Euro, OECD Economics Department Working Papers No. 298.

Koppl, Roger (1991), Retrospectives: Animal Spirits, in: Journal of Economic Perspectives, Vol. 5, 203-210.

Krause, Laurence A. (1991), Speculation and the Dollar: The Political Economy of Exchange Rates, Boulder.

Krolzig, Hans-Martin (1997), Markov-Switching Vector Autoregressions: modeling, statistical inference, and application to business cycle analysis, Berlin.

Krüger, Malte (1996), Speculation, Hedging and Intermediation in the Foreign Exchange Market, Documento de Trabajo No. 9606, Banco de España.

Lawson, Tony (1985), Uncertainty and Economic Analysis, in: Economic Journal, Vol. 95, 909-927.

Leahy, Michael P. (1995), The Profitability of US Intervention in the Foreign Exchange Markets, in: Journal of International Money and Finance, Vol. 14, 823-844.

LeBaron, Blake (1999), Technical Trading Rule Profitability and Foreign Exchange Intervention, in: Journal of International Economics, Vol. 49, 125-143.

Lee, Chun I., Ming-Shiun Pan, and Y. Angela Liu (2001), On Market Efficiency of Asian Foreign Exchange Rates: Evidence from a Joint Variance Ratio Test and Technical Trading Rules, in: Journal of International Financial Markets, Institutions and Money, Vol. 11, 199-214.

Leitner, Johannes and Robert Schmidt (2004), A Sytematic Comparison of Profesional Exchange Rate Forecasts With Judgmental Forecasts of Novices - Are There Substantial Differences?, Wuerzburg Economic Papers No. 49, University of Wuerzburg.

Leitner, Johannes and Robert Schmidt (2005), Expectation Formation in Foreign Exchange Markets: A Comparision of Professional Exchange Rate Analysts and Novices, mimeo.

Lequeux, Pierre (1998), Informative Spillovers in the Currency Markets: A Practical Approach Through Exogenous Trading Rules, in: Emmanuel Acar and Stephen Satchell (eds.), Advanced Trading Rules, Oxford, 143-175.

Lequeux, Pierre and Emmanuel Acar (1998), A Dynamic Index for Managed Currencies Funds Using CME Currency Contracts, in: European Journal of Finance, Vol. 4, 311-330.

Levich, Richard M. (1989), Is the Foreign Exchange Market Efficient?, in: Oxford Review of Economic Policy, Vol. 5, 40-60.

Levich, Richard M. (2001), International Financial Markets: Prices and Policies, Singapore.

Levich, Richard M. and L. R. Thomas (1993), The Significance of Technical Trading-Rule Profits in the Foreign Exchange Market: A Bootstrap Approach, in: Journal of International Money and Finance, Vol. 12, 451-474.

Lewis, David K. (1969), Convention , Cambridge.

Lichtenstein, Sarah and Paul Slovic (1971), Reversals of Preference Between Bids and Choices in Gambling Decisions, in: Journal of Experimental Psychology, Vol. 89, 46-55.

Liu, Christina Y. and Jia He (1991), A Variance-Ratio Test of Random Walks in Foreign Exchange Rates, in: Journal of Finance, Vol. XLVI, 773-785.

Liu, Peter C. and G. S. Maddala (1992a), Rationality of Survey Data and Tests for Market Efficiency in the Foreign Exchange Markets, in: Journal of International Money and Finance, Vol. 11, 366-381.

Liu, Peter C. and G. S. Maddala (1992b), Using Survey Data to Test Market Efficiency in the Foreign Exchange Markets, in: Empirical Economics, Vol. 17, 303-314.

Lo, Andrew W. and A. Craig MacKinlay (1988), Stock Market Prices Do Not Follow Random Walks: Evidence from a Simple Specification Test, in: The Review of Financial Studies, Vol. 1, 41-66.

Lo, Andrew W. and A. Craig MacKinlay (1989), The Size and Power of the Variance Ratio Test in Finite Samples: A Monte Carlo Investigation, in: Journal of Econometrics, Vol. 40, 203-238.

Lo, Andrew W. and A. Craig MacKinlay (1999), A Non-Random Walk Down Wall Street, New Jersey.

Lo, Andrew W., Harry Mamaysky, and Jiang Wang (2000), Foundations of Technical Analysis: Computational Algorithms; Statistical Inference, and Empirical Implementation, in: Journal of Finance, Vol. LV, 1705-1765.

Lorenzen, Hans Peter and Niels Thygesen (2000), The Relation Between the Euro and the Dollar, Paper for EPRU Conference, Copenhagen, mimeo.

Lothian, James R. and Mark P. Taylor (1996), Real Exchange Rate Behavior: The Recent Float From the Perspective of the Past Two Centuries, in: Journal of Political Economy, Vol. 104, 488-509.

Luca, Cornelius (2000), Trading in the Global Currency Markets, New York.

Lucke, Bernd (2003), Are Technical Trading Rules Profitable? Evidence for Head-and-Shoulder Rules, in: Applied Economics, Vol. 35, 33-40.

Lui, Yu-Hon and David Mole (1998), The Use of Fundamental and Technical Analyses by Foreign Exchange Dealers: Hong Kong Evidence, in: Journal of International Money and Finance, Vol. 17, 535-545.

Lyons, Richard K. (1995), Tests of Microstructural Hypotheses in the Foreign Exchange Market, in: Journal of Financial Economcis, Vol. 39, 321-351.

Lyons, Richard K. (1996), Foreign exchange Volume: Sound and Fury Signifying Nothing?, in: Jeffrey A. Frankel, Giampaolo Galli, and Alberto Giovannini (eds.), The Microstructure of Foreign Exchange Markets, Chicago, 183-201.

Lyons, Richard K. (1997), A Simultaneous Trade Model of the Foreign Exchange Hot Potato, in: Journal of International Economics, Vol. 42, 275-298.

Lyons, Richard K. (2001a), New Perspective on FX Markets: Order-Flow Analysis, in: International Finance, Vol. 4, 303-320.

Lyons, Richard K. (2001b), The Microstructure Approach to Exchange Rates, Cambridge.

Lyons, Richard K. (2002a), Foreign Exchange: Macro Puzzles, Micro Tools, in: FRBSF Economic Review 51-69.

Lyons, Richard K. (2002b), The Failure of Empirical Exchange Rate Models: Room for Optimism?, Economic Policy Web Essay, http://www.economic-policy.org/pdfs/responses/Lyons.pdf.

MacDonald, Ronald (2000), Expectations Formation and Risk in Three Financial Markets: Surveying What Surveys Say, in: Francois Gardes and Georges Prat (eds.), Price Expectations in Goods and Financial Markets: New Developments in Theory and Empirical Research, Cheltenham, 172-212.

MacDonald, Ronald and Mark P. Taylor (1992), Exchange Rate Economics, in: IMF Staff Papers, Vol. 39, 1-57.

MacKinnon, James G. (1991), Critical Values for Cointegration Tests, in: Robert F. Engle and Clive W. J. Granger (eds.), Long-Run Economic Relationships, Oxford, 267-276.

Malkiel, Burton G. (1992), Efficient Market Hypothesis, in: Peter Newman, Murray Milgate, and John Eatwell (eds.), The New Palgrave Dictionary of Money and Finance, London, 739-744.

Malkiel, Burton G. (1999), A Random Walk Down Wall Street, New York.

Mark, Nelson C. (1995), Exchange Rates and Fundamentals: Evidence on Long-Horizon Predictability, in: American Economic Review, Vol. 85, 201-218.

Mark, Nelson C. (2001), International Macroeconomics and Finance, Oxford.

Mark, Nelson C. and Doo-yull Choi (1997), Real Exchange-Rate Prediction Over Long-Horizons , in: Journal of International Economics, Vol. 43, 29-60.

Mark, Nelson C. and Donggyu Sul (2001), Nominal Exchange Rates and Monetary Fundamentals: Evidence from a Small Post-Bretton Woods Panel, in: Journal of International Economics, Vol. 53, 29-52.

Marsh, Barnaby (2002), Heuristics as Social Tools, in: New Ideas in Psychology, Vol. 20, 49-57.

Marsh, Barnaby, Peter M. Todd, and Gerd Gigerenzer (2004), Cognitive Heuristics: Reasoning the Fast and Frugal Way, in: Jaqueline P. Leighton and Robert J. Sternberg (eds.), The Nature of Reasoning, Cambridge, 273-287.

Mas-Colell, Andreu, Michael D. Whinston, and Jerry R. Green (1995), Microeconomic Theory, New York.

Mattern, Conrad (2000), Praktiker-Handbuch Investment Research: Wirtschafts- und Finanzmarktindikatoren als Market Movers, Stuttgart.

McFadden, Daniel (1999), Rationality for Economists?, in: Journal of Risk and Uncertainty, Vol. 19, 73-105.

Meade, James E. (1951), The Balance of Payments, London.

Meese, Richard A. (1990), Currency Fluctuations in the Post-Bretton Woods Era, in: Journal of Economic Perspectives, Vol. 4, 117-134.

Meese, Richard A. and Kenneth Rogoff (1983a), Empirical Exchange Rate Models of the 1970s: Do They Fit Out of Sample?, in: Journal of International Economics, 14, 3-24.

Meese, Richard A. and Kenneth Rogoff (1983b), The Out-of-Sample Failure of Empirical Exchange Rate Models: Sampling Error or Misspecification?, in: Jacob A. Frenkel (ed.), Exchange Rates and International Macroeconomics, Chicago, 67-105.

Mehta, J., C. Starmer, and R. Sugden (1994), The Nature of Salience: An Experimental Investigation of Pure Coordination Games, in: American Economic Review, Vol. 84, 658-673.

Menkhoff, Lukas (1995), Spekulative Verhaltensweisen auf Devisenmärkten, Tübingen.

Menkhoff, Lukas (1997), Examining the Use of Technical Currency Analysis, in: International Journal of Finance and Economics, Vol. 2, 307-318.

Menkhoff, Lukas (1998), The Noise Trading Approach - Questionnaire Evidence from Foreign Exchange, in: Journal of International Money and Finance, Vol. 17, 547-564.

Miah, Fazlul, M. Kabir Hassan, and S. M. Ikhtiar Alam (2004), Testing the Rationality of Exchange Rate Expectations: Evidence from Survey Data, in: American Business Review, Vol. 22, 11-20.

Moosa, Imad A. (2000), Exchange Rate Forecasting: Techniques and Applications, Basingstoke .

Muchlinski, Elke (1997), Some Remarks on Convention in Keynes's Economic Thinking, Diskussionsbeiträge der Freien Universität Berlin, Fachbereich Wirtschaftswissenschaften, 1997 No. 10.

Mullainathan, Sendhil and Richard H. Thaler (2000), Behavioral Economics, NBER Working Paper Series No. 7984.

Mundell, Robert A. (1968), International Economics, New York.

Mundell, Robert A. (1998), What the Euro Means for theDollar and the International Monetary System, in: Atlantic Economic Journal, Vol. 26, 227-237.

Munier, Bertrand and Reinhard Selten (1999), Bounded Rationality Modeling, mimeo.

Muradoglu, Gülnur (2002), Portfolio Managers' and Novices' Forecasts of Risk and Return: Are There Predictable Forecast Errors?, in: Journal of Forecasting, Vol. 21, 395-416.

Murphy, John F. (1999), Technical Analysis of the Financial Markets, New York.

Murray, Christian J. and David H. Papell (2002), The Purchasing Power Parity Persistence Paradigm, in: Journal of International Economics, Vol. 56, 1-19.

Mussa, Michael (1976), The Exchange Rate, the Balance of Payments and Monetary and Fiscal Policy Under a Regime of Controlled Floating, in: Scandinavian Journal of Economics, Vol. 78, 229-254.

Mussa, Michael (1979), Empirical Regularities in the Behavior of Exchange Rates and Theories of the Foreign Exchange Market, in: Karl Brunner and Alan Meltzer (eds.), Policies for Employment, Prices, and Exchange Rates, Amsterdam, 9-57.

Mussa, Michael (1984), The Theory of Exchange Rate Determination, in: John F. O. Bilson and Richard C. Marston (eds.), Exchange Rate Theory and Practise, Chicago, 13-58.

Mussweiler, Thomas and Fritz Strack (2000), Numeric Judgmnets under Uncertainty: The Role of Knowledge in Anchoring, in: Journal of Experimental Social Psychology, Vol. 36, 495-518.

Mussweiler, Thomas, Fritz Strack, and Tim Pfeiffer (2000), Overcoming the Inevitable Anchoring Effect: Considering the Opposite Compensates for Selective Accessibility, in: Personality and Social Psychology Bulletin, Vo. 26, 1142-1150.

Muth, John F. (1960), Optimal Properties of Exponentially Weighted Forecasts, in: Journal of The American Statistical Association, Vol. 55, 299-306.

Muth, John F. (1961), Rational Expectations and the Theory of Price Movements, in: Econometrica, Vol. 29, 315-335.

Muthoo, Abhinay (1999), Rationality in the Face of Uncertainty, in: Peter Earl and Simon Kemp (eds.), The Elgar Companion to Consumer Research and Economic Psychology, Cheltenham , 487-495.

Neely, Christopher J. (1997), Technical Analysis in the Foreign Exchange Market: A Layman's Guide, in: Review - Federal Reserve Bank of St.Louis, Vol. 79, 23-38.

Neely, Christopher J. (1998), Technical Analysis and the Profitability of U.S. Foreign Exchange Intervention, in: Review - Federal Reserve Bank of St.Louis, Vol. 80, 3-17.

Neely, Christopher J. (2002), The Temporal Pattern of Trading Rule Returns and Exchange Rate Intervention: Intervention Does Not Generate Technical Profits, in: Journal of International Economics, Vol. 58, 211-232.

Neely, Christopher J. and Lucio Sarno (2002), How well Do Monetary Fundamentals Forecast Exchange Rates?, in: Federal Reserve Bank of St.Louis Review, Vol. 84, 51-74.

Newey, Withney K. and Kenneth D. West (1987), A Simple Positive Semi-Definite Heteroskedasticity and Autocorrelation Consistent Covariance Matrix, in: Econometrica, Vol. 55, 703-708.

Noussair, Charles N., Charles R. Plott, and Raymond G. Riezman (1997), The Principle of Exchange Rate Determination in an International Finance Experiment, in: Journal of Political Economy, Vol. 105, 822-861.

Oberlechner, Thomas (2001), Importance of Technical and Fundamental Analsysis in the European Foreign Exchange Market, in: International Journal of Finance and Economics, Vol. 6, 81-93.

Obstfeld, Maurice and Kenneth Rogoff (2000), The Six Major Puzzles in International Macroeconomics: Is There a Common Cause, in: National Bureau of Economic Research (ed.), NBER macroeconomic annual, Cambridge, 339-390.

Oh, Keun-yeob (1996), Purchasing Power Parity and Unit Root Tests Using Panel Data, in: Journal of International Money and Finance, Vol. 15, 405-418.

Okunev, John and Derek White (2003), Do Momentum-Based Strategies Still Work in Foreign Currency Markets?, in: Journal of Financial and Quantitative Analysis, Vol. 38, 425-447.

Organisation for Economic Co-operation and Development (2003), OECD Economic Outlook, Volume 2003/2, No. 74, December, Paris.

Osler, Carol L. (2000), Support for Resistence: Technical Analysis and Intraday Exchange Rates, in: FRBNY Economic Policy Review, Vol. 6, 53-68.

Osler, Carol L. and P. H. Kevin Chang (1995), Head and Shoulders: Not Just a Flaky Pattern, Federal Reserve Bank of New York Staff Papers No. 4.

Osterberg, William P. (2000), New Results on the Rationality of Survey Measures of Exchange-Rate Expectations, in: Economic Review, Vol. 36, 14-21.

Önkal, Dilek and Gülnur Muradoglu (1994), Evaluating Probabilistic Forecasts of Stock Prices in a Developing Stock Market, in: European Journal of Operational Research, Vol. 74, 350-358.

Önkal, Dilek and Gülnur Muradoglu (1996), Effects of Task Format on Probabilistic Forecasting of Stock Prices, in: International Journal of Forecasting, Vol. 12, 9-24.

Pan, Ming-Shiun, Y. Angela Liu, and Hamid Bastin (1996), An Examination of the Short-Term and Long-Term Behavior of Foreign Exchange Rates, in: The Financial Review, Vol. 31, 603-622.

Papell, David H. (1997), Searching for Stationarity: Purchasing Power Parity under the Current Float, in: Journal of International Economics, Vol. 43, 313-332.

Papell, David H. and Hristos Theodoridis (1998), Increasing Evidence of Purchasing Power Parity over the Current Float, in: Journal of International Money and Finance, Vol. 17, 41-50.

Payne, Richard (1999), Informed Trade in Spot Foreign Exchange Markets: An Empirical Investigation, London School of Economics, mimeo.

Pesaran, M. Hashem (1988), The Limits to Rational Expectations, New York.

Pingle, Mark (1997), Submitting to Authority: Its Effect on Decision-Making, in: Journal of Economic Psychology, Vol. 18, 45-68.

Pingle, Mark and Richard H. Day (1996), Modes of Economizing Behavior: Experimental Evidence, in: Journal of Economic Behavior & Organization, Vol. 29, 191-209.

Piron, Robert (1991), Keynes as a Noise Trader, in: Journal of Economic Perspectives, Vol. 5, 215-217.

Plous, Scott (1993), The Psychology of Judgement and Decision Making, New York.

Portes, Richard and Hélène Rey (1998), The Emergence of the Euro as an International Currency, in: David Begg, Jürgen von Hagen, Charles Wyplosz, and Klaus Zimmermann (eds.), Prospects and Challenges for the Euro, Oxford, 305-343.

Poterba, James M. and Lawrence H. Summers (1988), Mean Reversion in Stock Prices - Evidence and Implications, in: Journal of Financial Economicis, Vol. 22, 27-59.

Pring, Martin J. (2003), Technical Analysis Explained: The Succesful Investor's Guide to Spotting Investment Trends and Turning Points, New York.

Rabin, Matthew (1998), Psychology and Economics, in: Journal of Economic Literature, Vol. 36, 11-46.

Rabin, Matthew (2002), Inference by Believers in the Law of Small Numbers, in: Quarterly Journal of Economics, Vol. 117, 775-816.

Rabin, Matthew and Joel L. Schrag (1999), First Impressions Matter: A Model of Confirmatory Bias, in: Quarterly Journal of Economics, Vol. 114, 37-82.

Rabin, Matthew and Richard H. Thaler (2001), Anomalies: Risk Aversion, in: Journal of Economic Perspectives, Vol. 15, 219-232.

Richardson, Matthew and James H. Stock (1989), Drawing Inferences from Statistics Based on Multiyear Asset Returns, in: Journal of Financial Economcis, Vol. 25, 323-348.

Rime, Dagfinn (2000), Private or Public Information in Foreign Exchange Markets? An Empirical Analysis, University of Oslo, Memorandum 14/2000.

Rime, Dagfinn (2001), U.S. Exchange Rates and Currency Flows, mimeo.

Roberts, Harry V. (1959), Stock Market 'Patterns' and Financial Analysis: Methodological Suggestions, in: Journal of Finance, Vol. 14, 1-10.

Rogoff, Kenneth (1996), The Purchasing Power Parity Puzzle, in: Journal of Economic Literature, Vol. XXXIV, 647-668.

Rogoff, Kenneth (1999), Monetary Models of Dollar/Yen/Euro Nominal Exchange Rates: Dead or Undead?, in: Economic Journal, Vol. 109, F655-F659.

Rogoff, Kenneth (2001), The Failure of Empirical Exchange Rate Models: No Longer New but Still True, Economic Policy Web Essay, October 2001, Issue 1, volume 1.

Rosenberg, Michael (1996), Currency Forecasting: A Guide to Fundamental and Technical Models of Exchange Rate Determination, Boston.

Rosser, J. Barkley (2001), Alternative Keynesian and Post Keynesian Perspectives on Uncertainty and Expectations, in: Journal of Post Keynesian Economics, Vol. 23, 545-566.

Rosser, J. Barkley (2003), A Nobel Prize for Asymmetric Information: The Economic Contributions of geroge Akerlof, Michael Spence, and Joseph Stiglitz, in: Review of Political Economy, Vol. 15, 3-21.

Rubin, Robert E. and Jacob Weisberg (2003), In an Uncertain World: Tough Choices from Wall Street to Washington, New York.

Rundes, Jochen (1991), Keynesian Uncertainty and the Instability of Beliefs, in: Journal of Political Economy, Vol. 3, 125 145.

Saacke, Peter (1999), Technical Analysis, Central Bank Interventions and Exchange Rate Regimes, PhD Dissertation, University of Hamburg.

Saacke, Peter (2002), Technical Analysis and the Effectiveness of Central Bank Intervention, in: Journal of International Money and Finance, Vo. 21, 459-479.

Salvatore, Dominick (2002), The Euro: Expectations and Performance, in: Eastern Economic Journal, Vol. 28, 121-136.

Samuelson, Paul A. (1965), Proof That Properly Anticipated Prices Fluctuate Randomly, in: Industrial Management Review, Vol. 6, 41-49.

Samuelson, Paul A. (1970), The Fundamental Approximation Theorem of Portfolio Analysis in Terms of Means, Variances, and Higher Moments, in: Review of Economic Studies, Vol. 38, 537-542.

Sanders, Nada R. and Karl B. Manrodt (1994), Forecastin Practices in US Corporations - Survey Results, in: Interfaces, Vol. 24, 92-100.

Sargent, Thomas J. (1993), Bounded Rationality in Macroeconomics, Oxford.

Sarno, Lucio and Mark P. Taylor (1998), Real Exchange Rates under the Recent Float: Unequivocal Evidence of Mean Reversion, in: Economics Letters, Vol. 60, 131-137.

Sarno, Lucio and Mark P. Taylor (2001), Official Intervention in the Foreign Exchange Market: Is It Effective and, If So, How Does It Work?, in: Journal of Economic Literature, Vol. XXXIX, 839-868.

Sarno, Lucio and Mark P. Taylor (2002), The Economics of Exchange Rates, Cambridge.

Schelling, Thomas C. (1960), The Strategy of Conflict, Cambridge.

Schmalensee, Richard (1976), An Experimental Study of Expectation Formation, in: Econometrica, Vol. 44, 17-41.

Schmidt, Robert and Timo Wollmershäuser (2005), Sterilized Foreign Exchange Market Interventions in a Chartist-Fundamentalist Exchange Rate Model, in: Kredit und Kapital, Vol. 38, Heft 1, 53-85.

Schneider, Stefan (2003), The Euro - What Went Down Must Go Up?, Deutsche Bank Research, Frankfurt Voice, March 5, 2003.

Schotter, Andrew R. (1997), Microeconomics: A Modern Approach, Reading.

Schröder, Bernd (2004), Interview: Transaction costs in asset markets, Dresdner Bank Asset Management, Frankfurt a.M., Interview 15.06.2004.

Schulmeister, Stephan (2000), Die Kaufkraft des Euros innerhalb und außerhalb der Währungsunion, Studie des Österreichischen Instituts für Wirtschaftsforschung.

Schwartz, Hugh (2002), Herbert Simon and Behavioral Economics, in: Journal of Socio-Economics, Vol. 31, 181-189.

Selten, Reinhard (1998), Features of Experimentally Observed Bounded Rationality, in: European Economic Review, Vol. 42, 413-436.

Shafir, Eldar, Peter Diamond, and Amos Tversky (2004), Money Illusion, in: Colin F. Camerer, George Loewenstein, and Matthew Rabin (eds.), Advances in Behavioral Economics, Princeton, 483-509.

Sharpe, William F. (1966), Mutual Fund Performance, in: Journal of Business, Vol. 39, 119-138.

Shefrin, Hersh M. and Richard H. Thaler (2004), Mental Accounting, Saving, and Self Control, in: Colin F. Camerer, George Loewenstein, and Matthew Rabin (eds.), Advances in Behavioral Economics, Princeton, 395-428.

Shiller, Robert (1987), Expectations, in: John Eatwell, Murray Milgate, and Peter Newman (eds.), The New Palgrave: A Dictionary of Economics, London, 224-229.

Shiller, Robert (1998), Human Behavior and the Efficiency of the Financial System, NBER Working Paper Series, No. 6375.

Shleifer, Andrei (2000), Inefficient Markets - An Introduction to Behavioral Finance, Oxford.

Shleifer, Andrei and Lawrence H. Summers (1990), The Noise Trader Approach to Finance, in: Journal of Economic Perspectives, Vol. 4, 19-33.

Simon, Herbert A. (1955), A Behavioral Model of Rational Choice, in: Quarterly Journal of Economics, 69, 99-118.

Simon, Herbert A. (1956), Rational Choice and the Structure of the Environment, in: Psychological Review, Vol. 63, 129-138.

Simon, Herbert A. (1957), Models of Man, New York.

Simon, Herbert A. (1976), From Substantive to Procedural Rationality, in: Spiro J. Latsis (ed.), Method and Appraisal in Economics, Cambridge, 129-148.

Simon, Herbert A. (1978), Rationality as Process and as Product of Thought, in: American Economic Review, Papers & Proceedings, Vol. 68, 1-16.

Simon, Herbert A. (1979), Rational Decision Making in Business Organizations, in: American Economic Review, Vol. 69, 493-513.

Simon, Herbert A. (1982), Models of Bounded Rationality, Vol. 1 Economic Analysis and Public Policy, Cambridge.

Simon, Herbert A. (1986), Rationality in Psychology and Economics, in: Journal of Business , Vol. 59, 209-224.

Simon, Herbert A. (1987a), Behavioural Economics, in: John Eatwell, Murray Milgate, and Peter Newman (eds.), The New Palgrave: A Dictionary of Economics, London, 221-225.

Simon, Herbert A. (1987b), Bounded Rationality, in: John Eatwell, Murray Milgate, and Peter Newman (eds.), The New Palgrave: A Dictionary of Economics, London, 266-268.

Simon, Herbert A. (1990), Invariants of Human Behavior, in: Annual Review of Psychology, Vol. 41, 1-19.

Simon, Herbert A. (1995), The Information-Processing Theory of Mind, in: American Psychologist, Vol. 50, 507-508.

Slovic, Paul (1995), Construction of Preference, in: American Psychologist, Vol. 50, 364-371.

Snyder, Mark and William B. Swann (1978), Hypothesis-Testing Processes in Social Interaction, in: Journal of Personality and Social Psychology, Vol. 36, 1202-1212.

Sobiechowski, David (1996), Rational Expectations in the Foreign Exchange Market? Some Survey Evidence, in: Applied Economics, Vol. 28, 1601-1611.

Soros, George (1994), The Alchemy of Finance, New York.

Sosvilla-Rivero, Simón, Julián Andrada-Félix, and Fernando Fernández-Rodríguez (2002), Further Evidence on Technical Trade Profitability and Foreign Exchange Intervention, in: Applied Economics Letters, Vol. 9, 827-832.

Spiwoks, Markus (2003a), Die Währungs-, Anleihen- und Aktienmarktprognosen des Zentrums für Europäische Wirtschaftsforschung, forthcoming in Zeitschrift für betriebswirtschaftliche Forschung.

Spiwoks, Markus (2003b), Qualität der Zinsprognosen deutscher Banken - Eine empirisache Analyse, in: Kredit und Kapital, Vol. 36, 289-308.

Stadtmann, Georg (2002), Noise-Trader auf Devisenmärkten: viel Lärm um Nichts?, Frankfurt am Main.

Stael von Holstein, Carl-Axel S. (1972), Probability Forecasting: An Experiment Related to the Stock Market, in: Organizational Behavior and Human Performance, Vol. 8, 139-158.

Starmer, Chris (1999), Experimental Economics: Hard Science or Wasteful Tinkering?, in: Economic Journal, Vol. 109, F5-F15 .

Starmer, Chris (2004), Developments in Nonexpected-Utility Theory: The Hunt for a Descriptive Theory of Choice under Risk, in: Colin F. Camerer, George Loewenstein, and Matthew Rabin (eds.), Advances in Behavioral Economics, Princeton, 104-147.

Stein, Jerome L. (2002), The Equilibrium Real Exchange Rate of the Euro: An Evaluation of Research, in: ifo-Studien: Zeitschrift für empirische Wirtschaftsforschung , Vol. 48, 349-381.

Stigler, George J. (1961), The Economics of Information, in: Journal of Political Economy, Vol. 69, 213-225.

Stracca, Livio (2004), Behavioral Finance and Asset Prices: Where Do We Stand?, in: Journal of Economic Psychology, Vol. 25, 373 405.

Strack, Fritz and Roland Deutsch (2002), Urteilsheuristiken, in: Dieter Frey and Martin Irle (eds.), Theorien der Sozialpsychologie. Band III: Motivations- und Informationsverarbeitungstheorien, Bern, 352-384.

Stramer, Chris (1999), Experimental Economics: Hard Science or Wasteful Tinkering?, in: Economic Journal, Vol. 109, F5-F15 .

Surajaras, Patchara and Richard J. Sweeney (1992), Profit-Making Speculation in Foreign Exchange Markets, Boulder.

Swann, Christopher (2000), Financial Times, June 2, 2000, p. 4.

Sweeney, Richard J. (1986), Beating the Foreign Exchange Market, in: Journal of Finance, Vol. 41, 163-182.

Sweeney, Richard J. (2000), Does the FED Beat the Foreign Exchange Market?, in: Journal of Banking & Finance, Vol. 24, 665-694.

Szakmary, Andrew C. and Ike Mathur (1997), Central Bank Intervention and Trading Rule Profits in Foreign Exchange Markets, in: Journal of International Money and Finance, Vol. 16, 513-535.

Takagi, Shinji (1991), Exchange Rate Expectations: A Survey of Survey Studies, in: IMF Staff Papers, Vol. 30, 156-183.

Tanner, Glenn (1997), A Note on Economic News and Intraday Exchange Rates, in: Journal of Banking & Finance, Vol. 21, 573-585.

Taylor, Alan M. (2001), Potential Pitfalls for the Purchasing Power Parity Puzzle? Sampling and Specification Biases in Mean-Reversion Tests of the Law of One Price, in: Econometrica, Vol. 69, 473-498.

Taylor, Mark P. (1995), The Economics of Exchange Rates, in: Journal of Economic Literature, Vol. XXXIII, 13-47.

Taylor, Mark P. and Helen Allen (1992), The Use of Technical Analysis in the Foreign Exchange Market, in: Journal of International Money and Finance, Vol. 11, 304-314.

Taylor, Mark P., David A. Peel, and Lucio Sarno (2001), Nonlinear Mean-Reversion in Real Exchange Rates: Toward a Solution to the Purchasing Power Parity Puzzles, in: International Economic Review, Vol. 42, 1015-1042.

Taylor, Mark P. and Lucio Sarno (1998), The Behaviour of Real Exchange Rates During the Post-Bretton Woods Period, in: Journal of International Economics, Vol. 46, 281-312.

Thaler, Richard H. (1991), The Psychology of Choice and the Assumptions of Economics, in: Richard H. Thaler (ed.), Quasi-Rational Economics, New York, 137-166.

Thaler, Richard H. (1992), The Winner's Curse - Paradoxes and Anomalies of Economic Life, New York.

Thomson, Mary E., Dilek Önkal-Atay, Andrew C. Pollock, and Alex Macaulay (2003), The Influence of Trend Strength on Directional Probabilistic Currency Predictions, in: International Journal of Forecasting, Vol. 19, 241-256.

Tirole, Jean (1992), Speculation, in: Peter Newman, Murray Milgate , and John Eatwell (eds.), The New Palgrave Dictionary of Money & Finance, Vol. 3, New York, 513-515.

Tivegna, Massimo (2001), Political and Economic News and Lira Fluctuations: The Recent Experience - 29 March 1994 - 29 December 1995, in: Mario Baldassarri, Michele Bagella, and Luigi Paganetto (eds.), Financial Markets: Imperfect Information and Risk Management, Basingstoke, 271-313.

Todd, Peter M., Laurence Fiddick, and Stefan Krauss (2000), Discussion: Ecological Rationality and its Contents, in: Thinking & Reasoning, Vol. 6, 375-384.

Todd, Peter M. and Gerd Gigerenzer (2000), Précis of Simple Heuristics That Make Us Smart, in: Behavioral and Brain Sciences, Vol. 23, 727-741.

Todd, Peter M. and Gerd Gigerenzer (2003), Bounding Rationality to the World, in: Journal of Economic Psychology, Vol. 24 , 143-165.

Trope, Yaacov and Akiva Liberman (1996), Social Hypothesis Testing: Cognitive and Motivational Mechanisms, in: E. Tory Higgins and Arie W. Kruglanski (eds.), Social Psychology: Handbook of Basic Principles, New York, 239-270.

Tversky, Amos and Daniel Kahneman (1974), Judgment under Uncertainty: Heuristics and Biases, in: Science, Vol. 185, 1124-1131.

Tversky, Amos and Daniel Kahneman (1981), The Framing of Decisions and the Psychology of Choice, in: Science, Vol. 211, 453-458.

Tversky, Amos and Daniel Kahneman (1999), Judgment Under Uncertainty: Heuristics and Biases, in: Daniel Kahneman, Paul Slovic, and Amos Tversky (eds.), Judgment Under Uncertainty: Heuristics and Biases, Cambridge, 3-20.

Van Hoek, Taco H. (1992), Explaining Mark/Dollar and Yen/Dollar Exchange Rates in the 1980s, in: Economics Letters, Vol. 38, 467-472.

Verbeek, Marno (2000), A Guide to Modern Econometrics, Chichester.

von Neumann, John and Oskar Morgenstern (1947), Theory of Games and Economic Behavior, Princeton.

von Nitzsch, Rüdiger (2002), Entscheidungslehre: Wie Menschen entscheiden und wie Menschen entscheiden sollten, Stuttgart.

Vriend, Nicolaas J. (1996), Rational Behavior and Economic Theory, in: Journal of Economic Behavior & Organization, Vol. 29, 263-285.

Wärneryd, Karl (2001), Stock-Market Psychology: How People Value and Trade Stocks, Cheltenham.

Webby, Richard and Marcus O'Connor (1996), Judgemental and Statistical Time Series Forecasting: A Review of the Literature, in: International Journal of Forecasting, Vol. 12, 91-118.

Wei, Shang-Jin and David C. Parsley (1995), Purchasing Power Disparity during the Floating Rate Period: Exchange Rate Volatility and Trade Barriers, NBER Working Paper Series No. 5032.

Wren-Lewis, Simon and Rebecca Driver (1998), Real Exchange Rates for the Year 2000, Washington D.C.

Wright, Jonathan H. (2000), Alternative Variance Ratio Tests Using Ranks and Signs, in: Journal of Business and Economic Statistics, Vol. 18, 1-9.

Wu, Yangru (1996), Are Real Exchange Rates Non Stationary? Evidence from a Panel Data Test, in: Journal of Money, Credit and Banking, Vol. 28, 54-63.

Yao, Jian (1998a), Market Making in the Interbank Foreign Exchange Market, Salomon Center for the Study of Financial Institutions Working Paper S-98-3.

Yao, Jian (1998b), Spread Components and Deyaler Profits in the Interbank Foreign Exchange Market, Salomon Center for the Study of Financial Institutions Working Paper S-98-04.

Yates, J. Frank, Linda S. McDaniel , and Eric S. Brown (1991), Probabilistic Forecasts of Stock Prices and Earnings: The Hazards of Nascent Expertise, in: Organizational Behavior and Human Performance , Vol. 49, 60-79.

Young, H. Peyton (1996), The Economics of Convention, in: Journal of Economic Perspectives , Vol. 10, 105-122.

Zentrum für Europäische Wirtschaftsforschung (ZEW) (2004), ZEW Finanzmarktreport, February 2004, Jahrgang 13, February 2004; http://www.zew.de/de/publikationen/finanzmarktreport.php3.